The Ackerman Guide

The contents of this book are believed correct at the time of printing. Nevertheless, the publisher can accept no responsibility for errors or omissions or changes in the details given.

© Leading Guides Limited, 1996
35 Tadema Road, London SW10 0PZ

The right of Leading Guides Limited to be identified as author of this work has been asserted by the Company in accordance with the Copyright Designs and Patents Act 1988.

All rights reserved. No part of this publication may be reproduced, stored in a retrieval system or transmitted in any form or by any means – electronic, mechanical, photocopying, recording or otherwise – unless the written permission of the publisher has been given beforehand.

Designed and typeset in Great Britain
by Bookman Projects Ltd.

ISBN 898 71875 X

First published 1996 by Bookman Projects Ltd
Floor 22
1 Canada Square
Canary Wharf
London E14 5AP

Contents

4
Introduction by Roy Ackerman

5
Meat & Livestock Commission

10
How to Use this Guide

16
Scotch Beef Club

17
The Four-Leaf Clover

21
L!VE TV

22
Academy of Food & Wine Service

23
London Reviews

108
England Reviews

270
Scotland Reviews

304
Wales Reviews

318
Channel Islands & Isle of Man Reviews

325
Northern Ireland Reviews

332
Republic of Ireland Reviews

372
Index

Introduction

by ROY ACKERMAN

I hope you like the new pocket format of this year's Guide in which we have introduced some innovative ideas. Another novel aspect is the link with my new television show "Dish of the Day", which allows me to present restaurants in and around London in an entirely new way. Next year we hope to extend this coverage to other parts of the country and to regional cooking.

I have seen many changes since introducing this Guide 8 years ago. Having this year travelled the length and breadth of the country with the Wedgwood Chef & Potter Roadshow, I have had a rare opportunity to meet with literally hundreds of the best chefs in Britain and Ireland. It has given me further insight into the hospitality industry. I was struck by how some chefs have lost sight of the fundamentals of their craft, with over complication. Appearance, all too often, was put before taste, and a confusion of cooking styles gave grounds for concern. Whatever happened to the simple, good things that we all enjoyed so often – a simple piece of grilled meat or fish, cooked with fresh herbs and served with crisp, green salad; warm baked bread and some creamy unpasteurised cheese with fresh berries. Sounds easy – but how difficult they are to find. Ironically, if you ask most chefs what they enjoy when off duty, they yearn for the same simplicity.

I have a strong feeling that big changes lie ahead. Giving the customer what they want must become every good restaurateur's prime objective. Certainly at front of house there must be a greater awareness of the value of continuity and the importance of retaining good, professional staff to whom regular customers can relate.

Amongst the most exciting events in the past year have been the number of new restaurants that have opened their doors, such as Coast, L'Odeon, Alistair Little Lancaster Road, the mega Mezzo, The Avenue and B-Square to name but a few, whilst we have said farewell sadly to a few old friends – Mijanou, Joël Antunès at Les Saveurs and Overtons.

We know from the mountain of mail we receive annually that you have strong opinions of your own. I am always delighted to hear from you and to listen to your views. I hope this Guide contributes to many good meals in the coming year.

The Recipe FOR Excellence

The association of British Meat with The Ackerman Guide - bringing together a commitment to quality and the recognition of outstanding achievement - is wholly appropriate.

Eating out is special and every chef's aim is to ensure it is memorable - for the whole occasion, certainly, but above all for the excellence of the food.

Leading chefs continue to innovate, experiment and delight. British Meat, equally, is committed to innovation. We work closely with leading chefs to develop and refine new cuts, added value products and a host of recipe and serving suggestions to ensure British meat remains at the centre of the menu.

More than that, we involve everyone concerned in the production and supply chain to ensure the needs of chefs and restaurateurs are met and that, above all, the eating quality of British meat is second to none. Our quality programmes start with animal breeding and embrace all aspects of farming systems and animal welfare. Our 'Farm Assurance' schemes mean that caterers can have total confidence in the quality of the meat they buy while our 'Blueprint' programmes - which cover beef, lamb, pork and veal - are designed to improve the eating quality of British meat so as to satisfy consumer expectations. And through our highly successful consumer advertising campaign - 'The Recipe For Love' - we maintain interest and also stimulate demand for British meat.

British Meat is, therefore, delighted to be associated with The Ackerman Guide and we look forward to continuing and developing our association with the country's leading chefs and restaurateurs in their pursuit of excellence.

BRIAN KILKENNY
Trade Marketing Manager
British Meat

The Ackerman Guide

*T*he trend to healthier eating has highlighted the nutritional benefits of lean red meat and British Meat's 'The Recipe For Love' advertising campaign - which promotes the 'emotional' appeal of British meat as a source of enjoyment - has been extended to include the 'rational' messages about the role lean red meat plays in today's healthy eating lifestyles.

Under the banner 'Meat Matters', the campaign in particular corrects the misconceptions with regard to fat, emphasising that red meat is low in fat. Lean, trimmed pork, for instance, has less fat than plain cottage cheese.

The campaign also promotes red meat as an excellent source of 'haem' iron as well as other important vitamins and minerals.

'Meat Matters' gives chefs and restaurateurs crucial support in making meat a central part of the menu with rational messages consumers will understand and appreciate - giving them every reason to make red meat part of their everyday healthy, balanced diet.

HEALTHY BENEFITS OF SERVING LEAN RED MEAT

Indeed, the information contained in the campaign affords the opportunity for those restaurants which offer a healthy choice or 'light eating' option on their menus to feature lean cuts of British meat and to highlight these choices on the menu.

Here are just three examples - featuring beef, lamb and pork - of delicious and nutritious recipes using British meat:

PORK IN SPICY YOGURT

Ingredients (10 portions)

10 x 127.5g lean, fully trimmed
  British pork steaks
200g natural yogurt
25g curry paste
50g mango chutney
15g coriander

METHOD
In a shallow dish, mix together all the marinade ingredients. Add the steaks and spread the marinade over to coat well. Cover and leave to marinate in a refrigerator for 3-4 hours. Remove steaks and cook under a preheated grill for 8-10 minutes each side.

Serve with rice, bread and a green salad. Garnish with lime wedges.

PAN COOKED LAMB WITH MUSHROOMS

Ingredients (10 portions)

10 x 112g lean, fully trimmed
  British lamb leg steaks
20g sliced garlic
240g button mushrooms
10g rosemary

METHOD

Heat some oil in a frying pan. Add garlic, rosemary and seasoning. Cook until garlic just starts to brown and flavours oil slightly. Add steaks and brown both sides over a high heat. Reduce heat and cook for 4-6 minutes each side. Add mushrooms about 5 minutes before the end of cooking. Serve with new potatoes and salad and a pre-made bought sauce of your choice, eg tomato or tomato and herb or garlic sauce.

BEEF AND SPINACH CURRY

Ingredients (10 portions)

1.5kg cubed, lean, fully trimmed
  British beef
300g chopped onion
25g crushed garlic
30g root ginger
80g curry paste - or -
  30g crushed coriander
  30g cumin
  10g turmeric
  12 cardamom pods
  20g chillies
800g tinned tomatoes
375ml stock
450g spinach
Salt and pepper to taste
30g chopped parsley or coriander

METHOD

Wipe the inside of a large pan with a very small quantity of oil (1tsp) and cook meat, onions, garlic and ginger until meat is sealed. Add the spices and chillies or curry paste and cook for 1-2 minutes. Stir in the tomatoes, stock, spinach and seasoning. Bring to the boil, cover and simmer for 1½ hours, stirring occasionally. Remove the lid and simmer for a further 30 minutes or until the sauce has thickened and meat is tender. Stir in the fresh coriander.

Serve with rice and/or naan bread and a selection of chutneys.

*B*ritish Meat's on-going work to help chefs and restaurateurs keep pace with the consumer's demand for new cuts, leaner meat and innovation is indicative of its wider commitment to the catering industry.

The Recipe FOR Quality

One of the major innovations pioneered by British Meat has been the development of product specifications designed to simplify the purchasing of British meat products and to ensure accurate portion control and consistent quality. 'The Meat Buyers' Guide for Caterers' covers the main red meats - beef, lamb, pork, veal, bacon and offal. The guide details degrees of trim and preparation, specifies fat cover or fat content in made up items and deals with both specialities of the catering business and new cuts.

There is a well established and proven portfolio of training workshops for kitchen staff at all levels to help restaurateurs and catering organisations minimise costs and maximise profits through improved knowledge and increased awareness of all the factors relating to meat quality.

British Meat is also working closely with caterers to introduce new seam butchery techniques - a procedure whereby whole muscles are separated by cutting via the natural seams between them, maximising the amount of lean muscle and eradicating excess fat, gristle and connective tissue. This method of butchery also helps to ensure consistent cooking and eating quality.

This work is allied to a commitment to developing added value, convenience and kitchen ready products as well as ready meals. Much of this work is done in close collaboration with chefs from all sectors of the catering industry working in the recently-opened state-of-the-art Catering Development Kitchen at British Meat's headquarters. This is an invaluable resource for new product development and evaluation under true catering conditions and will allow catering organisations to develop new British meat dishes to extend and excite their menus.

In these ways, British Meat strives to increase the profitable use of red meat and meat products throughout the catering sector and to stimulate their wider use in recipe development and menu planning.

NEWS FLASH

Britain's Top Independent Butchers

Who are the country's top butchers? Where are they? How can you be sure you're getting top quality, best advice and a service you can be confident of from a butcher?

These questions and more will be answered in the 1997 edition of the Ackerman Guide. Details have now been agreed on inspection criteria that will enable inspectors to visit independent butchers throughout the UK and determine which are good enough to be included in our Guide.

They will be listed in next year's Guide.

How to use this Guide

For those of you who are regular readers of the Guide, welcome to our new look. We hope you will find it easier to use and to carry around with you.

Reviews

Reviews are still set out very simply: London is arranged alphabetically by establishment name. Reviews in England, Scotland, Wales, Channel Islands & Isle of Man, Northern Ireland and the Republic of Ireland are arranged alphabetically by location, then by establishment name. The length of a review does not necessarily indicate the relevant importance of an establishment – everything included in this Guide is worth a visit. I have used a small team of reviewers who have worked with me for some years and whose judgement I trust, and who understand what I am seeking in standards of cuisine, atmosphere and service.

Clover Leaf Award Winners

The Clover Leaf Award Winners are listed on pages 17-21, and the symbol appears alongside entries for the winners, whose establishments are described more fully than others in the Guide.

Vital Statistics

These have been compiled from information supplied to us by the establishments themselves in response to our questionnaires. They have been checked and we have done our best to ensure that all information contained in this book is accurate. However, it is perfectly feasible that a restaurant or hotel may choose to change its last order times, or the days of the week that it is closed. Similarly, an owner, manager or chef may well move on. Even the style of food might be changed. We assume that in most cases you will book before going to a restaurant or hotel, and if you feel that any detail is especially important, we suggest you check it at the time of booking. When we have quoted particular dishes in a review, we cannot guarantee that they will be available on your visit - this is obviously true if you visit in a different season. In most cases, menus will be more comprehensive than the extracts we have chosen.

This year, to be more user friendly, we have introduced symbols to indicate the following statistics:

- ☎ Telephone number
- 📠 Fax number
- 🛏 Number of bedrooms
- £ Room price (see next paragraph)
- 🪑 Number of seats in restaurant
- 🏅 Meal price (see next paragraph)
- ☺ Opening times
- ☹ Closure times

Prices

Room prices are based on current high-season rates at the time of going to press and include VAT (also service if applicable), for a double room for 2 occupants with private bath and cooked breakfast, mid-week for one night only.

Restaurant prices, correct at the time of going to press, are for a 3-course meal for 2 people including one of the less expensive bottles of wine, coffee, service and VAT. The total is rounded up to the nearest £5.

Other Symbols

Additional symbols are used to highlight the following:

- 👪 Establishment welcomes families
- 🌱 Establishment enjoys an attractive setting
- ♣ Establishment given a Black Clover Leaf Award
- ♧ Establishment given a White Clover Leaf Award
- 🎒 As before, I have used the "vested interest" symbol to indicate restaurants in which I have a personal investment
- ❖ Academy of Food and Wine Service. This symbol indicates that an establishment is host to a member of the Academy of Food and Wine Service. More details on page 22
- 🐂 This symbol indicates that an establishment is a member of the Scotch Beef Club. More details of the Club are on page 16

SPECIALLY SELECTED SCOTCH BEEF

THE TRUE TASTE OF QUALITY

Scotland's world-wide reputation for producing prime beef cattle owes much to nature. Favoured with the ideal stock-rearing conditions of a temperate climate, an abundance of grass and pure water, and vast tracts of unspoiled countryside, generations of Scottish farmers have used their skills to produce beef for the discerning tables of the world.

300 YEARS OF TRADITION AND DEVELOPMENT

As far back as the 17th century, the beef from Scottish cattle was in demand, and each year tens of thousands were exported - on foot - to eager English markets. A century later agricultural improvements enabled whole herds to be fed through the winters, and attention was then turned to improving native cattle breeds.
The result, by the early 19th century, was beef breeds which were to become renowned throughout the world. Until the 19th century Scotch beef cattle continued to be walked to markets in the south, but the introduction of steam navigation, then railways, brought the cattle droving tradition of generations to an end. Prime Scotch beef could now travel to London in peak condition, and the modern meat industry began.
Now, one hundred years on, fleets of refrigerated vehicles daily transport Specially Selected Scotch Beef to markets throughout the UK and continental Europe.

REPUTATION FOR EXCELLENCE

Like other products with a reputation for excellence - such as vintage red wine and famous malt whiskies - it takes time and skill to produce Specially Selected Scotch Beef. Generations of experience in cattle rearing, backed by the quality assurance schemes of today, means that Specially Selected Scotch Beef is produced to the highest farming standards throughout. The Scotch meat industry has its own expertise, and Specially Selected Scotch Beef is matured in the traditional, time-honoured way to maximise the flavour and tenderness for which it is world renowned.

EUROPEAN QUALITY BEEF

The EC recognises the contribution of the Scottish meat industry in setting standards of quality. The use of the EC logo signifies that strict EC standards for quality control and product traceability from farm to consumer have been adhered to - further enhancing the reputation of Specially Selected Scotch Beef for consistent product quality.

A WHOLE NEW EATING EXPERIENCE

Specially Selected Scotch Beef is recognised as a popular choice for caterers around the world and many top class restaurants have enhanced their reputations with the quality of the Scotch beef they serve.

For the true taste of quality and a whole new eating experience, discover the flavour and tenderness of Specially Selected Scotch Beef at one of the many Scotch Beef Club restaurants, highlighted throughout this Guide.

FINANCED WITH THE ASSISTANCE OF THE EUROPEAN COMMUNITY

WELCOME TO THE SCOTCH BEEF CLUB

An elite club with over 600 members throughout the UK and continental Europe - each one a distinguished restaurant with an international reputation for excellence.

This Guide, recognised for the quality of its listed establishments and an indispensable aid to the discerning diner, features many of the Scotch Beef Club members. Chefs demand exacting standards of quality in the beef they buy. Scotch Beef Club members purchase not only one of the world's finest meat products, but a true taste of quality. This, together with their culinary expertise produces Specially Selected Scotch Beef dishes that enhance their international reputations and confirms their listing in the Guide.

D.S. Cameron

"At Turnberry we cater for the most discerning of both national and international clientele, and are proud to feature the finest of Scotch beef throughout the hotel's three restaurants. The Scotch Beef Club ensures that the highest standards are constantly maintained and protected for the future. Turnberry Hotel is proud to be a founder member of this prestigious Club".

**D.S. Cameron,
Executive Chef de Cuisine,
Turnberry Hotel.**

Look for the Black Bull symbol to identify members of the Scotch Beef Club. So whether you favour a succulent steak, a tender roast or a more exotic international recipe, visit a Scotch Beef Club member and experience the flavour and tenderness of Specially Selected Scotch Beef for yourself.

The Scotch Beef Club operates in Belgium, France, Germany, Great Britain, Holland, Italy and Spain - and each member restaurant is identified by a distinctive door sticker or plaque.

For a full list of all Scotch Beef Club members, please contact the Scotch Quality Beef and Lamb Association on

0131•333 5335

or write to: **Scotch Quality Beef and Lamb Association, Rural Centre-West Mains, Ingliston, Newbridge, Midlothian EH28 8NZ, Scotland.**

FINANCED WITH THE ASSISTANCE OF THE EUROPEAN COMMUNITY

Scotch Beef Club

A welcome addition to this year's Guide is the inclusion of the Scotch Beef Club. Initiated by the Scotch Quality Beef and Lamb Association to promote quality beef from Scotland, members of this prestigious Club make no compromise when it comes to quality.

Scotland is justifiably proud of the centuries-old reputation of its beef industry and only the finest, genuine Scotch Beef – naturally produced to the highest farming and quality standards – is served in Scotch Beef Club member establishments.

Originally started in Italy, the Scotch Beef Club has spread across Europe and now boasts members in France, Germany, Belgium and Holland. The UK Club membership reads like a veritable "who's who" of top restaurants and hotels nationwide.

Scotch Beef's traditional worldwide reputation for quality, tenderness and flavour is further enhanced by today's chefs in the skill and innovation used by Scotch Beef Club members in preparing the Scotch Beef dishes on their menus.

Discerning diners, particularly those who appreciate the taste and succulence of quality Scotch Beef, should look out for the Black Bull symbol which identifies members of the Scotch Beef Club throughout the Guide.

The Four-Leaf Clover

The four-leaf clover has been chosen because it is a symbol of luck and also a rare find. There is always a degree of luck involved when good ambience, excellent food, wine and service and the response of the customer combine to make a perfect occasion. A White Clover means that in my opinion, this is a very special place for many reasons, and made for a memorable experience. A Black Clover represents excellence in all aspects of food, service and decor, and these are the very best in Great Britain and the Republic of Ireland. With 17 new clovers this year marked [N] and 3 promotions to Black Clover from White Clover marked [P], The Ackerman Guide Clover Leaf Awards this year are given to:

LONDON:

Al San Vincenzo, W2		✿
Alastair Little, W1		♣
Atelier, W1	[N]	✿
Aubergine, SW10	[P]	♣
Belgo Noord, NW1		✿
The Berkeley, SW1		✿
Bibendum, SW3		✿
Bistrot 190, SW7		✿
Blakes Hotel, SW7		♣
Bombay Brasserie, SW7		✿
The Brackenbury, W6		✿
Café Royal Grill Room, W1		✿
The Canteen, SW10		✿
The Capital, SW3		♣
Le Caprice, SW1		✿
Chez Nico at Ninety Park Lane, W1		♣
Churchill Inter-Continental Hotel, W1		✿
Claridge's, W1		♣
Clarke's, W8		✿
The Connaught, W1		♣
dell'Ugo, W1		✿
The Dorchester, W1		♣
Elena's L'Etoile, W1	[N]	✿
Four Seasons Hotel, W1		✿
Frederick's, N1		✿
Fulham Road, SW3		✿
Le Gavroche, W1		♣
Gay Hussar, W1		✿
The Halcyon, W11		✿
The Halkin, SW1		✿
Hilaire, SW7		✿
L'Incontro, SW1		✿
Inter-Continental London, W1		✿
The Ivy, WC2		✿
Kensington Place, W8		✿
The Lanesborough, SW1		✿
Langan's Brasserie, W1		♣

LONDON (Contd):

The Langham Hilton, W1
Leith's, W11
Restaurant Marco Pierre White, SW1
Mimmo d'Ischia, SW1 [N]
Mon Plaisir, WC2
Mosimann's Club, SW1
Neal Street Restaurant, WC2
Nico Central, W1
Odette's, NW1
Odin's Restaurant, W1
Osteria Antica Bologna, SW11
Le Palais du Jardin, WC2
People's Palace, SE1 [N]
Pied à Terre, W1
Poissonnerie de l'Avenue, SW3
Le Pont de la Tour, SE1
Quality Chop House, EC1
Quincy's, NW2
Ransome's Dock, SW11
The Ritz, W1
Riva, SW13
River Café, W6
San Lorenzo, SW3
The Savoy, WC2
Shaw's, SW7
Shepherd's, SW1
Simply Nico, SW1
Snows on the Green, W6
The Square, SW1
Star of India, SW5 [N]
Stephen Bull, W1
Le Suquet, SW3
La Tante Claire, SW3
Turner's, SW3
Walton's of Walton Street, SW3

ENGLAND:

Amberley, Amberley Castle
Aston Clinton, The Bell Inn
Aylesbury, Hartwell House
Barnstaple, Lynwood House
Baslow, Fischer's Baslow Hall
Bath, Bath Spa Hotel
Bath, Clos du Roy
Bath, Queensberry Hotel
Bath, Royal Crescent Hotel
Bibury, The Swan
Birmingham, Swallow Hotel
Bradford-on Avon, Woolley Grange
Bradford, Restaurant 19
Bray-on-Thames, The Waterside Inn
Brimfield, Poppies Restaurant
Bristol, Harveys Restaurant
Bristol, Restaurant Lettonie

Bristol, Swallow Royal Hotel ❀
Broadway, Lygon Arms ❀
Brockenhurst, Le Poussin ❀
Bury, Normandie Hotel & Restaurant ❀
Calstock, Danescombe Valley Hotel [N] ❀
Castle Combe, Manor House ❀
Chaddesley Corbett, Brockencote Hall ❀
Chagford, Gidleigh Park ♣
Charingworth, Charingworth Manor ❀
Cheltenham, Le Champignon Sauvage ❀
Chester, Chester Grosvenor ❀
Chester, Crabwall Manor [N] ❀
Colerne, Lucknam Park ❀
Corse Lawn, Corse Lawn House ❀
Dartmouth, Carved Angel ♣
Dedham, Le Talbooth Restaurant ❀
Dorrington, Country Friends ❀
East Grinstead, Gravetye Manor ♣
Evershot, Summer Lodge ❀
Faversham, Read's ❀
Fressingfield, Fox and Goose ❀
Gillingham, Stock Hill House ❀
Goring-on-Thames, The Leatherne Bottel ❀
Grasmere, Michael's Nook ❀
Great Milton, Le Manoir aux Quat'Saisons ♣
Grimston, Congham Hall ❀
Gulworthy, Horn of Plenty ❀
Hambleton, Hambleton Hall ♣
Hastings, Röser's Restaurant ❀
Herstmonceux, Sundial Restaurant ❀
Hetton, Angel Inn ❀
Hintlesham, Hintlesham Hall ♣
Hunstrete, Hunstrete House ❀
Huntsham, Huntsham Court ❀
Ilkley, Box Tree [N] ❀
Kenilworth, Restaurant Bosquet [N] ❀
Langho, Northcote Manor ❀
Leamington Spa, Mallory Court ❀
Ledbury, Hope End ❀
Leeds, Pool Court at 42, The Calls ❀
Liskeard, Well House ❀
Longridge, Paul Heathcote's Restaurant [P] ♣
Lower Slaughter, Lower Slaughter Manor ❀
Ludlow, The Merchant House [N] ❀
Malvern, Croque-en-Bouche ❀
Melbourn, Pink Geranium ❀
Moulsford-on-Thames, Beetle & Wedge ❀
New Milton, Chewton Glen ♣
Newcastle-upon-Tyne, 21 Queen Street ❀
Northleach, Old Woolhouse ♣
Norwich, Adlard's ❀
Oxford, Gee's Restaurant ❀
Padstow, Seafood Restaurant ♣
Plymouth, Chez Nous ❀
Pulborough, Stane Street Hollow ❀

ENGLAND (Contd):

Ridgeway, Old Vicarage
Romsey, Old Manor House
Shinfield, L'Ortolan
South Molton, Whitechapel Manor
Speen, The Old Plow Inn at Speen
Staddlebridge, McCoy's
Stapleford, Stapleford Park
Ston Easton, Ston Easton Park
Storrington, Manleys
Taplow, Cliveden
Taunton, Castle Hotel
Thornbury, Thornbury Castle
Thundridge, Hanbury Manor
Torquay, Remy's Restaurant Français
Tunbridge Wells, Thackeray's House
Twickenham, McClements
Uckfield, Horsted Place
Ullswater, Sharrow Bay
Warminster, Bishopstrow House
Waterhouses, Old Beams
Winchester, Hotel du Vin & Bistro [N]
Windermere, Miller Howe
Windermere, Roger's Restaurant
Winteringham, Winteringham Fields
Witherslack, Old Vicarage
Woburn, Paris House
Woodstock, Feathers Hotel
Woolton Hill, Hollington House Hotel [N]
Worcester, Brown's
York, Melton's
York, Middlethorpe Hall

SCOTLAND:

Auchterarder, Gleneagles Hotel
Crinan, Crinan Hotel
Dunkeld, Kinnaird [N]
Edinburgh, The Atrium [N]
Edinburgh, Martin's
Edinburgh, The Witchery by the Castle [N]
Fort William, Inverlochy Castle
Glasgow, One Devonshire Gardens
Gullane, La Potiniere
Kingussie, The Cross
Linlithgow, Champany Inn
Peat Inn, The Peat Inn
Port Appin, Airds Hotel
Turnberry, Turnberry Hotel
Ullapool, Altnaharrie Inn

WALES:

Abergavenny, Walnut Tree Inn
Llandudno, Bodysgallen Hall
Llyswen, Llangoed Hall
Portmeirion, Hotel Portmeirion
Pwllheli, Plas Bodegroes

CHANNEL ISLANDS & ISLE OF MAN:
   Jersey, Longueville Manor ❀
NORTHERN IRELAND:
   Belfast, Roscoff ❀
   Portrush, Ramore ❀
REPUBLIC OF IRELAND:
   Adare, Adare Manor ❀
   Castlebaldwin, Cromleach Lodge [N] ❀
   Dingle, Doyle's Seafood Bar & Townhouse ❀
   Dublin, Le Coq Hardi ❀
   Dublin, Patrick Guilbaud [P] ♣
   Dublin, Roly's Bistro ❀
   Dublin, La Stampa ❀
   Kenmare, Park Hotel Kenmare ❀
   Mallow, Longueville House ❀
   Shanagarry, Ballymaloe House ♣
   Straffan, Kildare Hotel [N] ❀

L!VE TV: THE FACTS

- L!VE TV is Britain's first national 24-hour live cable exclusive entertainment channel

- L!VE TV is owned by Mirror Television, part of the Mirror Group

- L!VE TV is carried by 96% of cable systems as part of the basic package and as such is free to over <u>1.25 million cable viewers</u>

- L!VE TV broadcasts all day, every day, from both a multi-million purpose-built in London's Canary Wharf and roving broadcast vans

- L!VE TV has both national network and local versions, including Birmingham and Westminster Live

- Investment in L!VE TV is over £30m

- L!VE TV produces virtually all of its output using an in-house staff of trained TV professionals

The Academy of Food & Wine Service

The Academy of Food & Wine Service was formed 7 years ago as a joint initiative by the Hotel and Restaurant Industry and the Wine and Spirit Trade.

The objective of the Academy is to increase the level of knowledge, and in particular, service skills, of those waiting staff employed in restaurants throughout the United Kingdom to benefit both the Industry and, more importantly, the Customer, by ensuring that there develops a network of waiting staff throughout the country who have been trained to National Vocational Qualifications Standards, initially at levels One and Two, and ultimately to even higher levels.

The Academy first set about this task by producing an open learning programme for Wine Waiters, which is available as a complete self-study pack, including a skills video, knowledge competence book and work book. This programme has been greeted by the Industry with much enthusiasm and has encouraged the Academy to further pursue research into a similar open learning programme on Food Service. Development of this new initiative is now completed and the pack is currently available.

This edition of The Ackerman Guide to the Best Hotels & Restaurants in Great Britain sees another step forward for the Academy. Readers will notice that certain symbols are marked with the symbol ❖. This denotes that the establishment employs a current member of the Academy or works closely with the organisation and supports its aims and objectives.

You will be able to identify our members by a small uniform lapel badge - green and gold for food service associate members, burgundy and gold for wine service associate members and a combined burgundy, green and gold badge for a full member. Membership is only available to those members of the waiting profession who have been trained and assessed to a National Standard and on whom you should rely for professional service when you are dining out. Please look out for these badges recognising competence and skills and start to demand that your favourite restaurant employs these dedicated, professional staff.

If you would like to obtain further information on the work of the Academy of Food & Wine Service, or as an employer wish to become an Establishment Member and involve your own staff in the training programmes, please contact the Academy at the address below:

The Academy of Food & Wine Service
Chelsea Chambers
262a Fulham Road
London SW10 9EL
Tel: 0171-352 6997 Fax: 0171-351 9678

London

W2 Abbey Court

20 Pembridge Gardens, W2 4DU
☎ 0171-221 7518   📠 0171-792 0858
▯ 22 £ £138

Stylish, small hotel in an elegant Victorian house just off Bayswater Road. Elegant bedrooms are provided with all amenities. There's no restaurant in the hotel: instead, a short menu for room service, including some hot dishes. In the Conservatory, serve yourself with drinks from the honesty bar.

W2 L'Accento Italiano

16 Garway Road, W2 4NH
☎ 0171-243 2201   📠 0171-243 2201
🪑 65 🍽 £55
☺ Lunch 12-3, Dinner 6.30-11.30   ☹ Bank Holidays

Useful neighbourhood Italian restaurant – set menu changes weekly; home-made pasta and breads; good seafood. House wine from Sicily.

W12 Adam's Café

77 Askew Road, W12
☎ 0181-743 0572
🪑 60 🍽 £30
☺ Lunch English café 7.15am-6.30pm (Sat 8-2), Dinner Tunisian restaurant 7-11   ☹ Bank Holidays

Mediterranean evenings, Tunisian specialities (including wines) at this unusual little café. Now open 7 days a week.

SW1 Al Bustan

27 Motcomb Street, SW1X 8JU
☎ 0171-235 8277
🪑 70 🍽 £60
☺ Noon-11pm   ☹ Bank Holidays

Lebanese cuisine, extensive menu, carefully cooked and presented in comfortable surroundings – useful opening hours.

W2 Al San Vincenzo

30 Connaught Street, W2 2AF

☎ 0171-262 9623

🍴 22 ⏱ £80

☺ Lunch 12.30-1.45, Dinner 7-9.45 ☹ Lunch Sat, all Sun, 1 wk Xmas

An intimate Italian restaurant run by the Borgonzolo family. Here you will find some of the most authentic Southern Italian cooking in London. Thinly sliced smoked sturgeon in a warm olive oil and lemon dressing, fresh snails cooked with cannellini beans in a slightly spicy sauce or gnocchi with caviar, chives and nutmeg are typical starters. Black noodles with crabmeat are served in a tomato sauce with Parmesan and a touch of cream, an octopus and potato stew, a breast of pheasant with apples and chestnuts are superb main courses and Vincenzo makes sure that he buys the English grey-legged partridge rather than the inferior red-legged to cook with broccoli. Afterwards try the very unusual slices of aubergine dipped in dark chocolate or mango with dolcelatte cheese. An excellent list of all Italian wines.

W1 Alastair Little

49 Frith Street, W1V 5TE

☎ 0171-734 5183

🍴 38 ⏱ £85

☺ Lunch 12-3, Dinner 6-11.30

☹ Lunch Sat, all Sun, Bank Holidays, Xmas

A Soho original (though many of us remember him at previous establishments, too!), Alastair is definitely part of the scenery and has thankfully endured in his minimalist setting, serving up eclectic (which came first, the food or the word?) cooking to a dedicated following. From the starting point of the ground floor, he was also one of the first to open a lighter, more relaxed outlet downstairs, to meet the demand for shorter meals of high quality. A 2-course lunch downstairs is still incredible value at only £12.50 and gives you a choice between pasta ceci, pizzetta bianca, green leaf salad with parmesan or ham-hock terrine; followed by bouillabaisse, sauté of beef with polenta, or crispy asparagus rolls with salad. Some of these dishes reappear on the carte, which is always available; and the upstairs set lunch is a well-balanced no-choice 3-course affair for £25: marinated tuna tataki with shredded vegetables and mustard soy; calves' liver persillade with a potato and bacon cake; then a choice between pudding and cheese (which may well include a Spanish variety). Other dishes which have been praised this year include potato pancake with smoked eel, bacon and horseradish, saltimbocca of monkfish with haricot beans and a pepper sauce, breast of duck with spring greens and rosemary gravy, rhubarb and pistachio trifle, and pannetone and butter pudding. The concise wine list is simply laid out and reasonably priced.

W11 Alastair Little Lancaster Road

136A Lancaster Road, W11 1QU

☎ 0171-243 2220

🍴 50 🍽 £70

☺ Lunch 12.30-2.30 (Sat till 3), Dinner 7-11   ☹ Sun & Bank Holidays

A return to his Notting Hill roots for Alastair Little, in another plain, white setting, the better to display the intensity of flavours in his Italian-dominated menus, cooked here by Toby Gush. Super food, wines and service. Outside seating is an added attraction.

EC1 Alba

107 Whitecross Street, EC1Y 8JD

☎ 0171-588 1798

🍴 40 🍽 £60

☺ Lunch 12-3, Dinner 6-11   ☹ Sat & Sun, Bank Holidays, 1 wk Xmas

Piedmontese specialities (especially truffles and risotti) from a refitted kitchen at this comfortable restaurant, handy for the Barbican.

SW3 Albero & Grana

Chelsea Cloisters, 39 Sloane Avenue, SW3 3DX

☎ 0171-225 1048/9   📠 0171-581 3259

🍴 150 🍽 £70

☺ Dinner only 7.30-11 (Tapas 6-12), Sat & Sun Tapas 12-11.30

☹ Some Bank Holidays

Contemporary and traditional Spanish cooking, available as tapas in the bar or from the carta in the restaurant. Cool setting, bright colours, lively and busy atmosphere.

WC2 Alfred

245 Shaftesbury Avenue, WC2H 8EH

☎ 0171-240 2566   📠 0171-497 0672

🍴 67 🍽 £60

☺ Lunch 12-3.30, Dinner 6-11.30

☹ Lunch Sat, all Sun, Bank Holidays & few days Xmas

Inspired cooking by Robert Gutteridge in an inspired setting: that of a working men's caff! But don't be fooled: this is one of London's most original restaurants where English food has been elevated to new heights with some exciting interpretations of traditional dishes. While a modest wine list has a few English representatives alongside the French, the list of beers is very impressive and should provide something for every palate. Usefully situated for the British Museum, Covent Garden and theatreland.

W1 Andrew Edmunds

46 Lexington Street, W1R 3LH

☎ 0171-437 5708   📠 0171-439 2551

🪑 40 🍽 £65

😊 Lunch 12-3, Dinner 6-10.45   ☹ 1 wk Christmas, 4 days Easter

Modest Soho basement bistro offering a largely Mediterranean menu and an interesting wine list. Candle-lit at night. Friendly service. Few seats outside.

N1 Anna's Place

90 Mildmay Park, Newington Green, N1 4PR

☎ 0171-249 9379

🪑 42 🍽 £50

😊 Lunch 12.15-2.15, Dinner 7.15-10.30

☹ all Sun & Mon, 1 wk Xmas, 1 wk Easter, Aug

A Swedish original, popular with regulars and first-timers. Lots of herrings, delicious puds and an international wine list.

W8 Arcadia

Kensington Court, 35 Kensington High Street, W8 5EB

☎ 0171-937 4294   📠 0171-937 4393

🪑 90 🍽 £65

😊 Lunch 12-2.30, Dinner 7-11.30   ☹ Lunch Sun

After a brief spell in the hands of the Barracloughs, this former site of The Ark is now staffed by a team from L'Artiste Assoiffé, so there's a familiar bohemian atmosphere to the decor and an equally familiar French flavour to the food.

W8 The Ark

122 Palace Gardens Terrace, W8 4RT

☎ 0171-229 4024

🪑 75 🍽 £45

😊 Lunch 12-3, Dinner 6.30-11

☹ all Sun, Lunch Sat, 4 days Easter, 4 days Xmas

Wooden exterior at this long-established neighbourhood bistro and restaurant serving mostly French-style dishes at excellent prices. Wine list is more international.

N8 Les Associés

172 Park Road, N8 8GT
☎ 0181-348 8944

🍴 38 🍽 £60

☺ Lunch 12.30-2, Dinner 7.30-10

☹ Lunch Sat, all Sun & Mon, 1 wk Xmas, 1 wk Easter, 2 wks Aug

Long-established neighbourhood restaurant offering bistro cooking at reasonable prices and a concise French wine list.

W1 Atelier

41 Beak Street, W1R 3LE
☎ 0171-287 2057

🍴 45 🍽 £70

☺ Lunch 12-2.30, Dinner 6-10.45

☹ Lunch Sat, all Sun, 2 wks Jan, 2 wks Aug

Stephen Bulmer & Joanna Shannon, both protégés of Raymond Blanc's Le Manoir, offer concise and well-priced menus to match and be enjoyed in warm, stylish surroundings. There's a modern European feel to the dishes, with less influence from the Orient than is customary these days, perhaps a brioche torte filled with pheasant, foie gras and juniper berries with a sherry vinegar sauce to start, followed by steamed brill with a wild mushroom mousse, leeks, mashed potato and spinach or a quail risotto with crisp pancetta and deep-fried sage. Fulfilling desserts lean towards the home country: apple and blackberry crumble with vanilla ice cream versus chocolate and walnut steamed pudding with a dark chocolate sauce. The enterprising set-priced meals (£15.50 for two courses, £18 for three, less if you order before 8pm) are particularly good value. Service charge here is only 10%.

W1 Athenaeum Hotel & Apartments

116 Piccadilly, W1V 0BJ
☎ 0171-499 3464 📠 0171-493 1860

🛏 156 £ £246 🍴 60 🍽 £70

☺ Lunch 12.30-2.30 (Sun brunch 8-3), Dinner 6-11.30 (Sun 7-10)
 (Tea 3-6)

☹ Lunch Sat & Sun

Grand hotel and apartments with a prestigious address. Luxurious, traditional atmosphere combined with modern amenities including a health spa. Cooking is modern British with Mediterranean influences.

SW1 The Atrium

4 Millbank Street, SW1P 3JA

☎ 0171-233 0032   📠 0171-233 0010

⌂ 155 🍽 £60

☺ Lunch 12-3.30, Dinner 6.30-11 (Café all day menu 8am-11pm)

☹ Sun, Sat before 7, Bank Holidays, 1 wk Xmas

Persevere when you come to the office building at this address: there is a restaurant inside it, and it's one where you can enjoy modern British and Irish cooking, including a roast of the day and a 'pot' of the day (which won't necessarily be a casserole!).

W1 Au Jardin des Gourmets

5 Greek Street, W1V 6NA

☎ 0171-437 1816   📠 0171-437 0043

⌂ 150 🍽 £75

☺ Lunch 12.15-2.30, Dinner 6-11.15

☹ Lunch Sat & Bank Holidays, all Sun

Long-established and much-loved Soho venue offering traditional French cuisine. Some dishes are only available to be shared; and the 6-course menu prestige really lets the kitchen display its talent to the full. Now on first floor only.

SW10 Aubergine

11 Park Walk, SW10 0AJ

☎ 0171-352 3449   📠 0171-351 1770

⌂ 40 🍽 £90

☺ Lunch 12.15-2.30, Dinner 7-11

☹ Lunch Sat, all Sun, Bank Holidays, 2 wks Xmas, 2 wks Aug

Another comparatively recent Chelsea flowering, this one run by Gordon Ramsay who learned his craft and style from, among others, Guy Savoy of Paris. However, Ramsay is very definitely his own man; and in a creamy, airy dining room you can enjoy cooking of style and flair accompanied by immaculate, attentive service and a good-value wine list. The best way to experience Aubergine is by taking the 6-course prestige menu at £44, which on a recent visit offered a cappuccino of haricots blancs with sautéd morels, then a mosaic of rabbit on a bed of cabbage and ceps; moving on to a delicate blanquette of turbot with cucumber and chives before a main course: papillote of best end of lamb in cabbage (the only recurring ingredient) with lentils and basil jus. Pause before the double puddings: a pistachio crème brulée then parfait of banana with bitter chocolate sorbet. Other popular dishes this year include salad of roasted langoustine with candied aubergine, roast canon of lamb with baby spinach and a millefeuille of aubergine (yes, they are used freely, but not to excess!), orange pyramid with blood orange sorbet. The set lunch at only £19.50 for 3 courses is excellent value for money.

NW8 L'Aventure

3 Blenheim Terrace, NW8 0EH
☎ 0171-624 6232
🍴 45 🕐 £65

☺ Lunch 12.30-2.30, Dinner 7.30-11

☹ Lunch Sat, 1 wk Xmas, 4 days Easter

Lovely little neighbourhood French restaurant, run with style by Catherine Parisot. The menu is short and changes twice-daily according to market availability, but always offers reliably-cooked classic dishes. Friendly atmosphere, accessible wine list. Some outside seating in summer.

SW1 The Avenue

7 St James's Street, SW1A 1EE
☎ 0171-321 2111 📠 0171-321 2500
🍴 180 (80 in bar) 🕐 £90

☺ Lunch 12-3 (Sun till 4), Dinner 6-12 (Sun 7-10) ☹ 4 days Xmas

Another larger than life London opening (around 250 seats) designed in hi-tech style by Rick Mather. Trendy food matches the decor, while noise levels match the prices – generally high.

W11 Avenue West Eleven

157 Notting Hill Gate, W11 3LF
☎ 0171-221 8144
🍴 56 🕐 £65

☺ Lunch 12.30-2.30, Dinner 7-11.15 (10.30 Sun)

☹ Lunch Sat, Bank Holidays, 4 days Xmas

Modern European cooking in a relaxed setting; Moroccan themed decor with modern sculptures and stone-tiled floor.

SW11 B Square

8 Battersea Square, SW11 3RA
☎ 0171-924 2288 📠 0171-924 6450
🍴 100 🕐 £60

☺ 12-11 (Sun till 10) ☹ 4 days Christmas & 4 days Easter

Another venture from Sebastian Snow (see also Snow's on the Green), this time renewing the partnership forged at 190 Queen's Gate with Ian McKerracher. An admirably simple menu (priced for 1, 2 or 3 courses, 4 choices per course) offers modern European cooking to accompany carefully-chosen wines in a bright and cheerful setting.

London 31

SW3 Basil Street Hotel

Basil Street, SW3 1AH

☎ 0171-581 3311   📠 0171-581 3693

🛏 93 £200 🍴 68 🍽 £55

☺ Lunch 12.30-2.15, Dinner 6.30-10.15   ☹ Lunch Sat

Privately owned hotel discreetly located behind Harrods; gracious decor and furnishings but not overwhelming – strong list of returning loyal clientele. Edwardian elegance in the Dining Room, fine wine cellar.

WC2 Belgo Centraal

50 Earlham Street, Covent Garden, WC2H 9HP

☎ 0171-813 2233   📠 0171-209 3212

🍴 140 🍽 £70

☺ Lunch 12-3, Dinner 6-11.30 (beer hall 12-11.30)

Covent Garden offshoot of the North London original, with the same appealing mix of moules frites, an endless beers list and waiters dressed as monks.

NW1 Belgo Noord

72 Chalk Farm Road, NW1 8AN

☎ 0171-267 0718

🍴 125 🍽 £50

☺ Lunch 12-3, Dinner 6-11.30 (Sat 12-11.30, Sun 12-10.30)

☹ 25 & 26 Dec, 1 Jan

If you don't like mussels, chips, lobsters and beer, forget it! If you do, join the queue and enjoy yourself at this ever popular Belgian-themed restaurant. Specialities are mussels served 10 different ways, Canadian lobsters in 4 variations, asparagus in 5 and chips with everything. An unbelievable, and even more unpronounceable range of fairly alcoholic beers, includes some produced by Trappist monks; and service is by habited waiters.

W8 The Belvedere

Holland Park, Abbotsbury Road, W8 6LU

☎ 0171-602 1238

🍴 120 🍽 £60

☺ Lunch 12-3, Dinner 7-11 (6-11 summer)

☹ Dinner Sun, 25 & 26 Dec, 1 Jan

One of the most attractive settings for a restaurant in London, amidst the lovely parkland of elegant Kensington – a perfect venue for parties or weddings, and unusually, there's even a complete party menu for vegetarians. Johnny Gold's bonhomie ensures a lively atmosphere, and some modern international cooking goes down well. The wine list tends towards the middle price bracket.

SW3 Benihana

77 Kings Road, SW3 4NX
☎ 0171-376 7799
🍴 150 🍽 £75
☺ Lunch 12.30-2.45, Dinner 7-11 ☹ 25 Dec

The Chelsea branch (there are now three in London) of Rocky Aoki's successful group of Japanese restaurants. Great fun can be had watching the chefs at work, producing traditional Japanese dishes served to the accompaniment of western cocktails.

W1 Bentley's

11 Swallow Street, W1R 7HD
☎ 0171-287 5025 📠 0171-287 2972
🍴 90 🍽 £80
☺ Lunch 12-2.30, Dinner 6-11.30, (Oyster Bar 12-11.30)
☹ Lunch Sat, all Sun, Bank Holidays, 3 days Xmas

New owners here but the same chef, Keith Stanley, ensures continuity at this well-established venue for good British seafood and oysters. Long established and perennially popular, the club-like dining room is on the first floor while the oyster bar is below it.

SW1 The Berkeley

Wilton Place, SW1X 7RL
☎ 0171-235 6000 📠 0171-235 4330
🛏 160 £ £332 🍴 65 🍽 £115
☺ Lunch 12.30-2.30 (Sun to 2.15), Dinner 6.30-10.45 ☹ Sat

So established is The Berkeley that it really doesn't look like a hotel, the impeccable doorman could easily be guarding apartments rather than one of The Savoy Group's flagships. There is a new management team in place under the direction of Ramon Pajares and an extensive refurbishment programme is under way that will revitalise the hotel without changing its image. The superb rooftop pool and in-house cinema will naturally remain and already in situ is Vong restaurant, offering superlative Thai French cooking under the direction of Jean-Georges Vongerichten of New York.

W1 Berkshire Hotel

350 Oxford Street, W1N 0BY
☎ 0171-629 7474 📠 0171-629 8156
🛏 147 £ £231 🍴 38 🍽 £75
☺ Lunch 12.30-2.30, Dinner 5.30-10.30 (Sun to 10)
☹ Lunch Sat & Sun

Heart-of-town Radisson Edwardian hotel and first-floor restaurant serving modern European food in an elegant setting.

WC2 Bertorelli's

44a Floral Street, WC2E 9DA

☎ 0171-836 3969   📠 0171-836 1868

🍴 90 🍽 £60

☺ Lunch 12-3, Dinner 5.30-11.30 ☹ Sun, Xmas Day

Handy for the Opera House; modern and traditional Italian dishes; two floors for dining: a famous London name.

SW3 Bibendum

81 Fulham Road, SW3 6RD

☎ 0171-581 5817   📠 0171-823 7925

🍴 72 🍽 £120

☺ Lunch 12.30-2.30 (Sat & Sun to 3), Dinner 7-11.30 (Sun to 10.30)

☹ Closed: 4 days Xmas, Easter Mon

Simon Hopkinson now occupies a consultancy role at one of the Conran group's flagship restaurants in Chelsea, with head chef Matthew Harris coming up to 2 years at the helm. The style is modern-European-meets-classic-bistro, served up in a much-photographed and famous setting. Typical starters might include grilled mackerel with potatoes, lardons and beurre blanc; sauté of lamb's sweetbreads with spring vegetables and red wine sauce; marinated oriental chicken with yoghurt, mint and coriander dressing; ballotine of fresh foie gras; pappardelle with morels – I think you begin to get the picture! Lots of international influences, but a sound classic base. Main courses are just as inventive, as shown by roast veal with broad beans, artichokes and tarragon; andouillette au canard with mustard sauce; grilled calves' liver with salsa and guacamole; or a quintessentially English deep-fried plaice served with chips and tartare sauce. Puds range from cinnamon cream tart to passionfruit parfait; from rhubarb compote with crème fraiche and butter biscuits to chocolate pithiviers – well worth the 20-minute pause while it's cooked to order! Typically to the fore of current fashion, there's the Oyster Bar (see below) on the ground floor for light but trendy snacking; and as you would expect of Bibendum, the wine list is second to none.

SW3 Bibendum Oyster Bar

Michelin House, 81 Fulham Road, SW3 6RD

☎ 0171-581 5817   📠 0171-823 7925

🍴 45 🍽 £70

☺ 12-10.30 ☹ 24-28 Dec

Ground-floor sister of the main Bibendum upstairs – shortish menu (except for the range of oysters!) popular with Brompton Cross shoppers.

NW1 Big Night Out

148 Regent's Park Road, NW1 8XN
☎ 0171-586 5768   📠 0171-482 4176
🍴 65 🕐 £55

☺ Lunch 12-3, Dinner 7-11

☹ Lunch Mon (Oct-Mar), Dinner Sun, Bank Holidays, 25 Dec, 1 Jan

Modern British cooking – set menus change daily, the carte monthly. Good range of wines by the glass and good range of teas. Small outside eating area.

NW6 Billboard Café

222 Kilburn High Road, NW6 4JP
☎ 0171-328 1374
🍴 65 🕐 £40

☺ Lunch 12-3, Dinner 6.30-12am (Fri & Sat to 12.30)

☹ Lunch Mon-Fri, Dinner Sun, 25 & 26 Dec

Freshly-made pasta and other distinctive Italian dishes dominate the menu here, and fixed-price options offer good value for 3 courses. It's open for lunch only at the weekends, when it's really brunch, and you can be set up for the rest of the day for a mere £6.50! Live jazz on Wednesday nights and frequently-changing displays of aspiring artists' work (for sale) all add to the charm.

W1 Bistrot Bruno

63 Frith Street, W1V 5TA
☎ 0171-734 4545   📠 0171-287 1027
🍴 40 🕐 £70

☺ Lunch 12.15-2.30, Dinner 6.15-11.30

☹ Lunch Sat, all Sun, Bank Holidays, 1 wk Xmas

Changes and expansion planned as we go to press. Watch this space.

SW7 Bistrot 190

190 Queen's Gate, SW7 5EU
☎ 0171-581 5666   📠 0171-581 8172
🍴 55 🕐 £50

☺ 7am-12.30am (Sun to 11.30pm)   ☹ 24-26 Dec

A busy bistro and bar situated just behind the Albert Hall where the ubiquitous Anthony Worrall Thompson masterminds one of London's most popular venues. The menu is an international mix of dishes, cullen skink from Scotland, provencale soupe au pistou, Italian bresaola or British cod and chips, the repertoire is extensive, the standards high, prices surprisingly low by London standards. Wines change every few months to offer selections from different wine merchants and value is again in evidence, few are over £20. The bar is a great meeting place and offers a light menu of dishes throughout the day.

SW7 Blakes Hotel

33 Roland Gardens, SW7 3PF
☎ 0171-370 6701   0171-373 0442
51   £268   35   £150
☺ Lunch 12.30-3, Dinner 7.30-11.30   ☹ 25 & 26 Dec

Without doubt Blakes is one of London's most distinctive and dramatic hotels with decor that makes the rest seem somewhat drab to say the least! Bedrooms vary from the sublime to the totally theatrical, they are all the work of owner Anouska Hempel whose taste is quite exquisite. The hotel has been created within a row of Victorian houses between Fulham and Brompton Roads. The elegant restaurant and bar are situated downstairs and the menu is a mix of various cuisines, dishes from France, Italy, Japan, China and Indonesia blend happily together and are perfectly prepared. Look out for Anouska's new hotel in Bayswater which opens later this year.

SE1 Blue Print Café

Design Museum, Shad Thames, Butlers Wharf, SE1 2YD
☎ 0171-378 7031   0171-378 6540
86   £60
☺ Lunch 12-3 (Sun 3.30), Dinner 6-11   ☹ Dinner Sun, 4 days Xmas

Smaller establishment within the Conran empire, ideally situated on the first floor of the Design Museum, with wonderful views over the river. Modern European cooking.

SW6 Blue Elephant

4-6 Fulham Broadway, SW6 1AA
☎ 0171-385 6595   0171-386 7665
250   £70
☺ Lunch 12-2.30, Dinner 7-12.30 (Sun to 10.30)
☹ Lunch Sat, 24-27 Dec, 1 Jan

Top-range, exotic Thai restaurant, complete with indoor waterfall. Ingredients and orchids flown in from Thailand, no MSG used, Sunday brunch especially popular, children under 4 are charged £2 per foot for their food!

SW7 Bombay Brasserie

Courtfield Close, Courtfield Road, SW7 4UH
☎ 0171-370 4040   0171-835 1669
175   £70
☺ Lunch 12.30-3, Dinner 7.30-12 (Sun to 11.30)   ☹ 25 & 26 Dec

The opulent Bombay Brasserie remains London's most stylish Indian restaurant with its large bar and attractive plant-filled conservatory. The varied cuisine offers Moghlai, Goan, Parsi and Tandoori dishes that vary in strength but are generally well prepared and seasoned. The luchtime buffet has bags of choice and is good value. Reasonable wine list – try the Omar Khayyam sparkling wine produced in India, it's surprisingly good.

SW7 La Bouchée

56 Old Brompton Road, SW7 3DY
☎ 0171-589 1929 📠 0171-584 8625
🪑 70 🍽 £50

🙂 9am-11pm (Sun 9.30am-10.30pm) 🙁 1 Jan

Popular French brasserie that's open from breakfast to late supper. Eat in the small, ground-floor dining room or in the larger basement, its wooden tables candle-lit by night and always with a buzzy atmosphere. Modern-style menu accompanied by a small selection of sensibly-priced wines, starting at around £7 a bottle.

W8 Boyd's

135 Kensington Church Street, W8 7LP
☎ 0171-727 5452 📠 0171-221 0615
🪑 40 🍽 £70

🙂 Lunch 12.30-2.30, Dinner 7-11 🙁 all Sun, Easter, 2 wks Xmas

In a light, bright, crisp conservatory setting, Boyd Gilmour has established a regular clientele for his stylish food – the room is long and narrow, with dark green wooden tables. Boyd's food is modern in style, eclectic in inspiration, and generally displays a sure touch. Excellent wine selection, with something for most pockets and palates.

W6 The Brackenbury

129-131 Brackenbury Road, W6 OBQ
☎ 0181-748 0107
🪑 55 🍽 £55

🙂 Lunch 12.30-2.45, Dinner 7-10.45

🙁 Lunch Mon & Sat, Dinner Sun, Bank Holidays, 1 wk Xmas

The decor is not pretentious, the prices are even less so, but the food is excellent and the service competent and friendly, a rare combination in London! Order a plate of nibbles to start with and a glass or 3 of the Hidalgo fino while you choose from the short menu. How about stir-fried squid, spaghetti, parsley and garlic, mussels marinière or eggs poached in red wine to start? Red mullet with saffron and rouille, pigeon breasts with celeriac mash and juniper berries or poached capon with salsa verde to follow. A highly original banana Yorkshire pudding with vanilla ice cream and hot chocolate sauce or buttermilk pudding with poached apricots should satisfy the sweet-toothed. Try a glass of different wine with each course, there are more than 25 to choose from. Why aren't there more user friendly restaurants like this one around town?

SW14 Le Braconnier

467 Upper Richmond Road West, SW14 7PU

☎ 0181-878 2853

🍴 30 🕜 £60

☺ Lunch Sun in winter only 12.30-2.30, Dinner 7-10.30

☹ all Mon, Dinner Sun, Bank Holidays, 1wk Xmas

Neighbourhood restaurant in Sheen offering French regional dishes. Lovely touch here: a special main course comprising small tastings of all the main dishes on the carte – perfect for the indecisive gourmet!

SW3 La Brasserie

272 Brompton Road, SW3 2AW

☎ 0171-581 3089 📠 0171-823 8553

🍴 130 🕜 £60

☺ 8am-midnight (Sun & Bank Holidays 10am-11.30pm) ☹ 25 Dec

While many places call themselves brasseries, very few truly fit that description. Peter Godwin's long-established corner of France, however, fits the bill perfectly. It's open long hours, you can sit outside (weather permitting), drink a coffee or a glass of wine, eat a sandwich or have a fully-fledged lunch or dinner of robust brasserie dishes. Even some of the waiters are authentically French – emphatically so!

SW3 Brasserie St Quentin

243 Brompton Road, SW3 2EP

☎ 0171-581 5131 📠 0171-584 6064

🍴 80 🕜 £55

☺ Lunch 12-3, Dinner 7-11.30

Shades of the Parisian Belle Epoque at this old favourite in Knightsbridge, where you can enjoy the atmosphere and bustle of a true French brasserie and appropriate menus (set and à la carte) of classics. Plenty of choice, too, on the hard-to-resist wine list. Just round the corner is the traiteur outlet of the same group, Les Specialités St Quentin, which makes superb croissants, amongst other things! See also the Grill St Quentin.

W1 Brown's Hotel

Albemarle Street, W1A 4SW

☎ 0171-493 6020 📠 0171-493 9381

🛏 116 £ £256 🍴 35 🕜 £85

☺ Lunch 12.30-2.30, Dinner 6-10 (Sun 6.30-9.30) (Tea 3-6)

☹ Lunch Sat

Dating back to 1837 and comprising two former town houses, this hotel is now a must on the afternoon tea circuit. Grand living and grand luxury.

EC1 Bubb's

329 Central Markets, EC1A 9NB
☎ 0171-236 2435
🪑 75 🍽 £75

🙂 12-2.30 ☹ Sat & Sun, Bank Holidays

Authentic French setting right by Smithfield market – but the menu here is just as strong on fish dishes. Plenty of other French classics, too, and an atmosphere created by decor and staff mean that with only a little stretch of the imagination, you could be in Paris.

SW11 Buchan's

62-64 Battersea Bridge Road, SW11 3AG
☎ 0171-228 0888 📠 0171-924 1718
🪑 70 🍽 £59

🙂 Lunch 12-2.45, Dinner 6-10.45 (Sun 7-10) ☹ 26 Dec

The Auld Alliance of Scottish and French in a popular Battersea venue – produce from the first, style from the second. Customers from the local area as well as further afield. Result: a jolly mixture for a fun night out in both the informal front area or more formal rear resturant.

SE1 Butlers Wharf Chop-House

36E Shad Thames Building, SE1 2YE
☎ 0171-403 3403 📠 0171-403 3414
🪑 115 🍽 £80

🙂 Lunch 12-3, Dinner 6-11 (Bar 12-3 & 6-11)
☹ Lunch Sat, Dinner Sun, Good Friday, New Year's Day

Within Sir Terence Conran's gastrodrome complex with a great view of Tower Bridge: British cooking at its old-fashioned best but with a singularly modern approach. Daily specials on the board; popular weekend brunch. Outside seating area.

SW1 Cadogan Hotel

75 Sloane Street, SW1X 9SG
☎ 0171-235 7141 📠 0171-245 0994
🛏 64 £170 🪑 40 🍽 £55

🙂 Lunch 12-2, Dinner 6-10 ☹ Lunch Sat, 24-29 Dec

Usefully located, full of historic references to Oscar Wilde and Lillie Langtry. Refurbishment during 1995 of lounges and some bedrooms. Traditional dishes, well cooked in modern style.

London 39

N8 Le Cadre

10 Priory Road, Crouch End, N8 7RD
☎ 0181-348 0606
🍴 40 🍽 £50

☺ Lunch 12-2.30, Dinner 7-11

☹ Lunch Sat, all Sun, Bank Holidays, 25-30 Dec

David Misselbrook runs a friendly local restaurant in French bistro style with modern overtones. Good value for money on the set menus (though a slightly higher price on Friday and Saturday evenings) and on the wine list, too.

SE1 Café dell'Ugo

56-58 Tooley Street, SE1 2SZ
☎ 0171-407 6001   📠 0171-357 8806
🍴 90 🍽 £60

☺ Lunch 12-3, Dinner 7-11 (Café/Bar: 10am-11pm)

☹ Lunch Sat, all Sun, Bank Holidays

Mediterranean food full of sunshine flavours with the Antony Worrall Thompson touch, served in a relaxed atmosphere on the first floor, with a busy bar on the ground floor.

EC1 Café du Marché

22 Charterhouse Square, Charterhouse Mews, EC1M 6AH
☎ 0171-608 1609
🍴 100 🍽 £55

☺ Lunch 12-2.30, Dinner 6.30-10

☹ Lunch Sat, all Sun, Bank Holidays, 1 wk Xmas

French brasserie cooking in the heart of the English meat market. Live jazz in the evenings.

NW3 Café Flo

205 Haverstock Hill, NW3 4QY
☎ 0171-435 6744
🍴 40 🍽 £40

☺ 10am-11pm (Sun to 10.30)   ☹ 3 days Xmas

Right formula, right price, right time: the Cafés Flo are just about spot on, with simply-prepared dishes offering good value for money, to the accompaniment of appropriate wines in a very friendly atmosphere. No surprise, then, that the group has now expanded so that branches are as follows:

334 Upper Street, Islington Green, N1 8EA	Tel: 0171-226 7916
51 St Martins Lane, WC2N 4EA	Tel: 0171-435 6744
127-129 Kensington Church Street, W8 7LP	Tel: 0171-727 8142
676 Fulham Road, SW6 5SA	Tel: 0171-371 9673
13-14 Thayer Street, W1M 5LD	Tel: 0171-935 5023
26 Chiswick High Road, W4 1TE	Tel: 0181-995 3804

Les vrais bistros indeed!

W1 Café Royal Grill Room

68 Regent Street, W1R 6EL
☎ 0171-437 9090 📠 0171-439 7672
🍴 45 🍽 £135
☺ Lunch 12-2.30, Dinner 6-10.15
☹ Lunch Sat, all Sun, Bank Holidays, 3 days Xmas

The luxurious surroundings of the famous Café Royal are a fine stage for the superb cooking of Herbert Berger and the skilled service from David Arcusi's team of staff. Classic dishes have modern touches and there are the simple grills and perhaps Bresse chicken or chateaubriand for two on his compact menu. A wonderful venue in which to impress a business associate or to celebrate a special occasion.

NW1 Camden Brasserie & Underground Café

214/216 Camden High Street, NW1
☎ 0171-482 2114 📠 0171-284 2484
🍴 100 🍽 £55
☺ Lunch 12-3 (Sun-4), Dinner 6-11.30 (Sun-10.30) ☹ 25, 27 & 31 Dec

Two floors, two different names, similar style of Mediterranean food and arguably the best fries in London. Charcoal grill much used; concise, fairly-priced wine list.

SW19 Cannizaro House

West Side, Wimbledon Common, SW19 4UF
☎ 0181-879 1464 📠 0181-879 7338
🛏 46 £160 🍴 36 🍽 £95
☺ Lunch 12-2.30 (Sun 12.30-2), Dinner 7-10.30 (Sun to 10)

Elegant house set in its own parkland and backing onto the Common – country house style with a London address. Traditional classic cooking, including flambés.

SW10 The Canteen

Harbour Yard, Chelsea Harbour, SW10 0XD
☎ 0171-351 7330 📠 0171-351 6189
🍴 135 🍽 £75
☺ Lunch 12-3 (Sun 12.30-3.30), Dinner 6.30-12 (Sun 7-11)

The proximity of this restaurant to our offices sets many a heart soaring at the thought of great food on a daily basis (chance would be a fine thing!), but while you can just pop in for a bowl of risotto, such a snack would hardly do justice to some of the great cooking on offer here, which deserves close attention, though Marco Pierre White is no longer involved in the operation. However, the good news is that new chef Tim Powell is a talent to watch – try perhaps his rabbit terrine with pear chutney or rare grilled tuna served with sweet pickles and sesame dressing, and follow with a hearty navarin of lamb with parsley dumplings or the more delicate steamed fillet of brill with a velouté of oysters. Desserts deserve serious attention and the wine list includes the alcoholic strengths on each bin, an unusual and useful service; in addition a fine wine reserve list is available on request – for serious imbibers with deep pockets only!

London

SE1 Cantina del Ponte

Butlers Wharf Building, 36c Shad Thames,
Butlers Wharf, SE1 2YE
☎ 0171-403 5403   📠 0171-403 0267
🍴 95 🍽 £65

☺ Lunch 12-3, Dinner 6-11   ☹ Dinner Sun, Good Friday, 5 days Xmas

Part of Conran's Gastrodrome at Tower Bridge the Cantina offers a range of Mediterranean (mainly Italian) dishes and a super view of the Thames. There are pasta and pizza dishes together with a few more substantial main dishes such as braised oxtail with savoy cabbage and black pudding ravioli and rib-eye steak with plum tomato, black olive and parsley salad. Wines with the exception of champagne are all Italian, good but not cheap. Friendly service and lots of outside tables for the summer.

SW3 The Capital

22-24 Basil Street, SW3 1AT
☎ 0171-589 5171   📠 0171-225 0011
🛏 48 £ £257 🍴 40 🍽 £120

☺ Lunch 12-2.30, Dinner 7-11.15, (light meals 7.30am to 11.15pm)

At the heart of David Levin's mini empire (see also The Greenhouse, L'Hotel and People's Palace), the Capital has just undergone a facade-lift and benefits now from increased air-conditioning, as befits a small, luxury hotel in this part of London. Bedrooms and public rooms are all beautifully and individually furnished and decorated, with no attention to detail spared. Standards of upkeep are naturally impeccable. Chef Philip Britten has a discerning international clientele who dine in the sumptuous newly Margaret Levin-designed restaurant from a mixture of fixed-price menus (lunch at £22.50 or £25, dinner at £35 or £40) and the carte. The 6-course evening gourmet menu emphasises Philip's affection for fish, presented in his usual modern European way.
One such recent example offered consommé of scallops and beetroot with crème fraiche; then lobster salad with oranges and ginger; moving on to fresh spinach pasta and warm marinated salmon before a main course of baked seabass with braised fennel, basil and pinenuts, each course deliciously different and cleverly compiled. The pair of puddings were compote of pineapple with coconut tuiles and vanilla parfait with caramel syrup. Though not counted as one of the 6 courses, coffee and petits fours are also included at the price. The touch is just as sure with meat dishes: recently enjoyed have been a salad of grilled and thinly sliced fillet of beef on a bed of seasonal leaves and vegetables with fungi oil; best end of lamb on a sauté of courgettes, aubergines and coriander with a touch of mint and yoghurt; and pot-roasted saddle of rabbit with mushrooms and champagne. A superb wine list matches the stature of both the cooking and the environment.

SW1 Le Caprice

Arlington House, Arlington Street, SW1A 1RT
☎ 0171-629 2239   📠 0171-493 9040
🍴 70   🍽 £70

☺ Lunch 12-3 (Sun to 3.30), Dinner 6-12   ☹ 1 wk Xmas

Another desperately fashionable haunt for the jet-set and wannabees, Le Caprice actually also turns out some jolly good food. Under the same ownership as The Ivy, it shares a similar atmosphere in which modern European cooking by Tim Hughes is enjoyed. There are no set menus here, just the carte, and it has plenty of variety. There are even two grades of frites: pommes allumettes and medium-cut chips! Typical starters could be roasted Italian onions with San Daniele ham; seared scallops with Alsace bacon and sorrel; sautéed foie gras with Sauternes jus; smoked ham hock and split pea soup, ensuring something for most palates and pockets. Pasta and other light dishes can be taken as starter, main-course or between-course, and range from eggs Benedict to fettucine with langoustine tails. Main courses proper go from tournedos Rossini back to bangers and mash with bubble and squeak and onion gravy, but the sausages will be Lincolnshire's finest: the quality of the raw ingredients is what lifts the cooking here. A concise wine list covers Europe and the New World at relatively reasonable prices.

SW3 Carnegie Club London Outpost

69 Cadogan Gardens, SW3 2RB
☎ 0171-589 7333   📠 0171-581 4958
🛏 12   £154

Luxuriously and stylishly appointed town house, home-from-home (if you're lucky!), in leafy Chelsea setting. Offshoot of Peter de Savary's Skibo Castle in Scotland. Serves breakfast. Light meals also available through room service.

N1 Casale Franco

134-127 Upper Street, N1 1PQ
☎ 0171-226 8994   📠 0171-359 5569
🍴 140   🍽 £60

☺ Lunch 12.30-2.30, Dinner 6.30-11.30 (Sun to 11)
☹ Lunch Tue-Thu, all Mon, Bank Holidays, 1 wk Aug, 1 wk Xmas

Useful Islington local Italian restaurant, specialising in Pugliese and Venetian dishes. Menu changes seasonally. Brick walls, simple setting with some outside tables.

SW10 Chapter 11

47 Hollywood Road, SW10
☎ 0171-351 1683   📠 0171-376 5083
🍴 60   🍽 £50

☺ Dinner 7-11.30   ☹ Lunch daily, Dinner Sun, Bank Holidays

Concise menu of modern English dishes in popular Fulham/Chelsea borders venue. Well-priced wine list. 35 seats in the garden for summer eating and drinking.

London 43

W5 Charlotte's Place

16 St Matthew's Road, W5 3JT

☎ 0181-567 7541   📠 0181-567 0346

🪑 40 🍽 £50

☺ Lunch 12.30-2, Dinner 7.30-10   ☹ Check when booking

Long-established, modern British neighbourhood restaurant – simple menu, good-value set lunches, concise wine list.

SW1 The Chelsea

17-25 Sloane Street, SW1X 9NU

☎ 0171-235 4377   📠 0171-235 3705

🛏 225 £ £200 🪑 90 🍽 £60

☺ Lunch 12-2.30, Dinner 6-10.30

This modern hotel has had a chequered ownership history over the last 10 years but now seems to have settled down with its Hong Kong-based group, which has retained such features as the stunning central art deco-style staircase. It enjoys a useful, central location; and the Sunday jazz brunch is popular.

W1 Chesterfield Hotel

35 Charles Street, W1X 8LX

☎ 0171-491 2622   📠 0171-491 4793

🛏 110 £ £210 🪑 60 🍽 £80

☺ Lunch 12.30-2.15 (Sun to 2), Dinner 6.30-10.30 (Sat 5.30-9.30, Sun 7-10)   ☹ Lunch Sat

An elegant, very British hotel furnished and decorated in what is almost London Club-style, recreating the ambience of days gone by – no surprise, then, to discover that it's American owned. The main dining room is the Butler's Restaurant, and there's also an attractive conservatory where you can have a buffet lunch or afternoon tea.

W1 Chez Gerard

8 Charlotte Street, W1P 1HE

☎ 0171-636 4975

🪑 86 🍽 £55

☺ Lunch 12-3, Dinner 6-11.30   ☹ Lunch Sat, Bank Holidays

Simplicity and quality are the keynotes to success at this stylish, bright restaurant which claims to offer the best steak frites this side of Paris. At only £15, the fixed-price menu is certainly a snip. Good wines on the list start at under £10, with plenty of good bottles under £20. The flagship outlet of this undeniably successful Groupe.

W1 Chez Gerard

31 Dover Street, W1X 3RA

☎ 0171-499 8171

🪑 130 🍽 £55

☺ Lunch 12-3, Dinner 6-11.30   ☹ Sun, Bank Holidays

The menu at this branch is similar to that at Charlotte Street – a wide range of grills, in particular. There's a charming room with a vaulted brick ceiling that is especially popular for private parties.

WC2 Chez Gerard

119 Chancery Lane, WC2A 1PP

☎ 0171-405 0290

🪑 160 🍽 £55

☺ Lunch 12-3, Dinner 6-10 (breakfast 8-11.30, tea 3-5.30, wine bar 5.30-11)   ☹ Sat & Sun, Bank Holidays

Business at the city branch of the trio focuses on the wine bar which offers a range of simpler dishes; though at the main restaurant, the full gamut of traditional grills is available.

N4 Chez Liline

101 Stroud Green Road, N4 3PX

☎ 0171-263 6550

🪑 50 🍽 £45

☺ Lunch 12.30-2.30, Dinner 6.30-10.30   ☹ Sun, Bank Holidays

Mauritian seafood restaurant that has now become an established part of the culinary scene. Tropical fish are cooked to order in a variety of ways and with tasty flavourings, and as you can imagine with such warm sources, service is laid-back and friendly.

W11 Chez Moi

1 Addison Avenue, Holland Park, W11 4QS

☎ 0171-603 8267

🪑 45 🍽 £85

☺ Lunch 12.30-2, Dinner 7-11   ☹ Lunch Sat, all Sun, Bank Holidays

One of London's longest-established restaurants, with a reputation built solidly on attentive service from the patrons, Richard Walton & Colin Smith, who look after their loyal clientele as carefully now as they did some 28 years ago! On the good-value set menus, classics sit comfortably alongside newcomers: a case of menu mimics guests, or the reverse?

W1 Chez Nico at Ninety Park Lane ♣

90 Park Lane, W1A 3AA
☎ 0171-409 1290   📠 0171-355 4877
🍴 70   ⏱ £135

☺ Lunch 12-2, Dinner 7-11

☹ Lunch Sat, all Sun, Bank Holidays, 11 days Xmas, 4 days Easter

This is another occasion on which I quickly run out of superlatives: the man's a genius and there are no two ways about it. Despite the surprise with which cynics greeted his lodging here at the Grosvenor House Hotel. He does seem to have found a comfortable home and a perfect backdrop for his skilled cooking. Yes, it's expensive, but you get what you pay for. Merely describing a recent gastronomic lunch doesn't really do the execution justice, but if it sets your taste buds tingling, that's no bad thing! The special menu at £45 each for a minimum of 2 people runs to 10 outstanding courses, starting with langoustine soup with truffle sabayon, moving on to marinated salmon with blini and Iranian caviar, then salad of haricot beans with truffle oil and a boudin of foie gras. Risotto flavoured with cep, then grilled scallops with chive velouté and fresh vermicelli bring you to a refreshing lime and champagne sorbet. Steamed sea bass with olive crust and basil purée sets you up for a medallion of beef, served pink, with wild mushrooms. The simply described cheese and mini assiette gourmande bring the meal to a close. If it sounds overwhelming, remember that portions are not at all overpowering, and you invariably finish a course wanting more of that flavour; only for that desire to be replaced by sheer enjoyment of the next group of flavours. In addition, there are of course shorter menus as well as a carte. What more can I say? Simply go there and experience his cooking at first hand.

WC1 Chiaroscuro

Townhouse, 24 Coptic Street, WC1A 1NT
☎ 0171-636 2731   📠 0171-580 9160
🍴 59   ⏱ £65

☺ Lunch 12-3.30, Dinner 6-11.45   ☹ Lunch Sat, Dinner Sun

Edge-of-Covent-Garden setting where mobile phones are not tolerated! Concise menu offered in the first-floor dining room, especially good value at lunch and in the early evening. Modern international-style cooking.

W14 Chinon

23 Richmond Way, W14 0AS
☎ 0171-602 5968   📠 0171-602 4082
🍴 30   ⏱ £65

☺ Lunch 12.30-2, Dinner 6.30-10.30

☹ Sun, Xmas & Easter (check when booking)

Popular bar and restaurant serving an eclectic menu of modern-style European dishes with oriental influences. Predominantly French wine list.

W6 The Chiswick

131 Chiswick High Road, W4
☎ 0181-994 6887
🍴 70 🕐 £55
☺ Lunch 12.30-2.45, Dinner 7-11.30
☹ Lunch Sat, Dinner Sun, Xmas, New Year

A second outlet from the team which brought you the Brackenbury – modern European cooking at good-value prices, especially the early evening menu for only £8.50. Concise, reasonably-priced wine list.

W4 Christian's

Station Parade, Burlington Lane, W4 3HD
☎ 0181-995 0382   📠 0181-995 0208
🍴 42 🕐 £60
☺ Lunch 12-2.30, Dinner 7-10.30   ☹ Lunch Sat, all Sun & Mon

Light, simple decor combine with contemporary art on the walls and modern European food on the plate cooked in an open-plan kitchen at this friendly little neighbourhood restaurant. Soufflés are a speciality.

WC2 Christopher's American Grill

18 Wellington Street, WC2E 7DD
☎ 0171-240 4222   📠 0171-240 3357
🍴 120 🕐 £80
☺ Lunch 12-2, Dinner 6-11.30 (Café-Bar 11.30-11 Mon-Sat)
☹ Dinner Sun, Bank Holidays, 1 wk Xmas

Busy, stylish and popular, this bar and grill offers Classics and Specials on the menu, and a choice of New World or Old World on the wine list. The atmosphere is relaxed and friendly, so you can presumably mix these up and have a newer wine with a classic meal!

W1 Churchill Inter-Continental Hotel

30 Portman Square, W1A 4ZX
☎ 0171-486 5800   📠 0171-486 1255
🛏 448 £ £282 🍴 108 🕐 £80
☺ Lunch 12.30-3, Dinner 6-11   ☹ Lunch Sat

The recently refurbished Churchill now has even better facilities for business visitors with meeting rooms, boardroom and a business centre. Stylish suites and penthouses are comfortably furnished and staff are helpful and friendly. Idris Caldora cooks Mediterranean food in Clementine's restaurant, a bright and elegant room. Typical dishes may be a ravioli of egg and spinach with parmesan, steamed sea bass with spring vegetables in herb jus, roast fillet of beef with artichokes, sausage, potato and tomato. Well situated for the bustle of Oxford Street and the West End.

SW10 Chutney Mary

535 King's Road, SW10 0SZ
☎ 0171-351 3113 📠 0171-351 7694
🍴 110 🍽 £60

☺ Lunch 12.30-2.30 (Sun-3), Dinner 7-11.30 (Sun-10.30) (light meals Verandah Bar 6-7.30) ☹ Dinner 25 Dec, all 26 Dec

'The World's first Anglo-Indian Restaurant' now has some imitators, but the original leads the field. Colonial atmosphere in either the Conservatory, Club Room or Verandah Bar. Wines well chosen to complement spicy food.

W14 Cibo

3 Russell Gardens, W14 8EZ
☎ 0171-371 6271 📠 0171-602 1371
🍴 62 🍴 £65

☺ Lunch 12-3, Dinner 7-11 ☹ Dinner Sun

Popular local; lots of seafood amongst the Italian specialities here – no longer associated with L'Altro (qv). Set-price lunch offers good value – 2 courses for £12.50.

W1 Claridge's ♣

Brook Street, W1A 2JQ
☎ 0171-629 8860 📠 0171-499 2210
🛏 190 £ £316

The Restaurant:
🍴 120 🍴 £130

☺ Lunch 12.30-3, Dinner 7-11.15 (Fri & Sat to 1) ☹ Lunch Sat

The Causerie:
🍴 45 🍽 £85

☺ Lunch 12-3, Dinner 5.30-11 ☹ Lunch Sat, all Sun

To the outside world not much ever changes at Claridge's, though there has been a change in the kitchen: after 11 years chef Marjan Lesnik has moved on. The hotel continues despite this, just as it has for the last 100 years, playing host to all the most important visitors to London. Royalty, Presidents, Prime Ministers and Heads of State use it as a club, service and surroundings are all that they could wish for and the hotel is full of antiques and works of art. The Causerie is always busy, whether for the lunchtime smörgåsbord or pre- and post-theatre suppers, while a meal in the lovely art deco restaurant is a relaxed and more formal event. A three-course luncheon (£29 inclusive of service) offers a daily speciality (Irish stew, Claridge's chicken pie) or something from the trolley (roast rib of Scottish beef with Yorkshire pudding on Wednesday and Sunday), while from the à la carte menu you could choose a risotto of wild mushrooms and asparagus or lobster salad
with oriental spices and mango confit or a classic tournedos. Fine cheeses and a handsome and enticing dessert trolley will round things off in fine style.

W8 Clarke's

124 Kensington Church Street, W8 4BH

☎ 0171-221 9225   📠 0171-229 4564

🍴 90 🍽 £90

☺ Lunch 12.30-2, Dinner 7-10

☹ Sat & Sun, Bank Holidays, 10 days Xmas, 2 wks Aug

Sally Clarke's lovely Kensington restaurant goes from strength to strength, and her determination to stay with a successful formula has shown dividends at a time when so many restaurateurs and chefs try to create or tag on to a new trend, only to flounder as fashions change. When she began here, Sally herself was at the forefront of a new wave, then called eclectic or later Cal-Ital, but her sensible dedication to quality ingredients, albeit prepared in innovative ways, is what has seen her through. There's a comfort in the familiarity of the menu style, too: fixed-price for 2 or 3 courses with a little choice at lunchtimes; fixed-price for 4 courses with no choice in the evenings, the menus for the whole week clearly displayed. Balance is another key to her success, so that putting your destiny – at least for the mealtime! – in Sally's hands assures you of some fine combinations. A spring example could be ravioli filled with ricotta, black olives and pine nuts served over baby spinach and parsley; then breasts of pigeon char-grilled with blood orange glaze, celery salad and roasted root vegetables; Neal's Yard farmhouse cheeses with home-made oatmeal biscuits and radishes; and to finish, port cream pot with fresh fruits and biscotti. The wine list is equally carefully chosen. Wonderful home-made breads, biscuits, chocolates, preserves, wines and the cheeses are available from the shop next door.

W1 Coast

26b Albemarle Street, W1

☎ 0171-495 5999

🍴 150 🍽 £80

☺ Lunch 12-3 (Sun 12-3.30), Dinner 6-12 (Sun 6-11)

☹ some Bank Holidays

Up-to-the-minute, minimalist decor and style at another recent West End opening, where modern menus are served by cheerful, designer-clad staff. Dishes, though sometimes with unusual combinations, nevertheless deliver a good punch.

W1 The Connaught

Carlos Place, W1Y 6AL
☎ 0171-499 7070   📠 0171-495 3262
▭ 90 £ £320 🍽 75 🕐 £160
☺ Lunch 12.30-2.30, Dinner 6.30-10.30 (Grill Room 6-10.45)
☹ Grill Room: Sat & Sun, Bank Holidays

One of the most distinguished hotels in London and certainly one of my favourites. It's the sort of place you find yourself recommending when someone asks you for a really special place – a suitable backdrop for a marriage proposal, or to celebrate the award of some honour. That it enjoys equal status with The Savoy within the Savoy Group plc is surely also a testament to its standing. The public rooms are reassuringly "establishment", as are the bedrooms and suites, and in the two air-conditioned restaurants (Grill Room and, simply, Restaurant) you can enjoy cooking from the immensely highly respected brigade of Michel Bourdin. "Brigade" is something of a misnomer – it's an education in itself merely to train with the Master, and his down-to-earth modesty when you meet the man is endearing. Classics abound, from the specialities to be ordered in advance like mignon de veau Prince Orloff, or zephyrs de sole Tout Paris; to the regular luncheon dishes like steak, kidney and mushroom pie on Mondays to boiled silverside on Thursdays. As well as sweets from the trolley, there are savouries or well-kept cheeses. The wine list is everything you would expect at a hotel of this stature.

SW10 Conrad International London

Chelsea Harbour, SW10 OXG
☎ 0171-823 3000   📠 0171-351 6525
▭ 160 £ £285 🍽 50 🕐 £85
☺ Lunch 12-3, Dinner 6-10.30

Luxurious and elegant all-suite modern hotel facing the marina, much favoured by media celebrities. Well-furnished private and public rooms, good business facilities, excellent leisure facilities. Equally elegant dining with outside eating on sunny days. One of the better modern hotels in London. Well-managed with a touch of style.

WC2 Cork & Bottle

44-46 Cranbourn Street, WC2H 4AN
☎ 0171-734 7807   📠 0171-483 2230
🍽 100 🕐 £45
☺ 11-midnight (Sun 12-10.30)   ☹ 25 Dec, 1 Jan

Don Hewitson's wine bar has been established for over 20 years and is still one of the best places to drink serious wines in town. Whichever you choose, you are unlikely to be disappointed. This is a venue to fit the food around the wine, and you could have great fun doing so. There's a lively atmosphere, and if you ask Don to share a bottle with you, you might learn a thing or two about New Zealand wines.

SW14 Crowthers

481 Upper Richmond Road West, SW14 7PU

☎ 0181-876 6372

🍴 32 🍽 £65

☺ Lunch 12-2, Dinner 7-10

☹ Lunch Sat, Sun, Mon, 1 wk Xmas, 2 wks Aug

Friendly, neighbourhood restaurant, with a strong, local following, offering a blend of pan-European and specifically-French dishes in a cosy atmosphere.

SW3 Dan's

119 Sydney Street, SW3 6NR

☎ 0171-352 2718 📠 0171-352 3265

🍴 52 🍽 £75

☺ Lunch 12.30-2.30, Dinner 7.30-10.30

☹ Lunch Sat, all Sun, Bank Holidays, 1 wk Xmas

Despite its location in bustling Chelsea, Dan's has a rustic feel and an intimate atmosphere, created by pine floors and furniture and attentive service. The garden is always popular in good (or even average!) weather. You can choose from a fixed-price, 2- or 3-course menu or a small carte which will probably have a few specials. Good value, all round.

SW3 Daphne's

112 Draycott Avenue, SW3 3AE

☎ 0171-589 4257 📠 0171-581 2232

🍴 120 🍽 £85

☺ Lunch 12-3 (Sun to 4), Dinner 7-11.30 (Sun to 10.30) ☹ 1 wk Xmas

Immortalised in the media, must-book, must-be-seen-at, terminally trendy restaurant. Modern European/Cal-Ital/Pacific Rim influences, with the strongest leanings towards Italy. Relaxed, summery setting. If you're somebody, expect a warm welcome from the front-of-house team.

SW6 De Cecco

189 New King's Road, SW6 4SW

☎ 0171-736 1145

🍴 92 🍽 £40

☺ Lunch 12.30-2.45, Dinner 7-10.45

☹ Sun, Bank Holidays, 2 wks Aug, 2 wks Xmas

Busy and buzzy neighbourhood Italian, overseen by Anthony Worrall Thompson and managed by Julian Peters, just off Parson's Green with walls crammed full of framed posters. Plenty of pasta and seafood, plus daily specials. All-Italian wine list. Outside seating on pavement.

London 51

SW15 Del Buongustaio

283 Putney Bridge Road, SW15 2PT

☎ 0181-780 9361

🍴 60 🍽 £60

☺ Lunch 12-3 (Sun 12.30-3.30), Dinner 6.30-11.30 (Sun-10.30)

☹ Lunch Sat, Bank Holidays, 10 days Xmas

Slightly more sedate branch (cf Osteria Antica Bologna) of the Italo-Australian partnership of food and wine – strong local following who enjoy the rustic food and ambience, friendly atmosphere and good value.

W1 dell'Ugo

56 Frith Street, W1V 5TA

☎ 0171-734 8300 📠 0171-734 8784

🍴 180 🍽 £40

☺ Ground Floor café: 11am-12.30pm (bar to 11pm)

  1st Floor: Lunch 12-3, Dinner 7-12.30

  2nd Floor: Lunch 12-3, Dinner 5.30-11

☹ Sun, Bank Holidays

Shortly after Tony Worrall Thompson had opened dell'Ugo, it was the place on the gastronomic itinerary of some visitors from Rome, so quickly had the word spread. Tony has long been at the forefront of gastronomic trends, ranging from little touches like offering "hippy teas" to breathtaking combinations like thyme muffins with glazed crab, oysters and crispy bacon – the cooking style is loosely described as rustic Mediterranean. There's a huge range of dishes, but turnover is accurately monitored so that freshness is guaranteed. Choose, if you can, between mussels with ginger, chili and garlic in a coriander and lentil broth; pan-fried chicken livers, goat's cheese and spinach on filo; or spaghetti with artichokes, prosciutto and peas. Move on to slow-cooked baby squid with fried polenta and wilted greens; pot-roast pig with garlic, bay and thyme, mash and roast vegetables; or glazed goat's cheese tart with chicory and potato. Desserts are irresistible: bitter-sweet chocolate silk; rhubarb and stem ginger tart with walnut crumble; sour cream cheesecake with spiced plums. Several dishes are priced as either starters or main courses, so that the menu drifts along rather than impose itself on you; and snackers can enjoy light dishes that range from tapas to meze. Good range of wines, including excellent-value house wines by the glass or by the pichet. The atmosphere too varies according to which of the 3 levels you choose, becoming gradually more serious the higher you get.

NW8 Don Pepe

99 Frampton Street, NW8 8NA

☎ 0171-262 3834 📠 0171-724 8305

🍴 45 🍽 £50

☺ Lunch 12-2.30, Dinner 7-11.30 (Tapas bar 12-11.30 (Sun 12-3))

☹ Dinner Sun, New Year's Eve, New Year's Day

Long established, much feted Spanish restaurant featuring both tapas and a full restaurant menu of regional specialities and wines. Lively atmosphere.

W1 The Dorchester

Park Lane, W1A 2HJ
☎ 0171-629 8888 📠 0171-409 0114
🪑 244 £ £298

The Grill Room:
🪑 81 🕐 £130

☺ Lunch 12.30-2.30, Dinner 6-11 (Sun & Bank Hols 7-10.30),
  (Promenade Tea: 3-6)

Oriental Room:
🪑 51 🕐 £120

☺ Lunch 12-2.30, Dinner 7-11   ☹ Lunch Sat, all Sun, Aug

The Dorchester seems to be a favourite with at least one person in any random group to whom you pose such a question. It hasn't an ancient history (going back just to the '30s but such a story to tell since! Host and home to visiting dignitaries; stars of stage, screen and sport; lovers of unique and sumptuous design; and more besides. You could meet your maiden aunt for tea in the Promenade or have an early evening business drink in the Bar. If your heart is with the Rising Sun, then the Oriental Room might be your preference; or for plainer English cooking, you can't beat the Grill Room. Willi Elsener is in overall charge of the kitchens (though with plenty of back-up for the individual restaurants) and of the hotel's banqueting and conference business, too. He manages it all apparently effortlessly, just like Ricci Obertelli, General Manager and is as much part of The Dorchester as the splendid flower display in the foyer. As is so often the case, the hard work here is invisible to the visitor. The individual styles of the restaurants – classic English and of course exquisite Oriental – all share the same high quality of raw ingredients and tip-top presentation; so whether you are eating escalope of salmon with a potato crust and a fennel and dill sauce, boiled silverside with caraway dumplings, or marinated pork ribs baked in a tangy barbecue sauce, you can be confident that you are eating some of the best food available in London, being cared for by some of the most professional service in town, in a dream-come-true setting.

W4 La Dordogne

5 Devonshire Road, W4 2EU
☎ 0181-747 1836 📠 0181-994 9144
🪑 80 🕐 £55

☺ Lunch 12-2.30, Dinner 7-11   ☹ Lunch Sat & Sun, Bank Holidays

A touch of the Dordogne in a corner of Chiswick: all but the address is Gallic! Local specialities (Dordogne, not Chiswick!) feature throughout the menu but not exclusively: oysters come from County Down or Brittany, as appropriate. Wines are all French and moderately priced; and there's a wonderful opportunity to taste a white Jurançon with which the children of French kings were traditionally baptized! Where did we go wrong?

London 53

NW1 Dorset Square Hotel

39 Dorset Square, NW1 6QN

☎ 0171-723 7874 📠 0171-724 3328

▯ 37 £ £150 ♟ 30 🍽 £65

☺ Lunch 12-3, Dinner 6-10.30 ☹ Lunch Sun, all Sat

Beautifully restored Regency building with English-style bedrooms and Italian marble bathrooms. The Potting Shed restaurant and bar offers modern British cooking at reasonable prices.

SW7 Downstairs at 190

190 Queen's Gate, SW7 5EU

☎ 0171-581 5666 📠 0171-581 8172

♟ 70 🍽 £60

☺ Dinner 7-12 ☹ Lunch daily, all Sun, Bank Holidays, 1 wk Xmas

Seafood part of the 190 set-up – fish from all corners of the globe served in all manner of ways, but all with Tony Worrall Thompson's unusual touch and under the steady hand of manager, Graham Wells. There are even three types of fishcake! Carnivores and veggies also served, as well as hippy teas.

SW1 Dukes Hotel

35 St James's Place, SW1A 1NY

☎ 0171-491 4840 📠 0171-493 1264

▯ 64 £ £213 ♟ 30 🍽 £80

☺ Lunch 12.30-2.30 (residents only), Dinner 6-10 (residents only) (Sun from 7) ☹ Lunch Sat

Privately-owned, dignified, small hotel (nearly as many suites as rooms), each room individually furnished and decorated to a high standard. Well situated between Green Park and St James Park. The Duke in question was of the Wellington ilk.

EC1 The Eagle

159 Farringdon Road, EC1R 3AL

☎ 0171-837 1353

♟ 55 🍽 £40

☺ Lunch 12.30-2.30, Dinner 6.30-10.30

☹ Sat & Sun, Bank Holidays, 2/3 wks Xmas

If you can get a table in the Eagle, I'd hang on to it as it's a seller's market when it comes to finding a quiet place to sit and enjoy some exciting Mediterranean food. So often this can mean just olives, tomatoes, garlic, basil: not here, where there are dishes of Andalucian, Portuguese and Egyptian origin too.

W1 Elena's L'Etoile

30 Charlotte Street, W1H 1HJ
☎ 0171-636 7189 📠 0171-637 0122
🍴 82 🍽 £80

☺ Lunch 12.30-2.30, Dinner 6.30-12
☹ Lunch Sat, all Sun, Bank Holidays

The legendary Elena Salvoni watches, eagle-eyed, over her beloved customers; whether international star or local ad agency director, her greeting is assured. John Wrobel runs the front-of-house, whilst chef Kevin Hopgood and his team produce some imaginative cooking and presentation. Popular dishes include salmon and leek fishcakes, grilled calf's liver and bacon and gnocchi "Elena" (gnocchi with spinach, walnut, pesto, sage and tomatoes).

SW3 English Garden

10 Lincoln Street, SW3 2TS
☎ 0171-584 7272 📠 0171-581 2848
🍴 70 🍽 £75

☺ Lunch 12.30-2.30 (Sun to 2), Dinner 7.30-11.30 (Sun to 10)
☹ 25 & 26 Dec

Quintessentially English cooking in a quintessentially English setting – outdoor atmosphere in the conservatory, traditional dishes on the menu.

SW3 English House

3 Milner Street, SW3 2QA
☎ 0171-584 3002 📠 0171-581 2848
🍴 30 🍽 £75

☺ Lunch 12.30-2.30 (Sun to 2), Dinner 7.30-11.30 (Sun to 10) ☹ 26 Dec

Cosier sister of the English Garden, perhaps, with an open fireplace, heavy drapes and brass candlesticks. English cooking of a bygone age evoked on the well-priced menu.

SW15 Enoteca

28 Putney High Street, SW15 1SQ
☎ 0181-785 4449
🍴 40 🍽 £45

☺ Lunch 12.30-2.30, Dinner 7-11 ☹ Sun, 25-30 Dec

Friendly, informal atmosphere combined with good Italian regional food and wine; good value just south of the Thames.

SW3 The Enterprise

35 Walton Street, SW3

☎ 0171-584 3148 📠 0171-584 1060

🪑 35 🍽 £55

☺ Lunch 12-2.30 (Sun to 3), Dinner 7.30-10.30 (Sun to 10)

☹ 25, 26 & 27 Dec

English, traditional and modern food, in clubby, comfortable surroundings with friendly service. Good local restaurant owned by the Kemps (see Dorset Square, The Pelham etc.).

W1 L'Escargot

48 Greek Street, W1V 5LQ

☎ 0171-437 6828 📠 0171-437 0790

🪑 85 🍽 £100

☺ Lunch 12-2.15, Dinner 6-11.15

☹ Lunch Sat, all Sun, 24-26 Dec, 1 Jan

Still on 2 floors with differing styles, L'Escargot has not lost its place in the hearts (should that be stomachs?) of its dedicated following, not to mention all those first-timers for whom a trip to L'Escargot is still a part of a visit to London.

W1 Est

54 Frith Street, W1V 5TE

☎ 0171-437 0666

🪑 41 🍽 £40

☺ Lunch 12-3, Dinner 6-11 (Fri & Sat to 11.30)

☹ Lunch Sat, all Sun, Bank Holidays

Popular with media types who enjoy observing passers-by (from the large windows) and taking in the cool, minimalist decor. They further enjoy trendy, robust Mediterranean cooking and a strongly Italian wine list.

WC2 L'Estaminet

14 Garrick Street, WC2E 9BJ

☎ 0171-379 1432

🪑 60 🍽 £60

☺ Lunch 12-2.30, Dinner 5.45-11.15 ☹ Sun, Bank Holidays

Traditional French bistro (plus La Tartine wine bar in the basement), useful for pre-theatre dinners.

W4 Fat Boys

10a-10b Edensor Road, W4

☎ 0181-994 8089

🪑 80 🍽 £30

☺ Dinner 6.30-11

You don't need to turn up on a Harley to enjoy Thai food in the evenings here, though since it's a regular caff during the daytimes, it might be appropriate! As with others of this genre, the food is cheap, plentiful, filling and pretty authentic, though it's the atmosphere that sets this one apart: it's very much a fun place.

SW1 Fifth Floor Restaurant

Harvey Nichols, Knightsbridge, SW1

☎ 0171-235 5250 📠 0171-235 5020

🪑 110 🍽 £80

☺ Lunch 12-3 (Sat to 3.30), Dinner 6.30-11.30

☹ Sun, Dinner Bank Holidays, 25 & 26 Dec

Henry Harris's modern British cooking holds court up here to a constant stream of admiring diners and weary shoppers. Prices match the Knightsbridge setting, but being seen is more important here than economy! Stylish bar.

N8 Florians

4 Topsfield Parade, Middle Lane, N8 8RP

☎ 0181-348 8348

🪑 60 🍽 £50

☺ Lunch 12-3, Dinner 7-11 (Sun to 10.30) (light meals wine bar 12-11)

☹ Bank Holidays, 3 days Xmas

Neighbourhood modern Italian restaurant featuring dishes from the north. Amazing range of grappas. Easy-going atmosphere and friendly service.

SW10 Formula Veneta

14 Hollywood Road, SW10 9HY

☎ 0171-352 7612 📠 0181-295 1503

🪑 55 🍽 £50

☺ Lunch 12.30-2.30, Dinner 7-11.45 ☹ Dinner Sun, Bank Holidays, Xmas

Traditional cooking in a modern setting from the Veneto, seafood and pasta specialities; risotti are worth the 20-minute wait. Delicious desserts, good value wines.

London

W1 47 Park Street

47 Park Street, W1Y 4EB
☎ 0171-491 7282 📠 0171-491 7281
🛏 52 £ £310

An exclusive block of serviced suites and luxury apartments with
the distinction of having room service supplied by Le Gavroche (qv)!
Parking provided courtesy of the Grosvenor House Hotel –
a nice touch of co-operation in such a competitive industry!

W1 Four Seasons Hotel

Hamilton Place, Park Lane, W1A 1AZ
☎ 0171-499 0888 📠 0171-493 1895
🛏 227 £ £331

Lanes Restaurant:
🍴 75 🍽 £80

☺ Lunch 12-3, Dinner 6-11 (Sun 6.30-10.30)

Four Seasons Restaurant:
🍴 55 🍽 £120

☺ Lunch 12.30-3, Dinner 7-10.30 (Lounge: 9am-2am, Sun 9am-1am)

This fine hotel at the Hyde Park Corner end of Park Lane is 25 years
old and now in the capable hands of John Stauss. One of London's
most elegant and modern hotels it has spacious suites and bedrooms
and all the services you expect from a top hotel. (An invitation to their
Christmas Party is still one of the hottest tickets in town). There are
2 dining rooms, Lanes Restaurant with the hard-working and modest
Eric Deblonde (awarded a much deserved Chevalier de l'Ordre du Mérit
Agricole in 1996) as executive chef and the Four Seasons where Jean-
Christophe Novelli remains chef de cuisine until October 1996. Lanes
is the more traditional of the two with good value at lunchtime and
pre- or post-theatre dining from an extensive menu and super buffet.
The Four Seasons has an exciting modern French menu, a light scallop
and oyster mousse topped with julienne of cucumber and caviar with
asparagus sauce and a cassoulet terrine wrapped with slivers of Toulouse
sausage, cabbage and carrots with flageolet vinaigrette are typical hors
d'Oeuvres. Finely judged cooking at its best from both chefs makes this
hotel a real gem.

N1 Frederick's

Camden Passage, N1 8EG
☎ 0171-359 2888 📠 0171-359 5173
🍴 130 🍽 £65
😊 Lunch 12-2.30, Dinner 6-11.30 ☹ Sun, Bank Holidays

A long-established Islington restaurant which has recently undergone a face-lift: newly refurbished, new chef (Andrew Jeffs previously with Nico Ladenis), and new lease of life for septuagenarian owner Louis Segal and his son Nick. You can now sit at the bar and have just a bite to eat, perhaps a plate of risotto or a salad niçoise, washed down with one of the many wines served by the glass, as well as sitting in the airy dining area that overlooks the patio garden. The menu is much more modern than of old with starters such as risotto of langoustines with crème fraiche or crispy duck with tabbouleh and plum sauce, followed by main courses that might include a fillet of steamed wild seabass with spiced aubergine, coriander and taglioni or honey-roasted breast of duck, choucroute and carrot and potato mash. In addition to the à la carte menu, there are other options: a set 2-course business lunch for £12 (also served as the pre-theatre menu before 7pm) or a £13.50 (£5.95 for children) 3-course Saturday lunch. Terrific wine list, a passion of Louis, who likes nothing better than an excuse to motor down to France and purchase direct. Professional but friendly staff.

W1 French House Dining Room

49 Dean Street, W1
☎ 0171-437 2477 📠 0171-287 9109
🍴 30 🍽 £50
😊 Lunch 12.30-3, Dinner 6.30-11.30
☹ Sun, Bank Holidays, 10 days Xmas

French name, British food at this first floor pub dining room. Straightforward decor and food – they're open for supper rather than dinner.

SW3 Fulham Road

257-259 Fulham Road, SW3 6HY
☎ 0171-351 7823 📠 0171-376 4971
🍴 80 🍽 £80
😊 Lunch 12.15-2.15, Dinner 7-11 ☹ Bank Holidays, 1 wk Xmas

Stephen Bull's Chelsea outlet (no prizes for guessing its address!) is still thriving despite the departure of chef Richard Corrigan and restaurant manager Marian Scrutton. Cooking is inventive – unusual combinations of familiar ingredients, as in starters like cappuccino of wild mushrooms or terrine of foie gras and pressed leeks; main courses that might include a rump of lamb with smoked bacon and Savoy cabbage; sea bass served with braised red cabbage and pancetta; or breast and boudin of Bresse chicken with pearl barley. Desserts are just as difficult to choose between (hot pistachio soufflé with bitter chocolate sorbet; warm apple cake with caramel cinnamon ice cream), and a wine list of some stature includes plenty by the glass.

W1 Le Gavroche

43 Upper Brook Street, W1Y 1PF
☎ 0171-408 0881   📠 0171-491 4387
🪑 60 🍽 £160

☺ Lunch 12-2, Dinner 7-11

☹ Sat & Sun, Bank Holidays, Xmas & New Year

The Roux dynasty – both as a blood-line and by training – continues to weave its not-too-obtrusive spell over the eating habits of London's citizens. Here it's the heir apparent, Michel Jr, son of Albert and nephew of Michel-le-patissier, who has inherited the family mantle and it fits him beautifully. The menus themselves are discreetly labelled: with the famous Roux gamin, with the logo of Relais & Chateaux, and with a third declaring Traditions et Qualité. This could be said to sum up neatly the philosophy behind a meal at Le Gavroche: a luxurious setting and top-class cooking. You could do no better than to put yourself in Michel's hands and opt for Le Menu Choisi par Michel; or instead a short carte called Hommage à Mon Père, which gives you, for example, the famous soufflé suissesse, l'assiette du boucher, and omelette Rothschild to finish. Michel's own specialities include such delights as salade de langoustines grillées et asperges à la vinaigrette au truffe; dodine de canard et sa gelée au madère, and agneau de lait roti aux trois sauces. Desserts are simply delicious: even a simple-sounding crème brulée à la vanille scales new heights when eaten at the conclusion of a meal here. Whilst it has been remarked that the wine list could hardly be described as excellent value for money, it certainly matches the stature of the restaurant. Go on, enjoy it!

W1 Gay Hussar

2 Greek Street, W1V 6NB
☎ 0171-437 0973   📠 0171-437 4631
🪑 60 🍽 £60

☺ Lunch 12.30-2.30, Dinner 5.30-10.45

☹ Sun, Bank Holidays

What can I say? I suppose I did a Victor Kayam here: I liked it so much I bought the restaurant, hence the Vest Symbol, of which I am very proud. One of the greatest compliments paid was that there was very little impact on the customer, due in no small part to the good offices of chef Laszlo Holecz, in place since 1977, while front of house is in the friendly and capable hands of Bela Molnar. The atmosphere is that of a gentlemen's club, with red banquette seating, swathed plush drapes and dark wood. What of the menu? The traditional Hungarian favourites are all here – chilled wild cherry soup, cold pike with beetroot sauce and cucumber salad as starters; creamed chicken paprika with thimble egg dumplings or roast duck with red cabbage, Hungarian potatoes and apple sauce as main courses; dobos torta or walnut pancakes for pudding. Wines are Hungarian, Bulgarian or French, and reasonably priced. All in all, a meal at the Gay Hussar is an experience not to be missed (but I would say that, wouldn't I!). Look out for the lighter summer menu.

W8 Geales Fish Restaurant

2 Farmer Street, W8 7SN
☎ 0171-727 7969 📠 0171-229 8632
🍴 100 🍽 £30
🙂 Lunch 12-3, Dinner 6-11
☹ Sun & Mon, 2 wks Xmas & 2 wks July

Long-established family-run Notting Hill fish restaurant. No nonsense, no frills, good fresh produce, great atmosphere.

SW7 Gilbert's

2 Exhibition Road, SW7 2HF
☎ 0171-589 8947 📠 0171-589 8947
🍴 30 🍽 £60
🙂 Lunch 12-3, Dinner 6-10
☹ Lunch Sat, all Sun (exc Dec), Bank Holidays, 1 wk Xmas, 5 days Easter

Usefully situated to accompany some of South Kensington's culture – a transworld menu that's mainly French but benefitting from some oriental touches. Regular wine dinners, fine list of New World wines.

SW7 The Gloucester

4 Harrington Gardens, SW7 4LH
☎ 0171-373 6030 📠 0171-373 0409
🛏 548 £ £221 🍴 156 🍽 £60
🙂 12-10.45

Swish hotel with two club floors that have their own lounge. Excellent bedrooms and bathrooms. Restaurant South West 7 offers Cal-Ital cuisine.

SW7 The Gore

189 Queen's Gate, SW7 5EX
☎ 0171-584 6601 📠 0171-589 8127
🛏 54 £ £166
☹ 25 & 26 Dec

Next door to and thus sharing food facilities with 190 Queen's Gate, the Gore offers gracious London living surrounded by some stylish and different decor in a useful location (near the Royal Albert Hall).

SW1 The Goring

17 Beeston Place, Grosvenor Gardens, SW1W 0JW
☎ 0171-396 9000 📠 0171-834 4393
🛏 78 £ £179 🍴 70 🍽 £95
🙂 Lunch 12.30-2.30, Dinner 6-10 (Garden Lounge: 7.30am-11pm)

Just a stone's throw from Victoria Station and Buckingham Palace, the Goring is a medium-sized, family-run hotel offering comfortable bedrooms and elegant lounges. Efficient staff look after you very well; and in the restaurant there's a mixture of classic and modern styles to suit all tastes. Excellent wines have been carefully chosen and are reasonably priced.

London 61

N1 Granita

127 Upper Street, N1 1QP

☎ 0171-226 3222

⏱ 60 🍽 £50

☺ Lunch 12.30-2.30, Dinner 6.30-10.30 (Sun to 10)

☹ Lunch Tue, all Mon, 10 days Xmas, 1 wk Easter, 2 wks Aug

Popular Islington venue for modern Mediterranean cooking at reasonable prices in a minimalist setting. Concise wine list includes a good showing from the New World. Friendly atmosphere.

SW1 Green's Restaurant & Oyster Bar

36 Duke Street, St James's, SW1Y 6DF

☎ 0171-930 4566   📠 0171-491 7463

⏱ 65 🍽 £75

☺ Lunch 12.30-3, Dinner 6-10.45

☹ Dinner Sun, 3 days Xmas, Easter & New Year

Traditional English eating house offering classic cooking of the best fare, particularly seafood and game. Comfortable banquets in the bar with polished wood partitions. Daily specials are of the old school, though the carte shows distinctly modern leanings.

W1 Greenhouse

27a Hays Mews, W1X 7RJ

☎ 0171-499 3331

⏱ 90 🍽 £80

☺ Lunch 12-2.30 (Sun 12.30 to 3), Dinner 7-11 (Sun 7-10)

☹ Lunch Sat, Bank Holidays & 1 wk Xmas

A few South of the channel touches to enhance the British cuisine at this hidden venue in Mayfair. A baked cod fillet on stewed vegetables has hollandaise sauce, pan-fried halibut comes with noodles in anchovy cream sauce and crispy Bayonne ham, sautéed black pudding is served with mushroom risotto and bearnaise sauce is the perfect accompaniment to the grilled rib-eye steak. The cooking is precise and well executed, make sure you have room for one of the traditional puddings, hot apple fritters with vanilla ice cream and apricot sauce or creamy rice pudding with coconut and raspberry ripple ice cream.

W1 alistair Greig's Grill

26 Bruton Place, W1X 7AA

☎ 0171-629 5613   📠 0171-495 0411

⏱ 60 🍽 £60

☺ Lunch 12.30-2.30, Dinner 6.30-11

☹ Lunch Sat, all Sun, 25 & 26 Dec, 1 Jan

Long-established grill room offering a familiar menu of good-quality steaks and chicken, though recently more fish dishes have appeared. The lunchtime "quickie" menu has proved popular – £12.95 for a main course, coffee and a glass of wine – so they will probably expand its range.

SW3 Grill St Quentin

3 Yeoman's Row, SW3 2AL
☎ 0171-581 8377   📠 0171-584 6064
🍽 140 🍴 £55

☺ Lunch 12-3 (Sun to 3.30), Dinner 6.30-11.30

Spacious, basement restaurant just behind Brompton Road benefiting from a bright and comfortable Parisian atmosphere in which to enjoy some favourite authentic French grills, usually simply cooked without elaborate sauces and fussy garnishes. Good value wine list. Pleasant and informed front-of-house staff. See also the Brasserie St Quentin.

W1 Grosvenor House

86-90 Park Lane, W1A 3AA
☎ 0171-499 6363   📠 0171-493 3341
🛏 454 £ £272 🍽 100 🍴 £60

☺ Lunch 12.30-2.30, Dinner 6-10 (Sat & Sun to 10.30)
(light meals 11-11) (Pasta Vino 12.30-2.30, 7.30-11.30)

☹ (Pasta Vino: Lunch Sat, all Sun), Bank Holidays, 1 & 2 Jan

An institution on Park Lane, with luxurious lounge areas, bedrooms and suites, banqueting and conference facilities – familiar through TV for hosting awards ceremonies. Eat in Pasta Vino or Café Nico for some imaginative, reasonably priced creations.

W11 The Halcyon

81 Holland Park, W11 3RZ
☎ 0171-727 7288   📠 0171-229 8516
🛏 43 £ £235 🍽 50 🍴 £90

☺ Lunch 12-2.30, Dinner 7-10.30 (Fri & Sat to 11), (bar 11am-2am)
☹ Lunch Sat

Unobtrusively situated in Holland Park where it blends well with its dignified neighbours, this fairly small but select town house hotel has been lovingly restored to its Belle Epoque heyday. Spacious and elegantly proportioned rooms are individually designed and furnished to high standards (most of them were completely refurbished by early 1995), and the conservatory is an ideal meeting place or venue for light refreshments. The main restaurant, simply called The Room, comes under the auspices of head chef Martin Hadden, and he offers English and French cooking with particular emphasis on good-quality fish and shellfish. Menus are à la carte or fixed price (£18 for 2 courses at lunchtime, £21 for 3 courses at dinner, or £32 for a 6-course menu degustation) and offer some interesting flavour combinations. Try Thai-spiced chicken and coconut milk soup flavoured with lemon grass and lime leaves; honey-roasted quail with green bean salad with a mustard and hazelnut dressing; roast squab pigeon with a morel mushroom sausage, broad beans, smoked bacon and sage; salmon fillet with tagliatelle and red pepper vinaigrette. Desserts could include an unusual iced aniseed parfait, caramelised lemon tart, mint mousse or a plate of chocolate desserts. Good farmhouse cheeses come with home-made walnut bread and biscuits. The wine list is of appropriate stature to a hotel of this calibre, and service on all fronts is exemplary.

SW1 The Halkin

5 Halkin Street, SW1X 7DJ
☎ 0171-333 1000 📠 0171-333 1100
🛏 41 £ £262 🍴 45 🕐 £100
☺ Lunch 12.30-2.30, Dinner 7.30-11 (Sun 7-10), (Bar 11-11)
☹ Lunch Sat & Sun, 25 & 26 Dec

A quite unique hotel that breaks with London tradition: within the Georgian styled frontage is Northern Italian modern architecture, marble and delightful woods that feature in the stunning design. The restaurant is similarly simplistic overlooking a small garden and provides Milanese cooking of very high standards. Chef Stefano Cavallini creates dishes that are as precise as the decor, pasta with rabbit and wild mushrooms, hand made Ferrara maccheroni with broccoli and red mullet, a scallop of foie gras with Castelluchio lentils or a salad of scallops with black truffle. Main dishes of venison with blueberries, soft polenta, chestnut ravioli and sautéed savoy cabbage with pancetta and vinegar or pan-fried sea bass with courgette flowers, broccoli tortellini and red pepper sauce are typical examples of the imaginative cooking. Naturally the wine list is predominantly Italian and quality wines too. A very special hotel and restaurant with an international, dedicated following – style, style and more style – if you've got it, baby, flaunt it!

WC2 Hampshire Hotel

31 Leicester Square, WC2 7LH
☎ 0171-839 9399 📠 0171-930 8122
🛏 124 £ £248 🍴 55 🕐 £75
☺ Lunch 12.30-2.30, Dinner 6-11 (light meals Oscars 12am-11pm)

Radisson Edwardian's very central hotel, well insulated from the West End hubbub. French and continental cooking in the formal Celebrities restaurant.

**BRITAIN'S TOP
INDEPENDENT BUTCHERS**
see page 9

SW7 Hilaire

68 Old Brompton Road, SW7 3LQ
☎ 0171-584 8993 📠 0171-581 2949
🪑 60 🍽 £85
☺ Lunch 12.15-2.30, Dinner 6.30-11.30
☹ Lunch Sat, all Sun, Bank Holidays

Bryan Webb has been at Hilaire since 1987 and has made it very much his own. At the end of last year he undertook a modest expansion of the ground floor restaurant area, complete refurbishment of carpets, curtains and air-conditioning, amongst other improvements. The room is now an even more inviting arena in which to sample Bryan's splendid modern European cooking, which he offers on a mixture of set-price and à la carte menus, all very well balanced and simply described. Top of the range is a 4-course dinner which, from its choices, could yield you griddled scallops with vegetable relish and rocket; rack of lamb with herb crust and creamed flageolets; a selection of excellent English farmhouse cheeses; then white and dark chocolate terrine to finish – all this for only £32.50. His is one of the few restaurants, even today, to offer a serious alternative for vegetarians: substitute for the starter and main course salad of fennel, sun-dried tomato, crispy artichoke and shaved parmesan; then wild mushroom and truffle risotto; and you have a meal worthy of sitting alongside the omnivore version. In no way are vegetarians treated like poor relations! But as ever, remember to ask for this menu when booking. The wine list is reasonably priced and comprehensive.

NW8 Hilton International Regent's Park

18 Lodge Road, St John's Wood, NW8 7JT
☎ 0171-722 7722 📠 0171-483 2408
🛏 377 £ £150 🪑 42 🍽 £55
☺ Lunch 11-2, Dinner 5.30-10 ☹ Mon, 25 & 26 Dec, 1-3 Jan

Modern hotel, close to Lord's, the park and the West End. Good business facilities; relaxed eating in Minsky's New York Deli restaurant.

EC3 Hospitality Suite

London Underwriting Centre, 3 Minster Court, Mincing Lane, EC3R 7DD
☎ 0171-617 5042 📠 0171-617 5050
🪑 30 🍽 £75
☺ 12-2.30 ☹ Sat & Sun, Bank Holidays, 1 wk Xmas

An impressive setting in which to entertain business contacts in the city, this stylish room at the top of the London Underwriting Centre has fabulous views over the river and a luxurious, intimate atmosphere. The added bonus is food by the Roux Brothers, and all that such a pedigree leads you to expect is amply fulfilled. Not surprisingly, booking is essential! Tables well spaced for discreet business dining.

SW3 L'Hotel

28 Basil Street, SW3 1AT

☎ 0171-589 6286 📠 0171-225 0011

⌷ 12 £ £145 🍴 40 🍽 £40

☺ 12-10.30 (coffee & breakfast 7.30am-11am)

☹ Sun, Bank Holidays

David Levin's smaller Knightsbridge hotel (as compared with The Capital next door) and Le Metro wine bar/brasserie also open for breakfast.

E1 The Hothouse

78-80 Wapping Lane, E19 NF

☎ 0171-488 4797 📠 0171-488 9500

🍴 150 🍽 £50

☺ Lunch 12-3.30, Dinner 6-11

☹ Lunch Sat, Dinner Sun, all Bank Holidays

Warehouse setting (beams and wooden floor) for a modern European menu with seasonal specialities. Downstairs is considered a hot venue for parties. Concise, reasonably priced wine list.

WC2 Howard Hotel

Temple Place, Strand, WC2R 2PR

☎ 0171-836 3555 📠 0171-379 4547

⌷ 135 £ £267 🍴 93 🍽 £100

☺ Lunch 12.30-3, Dinner 6.30-11

A type of international elegance, tranquillity and calm pervade this centrally-sited hotel: glistening chandeliers, cool Italian marble, marquetry furniture. Traditional French cuisine in the Quai d'Or restaurant, superb Thames views from some rooms if you're lucky.

SW1 Hyatt Carlton Tower

2 Cadogan Place, SW1X 9PY

☎ 0171-235 1234 📠 0171-245 6570

⌷ 224 £ £295

Rib Room:

🍴 84 🍽 £110

☺ Lunch 12.30-2.45, Dinner 6.30-11.15 (Sun 7-10.15) ☹ 1-3 Jan

One of London's best run hotels. The Rib Room is a favourite, clubby, lunch venue offering grills and roasts, wonderful Aberdeen Angus beef or try the fisherman's mixed grill. State-of-the-art health club with full health & beauty facilities. Spacious, well-appointed bedrooms and bathrooms.

SW1 Hyde Park Hotel

66 Knightsbridge, SW1Y 7LA

☎ 0171-235 2000 📠 0171-235 4552

☐ 185 ☐ £306 ⛶ 80 🍽 £90

☺ Lunch 12.30-2.30, Dinner 7.30-11 (Sun to 10.30)

A grand hotel with all the trimmings overlooking Rotten Row on the parkside and Knightsbridge shops on the other. Furnished, decorated and maintained in the grand style; often used by celebrities. Afternoon tea is a treat here. (See separate entry for Marco Pierre White's Restaurant).

SW1 L'Incontro

87 Pimlico Road, SW1W 8PH

☎ 0171-730 3663 📠 0171-730 5062

⛶ 55 🍽 £100

☺ Lunch 12.30-2.30, Dinner 7-11.30 (Sun to 10.30)

☹ Lunch Sat & Sun, 25 & 26 Dec

An eternally stylish and popular modern Italian (specifically Venetian) restaurant in Pimlico. The sparse menu descriptions, in keeping with the minimalist decor, belie the attention paid to the quality of the raw ingredients as well as the care taken in compiling the dishes. There are fixed prices at lunchtime (for 1, 2 or 3 courses) as well as the carte, though in the evening only the carte is offered. Dishes range from the familiar (prosciutto e melone) to the less so (baccala mantecato, fish mousse – salt cod – served with polenta). Home-made pasta is popular: a simple bigoli in salsa was thick spaghetti in a rich sauce of anchovy and onion. Nodino de vitello all brace, a veal chop grilled with fresh rosemary, had the full flavours of its major ingredients. To finish, torta di pinoli is a traditional Italian flan made with pine nuts – some would say Italy's answer to Bakewell pudding! Vegetarians get plenty of choice here, and lovers of Italian wine can be in seventh heaven. A change this year is the opening now for dinner on Sundays, but closure on Saturday lunchtimes.

L!VE TV: THE FACTS
see page 21

W1 Inter-Continental London

1 Hamilton Place, Hyde Park Corner, W1V 1QY
☎ 0171-409 3131   📠 0171-409 7460
▭ 460 [£] £277 🛏 80 🍽 £150

☺ Lunch 12-3 (Sun 12-4), Dinner 7-10.30 (Sat 7-11.15)

☹ Lunch Sat, Dinner Sun, all Mon, Aug, 2 wks Xmas

One of London's largest hotels commands Hyde Park Corner imperially, its architecture and graphics the epitome of clean lines. Luxury is the keyword here, in public rooms, bedrooms and suites, banqueting and conference facilities (some of the most comprehensive in town), and leisure facilities. The icing on the cake here (if that's not too banal a comparison) is superb cooking by Peter Kromberg in the flagship restaurant, Le Soufflé. Le Choix du Chef brings you an amazing 7 courses plus amuse-bouche plus coffee for only £43 – or any 4 courses for £37.50 – the full works certainly offer good value! You could thus enjoy croustillant de St Pierre a l'huile de Provence et confits de fenouil; noix de St Jacques, meunière d'endive parfumé à l'orange; a refreshing sorbet au pamplemousse rosé; then supreme de canard grillé au miel de lavande et jus au thym or canon d'agneau du printemps aux herbes fines, pommes au basilic et epinards aux cèpes; your choice from the chariot de fromages before a pair of desserts: gratin de fruits exotiques then pétale glacé, couronne au café. The wine list is at the top of the price range, as you might expect.

W1 Interlude de Chavot

5 Charlotte Street, W1P 1HD
☎ 0171-637 0222   📠 0171-637 0224
🛏 54 🍽 £80

☺ Lunch 12-2.30, Dinner 7-10.30   ☹ Lunch Sat, all Sun, Bank Holidays

Formerly simply called Interlude, and before that Walsh's, the new name here echoes that of the chef rather than the owning family. French but modern, with much attention paid to finer details, such as sourcing and saucing. This team has enormous potential and deserves continued success.

WC2 The Ivy

1 West Street, WC2H 9NE
☎ 0171-836 4751   📠 0171-497 3644
🛏 100 🍽 £70

☺ Lunch 12-3 (Sun to 3.30), Dinner 6-12   ☹ 1 Jan

Proving that everything which goes around, comes around, Chris Corbin & Jeremy King have revitalised The Caprice and The Ivy and restored them to the glory they enjoyed in the '30s under the inimitable Mario. Cooking styles, like fashion, have changed over the years and the menu is now a blend of modern British and Mediterranean. Simple potted shrimps, dressed Cornish crab, eggs benedict, steak tartare, osso bucco and grilled chateaubriand may well have appeared on an opening menu. Seared Orkney scallops with spinach, sorrel and crispy bacon, roasted Rosevale potatoes with duck livers, garlic and pancetta, corned beef hash with fried egg or salad of venison, artichokes and wild mushrooms probably didn't. The success of the restaurant is that well-judged combination of new and traditional, simple and complex, safe and adventurous: a great concept that everyone enjoys as everything is so well done. Booking essential.

WC2 Joe Allen

13 Exeter Street, WC2E 7DT
☎ 0171-836 0651 📠 0171-497 2148
🍴 150 🍽 £40

🙂 12-1am (Sun to 12) 🙁 24 & 25 Dec

Cool, busy and bustling US-themed basement restaurant in Covent Garden which moves slowly with the times (rather than being ahead of them). Not many places could get away with featuring "soggy lemon cake" on the menu, but this sure is one of them! No credit cards.

SW3 Joe's Café

126 Draycott Avenue, SW3 3AH
☎ 0171-225 2217
🍴 75 🍽 £70

🙂 Lunch 12-3 (Sat 12-4, Sun 11.30-5), Dinner 7-11

🙁 Dinner Sun, 2 days Xmas

Endlessly fashionable venue where the menu seems less important than the quality of the shopping bags. Style doesn't come cheap, but the Sunday brunch is good value. Good service and dedicated following.

W11 Julie's

135 Portland Road, W11 4LW
☎ 0171-229 8331 📠 0171-229 4050
🍴 120 🍽 £70

🙂 Lunch 12.30-2.45 (Sun to 3), Dinner 7.30-11.45 (Sun to 10.30)

🙁 Bank Holidays, 1 wk Xmas

Chintzy and cutesy, choice of dining areas but always very popular: English food in the champagne bar, private dining rooms or main restaurant. You have to go to experience this unusual, long standing and much loved venue.

W2 Kalamaras

76-78 Inverness Mews, W2 3JQ
☎ 0171-727 9122 📠 0171-221 9411
🍴 88 🍽 £40

🙂 Dinner 6-12 🙂 Sun, Bank Holidays

Low ceilinged, beamed and the authentic atmosphere of a taverna that manages to capture the essence of Greece.

SW10 Kartouche

329 Fulham Road, SW10 9QL

☎ 0171-823 3515   📠 0171-823 3991

🪑 78 🍽 £60

☺ Lunch 12-3 (Sat & Sun to 3.30), Dinner 6-12 (Sun to 11)

Another recent opening in a now very busy part of Chelsea, highly populated from Day One – modern European cooking served in a lively atmosphere. No bookings taken for the evening so be prepared to queue. Fun, fun, fun.

W1 Kaspia

18/18a Bruton Place, W1X 7AH

☎ 0171-493 2612

🪑 60 🍽 £70

☺ Lunch 12-3, Dinner 7-11.30   ☺ all Sun, Sat in Aug

Caviar shop and restaurant in the perfect Mayfair setting, with a classy, clubby decor and service to match. All kinds of caviar and its traditional accoutrements are available, usually best accompanied by top-quality champagne or vodka (or both if you want an Ab Fab time!).

W8 Kensington Place

201/207 Kensington Church Street, W8 7LX

☎ 0171-727 3184   📠 0171-229 2025

🪑 140 🍽 £70

☺ Lunch 12-3 (Sat & Sun to 3.30), Dinner 6.30-11.45 (Sun to 10.15)

☹ 24-26 Dec, 1 Jan

Still full of happy faces, still bright and bouncy: another reliable restaurant that has survived from the decadent '80s to the more caring and responsible '90s. Simple, modern European cooking is what Rowley Leigh continues to offer, often using less common ingredients (smoked eel, salsify, chard, purple sprouting, tamarillos) alongside the more familiar: pumpkin soup with croutons and gruyère, grilled squid with red onion salad, noisettes of venison with sweet and sour sauce, steamed chocolate pudding with custard, pineapple fritters with passion fruit. The concise wine list requires you to know already what you like but is very reasonably priced. A regular clientele jostles alongside first-timers (yes, even though it's been in situ since 1987), all of whom know good value when they see it!.

NW1 The Landmark London (formerly The Regent)

222 Marylebone Road, NW1 6JQ

☎ 0171-631 8000   📠 0171-631 8080

🛏 309 £ £245 🪑 100 🍽 £95

☺ Lunch 12-3, Dinner 7-11   ☹ Sat

Gracious and historic red-brick hotel near Regent's Park and several major railway termini; limousine and airport service. High standards of housekeeping throughout beautifully-equipped lounges and bedrooms. Formal meals in the Dining Room; a more informal meeting-place is the Winter Garden with its huge central atrium, full of plants.

SW1 The Lanesborough

Hyde Park Corner, SW1X 7TA
☎ 0171-259 5599 📠 0171-259 5606
⌘ 95 [£] £334 ♟ 106 🍽 £90

☺ Lunch 12.30-2.30 (Sun brunch 11-3), Dinner 7-12, (tea 3.30-6)

Hyde Park Corner is the ideal location for this elegant hotel that was created within the shell of the St. Georges Hospital. Regency in style, no expense has been spared to create a splendid, intimate hotel with just under 100 suites and bedrooms. Impeccable management by Geoffrey Gelardi and superb cooking by Paul Gayler ensure that high standards are maintained. The Conservatory restaurant offers breakfast, lunch and dinner with a range of international dishes in a bright, palm filled room.

W1 Langan's Bistro

26 Devonshire Street, W1N 1RJ
☎ 0171-935 4531
♟ 34 🍽 £65

☺ Lunch 12.30-2.30, Dinner 7-11.30

☹ Lunch Sat, all Sun, Bank Holidays

A tiny bistro next door to Big Brother, Odins, with a loyal following, who enjoy the cosy Parisian atmosphere and reasonably-priced, eclectic menu and wine list.

W1 Langan's Brasserie

Stratton Street, W1X 5FD
☎ 0171-491 8822
♟ 220 🍽 £85

☺ 12.15-11.45 (Sat 8-12.45am)

☹ Lunch Sat, all Sun, Bank Holidays, Xmas

During the last 20 years when London has seen many trends in restaurants and styles of food, Langan's has not changed yet remains one of the most popular venues in town. It has a very established, safe feel about it, that's why people keep going back, the atmosphere is great, the food is good and prices are affordable. The menu pleases everyone, true brasserie dishes with bags of choice, earthy plates of knuckle of gammon with butter beans, Langan's cod and chips or bangers and mash to a subtle souffle of spinach with anchovy sauce or simple grilled Dover sole. House wines start at under £10 but drink Chassagne-Montrachet or Dom Perignon if you wish, you can feel at ease with either. Still the place to be seen in, and if you're lucky you can rub shoulders with owners actor Michael Caine and restaurateur Richard Shepherd.

W1 The Langham Hilton

1 Portland Place, W1N 4JA

☎ 0171-636 1000   📠 0171-323 2346

⌂ 379   £ £240   🪑 48   🍽 £85

☺ Lunch 12-2.30, Dinner 6-10.30, (Palm Court Tea: 3-5.30 daily)

They often say that nostalgia ain't what it used to be, but it sure is here! Memories of the Empire is the name of one of the restaurants (commemorating the hotel's origins and heydey in 1865, especially celebratory Sunday brunches), doormen still wear Tsarist uniforms, the Tsar's Restaurant-Bar offers an array of caviars, champagnes, vodkas and vodka cocktails. Tea in the Palm Court should surely be accompanied by music from a wireless: dainty sandwiches, freshly baked scones, strawberry preserves, clotted cream and of course a huge range of teas from which to choose. For breakfast, you can choose traditional, healthy, continental, champagne (available for residents only – a wise move!) or even Japanese! Corner suites (with views over town, by the way) are being equipped with all the latest technology – into the 21st century with a vengeance!

W8 Launceston Place

1a Launceston Place, W8 5RL

☎ 0171-937 6912   📠 0171-938 2412

🪑 80   🍽 £65

☺ Lunch 12.30-2.30 (Sun to 3), Dinner 7-11.30

☹ Lunch Sat, Dinner Sun, Bank Holidays

Secluded Kensington setting (sister to Kensington Place), comfortable surroundings, safe, but not uninventive British cooking: excellent value. Good local restaurant.

NW2 Laurent

428 Finchley Road, NW2 2HY

☎ 0171-794 3603

🪑 36   🍽 £40

☺ Lunch 12-2, Dinner 6-11   ☹ Sun, Bank Holidays, 3 wks Aug

If couscous is your thing, then this is your restaurant: you can have it in several guises, but the royal version gives you a bit of everything. Try North African wine to accompany it, and enjoy the happy atmosphere that goes with good value for money and honest food.

W11 Leith's

92 Kensington Park Road, W11 2PN
☎ 0171-229 4481
🪑 70 🍽 £115

☺ Dinner 7.30-11.30 ☹ 2 days Aug, Bank Holidays, 4 days Xmas

Uncluttered, contemporary styling is the decor here, a light and airy restaurant (now delightfully cool and air-conditioned) in which to enjoy food which is robust in flavour yet delicate in execution. Alex Floyd's menus are well constructed, full of interesting ideas and a joy to eat. For just £25 you can enjoy 2 courses with a choice of 3 or 4 dishes at each course – try layers of salmon and crisp potato with tapenade and shellfish dressing, then poached guinea fowl with leeks, mushrooms and vegetable consommé. Vegetarians are thankfully treated seriously here too, with a full menu dedicated to their tastes: pithiviers of goat's cheese and spinach with tomato oil; cassoulet of white beans and lentils with a courgette galette; traditional British cheeses and a choice from the dessert menu. The wine list is much applauded, being well laid out and reasonably priced – the pride of co-owner Nick Tarayan.

W1 The Lexington

45 Lexington Street, W1R 3LG
☎ 0171-434 3401 📠 0171-287 2997
🪑 45 🍽 £65

☺ Lunch 12-3, Dinner 6-11.30
☹ Lunch Sat, all Sun, Bank Holidays, Xmas/New Year

A change of chef has not affected the style of the menus at this smartly-furnished restaurant between Oxford Street and Regent Street. A small menu has a variety of modern dishes. An early-evening menu is a snip at £10, and it might even include entertainment from the pianist! An interesting wine list offers plenty of choice by the glass.

W1 Lindsay House

21 Romilly Street, W1V 5TG
☎ 0171-439 0450 📠 0171-581 2848
🪑 30 🍽 £80

☺ Lunch 12.30-2.30 (Sun & Sat to 2), Dinner 6-12 (Sun 7-10)
☹ 25 & 26 Dec

Another branch of Roger Wren's Waltons group, ideal for lunch in a hurry: 2 courses guaranteed in under 45 minutes. Presumably, that's not including time for choosing, which can be difficult even though menus are concise, as they are full of old favourites.

W1 London Hilton on Park Lane

22 Park Lane, W1Y 4BE

☎ 0171-493 8000 📠 0171-493 4957

▯ 448 £250 ⑁ 105 🍽 £125

☺ Lunch 12.30-2.30, Dinner 7-11.30 (Fri & Sat to 12.30),

(Café/Brasserie 7am-12.45am (Fri & Sat to 1))

☹ Lunch Sat, Dinner Sun, some Bank Holidays

Large, luxury hotel in the heart of the West End, and its top-floor dining room Windows on the World which takes full advantage both of location and building style. French classic cooking, dress codes apply. More informal eating in the Park Brasserie, but without the staggering views, or Trader Vic's Polynesian-style restaurant.

SW5 Lou Pescadou

241 Old Brompton Road, SW5 9HP

☎ 0171-370 1057 📠 0171-244 7545

⑁ 69 🍽 £50

☺ Lunch 12-3, Dinner 7-12 ☹ Sun, Jul & Aug

A corner of provincial France in Earl's Court, where you can enjoy a predominantly fishy range of dishes from no fewer than 5 different fixed-price menus or the carte itself. A busy, very French atmosphere and no table reservations, so go early or be prepared to wait.

EC3 Luc's Restaurant & Brasserie

17-22 Leadenhall Market, EC3V 1LR

☎ 0171-621 0666 📠 0171-336 7315

⑁ 140 🍽 £50

☺ Lunch 11.30-3 ☹ Lunch Sat & Sun, Bank Holidays, 5 days Xmas

Simple, French brasserie which is always busy. Classic dishes in classic style; convenient location by Leadenhall market. Dinner is only available to pre-booked parties, but this can be a very good way of enjoying Luc's.

WC2 Magno's Brasserie

65a Long Acre, WC2E 9JH

☎ 0171-836 6077 📠 0171-379 6184

⑁ 60 🍽 £70

☺ Lunch 12-2.30, Dinner 5.30-11.30

☹ Lunch Sat, all Sun, Bank Holidays, 1 wk Xmas

Typically French brasserie style – but with the occasional Italian overtone. Relaxed, Mediterranean atmosphere.

W11 Manzara

24 Pembridge Road, W11 3HL
☎ 0171-727 3062
🍴 40 🍽 £25

☺ 8am-11.30 (Sun to 10.30) ☹ 25 & 26 Dec

Turkish menu which encourages the diner to be adventurous – replacement guaranteed if you should by chance be less than satisfied with your choice! Ever-popular meze available for more conservative natures.

WC2 Manzi's

1-2 Leicester Street, WC2H 7BL
☎ 0171-734 0224 📠 0171-437 4864
🍴 110 🍽 £70

☺ Lunch 12-2.45, Dinner 5.30-11.45 (Sun to 10.30)
☹ Lunch Sun, 25 & 26 Dec

Famous seafood restaurant in the heart of the West End. Traditional British dishes are available, including eels jellied or stewed, and there are also simple letting bedrooms, if you feel like a real night on the town.

SW1 Restaurant Marco Pierre White

66 Knightsbridge, SW1Y 7LA
☎ 0171-259 5380 📠 0171-235 4552
🍴 50 🍽 £175

☺ Lunch 12-2.30, Dinner 7-11
☹ Lunch Sat, all Sun, Bank Holidays, 2 wks Aug, 2 wks Xmas

Genius does not come cheap, and Marco is not a man to sell himself short. As with Nico Ladenis, many were surprised that White took on a hotel flagship restaurant, but as did Nico, he has made a sure-fire success of the venture. In luxurious surroundings, he proffers fixed-price and à la carte menus that stun in the reading, let alone the eating. How to choose between panaché of grilled sea scallops and calamari, sauce nero; terrine of foie gras en gelée, toasted brioche; tagliatelle of oysters with caviar? Then pot-roast pork with spices and ginger, new potatoes with chives; caramelized calves' sweetbreads, braised lettuce, capers and celeriac, sauce vinaigre; escalope of brill, soft herb crust, young spinach, sabayon of chives? Marco has always set great store by the standards of his desserts, and chef-patissier Thierry Busset does not let the side down. The simply-described tart of bitter chocolate is an experience in itself, warm and meltingly delicious. Vacherin of red fruits with a kirsch sabayon is an explosion in the mouth. Any wine list has a hard time to keep up with a menu of this calibre, but this one succeeds!

W1 May Fair Inter-Continental

Stratton Street, W1A 2AN

☎ 0171-629 7777   📠 0171-629 1459

▯ 287 ▯£ £258 🪑 65 🕙 £80

☺ Lunch 12.30-2.30, Dinner 7.30-11 (Café 7am-10.30pm)

☹ Lunch Sat, Restaurant August

Luxury hotel with sought-after, lavishly equipped suites – though that's not in any way to decry the regular bedrooms! High standards of furnishing and housekeeping throughout, excellent business and leisure facilities. Contemporary British cooking in The Chateau restaurant.

W1 Le Meridien

Piccadilly, W1V 0BH

☎ 0171-734 8000   📠 0171-437 3574

▯ 266 ▯£ £271

Oak Room:

🪑 45 🕙 £135

☺ Lunch 12-2.30, Dinner 7-10.30

☹ Lunch Sat, all Sun, Bank Holidays, 3 wks Aug, 1 wk Jan

Terrace Garden Restaurant:

🪑 130 🕙 £65

☺ 7am-11.30pm (Sun 11.30-2.30)   ☹ Dinner Sun, Bank Holidays

A central location for this hotel which still displays much influence from its previous (French) owners. There are good leisure facilities here, much sought-after on a non-resident basis! The Oak Room is still one of the most elegant dining rooms in London.

SE1 Meson Don Felipe

53 The Cut, SE1 8LF

☎ 0171-928 3237   📠 0171-386 0337

🪑 60 🕙 £40

☺ 12-11   ☹ Sun, 25 & 26 Dec, 1 Jan

A vibrant Spanish tapas bar run by Philip Diment and his Spanish wife Aña. The South Bank venue came before most others in London, and serves a menu of little nibbles and more substantial meals, accompanied by a well-researched range of wines by the glass. Great fun for a night out with friends. Busy, busy, busy.

EC1 Le Mesurier

113 Old Street, EC1V 9JR

☎ 0171-251 8117   📠 0171-608 3504

🪑 20 🕐 £65

☺ Lunch 12-3, Dinner parties only 6.30-11

☹ Lunch Sat & Sun, Bank Holidays, 10 days Xmas, 2 wks Aug

Now well-established and very popular – booking essential for traditional and modern French food. Soufflés highly praised; menus change fortnightly. Wine list all French. Good for private dinners.

W1 Mezzo

100 Wardour Street, Soho, W1V 3LE

☎ 0171-314 4000   📠 0171-314 4040

🪑 350 🕐 £85

☺ Lunch 12-3, Dinner 6-1am (Thu-Sat to 3am, Sun to 11)

☹ Lunch Sat (but Mezzonine open), Dinner 24 Dec, all 25 & 26 Dec, 31 Dec & 1 Jan

The Conran machine continues to roll relentlessly around London (watch out for an imminent return to the Kings Road scene) but meanwhile, the former Marquee Club has been revamped as one of <u>the</u> places in which to be seen or to buy ashtrays. Modern menus offer good quality ingredients imaginatively combined, but it's the setting (and the cigarette girls!) which remain most strongly in the memory.

SW1 Mimmo d'Ischia

61 Elizabeth Street, Eaton Square, SW1 9PP

☎ 0171-730 5406   📠 0171-730 9439

🪑 70 🕐 £90

☺ Lunch 12-2.30, Dinner 7-11.30

☹ Sun, Bank Holidays, Easter, Xmas

Popular, lively Italian venue specialising in Neapolitan and Ischian dishes. The ever-present Mimmo works hard at pleasing everyone and you now have the choice of the elaborate new conservatory or the original restaurant. You can get so absorbed in identifying celebrities in the photos on the walls that you almost forget where you are – till the food arrives!

WC2 Mon Plaisir

21 Monmouth Street, WC2H 9DD
☎ 0171-836 7243 📠 0171-379 0121
🪑 95 🍽 £50

☺ Lunch 12-2.15, Dinner 5.50-11.15

☹ Lunch Sat, all Sun, Bank Holidays, Xmas/New Year

A quintessentially French bistro in Covent Garden (with branches in Kensington – Mon Petit Plaisir – and Islington – Mon Plaisir du Nord) where you can enjoy classic fare in authentic surroundings. There's good value to be had on the lunch and early-evening menus, which is not to say that the carte is particularly expensive, either! Try a superb gratinée à l'oignon, or rillettes de canard, followed by tulipe de St Jacques au safran, or magret de canard aux sésames et grillottes. A toothsome pudding might be le succès au chocolat (rich chocolate truffle on a light genoise base) or délice aux pommes et calvados (apple and calvados on a cream-filled almond sponge base) – all desserts are made in-house by the pastry chef. The all-French wine list is fairly priced – even the house's special reserves come in at under £50.

SW3 Monkeys

1 Cale Street, SW3 3QT
☎ 0171-352 4711
🪑 40 🍽 £80

☺ Lunch 12.30-2.30, Dinner 7.30-11

☹ Sat & Sun, Bank Holidays, 2 wks Easter, 3 wks Aug

Friendly, local restaurant on Chelsea Green with decor part reminiscent of Victorian style. Good, home cooking in classic European mode draws the regulars and keeps them coming back. Thomas & Brigitte Benham co-ordinate their activities to make this a popular destination for good food at good prices.

W1 Montcalm Hotel

Great Cumberland Place, W1A 2LF
☎ 0171-402 4288 📠 0171-724 9180
🛏 116 £ £234 🪑 60 🍽 £80

☺ Lunch 12.30-2.30, Dinner 6-10 ☹ Lunch Sat, all Sun

Japanese-owned, but named after the 18th-century Marquis de Montcalm who was the epitome of dignity and style, qualities to which the hotel aspires today. The Crescent restaurant offers modern British cooking in elegant surroundings.

SW1 Mosimann's Club ♣

11b West Halkin Street, SW1X 8JL
☎ 0171-235 9625 📠 0171-245 6354
🪑 100 🍽 £105
☺ Lunch 12-2.30, Dinner 6-11.30
☹ Lunch Sat, all Sun, Bank Holidays

An elegant and exclusive club where the legendary Anton Mosimann produces superb cooking in the dining room or for parties in the 4 beautiful private rooms. Inventive dishes include penne with smoked chicken hoisin style, tuna carpaccio with wasabi vinaigrette or spicy prawns with black bean sauce and couscous. Main courses like a salad of roast sesame sea bream with Thai dressing, grilled swordfish with spinach and artichokes or sautéed veal chop with salsify and asparagus display his talent. A unique experience with perfect food, wines and service in a lovely setting.

SW1 Motcomb's

26 Motcomb Street, SW1X 8JU
☎ 0171-235 9170 📠 0171-245 6351
🪑 70 🍽 £60
☺ Lunch 12.30-3, Dinner 7-11 ☹ Dinner Sun, Bank Holidays

Wine bar menu; clubby, stylish ambience and international-style cooking. Shorter menu on the ground floor but the famous fish cakes are available throughout this good local restaurant!

W1 Le Muscadet

25 Paddington Street, W1M 3RF
☎ 0171-935 2883
🪑 36 🍽 £60
☺ Lunch 12.30-2.30, Dinner 7.30-10.30
☹ Lunch Sat, all Sun, Bank Holidays, 2 wks Xmas, 3 wks Aug

Traditional French bistro menu, wine list and decor under the watchful eye of patron François Bessonard. Choices vary with market availability but invariably include all those comforting dishes you can enjoy in Parisian street-corner bistros.

WC1 Museum Street Café

47 Museum Street, WC1A 1LY
☎ 0171-405 3211
🪑 37 🍽 £55
☺ Lunch 12.30-2.30, Dinner 6.30-9.30
☹ Sat & Sun, 2 wks Aug, 1 wk Xmas, 1 wk Feb, Bank Holidays

Unpretentious setting, simple cooking, well executed and always enjoyable: a sure-fire recipe for success, but also for disaster if your aim is not true. Happily, it's the bull's eye here: short, fixed-price menus with a modern twang, properly cooked. Super range of unpasteurised cheeses that go well with home-made breads. Small, good-value, well-chosen wine list.

WC2 Neal Street Restaurant

26 Neal Street, WC2H 9PH
☎ 0171-836 8368 📠 0171-497 1361
🪑 60 🍽 £100

☺ Lunch 12.30-2.30, Dinner 7.30-11

☺ Sun, Bank Holidays, 1 wk Xmas/New Year

Antonio Carluccio's Covent Garden restaurant is still a firm favourite, and the gregarious patron finds time to converse with regular customers despite his busy schedule of television appearances, book writing and mushroom hunting. Imaginative cooking features more than a whiff of the odd truffle: wild mushroom soup, pappardelle with funghi, turbot with honey- fungus and Judas ears, chicken scaloppine with shiitake and oyster mushrooms, veal kidney with morels and red wine or medallions of venison with porcini and polenta chips. There are many more dishes that don't include the unbelievable range of mushrooms that Antonio discovers, and these are equally exciting: fritto misto of scallops and prawns with seaweed and lime, stuffed calamari on rocket, nuggets of lamb en croute or an entrecote with freshly grated wild horseradish. Shop next door at the deli to relive all those memories at home.

SW4 Newton's

33-35 Abbeville Road, SW4 9LA
☎ 0181-673 0977
🪑 70 🍽 £55

☺ Lunch 12.30-2.30, Dinner 7-11.30 (Sat & Sun 12.30-4 & 7-11.30)

☹ 3 days Xmas, 3 days Easter

Modern European with a touch of Thai aptly describes the style at this busy bistro, which offers fixed-price menus for lunch and dinner. There are 11 house wines at under a tenner on a most imaginative list. Saturday lunchtime is especially popular with families: a resident clown entertains the younger gourmets!

W1 Nico Central

35 Great Portland Street, W1N 5DD
☎ 0171-436 8846 📠 0171-355 4877
🪑 50 🍽 £60

☺ Lunch 12-2.30, Dinner 7-11 ☹ Lunch Sat, all Sun, 10 days Xmas

This is Middle Billy Goat Gruff as far as Nico's small (but beautifully put together) empire is concerned, driven by head chef Andre Garret in a useful West End location – smart, modern, brightly lit and buzzy under the direction of the suave Jean-Francois Girard. The set menus are amazingly good value – dinner can be only £26 for 3 courses – and for this you are getting the Great Man's creations prepared by a very expert disciple. Try boned devilled quail with pickled red cabbage, or soufflé of roquefort with roasted walnuts and ears; then noisette of ox tongue braised in madeira with spinach and beetroot, or baked fillet of brill with croutons and provensale vegetables. Desserts like hot ginger and walnut sponge with whisky ice cream, or a warm terrine of croissant and apricots are simply irresistible. The wine list has all the hallmarks of Nico's usual care and attention to detail.

W1 Nicole's

158 New Bond Street, W1Y 9AP

☎ 0171-499 8408 📠 0171-499 7522

🪑 70 🍽 £75

☺ Lunch 12-3.30, Dinner 6.30-11

☹ Dinner Sat, all Sun, 24, 25 & 26 Dec

In-store restaurant with the highest credentials: designer Nicole Farhi's store, chic monochrome decor, chef Annie Wayte. Not cheap, but a very desirable venue among the lunch set. Modern European cooking, predominantly Italian in style and flavour.

SW10 Nikita's

65 Ifield Road, SW10 9AU

☎ 0171-352 6326 📠 0181-993 3680

🪑 58 🍽 £70

☺ Lunch by arrangement, Dinner 7.30-11.30

☹ Sun, Bank Holidays, 3 wks Aug

I suggest you order from the menu before you start tasting the vast range of flavoured vodkas at one of London's oldest outposts of Russian cuisine! All the traditional favourites are here in abundance, served in an atmosphere of slightly faded decadence in an opulent basement setting. If you wish, you can hire a Russian gypsy balalaika band. When booking, a natural enquiry is about local parking: take my advice, and use a taxi...

W1 L'Odeon

65 Regent Street, W1R 7HH

☎ 0171-287 1400 📠 0181-287 1300

🪑 205 🍽 £90

☺ Lunch 12-3, Dinner 5.30-00.30

☹ 25 & 26 Dec, Bank Holidays

Another new opening within the last year, but here the protagonists are well known in the capital. Pierre & Kathleen Condou, and chef Bruno Loubet. Interesting and innovative dishes, on set price and à la carte menus, with prices that have actually come down slightly since opening. Good views over Regent Street from the windows of this first floor, modern and buzzy restaurant.

NW1 Odette's

130 Regent's Park Road, NW1 8XL

☎ 0171-586 5486

🏠 60 🍴 £65

☺ Lunch 12.30-2.30, Dinner 7-11

☹ Lunch Sat, Dinner Sun, Bank Holidays, 10 days Xmas

Primrose Hill setting for a friendly neighbourhood and destination venue. Simone Green changes the menu daily (though the style can always be called modern British or eclectic), and you can eat either in the first-floor restaurant or the ground-floor wine bar. Typical of early spring offerings were smoked haddock and artichoke fishcake, served with a poached egg and hollandaise sauce, or red mullet and blood orange terrine in a seaweed jelly, among the starters. Representative main courses might be honey-spiced hare with garlic potato pie, breast of corn-fed chicken served with butter beans, barley and wild mushrooms, scallop and salmon cannelloni with parsley sauce, or lemon and basil risotto with shaved parmesan. Influences are drawn from around the globe, and Simone is particularly proud of the range of specialist Spanish cheeses, served with sunflower seed biscuits and quince jelly. Wines are recommended on a monthly basis, with several available by the glass. This is a real favourite.

W1 Odin's Restaurant

27 Devonshire Street, W1N 1RJ

☎ 0171-935 7296

🏠 60 🍴 £65

☺ Lunch 12.30-2.30, Dinner 7-11.30 ☹ Sat & Sun, Bank Holidays

Not overpowered by big sister Langan's, Odin's shares the same gene pool. So you can find familiar dishes like steamed mussels in coriander and cream sauce, roast rack of English lamb with a herb crust and Mrs Langan's famous chocolate pudding in an even more relaxed and laid back atmosphere, if that's possible. Chef Sean Butcher is pretty handy with fish dishes, too, and has been here for 8 years, the last 3 or so as head chef. Richard Shepherd is confident to leave matters in his capable hands, and he does not let his mentor down. Familiar, fairly-priced wine list. All overseen by the suave Dieter Schuldt.

SW1 Olivo

21 Eccleston Street, SW1W 9LX

☎ 0171-730 2505

🏠 43 🍴 £55

☺ Lunch 12-2.30, Dinner 7-11

☹ Lunch Sat, all Sun, Bank Holidays, 1 wk Aug

One of the new-wave Italian restaurants, this time with Sardinian influences on an interesting menu. Fixed-price arrangements at lunchtime give way to an extensive evening carte. 6 Sardinian wines are featured on the all-Italian list. Little sister, Olivetto, was due to open as we went to press, around the corner in Elizabeth Street, offering pasta, salads and pizzas.

W11 192

192 Kensington Park Road, W11 2JF
☎ 0171-229 0482
⌂ 100 ⓘ £75
☺ Lunch 12.30-3, Dinner 7-11.30

Notting Hill's beloved favourite offering modern European cooking in a trendy setting at reasonable prices. Recent refurbishment in the kitchens injected new enthusiasm to the menu; and there's an excellent range of wines by the glass.

W11 Orsino

119 Portland Road, W11 4LN
☎ 0171-221 3299
⌂ 106 ⓘ £60
☺ 12-10.45 (Sun to 9.45) ☹ 25 Dec

Regional Italian variations featuring lots of grills as well as pizzas. Excellent value all-afternoon lunch menu (noon to 6.30pm), interesting Italian wine list, no credit cards.

WC2 Orso

27 Wellington Street, WC2E 7DA
☎ 0171-240 5269 0171-497 2148
⌂ 100 ⓘ £65
☺ 12-12 ☹ 24 & 25 Dec

Italian basement restaurant adorned with monochrome photographs and stylish waiters. Concise, well-priced wine list.

SCOTCH BEEF CLUB
see page 16

SW11 Osteria Antica Bologna

23 Northcote Road, SW11 1NG
☎ 0171-978 4771
🍴 75 🍽 £45
☺ Mon-Thur 12-11, Sat 12-11.30, Sun 12.30-10.30
☹ 10 days Xmas/New Year

One of a kind, really, despite the branch in SW15 (which covers Italy a little more broadly). This aims to be a true Bolognese hostelry, from the rustic styling of pine, with tables and chairs somewhat haphazardly set out, the overspill to the pavement, and of course the menu, which starts with assaggi – small dishes ideal for sharing, while you're waiting for the rest of your group to arrive and to help soak up some robust Italian house wine, not dissimilar in style to the Spanish tapas which took London over in the '80s. These change seasonally, number around a dozen and could include polpino con rucola (freshly boiled octopus with rocket, olive oil and chilis), torta pugliese (baked potato, mushroom, fresh basil and pecorino cheese tart), or asparagi con salsa mandorlata (fresh asparagus with lemon, garlic and almond sauce). Inventive salads like stromboli (a volcanic combination of warm salad greens with gorgonzola, bacon, mushrooms and avocado); home-made pastas like strozzapreti con sarde e pomodori al forno (pasta scrolls with fresh boned sardines, roast tomatoes, fresh basil and olives); and we haven't even got to the main courses yet! A speciality here is capretto alle mandorle – goat cooked in a rich tomato and almond pesto; and another firm favourite is tonno alla griglia con radicchio e salsa verde – grilled fresh tuna steak served on marinated grilled radicchio (a million miles removed from the slightly tough red leaves so often left on the side of a salad) and served with green olive and garlic sauce. Desserts are enough to test even the strongest will: dark chocolate cake filled with espresso cream, served with fresh cream and warm chocolate sauce; warm apple and walnut cake; panna cotta with fresh strawberries and caramel sauce. Do go.

SW18 Le P'tit Normand

185 Merton Road, SW18 5EF
☎ 0181-871 0233
🍴 35 🍽 £50
☺ Lunch 12-2.30, Dinner 7-10.30 (Sun to 10) ☹ Lunch Sat

Useful neighbourhood bistro offering traditional French cooking, wines and atmosphere. Excellent value for money, extensive range of top-quality cheeses kept in prime condition.

WC2 Le Palais du Jardin

136 Long Acre, WC2E 9AD
☎ 0171-379 5353 📠 0171-379 1846
🍴 220 🕐 £60

🙂 12 midday to 12 midnight 🙁 25 & 26 Dec

Great moves afoot at Covent Garden's own people's palace, with chef-patron Winston Matthews overseeing expanded restaurant areas and consequently kitchens too. It's a very slick operation, with up-to-the-moment reserved, airy decor brightened by a flowers on tables. The Oyster Bar part of the operation is nearer to the entrance, while the restaurant proper extends towards the rear, rising to a second level. Service is slick and professional, and the food on the plate, modern European in style, places much emphasis on fish and shellfish with most inspiration coming from France. Typical starters could be baby scallops with bacon and spinach in garlic butter, carpaccio, onion soup, an unusual baked gateau of goat's cheese in a hazelnut cust with roasted pear, or tiger prawns, mussels, shrimps, scallops and squid in an aromatic glaze served as a timbale. Daily specials for main courses range from a robust dish of grilled fillets of red mullet in a parsley crust with creamed sauerkraut and bacon to simply grilled fish of the day served with gren vegetables in a basil vinaigrette. Bangers and mash, fish cakes, confit, steaks and calves' liver all jostle for attention on the menu, which is as reasonably priced as the concise, accompanying wine list. There is a section on the menu for ice creams as distinct from desserts – they are made in-house and can often be quite inventive: brown bread and cinnamon ice served with a hazelnut coulis; while on the regular dessert menu the likes of pear tarte tatin, raspberry mille feuille, dark chocolat soufflé with a white chocolate sauce or Ricard parfait with mango coulis round off an enjoyable meal. Booking is essential – this place is lively and popular.

W1 The Park Lane Hotel

Piccadilly, W1Y 8BX
☎ 0171-499 6321 📠 0171-499 1965
🛏 307 £249 🍴 60 🕐 £70

🙂 Lunch 12.30-2.30, Dinner 7-10.30 🙁 all Sun, Bank Holidays

Enjoy afternoon tea or snacks at any time in the Palm Court Lounge, which has a vaulted ceiling with glorious art deco stained glass – there are several distinctive features from that period throughout the hotel, though the overall feel is traditional. Eat formally in Bracewells, or more informally in the Brasserie.

EC1 The Peasant

240 St John Street, EC1V 4PH
☎ 0171-336 7726
🍴 80 🕐 £50

🙂 Lunch 12.30-2.30, Dinner 6.30-11
🙁 Lunch Sat, all Sun, Bank Holidays, 10 days Xmas

Another of those London traditional public houses that now sport interesting restaurants. This one offers Mediterranean flavours and textures in a relaxed setting and a lively atmosphere. May there be many more.

SW7 Pelham Hotel

15 Cromwell Place, SW7 2LA
☎ 0171-589 8288 📠 0171-589 8444
🛏 41 £ £194 🍴 30 🍽 £50

☺ Lunch 12-2.30, Dinner 6-10.30 (light meals 7am-10.30pm)

☹ Sat, Lunch Sun & Bank Holidays, 25 & 26 Dec

Another of Tim & Kit Kemp's small and friendly town house hotels, this one usefully located for museum-hopping. Fine antiques and paintings adorn the well maintained rooms; while in Kemp's basement restaurant a concise menu of modern British food is available at very reasonable prices.

SE1 People's Palace

Level 3, Royal Festival Hall, Southbank Centre, SE1 8XX
☎ 0171-928 9999 📠 0171-928 2355
🍴 180 🍽 £70

☺ Lunch 12-3, Dinner 5.30-11

Famous now as one of the few places you can eat well in this stretch, for this venue is now under the guidance of Joseph Levin and chef Stephen Carter. It's on Level 3 of the Royal Festival Hall, so there's a guaranteed clientele jostling alongside destination diners. Simple, good, modern British food, good, clean flavours and a huge range of wines by the glass. Wonderful views over the Thames

W8 Phoenicia

11-13 Abingdon Road, W8 6AH
☎ 0171-937 0120 📠 0171-937 7668
🍴 80 🍽 £60

☺ 12-11.45 ☹ 24 & 25 Dec

A well-patronised, family-run, long-established Lebanese restaurant that always has a large range of mezze and charcoal-grilled main courses, washed down with an interesting Lebanese wine. Finish with Turkish coffee. The set meals are great fun if you're in a group.

SW15 The Phoenix

Pentlow Street, SW15 1LY
☎ 0181-780 3131 📠 0181-780 1114
🍴 100 🍽 £65

☺ Lunch 12.30-2.30 (Sun 12-3), Dinner 7-11.30 (Sun 7-10) ☹ Lunch Sat

A welcome addition to the Putney eating scene is Rebecca Mascarenhas's second London outlet (after Sonny's in nearby Barnes). Relaxed, informal style; friendly service; some well-cooked, up-to-the-minute food and a short wine list. Tables outside under big umbrellas on a plant-filled terrace.

W1 Pied à Terre

34 Charlotte Street, W1P 1HJ

☎ 0171-636 1178   📠 0171-916 1171

🍴 36 🍽 £110

☺ Lunch 12.15-2.15, Dinner 7-10.30

☹ Lunch Sat, all Sun, Bank Holidays, 2 wks Aug, 1 wk Dec, 1 wk Jan

Despite the departure of chef Richard Neat, you can still enjoy some very exciting food here, in a calm and relaxing ambience. The main thrust is modern French, the favourite ingredients fish, shellfish and offal. Set menus are well balanced, and the carte allows you to put together your own favourite style of meal from what's on offer. Fixed-price menus tend to become pricy – lunch as we went to press was £16.50, £19.50 or £39.50; and dinner £33.00 for 2 courses, £39.50 for 3 – but cooking of this quality does not come cheap. Try snails with morille, girolle, asparagus and garlic purée; deep-fried crab with smoked salmon sauce; duck breast, a confit of the gizzard and neck with rösti potatoes and wild mushrooms; roasted brill fillet with marinated red mullet and fennel sauce; venison fillet with deep-fried beetroot and grape wine juice. Puddings could be an unusual grapefruit parfait or roasted plum tart with crème fraiche. The wine list includes a good showing from the New World.

SW3 Poissonnerie de l'Avenue

82 Sloane Avenue, SW3 3DZ

☎ 0171-589 2457   📠 0171-581 3360

🍴 100 🍽 £95

☺ Lunch 12-3, Dinner 7-11.30   ☹ Sun, Bank Holidays, 10 days Xmas

The Avenue is Sloane Avenue, the Poissonerie is one of the capital's longest established fish restaurants where for 30 years Peter Rosignoli has looked after his regular customers. The restaurant has been refurbished recently, a modern bar, new shop front and bright blinds have cheered up the image. The menu is large and has a wide range of fish dishes as first and main courses with a few concessions to meat eaters. A good selection of oysters, natives in season and almost everything that swims is prepared in one way or another, even a couple of fishy savouries to finish in addition to the puddings. White wines naturally predominate on the mainly French list.

SW1 Pomegranates

94 Grosvenor Road, SW1V 3LE

☎ 0171-828 6560   📠 0171-828 2037

🍴 50 🍽 £80

☺ Lunch 12.30-2, Dinner 7-11.15

☹ Lunch Sat, all Sun, Bank Holidays

Travel the world from Victoria but don't go near the station – pop into Patrick Gwynn-Jones's friendly restaurant which offers you the summary of the best of his lifetime's worldwide gastronomy. They are justifiably proud of their own gravad lax. Chefs change, but such is Patrick's style that a strong element of continuity is assured in this warm, clubby, basement restaurant.

SE1 Le Pont de la Tour

Butlers Wharf Building, 36D Shad Thames,
Butlers Wharf, SE1 2YE

☎ 0171-403 8403   0171-403 0267

105   £95

☺ Lunch 12-3, Dinner 6-11.30 (Sun to 11), (Bar & Grill 12-11.30 daily
(Sun to 11) ☹ Lunch Sat, 5 days Xmas, Good Friday

On a balmy summer evening the view alone is almost worth the price, sit outside on the wide terrace that borders the Thames and admire Tower Bridge whilst the World floats gently past. You can eat in the main restaurant or the slightly cheaper bar and grill, both have outside tables. The cooking from David Burke's kitchen is modern in concept, halibut with clams, olive oil, parsley and garlic, braised lamb shank with roast onions and rosemary or perhaps fillet of red mullet baked in a salt crust with carrots and thyme are typical. In the grill the speciality is seafood, try a mammouth fruits de mer, oysters, crab or lobster – the crab's hard work, however, as the chef doesn't do much preparation. The grill is a more relaxed atmosphere, a pianist plays during the evening. The wine list is a very lengthy item with a huge variety of fairly expensive offerings but lacks nothing. Have a glass of champagne and watch the sun go down on the glistening Canary Wharf! This place has style and finesse.

W1 La Porte des Indes

32 Bryanston Street, W1H 7AE

☎ 0171-224 0055

300   £80

☺ Lunch 12-2.30, Dinner 6-12 (Sun to 10.30) ☹ 25 Dec

Stunning and sumptuous West End venue in a restaurant backwater, from the team who brought you the Blue Elephant in SW6. Orchids, palm trees and fountains create the backdrop for Creole and other regional Indian cooking, served with style and charm. Walk on peanut shells into the Jungle Bar, then add your own over an aperitif.

WC2 Porters English Restaurant

17 Henrietta Street, WC2E 8QH

☎ 0171-836 6466   0171-379 4296

210   £35

☺ 12-11.30 (Sun to 10.30) ☹ 25 Dec

Old English favourites such as steak and kidney pie, roast beef and Yorkshire pudding and bangers and mash are all to be found in a perfect setting in Covent Garden, in the honour of whose market porters the Earl of Bradford named his restaurant. The menu is also available in Japanese, Italian and French, reflecting the nationalities of the area's greatest numbers of tourists. Wonder what the Japanese is for suet?

SW1 La Poule Au Pot

231 Ebury Street, SW1W 8UT
☎ 0171-730 7763   📠 0171-259 9651
🪑 65 🍽 £55
☺ Lunch 12.30-2.30, Dinner 7-11.15   ☹ 24-26 Dec, New Year's Day

Long-established, friendly and romantic French bistro offering robust, traditional, regional dishes cooked and served with Gallic flair and charm. Cosy atmosphere; seating in Orange Square on warm days.

SW1 Quaglino's

16 Bury Street, St James's, SW1Y 6AL
☎ 0171-930 6767   📠 0171-839 2866
🪑 338 🍽 £70
☺ Lunch 12-3, Dinner 5.30-12 (Fri & Sat to 1, Sun to 11)
  (Bar 11.30am-midnight (Sun 12-11))
☹ 3 days Xmas

Probably Sir Terence Conran's largest restaurant – at the time of going to press, at least! An unqualified success, the restaurant demands an entrance be made, the antipasti bar (no booking) is an interesting place from which to spot all types of diners. Modern international cooking – daily specials supplement the printed menu. Now that you can buy the ashtrays, more of them stay on the tables!

EC1 Quality Chop House

94 Farringdon Road, EC1R 3EA
☎ 0171-837 5093
🪑 48 🍽 £45
☺ Lunch 12-3 (Sun to 4), Dinner 6.30-11.30 (Sun from 7)
☹ Lunch Sat & Bank Holidays, 24 Dec-3 Jan

"Progressive working class caterer" is the sub-title on Charles Fontaine's menu, which also guarantees "quality" and "civility". I absolutely agree on the last points, but must observe that working class food has come on in leaps and bounds since I was last sent up a chimney with only bread and scrape for my supper! Today's artisans can feast on warm asparagus with pecorino, roast snails with garlic butter, scrambled eggs with smoked salmon, roast hake with garlic and tomato, or confit of duck. But the point here is "progressive", for Charles takes a traditional idea and gives it his own individual twist, occasionally with a touch of France where the style of restaurants regularly used by workers has long been an example to which British restaurateurs aspire. To be sure, there's egg, bacon and chips on the menu, there's corned beef hash and fried egg, there's sausage and mash: but the sausages are Toulouse, the fish in the fishcakes is salmon (once indeed a working man's fish when the Thames still supported them), and the chips are the real thing: thick, crisp and tasty, not stringy and salty. Finish with proper treacle pudding, and some Traditional English Tea. A pint of Ruddles' or Sam Smith's best might seem most appropriate, but in fact the wine list is concise and carefully chosen. Sunday brunch, starting with jugs of Bloody Mary or Bucks Fizz, is very popular. It's good to be able to cheer on the continuing revival of the Best of British, in the capable hands of an eccentric Frenchman.

NW2 Quincy's

675 Finchley Road, NW2 2JP
☎ 0171-794 8499
⌸ 30 ⏱ £60
☺ Dinner 7-11 ☹ Sun & Mon, Xmas

Quincy's is a good local restaurant with a simple operating policy: a set-priced dinner menu with no hidden extras served 5 nights a week, the menu changing monthly – the chef here, David Philpott, knows his clientele and is rewarded by plenty of returnees. In fact, there's sufficient choice amongst the courses (at least 5 a time) to allow you to go several times within a month and never eat the same meal twice – then when the new menu arrives, off you go again! This would only work if the standards of cooking and service were spot on: needless to say, here they are just that. No specific nationality or style of food is claimed, but the presentation veers towards the modern, the ingredients towards the European. Try for instance potato pancakes with chicken livers, salad of quail and leeks in hazelnut dressing, smoked haddock mousse with french beans and chive cream, or a delicious home-made soup of the day. Main courses always include a fish of the day and one vegetarian option, with the remaining meat dishes making you choose between, say, roast venison with spiced quince and peppercorns, lamb with mint couscous and sun-dried tomato butter, or duck with lentils, red wine and garlic confit. Desserts are enticing, to say the least: coulibiac of winter fruits and rice pudding; chocolate and cherry clafoutis tart with white chocolate ice cream, pithiviers of pear with ginger sauce, caramelized apple and cider sorbet all being typical. A concise, simply described wine list is very reasonably priced, with scarcely anything over £20. London needs more of these!

WC2 Radisson Mountbatten Hotel

20 Monmouth Street, WC2H 9HD
☎ 0171-836 4300 📠 0171-240 3540
🛏 127 [£] £207 ⌸ 75 ⏱ £55
☺ Lunch 12.30-2.30, Dinner 5.30-11.30 ☹ Lunch Sat & Sun

Corner site for smart, comfortable themed hotel. Ad Lib restaurant offers traditional British dishes presented in modern style.

W1 Radisson SAS Portman Hotel

22 Portman Square, W1H 9FL
☎ 0171-208 6000 📠 0171-208 6001
🛏 279 [£] £225 ⌸ 62 ⏱ £65
☺ Lunch 12-3.30 (Sun from 12.30), Dinner 7-11 (Sun to 10.30)

Modern, luxurious hotel behind Oxford Street, a welcome retreat from the hurly-burly. Airline check-in desk. Bedrooms in Oriental, Scandinavian or British style, good conference facilities. Corner restaurant open all day for mid-priced meals and snacks.

SW11 Ransome's Dock

35-37 Parkgate Road, SW11 4NP

☎ 0171-223 1611 📠 0171-924 2614

🪑 65 🍲 £65

🙂 12-11pm (Sat to 12, Sun to 3.30)

☹ Dinner Sun, 25-27 Dec, Bank Holidays

In a waterside setting just south of Battersea Bridge, Martin Lam has established a very popular restaurant that is always full, so book, especially if you want a terrace table during the summer. His short menus feature modern cooking of homely dishes such as roast chicken stuffed with smoked bacon and thyme with wild mushroom polenta, calf's liver with crisp bacon and parslied mashed potato or grilled lamb with braised flageolets and turnips. Appealing puddings like a hot prune and armagnac souffle with armagnac sauce, apricot and ratafia trifle or cherry and almond frangipane tart are delicious. A good selection of wines at reasonable mark ups.

W1 Red Fort

77 Dean Street, W1V 5HA

☎ 0171-437 2115 📠 0171-434 0721

🪑 130 🍲 £70

🙂 Lunch 12-2.45, Dinner 6-11.30

Moghul cuisine in the grand manner, named after the Delhi original. Sunday buffet lunch is very popular.

W2 Los Remos

38A Southwick Street, W2 1JQ

☎ 0171-723 5056

🪑 50 🍲 £45

🙂 Lunch 12-3, Dinner 7-12 ☹ Sun

Traditional Spanish restaurant and tapas bar offering an extensive range of dishes from which you can put together a light snack or a substantial meal. Good range of wines to accompany, and a lively atmosphere.

**THE ACADEMY OF
FOOD & WINE SERVICE**
see page 22

London   91

W1 The Ritz

150 Piccadilly, W1V 9DG
☎ 0171-493 8181 📠 0171-493 2687
🚪 130 £ £249 🪑 110 🍽 £120
☺ Lunch 12.30-2.30, Dinner 6-11.15

Another institution, for the West End, for London, even for England itself; and the change of ownership (to the Hong-Kong based Mandarin group) has given this stately grande dame a new lease of life, though there's continuity in the kitchen under the watchful eye of the talented David Nicholls. The fine dining areas have been expanded to include the Terrace and Italian Gardens in fine weather, and on Sundays you can now have brunch in the famous Palm Court, hitherto largely a preserve of the afternoon tea brigade. The £16 menu is offered from 10.30am to 1.30pm, so the relaxed atmosphere has time to metamorphose back to grandeur for 4pm. The brunch menu adds one main dish and one flavoured crème brulée (pistachio, white chocolate, raspberry) to a fairly standard breakfast framework: try Yorkshire duckling pudding with pearl onions and pancetta, or crab cakes with mustard sauce – ideal for reviving you after Saturday night! The same venue offers a healthy breakfast from 7-10.30am on weekdays – all this in addition to the main Louis XVI restaurant, one of the most attractive hotel dining rooms in the world, which serves a mixture of fixed-price and à la carte menus of classic cuisine in splendidly luxurious surroundings – there are daily and trolley specials for those who can tell the day of the week by their lunch menu. Signature dishes from the carte include crab and lobster Antoinette; crown of asparagus with lobster and truffles; fillet of seabass with potato, langoustine and basil; and ceps in puff pastry with aubergine béarnaise, asparagus and truffles.

SW13 Riva

169 Church Road, SW13 9HR
☎ 0181-748 0434
🪑 50 🍽 £75
☺ Lunch 12-2.30, Dinner 7-11
☹ Lunch Sat, Bank Holidays, 2 wks Aug, 1 wk Xmas

Just south of the Thames, but you could be well far south of the Channel for the atmosphere is authentically Italian atmosphere! Simple, stylish decor and rather more complex cooking has made Riva one of the most popular local restaurants in the area and booking is essential. Have one of the platters for 2 to start: an antipasto of prosciutto, smoked mozzarella, venison bresaola with goat's cheese and mostarda, coppa, speck, salami with artichokes, nuts and sottaceti; or earth and sea, which is lobster and porcini, salt cod and grilled polenta, cuttlefish and spinach, mussels with tomato pesto and spicy oysters. All those flavours and you're still on a starter! For main courses, squid is grilled with wild herbs; pan-roast cod is served with Swiss chard au gratin and pink peppercorn sauce; roast quails have been wrapped in Parma ham and sit beside cabbage and lentils; calves' liver comes with soft polenta and porcini; and a braised shin of pork with mashed potato and mushrooms. If choosing one of those dishes is difficult, the dessert menu is no easier: sweet milk gnocchi with honey-butter sauce; maize and almond crumble soaked in vin santo with mascarpone, a blood orange sorbet with grappa; or a delicious savoury/sweet combination of a crostone with gorgonzola and chestnut honey. When someone takes so much trouble to prepare food like this the wine list is no afterthought. It's an exciting selection of top-quality Italian wines which blend perfectly with the dishes.

W6 River Café

Thames Wharf Studios, Rainville Road, W6 9HA

☎ 0171-381 8824   📠 0171-381 6217

🍴 100 🍽 £80

☺ Lunch 12.30-3, Dinner 7.30-9.30

☹ Dinner Sun, Bank Holidays, 25 Dec-31 Jan

Ruthie Rogers & Rose Gray are two more representatives of an enduring band of women chefs who set up in the late '80s and live to tell the tale. Again, the secret of their success here was to identify a market opportunity (robust Italian food), come up with the perfect solution (well cooked, at reasonable prices, served in straightforward surroundings), and never to believe that it's absolutely right (gradual development of both the room housing the restaurant – part of Richard Rogers' architectural practice – and the menu itself, which uses different ingredients in a variety of ways but always bound by one watchword: quality). Attention to detail showed in a spring menu which offered pappa pomodoro: a Tuscan soup made of bread, plum tomatoes, basil, and olive oil – but not just any olive oil. It was new season's olive oil, and its village of origin was also declared. Such a simple dish: such care in its compilation; and the results showed deliciously on the plate. The same lunch progressed to maialle all'latte: loin of pork, slow-cooked in milk with lemon zest and bay, served with spinach, oil and lemon (the meat tender, infused with flavour). Some Sienese panforte with good strong coffee completed a gastronomic tour of the glories of northern Italy. It's easy to forget you're right by the Thames.

SE1 RSJ

13a Coin Street, SE1 8YQ

☎ 0171-928 4554

🍴 90 🍽 £65

☺ Lunch 12-2, Dinner 6-11   ☹ Lunch Sat, all Sun, Bank Holidays

Useful location for South Bank arts complex – English and French food and wine tastings in restaurant named after its essential architectural feature! Excellent list of Loire wines.

WC2 Rules

35 Maiden Lane, WC2E 7LB

☎ 0171-836 5314   📠 0171-497 1081

🍴 140 🍽 £60

☺ 12-11.30 (Sun 10.30)   ☹ 4 days Xmas

One of London's oldest eating houses, specialising in classic game cookery. The elegant ground floor restaurant also has a choice of private rooms. Steeped in history and with several visitors from the world of the Arts, a "must" on every American tourist's itinerary.

W1 St George's Hotel

Langham Place, W1N 8QS

☎ 0171-580 0111   📠 0171-436 7997

🛏 86   £166   🍴 85   🍽 £70

☺ Lunch 12-2.30, Dinner 7-10   ☹ Lunch Sat, all Sun, Bank Holidays

Wide-ranging refurbishment here since 1995; new chef Nick Evenden in the Heights restaurant cooks modern-style with flair and panache to be enjoyed in the airy, relaxed atmosphere – magnificent views over London from its 15th floor location.

SW1 St James Court

41 Buckingham Gate, SW1E 6AF

☎ 0171-834 6655   📠 0171-630 7587

🛏 471   £180   🍴 65   🍽 £90

☺ Lunch 12.30-2.30, Dinner 7.30-11

☹ Lunch Sat, all Sun, Bank Holidays, 2 wks Aug

Usefully located for tourists and business delegates, this grand Edwardian hotel contains within its heart an open-air courtyard complete with fountain and trees – just the place to feel as regal as the near neighbours in BP! There's a splendid health club, and eating choices range from Mediterranean to Far Eastern. Grand hotel wine list to accompany formal dining.

SW3 Sambuca

6 Symons Street, SW3 2TJ

☎ 0171-730 6571

🍴 75   🍽 £70

☺ Lunch 12-2.30, Dinner 7-11.30   ☹ Sun, Bank Holidays

Traditional Italian cooking (sweetbreads a speciality), mostly-Italian wine list. Sister to Sale e Pepe and Sandrini. A favourite with the customers from Peter Jones, opposite

SW3 San Frediano

62 Fulham Road, SW3 6HH

☎ 0171-584 8375   📠 0171-589 8860

🍴 120   🍽 £55

☺ Lunch 12.15-3, Dinner 7-11.45

☹ Sun except Mothering, some Bank Holidays

Long-established, perennially popular Chelsea venue where Northern Italian specialities are to the fore.

SW3 San Lorenzo

22 Beauchamp Place, SW3 1NL
☎ 0171-584 1074 📠 0171-584 1142
🪑 150 🕐 £100
☺ Lunch 12.30-3, Dinner 7.30-11.30 ☹ Sun, Bank Holidays

Run by Lorenzo & Mara Berni, this eternally popular Knightsbridge venue for the see-and-be-seen-set, often has papparazi hanging about to spot the latest celeb eat very little, drink not much more, but have a simply splendid time amongst like-minded folk. Cooking is eye-catching rather than substantial, and regular favourites include the likes of spaghetti with langoustines, bollito misto, polenta-based dishes and home-made pastas. Grills are also good. Regulars return time and time again to this clubby, Italian restaurant.

SW3 San Martino

103-105 Walton Street, SW3 2HP
☎ 0171-589 3833 📠 0171-584 8418
🪑 130 🕐 £60
☺ Lunch 12-3, Dinner 6.30-11.30
☹ Lunch Sun, 25 & 26 Dec, Easter Mon

Tuscan specialities at this popular venue – many of the ingredients (especially courgette flowers) come from their own gardens. It was here that spaghetti cooked in a paper bag was invented.

SW3 Sandrini

260 Brompton Road, SW3 2AS
☎ 0171-584 1724
🪑 80 🕐 £70
☺ Lunch 12-2.30, Dinner 7-11.30 ☹ 25 & 26 Dec

Traditional Italian cooking (good pasta) and wine list at this deservedly popular Knightsbridge branch of Sandro Tobi's group. Pavement seating in summer and a warm welcome from Basilio and the staff.

SW1 Santini

29 Ebury Street, SW1W 0NZ
☎ 0171-730 4094 📠 0171-730 0544
🪑 55 🕐 £100
☺ Lunch 12.30-2.30, Dinner 7-11.30 (Sun to 10.30)
☹ Lunch Sat & Sun, 25 & 26 Dec

Endlessly fashionable but not cheap Belgravia restaurant, featuring Venetian dishes especially on the monthly-changing list of specialities.

W1 Les Saveurs

37a Curzon Street, W1Y 7AF
☎ 0171-491 8919 📠 0171-491 3658
🍴 50 🍽 £120

☺ Lunch 12-2.30, Dinner 7-11

☹ Sat & Sun, 2 wks Xmas/New Year, 2 wks Aug

New chef, Richard Stuart, has recently taken over. Check next year's Guide for an update.

WC2 The Savoy

Strand, WC2
☎ 0171-836 4343 📠 0171-240 6040
🛏 202 £ £303

Upstairs at the Savoy:
🍴 38 🍽 £60

☺ 12-12 Mon-Fri (Sat from 3) ☹ Lunch Sat, all Sun, Bank Holidays

The River Restaurant:
🍴 160 🍽 £130

☺ Lunch 12.30-2.30, Dinner 7.30-11.20 (Sun 7 to 10.30)

Grill Room:
🍴 100 🍽 £120

☺ Lunch 12.30-2.30, Dinner 6-11.15 ☹ Sun, Aug

A London landmark since 1650, this grand hotel has cleverly combined maintaining its innate sense of history with moving determinedly forwards as time marches on. The lovely rooftop pool within the new leisure centre reflects the feeling of an establishment at the peak of its potential, though even in the traditional haunts of the River Room or the Grill Room, time has stood still only in food styling: service and maintenance are as on-the-spot as you could wish for, a testament to the the need for establishments like this to respond to the mood of the clientele or simply get left behind. The Grill Room's daily specials at lunch and dinner are the sort of stuff by which to set your watch: rib of beef for lunch and roast duck for dinner mean it must be Thursday, and you can even enjoy these trolley specials as part of the pre-theatre menu served between 6pm and 7pm. There's no obligation to go to the Savoy theatre after eating here though many, obviously, do! Excellent cheeses and classic desserts complete a meal. Maitre Chef Anton Edelmann is another modest star, preferring to stay in his kitchen and oversee the future of the profession through his young protégés rather than seeking the limelight. The hotel itself naturally keeps standards up (ongoing refurbishment of rooms and suites) under the stewardship of one of the hotel industry's most respected figures, Ramon Pajares.

SW3 Scalini

1-3 Walton Street, SW3 2JD

☎ 0171-225 2301

🍴 100 🕑 £70

🙂 Lunch 12-3, Dinner 7-12 (Sun to 11.30) ☹ Bank Holidays

Busy, bustling, chic and popular Italian restaurant in Chelsea; risotti and pasta are home-made and just a cut above average. Its late closing is particularly useful in this area.

W1 Scott's Restaurant & Oyster Bar

20 Mount Street, W1Y 6HE

☎ 0171-629 5248 📠 0171-499 8246

🍴 115 🕑 £60

🙂 Lunch 12-3, Dinner 6-11

☹ Lunch Sat, all Sun, Bank Holidays, Xmas-New Year

Now part of the Groupe Chez Gerard. Oysters, seafood and shellfish are the mainstay of the menu, though there are now also some meat dishes. The wine list is exceptional and it's worth spending time over it.

W1 The Selfridge

Orchard Street, W1H 0JS

☎ 0171-408 2080 📠 0171-409 2295

🛏 295 £181 🍴 65 🕑 £65

🙂 Lunch 12.30-2.30, Dinner 6-10.30 ☹ Lunch Sat, all Sun

Thistle hotel in the heart of the West End; all rooms are sound-proofed and very comfortable. An air of discreet luxury in the lounges and bar. Fletchers restaurant offers modern British food.

SW7 Shaw's   ❀

119 Old Brompton Road, SW7 3RN

☎ 0171-373 7774 📠 0171-370 5102

🍴 44 🕑 £70

🙂 Lunch 12-2 (Sun to 3.30), Dinner 7-10

☹ Lunch Sat, Dinner Sun, 2 wks Xmas, 2 wks Aug

Now well and truly part of the South Kensington scene (the number of people who recall Chanterelle on this site diminishes with each day!), Bill & Frances Atkins' charming restaurant offers English cooking in the modern vein on a mixture of fixed-price and à la carte menus, which are marked to indicate those dishes prepared in lighter style. Thus you may choose between a light charlotte of asparagus, leek and artichoke or a more traditional timbale of calves' sweetbreads and mushrooms; followed by char-grilled fillet of red mullet with grilled vegetables and tomato and basil oil or braised rabbit and ham shank with leeks and prunes. Delicious desserts range from a plate of sorbets and berries to chocolate tart with caramelized oranges and crème fraiche. Coffee or tea comes with hand-made petits fours, and the wine list, sensibly priced, includes a good few representatives from the New World.

WC2 Sheekey's Restaurant

28-32 St Martins Court, Leicester Square, WC2N 4AL
☎ 0171-240 2565   📠 0171-379 1417
🪑 90 🍽 £65
☺ Lunch 12-3, Dinner 5.30-11.30 (light meals 12-11.30 (Sat 6-11.15)
☹ Sun (exc May-Aug), 25 & 26 Dec, Easter, Bank Holidays

English and French seafood restaurant in a theatre-land setting where the early-evening and late-night suppers are particularly popular. There are a couple of meat dishes for dedicated carnivores. Sheekey's celebrates its centenary in 1996 – congratulations! Seating outside in the courtyard on sunny days.

SW1 Shepherd's

Marsham Court, Marsham Street, SW1P 4LA
☎ 0171-834 9552   📠 0171-233 6047
🪑 75 🍽 £60
☺ Lunch 12.30-2.45, Dinner 6.30-11.30 (bar 5.30-8)
☹ Sat & Sun, Bank Holidays, Xmas

Many thought that the Langan's formula couldn't be repeated, but the remaining partners from that original triumvirate, Richard Shepherd & Michael Caine, have struck lucky again, by providing a slightly scaled-down version of the same idea: good British cooking at reasonable prices in a canny location. (Peter Langan's heritage is acknowledged by his portrait on the menu.) Try crab and brandy soup, an unusual octopus and hot red pepper salad, black pudding with bubble and squeak; then baked aubergine with oyster mushrooms, kipper and haddock fishcakes with egg sauce, or haunch of venison with chestnuts and port sauce, although I often opt for the conventional oysters followed by excellent roast beef from the trolley. Desserts range from a comforting home-made raspberry jelly and ice-cream (who else would have the audacity to serve this?!), bread and butter pudding, or chocolate and passion fruit mousse. There's a good range of wines by the glass, enabling you to sip your way around an interesting list. The atmosphere created by polished wood and shining glass is very much for grown-ups (as befits its being within sound of Parliament's Division Bell), and it still manages to be great fun, too.

SW1 Sheraton Park Tower

101 Knightsbridge, SW1X 7RN
☎ 0171-235 8050   📠 0171-235 8231
🛏 295 £ £308 🪑 80 🍽 £70
☺ 12-11

Circular Knightsbridge hotel, commanding great views from the upper floors – all carefully furnished and maintained. Restaurant 101 is light and airy, almost a conservatory. Grand wine list.

SW1 Signor Sassi

14 Knightsbridge Green, SW1X 7LG

☎ 0171-584 2277 📠 0171-225 3953

🪑 80 🍽 £60

☺ Lunch 12-2.30, Dinner 7-11.30 ☹ Sun, Bank Holidays

Handy for hungry bargain-hunters from Harrods or Harvey Nichols, this homely haunt offers a traditional taste of Italy at sensible prices.

SW1 Simply Nico

48A Rochester Row, SW1P 1JU

☎ 0171-630 8061 📠 0171-355 4877

🪑 45 🍽 £65

☺ Lunch 12-2, Dinner 7-11

☹ Lunch Sat, all Sun, Bank Holidays, 11 days Xmas, 4 days Easter

So bringing up the rear is Pimlico's passport to fine dining within the Ladenis style: simple surroundings, good ingredients simply cooked by head chef Tim Johnson, a simple pricing structure (lunch at £21 for 2 courses, £24 for 3; dinner £26 for 3). Again, examples from the Nico school of cooking turn up as in terrine of fresh and smoked salmon with cucumber salad, gratin of crab with fresh pasta and lobster sauce, seared escalope of foie gras with brioche and chopped oranges; escalope of brill with sweet onion purée, breast of duck with honey, peppercorns and a maize pancake, best end of lamb with a herb crust and couscous, seared salmon fillet with lettuce and oriental sauce. Desserts might include the infamous double chocolate tart with orange crème anglaise, assorted sorbets served with lime syrup, diplomate of apricots and flaky pastry, or a selection of cheeses. Simply, one of the best!

WC2 Simpson's-in-the-Strand

100 Strand, WC2R 0EW

☎ 0171-836 9112 📠 0171-836 1381

🪑 240 🍽 £75

☺ Lunch 12-2.30, Dinner 6-11 (Sun to 9) ☹ Bank Holidays

Simpson's has been 'restoring' customers since 1828, when it offered only coffee and cigars. Gradually, over the years, its range has expanded considerably up to the most recent addition of the Great British Breakfast, or any combination of the Ten Deadly Sins. The daytime bill of fare brings traditional favourites including joints carved from the trolley, and wonderful nursery puddings. All in all, a wonderful piece of heritage and history. Well worth a trip down memory lane.

W6 Snows on the Green

166 Shepherds Bush Road, W6 7PB

☎ 0171-603 2142

🍴 70 ‖⊘‖ £70

☺ Lunch 12-3, Dinner 7-11

☹ Lunch Sat, Dinner Sun, Bank Holidays, 1 wk Xmas

More than a touch of the Mediterranean in Shepherd's Bush with light warm colours, pictures of lavender fields and owner, Sebastian Snow's flavours of the sunny South. Ingredients like salt cod, snails, carpaccio of beef, foie gras and goat's cheese team up with flavours of saffron, truffle oil, parmesan and sweet peppers for authenticity amongst first courses, do try the foie gras with fried egg and vinegar – delicious! Main dishes might include a partridge with savoy cabbage and sausage, John Dory with mussels and chives, char-grilled squid with crispy vegetables and aioli or a simple steak frites. Friendly, attentive service and reasonably-priced wines make this a popular choice with locals.

W1 Soho Soho

11-13 Frith Street, W1

☎ 0171-494 3491 📠 0171-437 3091

🍴 60 ‖⊘‖ £70

☺ Lunch 12-3, Dinner 6-12, (Ground Floor: Rotis 12-12.45am Mon-Sat, Wine Bar 11-11 Mon-Sat)

☹ all Sat & Sun, Bank Holidays

A restaurant, café/bar, rotisserie and salon privé that has captured the mood of the moment and serves its purpose admirably. As the floors rise, the emphasis towards serious eating grows away from the light snacks which accompany drinks on the ground floor. Standards are consistent wherever you choose to eat. Wines are fairly priced, service is smart and friendly – all in all, a fun place to be. A great achievement.

SW13 Sonny's

94 Church Road, SW13 0DQ

☎ 0181-748 0393

🍴 100 ‖⊘‖ £65

☺ Lunch 12.30-2.30 (Sun to 3), Dinner 7.30-11 (light meals in café 10.30-6)

☹ Dinner Sun, Bank Holidays

Perennially popular for modern British cooking in a lively setting. Recent changes of chef seem not to have adversely affected standards. There's usually a new twist each time regulars go, though old favourites like fish soup with rouille and croutons are always available. Daytime café operation and adjoining deli also successful.

SW1 The Square

32 King Street, St James's, SW1Y 6RJ
☎ 0171-839 8787
🪑 65 🍽 £80

☺ Lunch 12-3, Dinner 6-11.45   ☹ Lunch Sat & Sun

A coolly modern setting for some lively modern cooking by Philip Howard. A la carte lunches and set-price dinners (£32 for 2 courses, £38 for 3) offer simple descriptions of some quite complex executions. White bean soup with foie gras croutons, warm salad of game with port and raisins, mille feuille of caramelized sweetbreads show the style. Main courses range from roast cod with savoy cabbage, button onions and lardons; by fillet of plaice with parsley mash and buttered carrots; to roast Tuscan squab with a sauté of trompettes and balsamic jus. Desserts are just as attractive: soup of fruits with vanilla ice cream, baked chocolate sponge with orange sauce, tarte tatin all being typical. A concise wine list matches the food well. Due to move to 6 Bruton Street, W1 in September 1996.

SW1 The Stafford

16-18 St James's Place, SW1A 1NJ
☎ 0171-493 0111   📠 0171-493 7121
🛏 74 £223 🪑 58 🍽 £75

☺ Lunch 12.30-2.30, Dinner 6-11   ☹ Lunch Sat

Terry Holmes has returned to this clubby hotel, which is undergoing sympathetic refurbishment to include air-conditioning. Famous American Bar for cocktails, and the wine cellar with its 350-year history. This will be a winner with the recruitment of the talented Chris Oakes to head up the kitchen. I'm looking forward to its opening at the end of June 1996.

SW1 Stakis St Ermin's

Caxton Street, SW1H OQW
☎ 0171-222 7888   📠 0171-222 6914
🛏 290 £159 🪑 150 🍽 £55

☺ Lunch 12.30-2.30, Dinner 6-9.30

Elegant and usefully situated hotel near the House of Commons. Good conference and leisure facilities. Wonderful internal staircase and balcony used in many feature films.

SW5 Star of India

154 Old Brompton Road, SW5 0BE
☎ 0171-373 2901   📠 0171-373 5664
🪑 80 🍽 £70

☺ Lunch 12-3, Dinner 6-12 (Sun 7.30-11.30)   ☹ Bank Holidays

Reza Mahammad and his brothers run the Star with style. Good service and some sparkling food. Try the chicken and lentil kebabs with a cashew nut heart as a starter, followed by roast leg of lamb marinated in spices, cooked in a rich onion and tomato gravy flavoured with nutmeg and flambéed with rum. Fun decor – great local restaurant.

EC1 Stephen Bull's Bistro

71 St John Street, EC1M 4AN

☎ 0171-490 1750   📠 0171-490 3128

🪑 120   🍴 £60

☺ Lunch 12-2.30, Dinner 6-10.30   ☹ Sun, Bank Holidays, 1 wk Xmas

Now virtually doubled in size (since its expansion into an adjoining property), Stephen Bull's Anglo-European style of menu is thus available to a larger clientele. A shorter carte is offered in the bar, while an interesting, wide-ranging wine list complements the food. Served in minimalist, cool decor.

W1 Stephen Bull

5-7 Blandford Street, W1H 3AA

☎ 0171-486 9696   📠 0171-490 3128

🪑 55   🍴 £80

☺ Lunch 12.15-2.15, Dinner 6.30-10.45

☹ Lunch Sat, all Sun, Bank Holidays, 1 wk Xmas

Another builder of small empires, Stephen Bull was a comparative latecomer to cooking for a living, but he has certainly made up for lost time since (see also his Bistro and Fulham Road) 3 seems an optimum number of London outlets over which any one emperor can comfortably rule. Here at his first West End site (ie after moving in from Richmond), a daily-changing menu offers reliable modern British cooking with European overtones, such as twice-cooked goat's cheese soufflé; pizza of smoked salmon, mascarpone cheese and shallots; terrine of chicken, pork and sage with cranberry sauce; or a plate of Spanish delicacies comprising salchicon, Serrano ham, Mahon cheese, chorizo and quince paste. Sturdy main courses like supreme of free-range, black-leg chicken with roast garlic, flageolets and marjoram; roast grey mullet with lentils, ceps and black muscat; and John Dory and scallops with saffron cream and shallots continue the journey. Come to rest with an apricot tarte tatin, baked lemon and ginger pudding, or iced apple and hazelnut parfait. Home-made oatcakes are served with farmhouse cheeses.

W8 Stratfords

7 Stratford Road, W8 6RF

☎ 0171-937 6388   📠 0171-938 3434

🪑 50   🍴 £70

☺ Lunch 12-3, Dinner 7-11   ☹ Sun

Formerly known as Le Quai St Pierre and still upholding that tradition of French seafood in a quiet Kensington backwater. There are daily specials and also a couple of meat dishes.

SW3 Le Suquet

104 Draycott Avenue, SW3 3AE
☎ 0171-581 1785   📠 0171-225 0838
🪑 70 🍽 £70
🙂 Lunch 12-2.30, Dinner 7-11.30

Little has changed in almost 20 years at Le Suquet save the fish, which arrives extremely fresh every day at this petit coin de Provence. Choose the classic fruits de mer or any of the fish or shellfish dishes that are the specialities of Pierre Martin's cheerful and authentic restaurant that could as easily be in France as downtown Chelsea. Always busy so book beforehand.

EC4 Sweetings

39 Queen Victoria Street, EC4N 4SA
☎ 0171-248 3062
🪑 65 🍽 £60
🙂 Lunch only 11.30-3   ☹ Lunch Sat & Sun, Bank Holidays, 1 wk Xmas

Quintessentially traditional English fish, seafood and oyster bar in the heart of the city. Fish is cooked to order, wines are mostly white (with plenty available by the glass, as is Black Velvet). Evening functions can be arranged – as can take-away! No credit cards.

SW3 La Tante Claire

68 Royal Hospital Road, SW3 4HP
☎ 0171-352 6045   📠 0171-352 3257
🪑 43 🍽 £140
🙂 Lunch 12.30-2, Dinner 7-11
☹ Sat & Sun, Bank Holidays, 1 wk Xmas, 3 wks Aug

An enduring favourite just near the river in Chelsea, with clean, crisp lines of decor and furnishing, impeccable and discreet service and some of the best food in London offered by Pierre Koffmann. The set lunch at only £25 represents excellent value and can give you a delightful meal such as one recently enjoyed, comprising mousseline de St Jacques au beurre d'herbes, then magret to canard au poivre vert, excellent French cheeses then blinis chocolat et fruits du mendiant, with coffee and petits fours included for the price. The carte (which is subject to a minimum charge of £45 per person in the evening) shows a full range: frivolité de la mer; coquilles St Jacques à la planche, sauce encre; tranche de foie gras et pain grillé are typical starters, while main courses could include thon confit aux haricots tarbais; homard roti, vendange tardive; the famous pied de cochon aux morilles; or filet de chevreuil au chocolat amer et vinaigre de framboise. Desserts keep to the same high standards, from croustade de pommes à l'Armagnac to feuilleté de poires caramelisées, or some immaculately kept French cheeses. An all-French wine list comes as no surprise: that the prices are quite modest for a restaurant of this calibre.

SW3 Thierry's

342 King's Road, SW3 5UR

☎ 0171-352 3365

🅷 65 🍽 £60

☺ Lunch 12.30-4.30 (Mon to 2.30), Dinner 7-11 (Fri & Sat to 11.30,
Sun to 10.30) (light meals 12.30-7.30)

☹ Bank Holidays, 4 days Xmas

A little toe-hold of Paris in Chelsea: much-loved French bistro where Hervé Salez and chef, Mark Keenan, look after their longtime regulars and first-timers with equal charm. Traditional and some modern bistro dishes appear on both the carte and the menu rapide which wows them at lunch-time. The private room downstairs is great for parties.

SW1 Tophams Ebury Court

28 Ebury Street, SW1W 0LU

☎ 0171-730 8147   📠 0171-823 5966

🛏 42   £ £115   🅷 30 🍽 £50

☺ Lunch 12-2.30, Dinner 6-9.30   ☹ Lunch Sat, all Sun

An English Country House in the heart of Belgravia – days of gracious living recalled, but complemented by modern amenities in the individually-styled rooms. Garden rooms are available for private meetings and parties. Well-priced menus offering both the traditional and modern in Tophams restaurant.

SW3 Turner's

87-89 Walton Street, SW3 2HP

☎ 0171-584 6711   📠 0171-584 4441

🅷 50 🍽 £100

☺ Lunch 12.30-2.30, Dinner 7.30-11.15 (Sun to 10)

☹ Lunch Sat, Bank Holidays, 1 wk Xmas

Brian Turner continues to combine the many threads of his career – chef, restaurateur, TV presenter and sometime culinary comic genius – with the flair that marks the versatility of so many Yorkshiremen. He remains down to earth first and foremost, and never loses track of the fact that at the end of the day (or more likely 3 times a day), what most people want is a good meal at a sensible price. He thus sticks to his guns by offering no-nonsense classics with not too many nods to trendy fashions, in a blue and yellow dining room which appears fresh and cheerful. Set-price lunches are especially good value, priced at £9.95, £13.50 and £19.50; while at dinner prices range from around £23 to around £37. Some fine examples of his recent dishes include a light salad of sautéed scallops with a beetroot dressing; terrine of fresh pressed salmon with a dill sauce; and a hot, strong, creamy crab soup. Main courses could be a duo of brill and scallops with baby spinach; roast rib eye of beef with Yorkshire pudding (what else!); sea bass on a bed of stewed leeks with a bacon dressing. Filling desserts could be a very light rosewater parfait; white chocolate torte; or mousse au caramel. This is an all-time favourite – see you there!

SW9 Twenty Trinity Gardens

20 Trinity Gardens, SW9 8DP
☎ 0171-733 8838
🪑 54 🍽 £45

☺ Lunch Sun only, Dinner 7-10.30 (Fri & Sat to 11)
☹ Lunch Mon-Sat, Bank Holidays, 26 Dec-1 Jan

Useful neighbourhood modern French restaurant in a somewhat barren area. Special menus on celebration days (from New Year's Eve to Ramadan!); outside delivery service; speedy menus for those in a rush.

W2 Veronica's

3 Hereford Road, W2 4AB
☎ 0171-229 5079 📠 0171-229 1210
🪑 60 🍽 £65

☺ Lunch 12-3, Dinner 7-12
☹ Lunch Sat, all Sun, Bank Holidays, 2 days Xmas

British historic and regional menus cooked and served with great care, especially to celebrate feast days; organic wines, dishes for vegans: a fascinating place. Worth a visit.

SW10 Village Taverna

196-198 Fulham Road, SW10 9TW
☎ 0171-351 3799
🪑 70 🍽 £60

☺ 12 noon-1am ☹ 4 days Xmas

My favourite Greek run by my favourite Greeks (and not just because it's handy for the office!). Reliable menu of traditional dishes, served in a jolly atmosphere. Share a meze or indulge in some kleftiko, washed down with retsina and finish with sweetened coffee.

W1 Villandry Dining Room

89 Marylebone High Street, W1M 3DE
☎ 0171-224 3799 📠 0171-486 1370
🪑 50 🍽 £45

☺ Lunch 12-2.30, Dinner once a month
☹ Sun, Bank Holidays, 24 Dec-5 Jan

Which came first, the delicatessen or the dining room? Whichever, you could take away but it's more fun to eat in, and try modern French, English and Italian foods in tightly-packed surroundings. There are over 70 cheeses available!

WC1 Wagamama

4 Streatham Street, WC1

☎ 0171-323 9223 📠 0171-323 9224

🪑 104 🍽 £25

☺ 12-11 (Sat 12.30-11, Sun 12.30-10)   ☹ 1 wk Xmas & Easter Sun

Positive eating and positive living are the buzz-words at this positively different noodle restaurant near the British Museum. Authentic Japanese ingredients and efficiency, quick turnaround, busy atmosphere. Be prepared to queue. Second branch now open in Lexington Street, W1.

WC2 The Waldorf Meridien

Aldwych, WC2B 4DD

☎ 0171-836 2400 📠 0171-836 7244

🛏 292 £ £212 🪑 67 🍽 £90

☺ Lunch 12.30-2.30, Dinner 6-11 (Sun 7-10) (light meals Palm Court: 7-6, Tea Dance Sat & Sun 3.30-6)

☹ Lunch Sun & Sat, 2 days Xmas, Bank Holidays

A piece of history – Edwardian elegance is alive and well and you can go to the Palm Court tea dance to prove it! The restaurant offers formal eating with Mediterranean influences.

SW3 Waltons of Walton Street

121 Walton Street, SW3 2PH

☎ 0171-584 0204 📠 0171-581 2848

🪑 90 🍽 £100

☺ Lunch 12.30-2.30 (Sun to 2), Dinner 7.30-11.30 (Sun 7-10)

☹ 26 Dec

A new chef at Waltons at the end of 1994, but such is the style of Roger Wren's small group of London restaurants (see also English House, English Garden and Lindsay House), that a newcomer to the team can be absorbed seamlessly especially at this, the founding establishment. In either the elegant, spacious main restaurant, or the smaller and cosier Red Room (silk-lined walls) or even more intimate Yellow Room, (these two usually used for private parties), an excellent menu of prime English cooking with a modern touch can be enjoyed. The traditional Sunday lunch is very popular, as is the shorter and speedier Simply Waltons Lunch (on weekdays); but it's the full carte that best shows the range. Try home-made chicken and tarragon sausage on a bed of potato and celeriac purée with a shallot and thyme sauce, or an unusual wild mushroom and muscat soup; followed by breast of Norfolk duck, served pink with sea haricot and lingonberries, or grilled calves' liver and bacon with a white wine and onion confit. Traditional puddings might include apple and calvados tart with cinnamon custard, or steamed chocolate and hazelnut sponge with white chocolate sorbet and a coffee and whisky sauce. All of these dishes show an inventive approach to traditional ingredients, and they work well. There's an extensive wine list and also an abbreviated version of their more popular bins to aid with the choosing – prices are in the medium range.

W1 The Westbury

Conduit Street, W1A 4UH

☎ 0171-629 7755 📠 0171-495 1163

🛏 244 £19 🍴 55 🍽 £65

☺ Lunch 12.30-2, Dinner 6-10 ☹ Dinner Sun

Forte Grand in the West End, polo-themed. Comfortable lounges and bedrooms, discreet service. Polo Lounge coffee shop a haven for weary but well-heeled shoppers.

W1 White Tower

1 Percy Street, W1P 0ET

☎ 0171-636 8141

🍴 75 🍽 £70

☺ Lunch 12.30-2.30, Dinner 6.30-10.30

☹ Lunch Sat, all Sun, Bank Holidays, 3 wks Aug, 1 wk Xmas

Greek and French cooking in a famous West End location, which celebrates its 100th birthday in 1996. Intricately-described main courses with menu desriptions from the 50s. Duck specialities range from confit to pressed and Greek roast. Traditional Mediterranean dishes on a platter a speciality. Private dining rooms on 3 floors are popular with the arty, film and advertising fraternity.

EC4 Whittington's

21 College Hill, EC4 2RP

☎ 0171-248 5855

🍴 52 🍽 £70

☺ 11.45-2.15 ☹ Sat & Sun, Bank Holidays

Another City venue at which it essential to book for lunch (in the evening, the entire restaurant is only available for party reservations). Anglo-French cooking is the order of the day; and the menu changes fortnightly.

SW1 Wilton's

55 Jermyn Street, SW1Y 6LX

☎ 0171-629 9955 📠 0171-495 6233

🍴 100 🍽 £110

☺ Lunch 12.30-2.30, Dinner 6.30-10.30 ☹ all Sat, 1 wk Xmas

British cooking (especially of game, fish and shellfish) at this stately outpost of the Savoy group, the original in nearby St James Street and dating back to 1742. Beloved by politicians and the old school tie it offers a daily-changing specials list, nearly as long as the carte itself.

W8 Wodka

12 St Alban's Grove, W8 5PN

☎ 0171-937 6513 📠 0171-937 8621

🪑 60 🍽 £45

☺ Lunch 12.30-2.30, Dinner 7-11

☹ Lunch Sat & Sun, Bank Holidays

Polish and East European cooking at a small restaurant tucked away behind Kensington High Street. No surprise that there's an extensive range of vodkas!

SW3 Ziani

45/47 Radnor Walk, SW3 4BP

☎ 0171-351 5297 📠 0171-244 8387

🪑 50 🍽 £65

☺ Lunch 12-2.45 (Sun to 3.15), Dinner 7-11.30 (Sun to 10.30)

☹ 25 & 26 Dec, 1 Jan

Venetian cooking is the prime attraction here, so lots of offal, fish, pasta, polenta and an interesting wine list of "specials" as opposed, presumably, to the more familiar labels.

W1 Zoë

St Christopher's Place, W1M 5HH

☎ 0171-224 1122 📠 0171-935 5444

🪑 150 🍽 £65

☺ Lunch 12.00-2.30 (Sat café only), Dinner 6.30-11.30

(Café 11.30am-11.30pm)

☹ Sun, Bank Holidays

Busy and fun – modern Mediterranean food combined with Antony Worrall Thompson's usual wit and flair. Menus change seasonally, game and seafood are specialities. Large outside seating area.

L!VE TV: THE FACTS
see page 21

England

Abberley Elms Hotel

Stockton Road, Abberley, Nr Worcester,
Hereford & Worcester, WR6 6AT
☎ (01299) 896666 📠 (01299) 896804
▯ 25 £ £120 🍴 70 🍽 £70
☺ Lunch 12-2 Sun only, Dinner 7.30-9.30

An elegant country house set in the beautiful Teme Valley with comfortably furnished rooms and suites, some in the converted coach house. Seasonal fixed-price menus include a good choice of ambitious dishes.

Aldeburgh Regatta

171-173 High Street, Aldeburgh, Suffolk, IP15 5AN
☎ (01728) 452011
🍴 80 🍽 £55
☺ Lunch 12-2, Dinner 6-10 (Sun 7-10)
☹ Mon & Tue (except Bank Holidays)

Robert Mabey's second restaurant follows very much the style of the Sudbury original – good, fresh ingredients used in simple but inventive ways, and served up in a friendly atmosphere. Children are always welcome here.

Alderley Edge Alderley Edge Hotel

Macclesfield Road, Alderley Edge, Cheshire, SK9 7BJ
☎ (01625) 583033 📠 (01625) 586343
▯ 32 £ £117 🍴 80 🍽 £90
☺ Lunch 12-2, Dinner 7-10

Built in 1850 for one of Manchester's wealthy cotton merchants, this red-stone house was refurbished to high standards and is well maintained throughout. An amazing wine cellar demands a lengthy read (and probably a lengthy stay, to put it through its paces!); and the hotel's own bakery supplies a staggering range of breads, cakes and pastries. Fish comes daily from Fleetwood; and the overall style of the cooking is modern European.

Alston Lovelady Shield Country House Hotel

Nenthead Road, Alston, Cumbria, CA9 3LF
☎ (01434) 381203 📠 (01434) 381515
▯ 12 £ £98 🍴 40 🍽 £60
☺ Lunch by arrangement only at 1, Dinner 7.30-8.30
☹ 4 wks Jan/Feb

Located just 2½ miles from Alston on the A689 where it meets the B6294 Hexham road, this country house hotel on the banks of the River Nent. The Lyons family and chef Barrie Garton, here since 1989, continue to woo regulars and newcomers alike with modern English style cooking.

Altrincham Francs

2 Goose Green, Altrincham, Cheshire, WA14 1DW
☎ 0161-941 1842   📠 0161-941 6610
🍽 90   ⏱ £45

☺ Lunch 12-3, Dinner 6-11 (10.30 Mon-Thurs)
☹ Dinner Sun, Bank Holidays

Special French-themed evenings whenever possible (Bastille Day, Beaujolais Nouveau, Valentine's Day) just in case you were in any danger of forgetting that this is a French restaurant. The latest thing here is Le Braziard – hot-stone cooking of steaks and chicken, which are then served with dauphinoise potatoes, salad or vegetables, and a choice of starter and dessert. Good, bustling atmosphere.

Altrincham The French Brasserie

24 The Downs, Altrincham, Cheshire, WA14 2QD
☎ 0161-928 0808   📠 0161-941 6154
🍽 140   ⏱ £35

☺ 11-12am

Lively brasserie in authentic style where you can enjoy a fixed-price menu with plenty of choice for just £5 at lunch or £9.95 at dinner. For more choice, eat from the carte and you still shouldn't spend much. Live jazz and monthly wine tastings add to the appeal.

Altrincham The French Restaurant

25 The Downs, Altrincham, Cheshire, WA14 2QD
☎ 0161-941 3355   📠 0161-941 6154
🍽 110   ⏱ £40

☺ Lunch 12-2.30, Dinner 6-10.30   ☹ Lunch Sat

Grown-up sister of the next-door Brasserie, here proprietor Chris Hume and chef Phil Berry produce some serious French food for the good burghers of the North West. One aspect that isn't typically French, though, is the provision of a separate menu for vegetarians. Lots of special deals such as short meal times or short menus, help make this an attractive venue.

Amberley Amberley Castle

Amberley, Nr Arundel, West Sussex, BN18 9ND
☎ (01798) 831992 (01798) 831998
15 £130 40 £110
☺ Lunch 12-2, Dinner 7-9.30

Live like a king for a while in the unique atmosphere of this twelfth century castle complete with portcullis and battlements. Martin & Joy Cummings acquired the castle in 1988 and continue the lengthy work of restoration that was begun by the Duke of Norfolk at the turn of the century. 14 bedrooms are named after Sussex Castles and are furnished in appropriate style with four posters and antiques. The Queen's room is a charming, baronial hall now used as the dining room where local produce is used by chef Mark Raffan. Dishes include homecured marinated salmon flavoured with fennel and pernod and served with a red pepper dressing, followed by roasted breast of guinea fowl with confit of leg and a sloe gin sauce, with iced roasted hazelnut parfait served with poached pears and a caramel sauce rounding off the meal.

Ambleside Rothay Manor Hotel

Rothay Bridge, Ambleside, Cumbria, LA22 0EH
☎ (01539) 433605 (01539) 433607
18 £113 70 £70
☺ Lunch 12.30-2 (Sun 12.45-1.30), Dinner 7.45-9 ☹ 3 Jan-9 Feb

Half-way between Ambleside and Lake Windermere, Rothay has been a family-run hotel and restaurant since 1967, and it has a regularly returning clientele who love the elegance of the Regency building and the standards within it. Menus tend to be traditionally English, but some French influence. Good range of New World wines on the list.

Ambleside Sheila's Cottage

The Slack, Ambleside, Cumbria, LA22 9DQ
☎ (01539) 433079 (01539) 434488
68 £55
☺ Lunch 12-2.45, Dinner 7-9 ☹ Dinner Sun & Mon, Jan

Run by Stewart & Jan Greaves since 1965, this is a lakeland institution, and chef David Clay has done very well to slip smoothly into the groove since 1995. They describe it as a country restaurant and tea rooms, which is a fair description of what's to be found, although it doesn't really do justice to either the setting, or to the care that is put into producing carefully constructed dishes. The wine list has some useful notes.

Ambleside Wateredge Hotel

Waterhead Bay, Ambleside, Cumbria, LA22 0EP
☎ (01539) 432332 📠 (01539) 431878
🛏 23 £98 🪑 50 🍽 £80
☺ Dinner 7-8.30 ☹ mid Dec-early Feb

Lovely views, as you would expect from the name! This hotel, on the very tip of Windermere, started life as a couple of fishermen's cottages in the 17th Century, and now ranks with the best in the Lake District. In addition to meals in the restaurant, you can have a light lunch, morning coffee or afternoon tea in one of the lounges or on the lakeside patio, thus enjoying British food and British views at their best.

Appleby-in-Westmorland Appleby Manor

Roman Road, Appleby-in-Westmorland, Cumbria, CA16 6JB
☎ (01768) 351571 📠 (01768) 352888
🛏 30 £98 🪑 70 🍽 £55
☺ Lunch 12-1.45, Dinner 7-9 ☹ 3 days Xmas

Extensive refurbishment of the annexe bedrooms has brought them into line with those in the main house, so you can be assured of top-notch care wherever and whenever you stay at this family owned and run country house. All the usual Lake District pursuits are on the doorstep: step back inside to enjoy imaginative British cooking on set menus served with charm.

Appleby-in-Westmorland Tufton Arms

Market Square, Appleby-in-Westmorland, Cumbria, CA16 6XA
☎ (01768) 351593 📠 (01768) 352761
🛏 21 £80 🪑 70 🍽 £50
☺ Lunch 12-2, Dinner 7-9.30

The fertile Eden Valley is the setting for this lovely privately-owned and run hotel, built in the 16th Century and extended in the late 19th Century when it was one of the foremost country houses of Victorian England. In 1989 the Milsom family took it into their care and since then have kept the ambience and atmosphere of bygone times. In the Conservatory restaurant you can enjoy the fixed-price 3-course dinner menu, the plainer grill menu (also served at lunchtime), or different menus again at lunch and dinner in the Victorian Bar.

Applethwaite Underscar Manor

Applethwaite, Keswick, Cumbria, CA12 4PH
☎ (01768) 775000 (01768) 774904
 11 £150 55 £65
☺ Lunch 12-1, Dinner 7-8.30

Detailed directions are available from the Harrisons when you book, and all we would add to those is follow your instincts: they'll doubtless lead you to this attractive country house set in some breathtaking scenery – it was built in the Italianate style in the last century. Attention to detail is paramount, and is evident in decor and furnishings, housekeeping, creature comforts. It's no less evident on the menus, which offer modern British interpretations of classic French dishes; all accompanied by a well-researched wine list.

Ascot Royal Berkshire

London Road, Sunninghill, Ascot, Berkshire, SL5 0PP
☎ (01344) 23322 (01344) 874240
 63 £217 35 £80
☺ Lunch 12-2, Dinner 7.15-9.30

Previous residents of note here have included members of the Churchill family, and the gentleman responsible for many a night of sweet dreams, Colonel Horlicks. The present incumbents also wish you a good night's sleep – not necessarily with a hot milky drink – but rather by having provided comfortable and elegant surroundings, a good-value set dinner, and maybe a decent bottle of wine to go with it.

Asenby Crab & Lobster

Asenby, Nr Thirsk, North Yorkshire, YO7 3QL
☎ (01845) 577286 (01845) 577109
 60 £60
☺ Lunch 11.30-3, Dinner 6.30-11 ☹ Dinner Sun, 25 Dec

Lively restaurant and brasserie in a thatched building in lovely countryside. Extensive brasserie menu includes no fewer than 5 soups among the 20 starters! Main course choices are half-and-half fish and meat. Specials listed on blackboard. Slightly less choice in the restaurant, but still the same high standards. Summer Sunday jazz barbecues.

Ashbourne Callow Hall

Mappleton Road, Ashbourne, Derbyshire, DE6 2AA
☎ (01335) 343403 (01335) 343624
 16 £105 80 £80
☺ Lunch Sun only 12-1.30, Dinner 7.30-9.15 (Sun residents only), (light meals 7.15-9.15) ☹ 25 & 26 Dec, 1 wk Feb

Victorian hall set in lovely gardens within 44 acres of unspoilt countryside, where a principle pasttime is fishing: Callow has its own beat on a tributary of the River Dove. Elegant lounges and comfortable bedrooms set the scene indoors, and in the dining room enjoy some traditional English cooking accompanied by an interesting wine list.

Ashburton Holne Chase Hotel

Ashburton, Devon, TQ13 7NS
☎ (01364) 631471   (01364) 631453
14 £90   50 £55
☺ Lunch 12.30-1.45, Dinner 7.15-9

The Bromage family have been dispensing hospitality here since 1972, much of it to fishermen of the River Dart. The house is comfortably furnished, and there's the kind of attention to detail that makes a hotel a home-from-home. Complete your day with an unpretentious 3-course set dinner, and a superb selection of wines.

Ashford Eastwell Manor

Eastwell Park, Boughton Aluph, Ashford, Kent, TN25 4HR
☎ (01233) 635751   (01233) 635530
23 £142   65 £95
☺ Lunch 12.30-2, Dinner 7-9.30 (Fri & Sat to 10)

Lovely, 1920s mansion in 62 acres of grounds within a 3,000-acre estate. Individually decorated bedrooms are elegant and comfortable, while the lounges feature carved or panelled ceilings, open stone fireplaces and chandeliers. Ian Mansfield's menus are modern in style but with a strong French influence, and the wine list is of appropriate stature to the setting.

Ashington The Willows

London Road, Ashington, West Sussex, RH20 3JR
☎ (01903) 892575
30 £55
☺ Lunch Sun only 12-2, Dinner 7-10   ☹ Dinner Sun, all Mon

The Illes' friendly little local restaurant now benefits from the A24 bypassing the pretty village of Ashington completely, so be sure to spot the signs and reach this converted 15th-century farmhouse. Set-price dinners and Sunday lunches offer an international menu.

Aston Clinton The Bell Inn

Aston Clinton, Buckinghamshire, HP22 5HP
☎ (01296) 630252   (01296) 631250
21 £64   150 £100
☺ Lunch 12.30-1.45, Dinner 7.30-9.45 (Sun & Mon to 9)

A cluster of buildings, some dating back to the 17th century, form this popular hostelry which has been in the same ownership for 50 years. The old brewery now houses bedrooms around a pretty, cobbled courtyard with pretty gardens around them. Local Aylesbury duckling is a speciality in the restaurant, bred especially by a certain Mr Whaller and served either plain roasted, flamed with brandy, peppered or with an orange glaze. Other dishes include best end of lamb with a shallot and asparagus mousse; John Dory roasted on a bed of lemon grass and cracked pepper and grilled fillet of beef with morels, stuffed with calf's tongue and sauce 'financier'. Extensive wine list.

Austwick The Traddock

Austwick, Nr Settle, North Yorkshire, LA2 8BY
☎ (0152 42) 51224
🛏 11 £60 🍴 34 🍽 £50
☺ Lunch 12-2, Dinner 7-9 (light meals all day)

Comfortable, family-run hotel in the lovely Dales. The bar menu is extensive and offers hearty dishes to hikers and walkers, while the dining room is slightly more formal and still has plenty of choice. Yorkshire breakfasts set you up for a day in this lovely area.

Avebury Stones Restaurant

Avebury, Nr Marlborough, Wiltshire, SN8 1RF
☎ (01672) 539514   📠 (01672) 539683
🍴 80 🍽 £30
☺ 10-6.30 (weekends only Nov-Mar to 5.30)
☹ weekdays Nov-Mar, all Jan

A truly pioneering, counter-service, vegetarian restaurant where you can enjoy natural foods, organic produce, country wines in a relaxed and friendly setting. Menus change daily. Hilary Howard's cook book of the restaurant's favourite recipes is deservedly popular.

Aylesbury Hartwell House

Oxford Road, Aylesbury, Buckinghamshire, HP17 8NL
☎ (01296) 747444   📠 (01296) 747450
🛏 45 £176 🍴 70 🍽 £100
☺ Lunch 12.30-2, Dinner 7.30-9.45

As much a trip back to the 1600 as a visit to a hotel, this architectural gem has been meticulously restored by Historic House Hotels whose chairman, Richard Broyd, scoured the country to find suitable furniture and pictures, some that even belonged to the house during its illustrious past. It has all been worthwhile, the hotel is simply magnificent, 45 suites and bedrooms are situated within the house or in Hartwell Court, once the menagerie in the grounds. The Hartwell Spa, incorporating full leisure facilities, including a 50-foot swimming pool, can be found 100 yards from the main house. Words can't do justice to the setting, go and see it and experience grand living. The menu offers British cooking soundly prepared by chef Alan Maw, with the likes of warm salad of roast pigeon with wild mushrooms to start, followed by medallions of venison with braised cabbage and a sloe and juniper sauce. Excellent wine list, albeit featuring wines at the higher end of the price range.

Barham Old Coach House

Dover Road, Barham, Nr Canterbury, Kent, CT4 6SA
☎ (01227) 831218   📠 (01227) 831932
🛏 6 £62 🍴 40 🍽 £50
☺ Dinner 7.30-9.30 ☹ Sun, 25 Dec & 1 Jan

You'll receive a warm welcome at this former coaching inn run by Jean-Claude & Angela Rozard. Set back off the A2 Canterbury to Dover Road, and very much along the lines of a friendly and informal French auberge, you're far better to stay here en route to France than closer to the Channel ports. As well as the normal menus you will find all manner of game birds in season, plus locally-caught river fish. This man can cook. Winners of the Gold Small Hotel Welcome to Kent Tourism Award for 1995.

Barnard Gate The Boot Inn

Barnard Gate, Nr Witney, Oxfordshire, OX8 6XE
☎ (01865) 881231
🍽 £50
☺ Lunch 12-2 (Sun-3), Dinner 7-10 ☹ 25 & 26 Dec

Just off the A40 between Oxford and Witney, this well-run hostelry offers an extensive blackboard menu of hearty dishes, including good moules marinière and rack of lamb, making it popular with locals and travellers alike. Reasonably-priced wines. Bustling atmosphere.

Barnsley Armstrongs

102 Dodsworth Road, Barnsley, South Yorkshire, S70 6HL
☎ (01226) 240113
🍴 60 🍽 £60
☺ Lunch 12-2, Dinner 7-10
☹ Lunch Sat, all Sun & Mon, Bank Holidays

A concise menu of modern European cooking, accompanied by some well-priced wines is on offer at this good, local restaurant, which has recently moved to larger premises.

Barnstaple Lynwood House

Bishop's Tawton Road, Barnstaple, Devon, EX32 9DZ
☎ (01271) 43695 📠 (01271) 79340
🛏 5 £61 🍴 60 🍽 £70
☺ Lunch 12-2, Dinner 7-10 ☹ Sun (except residents)

A real family enterprise with the Roberts family filling all key roles in the running of their Victorian house with restaurant and rooms. Cooking is the domain of Mrs Roberts and Matthew, they offer good value fixed-price lunch menus and a more extensive carte-in the evening. Plenty of local fish is featured, Dover sole, scallops, chunky fish soup or a pot of seafood cooked with white wine and cream. Good wines are very reasonably marked up.

England   117

Basingstoke Audleys Wood

Alton Road, Basingstoke, Hampshire, RG25 2JT
☎ (01256) 817555   📠 (01256) 817500
🛏 71   £128   🍴 70   🕐 £80
☺ Lunch 12-1.45 (Sun to 2), Dinner 7-9.45 (Sun to 9.15)
☹ Bank Holidays & 1 wk Xmas

A dramatic setting for Murder Weekends organised throughout the year, this impressive, Victorian mansion has oak panelling, carved fireplaces and a minstrel's gallery in the lounge. Eat in the unusual vaulted, timber-roofed conservatory, and keep an eye out for Poirot or the Butler!

Baslow Cavendish Hotel

Baslow, Derbyshire, DE45 1SP
☎ (01246) 582311   📠 (01246) 582312
🛏 23   £118   🍴 50   🕐 £75
☺ Lunch 12.30-2, Dinner 7-10 (light meals Garden Room: 11-11)

Eric Marsh describes himself as the tenant of Cavendish from the Chatsworth Estate, but since the tenancy has run so far to 20 years, he seems as much part of the history of the place as many other features! Another attraction is Nick Buckingham's cooking, which has the same longevity. You can eat in the main restaurant, the garden room (no bookings needed) or at the famous kitchen table, with dishes ranging from fresh scallops and scampi pan fried and served with their sauces, to sushi and home-made bangers and mash!

Baslow Fischer's Baslow Hall

Calver Road, Baslow, Derbyshire, DE4 1RR
☎ (01246) 583259   📠 (01246) 583818
🛏 6   £120   🍴 40   🕐 £95
☺ Lunch 12-2.30, Dinner 7-9.30, (Café Max: 10-10)
☹ all Sun (except residents), 25 & 26 Dec

Max Fischer's cooking is the reason to visit Baslow Hall though the setting is well worth consideration too, a stone built manor house with half a dozen comfortable bedrooms and stylishly furnished day rooms. Max's distinctive dishes are well composed and perfectly executed, a tian of sea bass with a potato galette is served with beurre blanc, a saddle of rabbit comes with herb risotto and two mustard sauce, Chinese five spice powder flavours roast venison that is served with a compote of lentils. For the sweet-toothed a 'tear drop' of white chocolate is served with warm raspberries and chocolate sorbet or a gratin of Yorkshire rhubarb comes with stuffed prunes and creme Anglaise. Great precision and skill go into each dish and wines are chosen with care and knowledge. Café Max provides a slightly less formal and cheaper deal.

Bassenthwaite Armathwaite Hall ❖ 🍴 👪

Bassenthwaite Lake, Nr Keswick, Cumbria, CA12 4RE
☎ (01768) 776551 📠 (01768) 776220
🛏 43 £ £100 🍽 80 🍴 £75
☺ Lunch 12.30-1.45, Dinner 7.30-9.30

Another lovely lakeland hotel and restaurant, owned and run by the Graves family since 1977. The Lake View restaurant shares the vista with some of the bedrooms; while the imposing almost baronial building is decorated and furnished in keeping with its grandeur. An ongoing programme of refurbishment ensures high standards are maintained.

Bath Bath Spa Hotel ❖ 👪 ✿

Sydney Road, Bath, Avon, BA2 6JF
☎ (01225) 444424 📠 (01225) 444006
🛏 98 £ £176 🍽 120 🍴 £90
☺ Lunch 12-2 (Sun 12.30-2), Dinner 7-10 (Sat to 10.30)
   (Alfresco: 6.30-9.30)

A splendid Georgian hotel, formerly residence-in-exile of Emperor Haile Selassie, in landscaped gardens on the edge of town that is well run by Robin Sheppard. Exceptionally comfortable bedrooms and suites, indoor pool, tennis, gymnasium, sauna and solarium will all help to make your stay a memorable one. Jonathan Fraser's cooking also contributes to a feeling of well being whether you choose to eat in the Vellore Restaurant or the more informal Colonnade. In the Vellore try one of the 'Collective' menus for two or more people where you can sample a variety of dishes, the 'Tasting of Duck' menu includes a caramelised breast of duck with orchard fruits, a confit of leg teriyaki and pan-fried liver parfait served on brioche. The wine list is wide ranging and well composed with selections from all the premier wine regions. The menu in the Colonnade is a mix of old English dishes like cod and chips and sticky toffee pudding, Mediterranean with barbecue roast Provencal vegetables and goat's cheese with shallot and walnut vinaigrette and Far Eastern with oriental crab salad with mungo bean noodles, coriander and ginger-fried spinach.

Bath Clos du Roy

1 Seven Dials, Sawclose, Bath, Avon, BA1 1EN
☎ (01225) 444450 📠 (01225) 460218
🍽 85 🍴 £65
☺ Lunch 12-2.30, Dinner 6-10.30 ☹ 25 Dec

Whilst Philippe Roy's formal training at catering school in Poitiers shows in his classic treatment of dishes at the new Clos du Roy, the modern setting and decor of the restaurant also reflects in some of the up to date additions to his repertoire. A warm terrine of pike and mushrooms is served with basil and white wine sauce, a cassolette of gambas and wild mushrooms come with Pernod sauce, fillet of Scotch beef is topped with foie gras and sauternes sauce and a supreme of Trelough duck is garnished with white peach and served with cabernet sauvignon agridulce vinegar. Though the cooking is French his wine list shows no bias, choices from the New World and other European countries are interspersed with some good French growers.

Bath Hole in the Wall

16 George Street, Bath, Avon, BA1 2EN
☎ (01225) 425242 📠 (01225) 425242
🍴 70 🍽 £70
☺ Lunch 12-2, Dinner 6-11
☹ Sun, Bank Holiday Mon, Xmas, 2 wks Jan

Chris & Gunna Chown hope to be concentrating on their Bath establishment fully in 1996, but it has to be said, they have a good team with them in this attractive, atmospheric restaurant, which offers modern British food with menus changing at least monthly and often weekly. A relaxed atmosphere makes this a popular destination.

Bath The New Moon

Seven Dials, Sawclose, Bath, Avon, BA1 1EN
☎ (01225) 444407 📠 (01225) 318613
🍴 70 🍽 £50
☺ Dinner 7-11 (Brasserie 11-7) ☹ 25 & 26 Dec, 1 Jan

Useful restaurant and brasserie near the Theatre Royal. The brasserie menu is available from 12noon-7pm, a carte in the evening. Both have similar style: modern British cooking, quite light in touch and flavour. Another place that is popular with Bath's increasingly knowledgeable diners.

Bath Priory Hotel

Weston Road, Bath, Avon, BA1 2XT
☎ (01225) 331922 📠 (01225) 448276
🛏 21 £155 🍴 60 🍽 £85
☺ Lunch 12.15-1.45, Dinner 7.15-9.15

Privately owned (and a change of hands since the last Edition) but continuity is maintained by general manager Thomas Conboy and chef Michael Collom. The Gothic-style, Bath-stone building, set in its own grounds, offers some very comfortable bedrooms and lounges, serviced by professional yet friendly staff. For the restaurant, the cooking is British with classic French influences, and is well matched by the wine list.

Bath Queensberry Hotel

Russel Street, Bath, Avon, BA1 2QT
☎ (01225) 447928 📠 (01225) 446065
🛏 22 £133 🍴 50 🍽 £55
☺ Lunch 12-2, Dinner 7-10 ☹ Lunch Sun, 1 wk Xmas

A small, intimate hotel in a Georgian terrace just off the city centre with 22 well appointed bedrooms and an impressive bistro called The Olive Tree. Stephen Ross cooks Mediterranean dishes, a spiced cous cous broth of chicken breast, red onions and peppers, risotto of seafood, braised beef with prunes and armagnac or vegetarian polenta layered with courgettes and mushrooms. Wines stray further than the Med. but stay mainly below £20 which is satisfying. A welcome change from large, group owned hotels.

Bath Royal Crescent Hotel

16 Royal Crescent, Bath, Avon, BA1 2LS
☎ (01225) 319090 📠 (01225) 339401
🛏 46 £188 🍽 60 🍴 £95
☺ Lunch 12.30-2, Dinner 7-9.30 (Sun to 10)

Housed in this quite unique sweep of Bath stone the hotel is marked by small plant tubs, nothing as vulgar as even a brass plaque is allowed to break the symmetry of John Wood's (the younger) 18th-century architectural masterpiece in crescent building. Within the hotel is the kind of elegance that you would expect from its exterior, 40 odd impeccable suites and bedrooms, some in the Dower House and Pavilion located in the grounds. The Dower House is home to Steven Blake's fine cooking, classic in style with modern interpretations. Dishes might include tortellini of woodland mushrooms in a truffle dressing with leaf spinach, followed by roast Lunesdale duckling with croutons, lardons and confit and finishing with a delicious hot raspberry soufflé with vanilla ice cream. The wine list is long and not cheap but then this is hardly an average hotel.

Bath Woods

9-13 Alfred Street, Bath, Avon, BA1 2QX
☎ (01225) 314812 📠 (01225) 443146
🍽 70 🍴 £40
☺ Lunch 12-3, Dinner 6-11 ☹ Sun, 24-26 Dec

A 3-course dinner menu for only £12 offers great value for money at the Prices' long-established city-centre restaurant. An alternative at around £20 might use more expensive ingredients, but is equally good value. There's a good choice of wines by the glass. Friendly, efficient service directed by David Price.

Battle Netherfield Place

Battle, East Sussex, TN33 9PP
☎ (01424) 774455 📠 (01424) 774024
🛏 14 £105 🍽 50 🍴 £70
☺ Lunch 12.30-2, Dinner 7-9.30 (Sun to 9) ☹ 2 wks Xmas

Lovely Georgian-style country house just 4 miles north of Battle, with pretty gardens including a walled kitchen garden which provides fruit, vegetables and herbs. Resident proprietors Helen & Michael Collier take great care with small details, which shows in the maintenance and equipping of the bedrooms as well as the presentation of chef Paul Madge's modern European cooking.

Beanacre Beechfield House

Beanacre, Nr Melksham, Wiltshire, SN12 7PU
☎ (01225) 703700 📠 (01225) 790118
🛏 24 £80 🍽 33 🍴 £60
☺ Lunch 12-2, Dinner 7-9.30 (Sun to 9)

Intricate, Victorian Bathstone house set in its own landscaped grounds (bedrooms are named after trees). Lounges are relaxing and comfortable, and the staff succeed in being professional yet discreet. Modern British food in the pretty restaurant.

England 121

Beaulieu Montagu Arms

Beaulieu, New Forest, Hampshire, SO42 7ZL
☎ (01590) 612324   (01590) 612188
24 £99 80 £65
☺ Lunch 12.30-2, Dinner 7.30-9.30 (Fri & Sat 7.30-10)

Idyllic setting in Beaulieu village and on the Beaulieu river, complete with waddling ducks and New Forest ponies which regularly stop the traffic. So if you are halted, pop into the Montagu Arms for a full meal or a light snack. Eat outside in summer, be warmed by log fires in the winter – it's one of those places which seems to suit all seasons.

Beckingham Black Swan

Hillside, Beckingham, Lincolnshire, LN5 0RF
☎ (01636) 626474
35 £55
☺ Lunch 12-2, Dinner 7-9.30
☹ Mon, Dinner Sun, 2 wks Aug, 1 wk Jan

Situated 6 miles east of Newark on the A17 Sleaford Road and with a lovely riverside garden, this converted village pub has been run by the Indans for 10 years, over which time Anton's cooking has evolved into a modern British style that is very much in keeping with the times. He uses local game in season, and soufflés (both savoury and sweet) are a speciality.

Bibury The Swan

Bibury, Gloucestershire, GL7 5NW
☎ (01285) 740695   (01285) 740473
18 £128 65 £100
☺ Lunch Sun only 12.30-2.30, Dinner 7.30-9.30, (Jankowskis: 10-10)

An old coaching inn that is now very much into the needs of the modern age. Hosts Alexander & Elizabeth Furtek have really created a stylish hostelry that retains its old World charm whilst providing all the necessities of a modern hotel. The River Coln drifts aimlessly past the hotel, a spring rises to supply water to the trout stream and gardens border the river, Cotswold charm at its very best. The unfortunate trout feature on the menus of the dining room and Jankowski's Brasserie which is open all day, it might come with almonds, a red wine and caper sauce or en papillotte with vermouth, fennel and tomato confit. Interesting contrasts of decor throughout the hotel change from Edwardian to art deco and a fine oak panelled bar. Delightful dining room.

Bigbury-on-Sea Burgh Island Hotel

Burgh Island, Bigbury-on-Sea, Devon, TQ7 4AU
☎ (01548) 810514   (01548) 810243
14 £208 60 £70
☺ Lunch 12-2, Dinner 7.30-9 ☹ midweek Jan & Feb

Wonderful state-of-the-art-deco hotel, restaurant, inn and island owned by the Porters, equally loved by movie-makers and holiday-makers. Set menus of modern European cooking are complemented by a fine wine list. Dress for dinner and make believe the fairytale that is Burgh Island.

Billesley Billesley Manor

Billesley, Alcester, Nr Stratford-upon-Avon,
Warwickshire, B49 6NF
☎ (01789) 400888   (01789) 764145
 41   £168   80   £85
☺ Lunch 12.30-2, Dinner 7.30-9.30 (Fri & Sat to 10)

A settlement on this site is recorded in Saxon times, and the Manor itself is listed in the Domesday Book. The present building dates from the late 16th Century, so you can expect plenty of low beamed ceilings, dark wood panelling, 4-posters and irregular ceilings. There are also some modern rooms and an indoor swimming pool, to create good business and leisure facilities.

Billingshurst The Gables

Pulborough Road, Parkbrook, Billingshurst, Kent, RH14 9EU
☎ (01403) 782571
 52   £60
☺ Lunch 12.15-1.45, Dinner 7.15-9 (Fri & Sat to 10)
☹ Lunch Sat, Dinner Sun, all Mon, 1 wk Jan/Feb

An innovation here is gourmet themed wine evenings, held every couple of months by partners Nicholas Illes & Rebecca Gilroy. Chef Nicholas doesn't do things the easy way – he goes up to Billingsgate, Smithfield and Covent Garden himself to ensure he gets the best quality for his international-style set-price menus.

Birdlip Kingshead House

Birdlip, Nr Cheltenham, Gloucestershire, GL4 8JH
☎ (01452) 862299
 1   £54   34   £55
☺ Lunch 12.30-1.45, Dinner 7.30-9.45
☹ Lunch Sat, Dinner Sun, all Mon, 24 Dec-2 Jan

Warren & Judy Knock have notched up 10 years at this pretty Cotswold restaurant that began life as a 17th century coaching inn. Judy cooks, constantly seeking new inspirations and refinements to existing ones, and prepares modern English dishes with a light touch. Local suppliers are treasured; all the bread is home made (and can be purchased), and themed evenings are very popular. Set on the delightful Cotswold Way, it's worth an overnight in the one and only room.

England **123**

Birmingham Hyatt Regency

2 Bridge Street, Birmingham, West Midlands, B1 2JZ
☎ 0121-643 1234   0121-616 2323
319 £144 75 £80

☺ Lunch 12.30-2.30, Dinner 6.30-11 (Court Café: 6.30am-12 midnight)
☹ Lunch Sat, all Sun

Ultra-modern hotel in the city-centre, featuring an atrium-reception with marble floor, carefully-designed and excellently-equipped bedrooms and good business facilities. Within its grounds, the Glassworks is an informal bar in a 19th-century glass factory, overlooking the Grand Union Canal. Back in the hotel, the top 3 floors are a kind of "hotel within a hotel": the Regency Club is exclusive and pampering. One suite has its own baby grand, private dining area and spa bath.

Birmingham Swallow Hotel

12 Hagley Road, Five Ways, Birmingham,
West Midlands, B16 8SJ
☎ 0121-452 1144   0121-456 3442
98 £145
Sir Edward Elgar:
60 £95

☺ Lunch 12.30-2.30, Dinner 7.30-10.30 (Sun to 10) ☹ Lunch Sat
Langtry's:
60 £60

☺ Lunch 11.30-3, Dinner 6-10 ☹ Sun, Bank Holidays, 1 wk Xmas

A superb hotel that lives up to the aspirations of the revitalised second city following the development of its business and cultural activities. The Swallow is Edwardian in style with Italian marble, mahogany, crystal chandeliers, period furnishings and oil paintings, no expense was spared to create a luxurious atmosphere. There are 2 restaurants, dedicated to 2 eminent Edwardians, Sir Edward Elgar and Lillie Langtry, the former is as classical as its namesake's music, trompe l'oeil, murals of The Malverns and a grand piano. In Langtry's the cuisine tends to be traditional British with a few modern variations, regional dishes feature daily and Jonathan Harrison's cooking achieves high notes.

Bishop's Tawton Halmpstone Manor

Bishop's Tawton, Barnstaple, Devon, EX32 0EA
☎ (01271) 830321   (01271) 830826
5 £100 24 £75

☺ Lunch by arrangement, Dinner 7-9 ☹ Nov & Jan

Jane & Charles Stanbury look after you well at Halmpstone, their lovely North Devon country house – the name derives from "Holy Boundary Stone". There's a pleasant, homely atmosphere to the place, not least because Jane cooks a delicious set dinner of 5 courses plus coffee, and there's also a short list of very reasonably priced wines.

Blackpool September Brasserie

15-17 Queen Street, Blackpool, Lancashire, FY1 1PU
☎ (01253) 23282
🍴 40 🍽 £65
🙂 Lunch 12-2, Dinner 7-9.30 ☹ Sun & Mon, 2 wks summer, 2 wks winter

Just a stone's throw from the Promenade, this first-floor dining room offers creative eclectic cooking to an enthusiastic audience. Special dates are comemmorated with special events and menus, but served always with Michael Golowicz's flair and style. Partner Pat Wood also runs the hair studio on the ground floor.

Bollington Mauro's

88 Palmerston Street, Bollington, Nr Macclesfield, Cheshire, SK10 5PW
☎ (01625) 573898
🍴 49 🍽 £60
🙂 Lunch 12-2, Dinner 7-10 ☹ Lunch Sun & Sat

Long-established traditional Italian restaurant in a slightly unusual north-west location, but Vincenzo Mauro is now certainly part of the scenery. A fine wine selection accompanies his classic menu, which makes a feature of seafood.

Bolton Abbey Devonshire Arms

Bolton Abbey, Nr Skipton, North Yorkshire, BD23 6AJ
☎ (01756) 710441 📠 (01756) 710564
🛏 41 £130 🍴 50 🍽 £80
🙂 Lunch 12-2, Dinner 7-10 (Sun 7-9.30) (Duke's Bar 12-2)

Part of the Devonshire estate since 1753, this comfortable country house reminds you of its origins but does not overpower. The historic setting; individually-themed bedrooms; good health, beauty and fitness facilities; and the Burlington Restaurant combine to take care of all aspects of guests' well being.

Bonchurch Winterbourne Hotel

Bonchurch, Isle of Wight, PO38 1RQ
☎ (01983) 852535 📠 (01983) 853056
🛏 14 £124 🍴 35 🍽 £50
🙂 Dinner 6.45-9 (later by arrangement) ☹ Hotel Nov-March

Charles Dickens wrote *David Copperfield* in this charming house and described it as the prettiest place that he ever saw in his life. Set near the sea, the gardens have extensive lawns, a stream and even waterfalls.

Boughton Monchelsea Tanyard Hotel

Wierton Hill, Boughton Monchelsea, Nr Maidstone, Kent, ME17 4JT
☎ (01622) 744705   📠 (01622) 741998
6   £90   28   £60
☺ Lunch by arrangement only, Dinner 7-9
☹ Lunch Mon, Tue & Sat, 1 wk Xmas, 2 wks winter

Medieval origins cannot be missed as soon as you see the Tanyard, though the ensuite bedrooms offer all modern amenities within the beamed and inglenooked interior. Set-price menus offer 4 courses plus coffee at dinner, fewer at lunchtime. The concise wine list is as well chosen as the menu – a credit to Jan Davies' spirit of enterprise.

Bournemouth De Vere Royal Bath Hotel

Bath Road, Bournemouth, Dorset, BH1 2EW
☎ (01202) 555555   📠 (01202) 554158
131   £115   300   £60
☺ Lunch Sun only 12.30-2.15, Dinner 7-9.15

Near the pier and beach with wonderful views and a private garden, this grand hotel is ideally located for those taking advantage of Bournemouth's assets. Good leisure and business facilities include an indoor swimming pool and health club and the two restaurants (the Garden Restaurant and Oscar's) offer seasonally changing menus. There's often a live pianist or dinner dance – check dates when booking.

Bowness-on-Windermere Gilpin Lodge

Crook Road, Bowness-on-Windermere, Cumbria, LA23 3NE
☎ (01539) 488818   📠 (01539) 488058
9   £120   45   £70
☺ Lunch 12-2, Dinner 7-8.45

Located on the B5284 between Crook and Bowness, Gilpin Lodge is set in 20 acres of beautiful lakeland countryside. Much love has been lavished on the house by the Cunliffes, and it shows in every detail. In the restaurant you can enjoy a classic menu which uses modern ingredients and techniques. Revised wine list has more components from the New World. Definitely a favourite.

Bowness-on-Windermere
Linthwaite House

Bowness-on-Windermere, Cumbria, LA23 3JA
☎ (01539) 488600   📠 (01539) 488601
18   £115   48   £68
☺ Lunch 12.15-1.45, Dinner 7.15-8.45

Charming lakeland hotel and restaurant with the kind of views about which you can almost become blasé up here! Calm and relaxing decor inside (bedrooms and lounges) are enhanced by friendly and professional service. 1995 saw a change in menu format: a 3-course table d'hote at around £22 or a 5-course gourmet menu for £35 now supplement the carte. Cooking is modern British.

Bracknell Coppid Beech Hotel

John Nike Way, Bracknell, Berkshire, RG12 8TF
☎ (01334) 303333 📠 (01334) 301200
🛏 205 £125 🪑 120 🍽 £70
☺ Lunch 12-2.30, Dinner 7-10.30 (Sun to 10), (Brasserie: 11-11)
☹ Lunch Sat

Just 5 minutes from Junction 10 of the M4 or Junction 3 of the M3, the ultra-modern Coppid Beech appeals to an international clientele. It has the appearance of a clean-cut, over-large, Swiss chalet, so perhaps it's no surprise to find that the extensive leisure facilities are geared to such things as a "get fit for ski-ing" break; and there's also an Olympic-sized ice rink! Above-average food in Rowans Restaurant, extensive wine list.

Bradford-on-Avon Leigh Park Hotel

Leigh Road West, Bradford-on-Avon, Wiltshire, BA15 1AR
☎ (01225) 864885 📠 (01225) 862315
🛏 22 £85 🪑 30 🍽 £50
☺ Lunch 12-2, Dinner 7-9.30 ☹ Lunch Sat

A lovely Georgian Country House and Vineyard set within 5 acres of grounds – not many places can claim such a title, but this is one! It's a relaxed, informal venue with good business and conference facilities, and is well favoured for private parties. Traditional menus are served in Winstons Restaurant.

Bradford-on-Avon Woolley Grange

Woolley Green, Bradford-on-Avon, Wiltshire, BA15 1TX
☎ (01225) 864705 📠 (01225) 864059
🛏 20 £140 🪑 50 🍽 £75
☺ Lunch 12-2, Dinner 7-10

A charming country house hotel built of Bath stone back in the 17th century, now the home of the Chapman family. Full of character, antiques and warmth the hotel combines high standards with friendly service and welcomes children which is a pleasant change! Fixed-price dinner menus usually offer 4 or 5 choices at each course, you might start with a bourride of fishes served with aioli and rouille then perhaps roast pigeon with confit cabbage and madeira sauce. Good cheeses or puddings like chocolate and Drambuie marquise with coffee bean sauce or bread and butter pudding.

Bradford Restaurant 19

Belevedere Hotel, 19 North Park Road, Heaton,
Bradford, West Yorkshire, BD9 4NT

☎ (01274) 492559   📠 (01274) 483827

▯ 4 £75   ⚲ 36 🍽 £70

☺ Dinner 7-9.30 (Sat to 10)   ☹ Sun, 2 wks Dec/Jan, 2 wks Sep

There's a simple but successful formula in operation here: dinner at a fixed price of £25 for 3 courses (an extra £3.75 for starter or cheese to make up 4 courses, £1.95 for coffee and home-made petits fours), with plenty of choice at each courses, interesting combinations of ingredients and a friendly and relaxed atmosphere; and 4 comfortable bedrooms into which to collapse. English cooking enjoys a modern touch on a classic base. There are substantial starters like grilled tuna steak with tomatoes, sautéed potatoes and fresh capers; sautéed chicken in 3 spices with noodles in a creamy mushroom sauce; or fillet of salmon wrapped in seaweed, lightly steamed with ginger and spring onions. Main courses sound equally robust but the execution is in fact quite light, so that you don't feel overfaced by the meal. Try fillet of beef with polenta, bacon chips, and Mediterranean roulade; roast saddle of rabbit with apple and a sausage of the leg meat with herbs and pine kernels; rack of spring lamb with a pistachio and mint crust and a ragout of vegetables; fillet of salmon with Puy lentils and a red wine sauce. Desserts are just as delicious: mascarpone mousse with strawberries and mint; panna cotta with rhubarb and ginger; twice-baked orange soufflé with vanilla custard. A serious wine list travels the world but is nevertheless reasonably priced.

Braithwaite Ivy House

Braithwaite, Nr Keswick, Cumbria, CA12 5SY

☎ (01768) 778338   📠 (01768) 778113

▯ 12 £60   ⚲ 32 🍽 £50

☺ Dinner at 7.30   ☹ Jan

Small and friendly 17th-century lakeland hotel offering traditionally furnished bedrooms and lounges. Set-price menus of local ingredients with international touches are served in the candle-lit dining room.

Bramley Garden Restaurant

4A High Street, Bramley, Nr Guildford, Surrey, GU5 0HB

☎ (01483) 894037

⚲ 24 🍽 £45

☺ Lunch 12-3, Dinner 7-9.30

☹ Lunch Mon-Fri, Dinner Sun-Thu, 2 wks Jan

Open only at the weekend, the Hirths' restaurant offers fixed-price menus of simple, well-prepared dishes. There's room for over 100 in the rear garden so if the weather is kind, this is an ideal place for a party or a wedding reception.

Brampton Farlam Hall

Hallbankgate, Brampton, Cumbria, CA8 2NG

☎ (0169 77) 46234   📠 (0169 77) 46683

🛏 12 £184   🍴 40 🕐 £60

☺ Dinner 8-8.30   ☹ Hotel 25-30 Dec

Another 21st anniversary, this time for the Quinion & Stevenson families who opened Farlam in 1975. It's a small lakeland hotel, beautifully furnished with antiques, offering friendly yet professional service, good standards of housekeeping, and English country house cooking of good, local ingredients, all in a lovely setting. Concise, reasonably priced wine list.

Bray-on-Thames The Waterside Inn

Ferry Road, Bray-on-Thames, Berkshire, SL6 2AT

☎ (01628) 20691   📠 (01628) 784710

🛏 7 £170   🍴 75 🕐 £130

☺ Lunch 12-2 (Sun 12-2.30), Dinner 7-10

☹ Lunch Tue, Dinner Sun in winter, all Mon, Bank Holidays, 5 wks after 24 Dec

"Un restaurant avec chambres" is how the patron modestly describes his inn. That it certainly is, but modest it most certainly is not! Michel Roux runs one of the finest French restaurants in the country his flair and enthusiasm continue to reflect his skill and art in producing the best in terms of food and service. A lovely Thameside setting has become a pilgrimage for gastronomes from around the World. Mark Dodson is Michel's disciple as head chef and the dishes that emanate from the kitchen are legendary, a soufflé of mussels with lemon thyme, breast of chicken with wild mushrooms and pistachios in jelly, a consommé of crab with girolles and foie gras or choucroute of seafood might feature amongst first courses. Grilled calf's kidney on braised lettuce with devilled or Bearnaise sauce, a pot-roast poussin with cepes and sweetbreads, fillets of rabbit grilled with marrons glacé or a slice of grilled turbot with olive oil perfumed with chives may follow. As if that were not enough the puddings are quite exquisite, a hot raspberry soufflé, a ravioli of citrus with a gratin of pears and bananas or featherlight 'floating islands' with dates and coffee flavoured sauce. There is a cottage in the grounds that may be hired for private functions or small conferences and of course there are the chambres to drift into and dream about the dinner!

Bridport Riverside Restaurant

West Bay, Bridport, Dorset, DT6 4EZ

☎ (01308) 422011

🍴 70 🕐 £40

☺ Lunch 11.30-2.30 (Sun to 3.30), Dinner 6.30-9

☹ Dinner Sun, all Mon (except Bank Holidays), late Nov-early Mar

One of my favourites: a relaxed, unusual and informal restaurant with good seafood, where the atmosphere is almost as important as the food – though the food is top-notch, too! You have to cross a footbridge to get here, and having made the journey I never want to leave. Janet & Arthur Watson have been joined this year by a couple of new young chefs who are also seafood experts so the fresh, local ingredients can be sure of good treatment. Sort of self-service!

England 129

Brightling Jack Fuller's

Oxley's Green, Brightling, Nr Robertsbridge,
East Sussex, TN32 5HD
☎ (01424) 838212
⏵ 70 🍽 £35

☺ Lunch 12-2, Dinner 7-11

☹ Dinner Sun, all Mon & Tue, 25 Dec, Bank Holidays, 2 wks Jan

Squire John Fuller, an MP for East Sussex in the last century, was most widely known for being a builder of follies, and he's buried beneath one of his own design in Brightling churchyard. However, the food at this evolved pub (situated 3 miles from Robertsbridge on the un-numbered Brightling road) is of a much more serious turn of mind. Roger and Shirl Berman have put their stamp firmly on the place which is now as well known for its straightforward food and concise, international wine list as its historic associations.

Brighton Brighton Thistle Hotel

King's Road, Brighton, East Sussex, BN1 2GS
☎ (01273) 206700 📠 (01273) 820692
⏵ 204 £ £160 ⏵ 45 🍽 £85

☺ Lunch 12-2, Dinner 7-10, (Promenade Brasserie 12-2.30, 7-10.00)

☹ Lunch Sat, all Sun

Large, modern hotel right on the seafront, backing on to the Lanes and overlooking the Palace Pier. A feature is the glazed atrium lounge, an ideal meeting place or afternoon tea venue. Bedrooms are all air-conditioned, and leisure facilities include a pool and fitness equipment. A modern international style of menu is served in La Noblesse Restaurant, with more relaxed eating available from the Promenade Brasserie.

Brighton Grand Hotel

King's Road, Brighton, East Sussex, BN1 2FW
☎ (01273) 321188 📠 (01273) 202694
⏵ 200 £ £165 ⏵ 130 🍽 £75

☺ Lunch 12-2, Dinner 7-10

A member of the De Vere group, the Grand stands proudly on Brighton's seafront, over which the balconied bedrooms have an uninterrupted view. The interior is equally gracious and imposing, and standards of maintenance are high. An overnight stay also gets you complimentary membership of the health spa and the night club. An international-style menu is served in the Kings Restaurant.

Brighton Topps Hotel

17 Regency Square, Brighton, East Sussex, BN1 2FG
☎ (01273) 729334 📠 (01273) 203679
15 £79 20 £50

☺ Dinner 7-9.20 ☹ Dinner Sun & Wed, Hotel 25 & 26 Dec, Jan

Lovely little hotel set back from, but still overlooking, the seafront. The Regency building has been impeccably restored and is continuously well maintained. The characters of owners Paul & Pauline Collins come through in the atmosphere and in the attention to detail. The light basement restaurant serves a mixture of French and English cooking with a homely touch. Excellent breakfasts.

Brimfield Poppies Restaurant

The Roebuck, Brimfield, Nr Ludlow,
Hereford & Worcester, SY8 4NE
☎ (01584) 711230 📠 (01584) 711654
3 £60 40 £75

☺ Lunch 12-2, Dinner 7-9.30 ☹ Sun & Mon, 25 & 26 Dec

Carole Evans' popular Poppies continues to make strides: the latest additional feature is a 16-seater terrace for coffee, drinks or full meals if the weather holds. The standard of cooking is equally high for either the bar or the restaurant menu, and organic produce is used whenever possible. From the former, try fish cakes with parsley sauce; crab pot with melba toast; soup of the day with delicious home-made bread rolls; old-fashioned steak and kidney pie; or an unusual savoury bread and butter pudding with a watercress sauce. A set lunch menu offers 3 courses for £20, with a choice of 2 dishes at each course, so you could enjoy spinach soufflé served with a light hollandaise sauce, roast fillet of pork stuffed with apricot and orange served on a bed of sage-flavoured Puy lentils with a cider sauce, with a chocolate and cardamom burnt cream to finish. The carte shows Carole's full range, as in baked lemon sole with a grape, wine and cream sauce served with fresh ribboned pasta; followed by roast fillet of Herefordshire beef served on a purée of horseradish and sugar-snap peas with a red wine sauce and glazed shallots; and to finish, a caramel pyramid with spiced brown bread ice cream. The accompanying wine list is well priced and extensive. Soothing and relaxing ensuite bedrooms ensure a sound night's sleep.

SCOTCH BEEF CLUB
see page 16

Bristol Harveys Restaurant

12 Denmark Street, Bristol, Avon, BS1 5DQ
☎ 0117-927 5003   📠 0117-925 3003
🍽 120 🍴 £80
☺ Lunch 12-1.45, Dinner 7-10.30
☹ Lunch Sat, all Sun, Bank Holidays, 1 wk Xmas

Harvey's of Bristol, a name so long synonymous with fine wines, has surely now broken through to rank alongside its peers as being among the finest in the land for food, too. New chef, Daniel Galmiche, joins here as we go to press, with long-time chef, Ramon Farthing, moving to 36 On The Quay, Emsworth. An experienced chef, Daniel looks set to maintain the standards set by Ramon, keeping this place a force to be reckoned with in Bristol.

Bristol Howard's

1A-2A Avon Crescent, Bristol, Avon, BS1 6XQ
☎ 0117-926 2921
🍽 65 🍴 £50
☺ Lunch 12-2.30, Dinner 7-11
☹ Lunch Sat, all Sun, Bank Holidays, 25 & 26 Dec

Close to the city centre in the newly revived docklands area, Chris & Gillian Howard's busy and bustling restaurant, in situ since 1977, has a grand view of Clifton Suspension Bridge. They offer modern French and English cooking featuring fish from Cornwall and local game; and recently they opened a sister establishment, Howard's Bistro just down the coast at Nailsea.

Bristol Hunt's

26 Broad Street, Bristol, Avon, BS1 2HG
☎ 0117-926 5580   📠 0117-926 5580
🍽 40 🍴 £65
☺ Lunch 12-2, Dinner 7-10
☹ Lunch Sat, all Sun & Mon, 10 days Xmas, 1 wk Easter, Aug

Anne & Andy Hunt have been at this city-centre locale since 1990, and they offer a simply described menu that is set at lunchtime (2 or 3 courses) and à la carte in the evening. Time is not wasted on elaborate descriptions – that time goes into the careful preparation of good basic ingredients, prepared to bring out their true flavours. The tone is mostly English, with nods across the channel, and fish is a speciality.

Bristol Restaurant Lettonie

9 Druid Hill, Stoke Bishop, Bristol, Avon, BS9 1EW
☎ 0117-968 6456 📠 0117-968 6943
🪑 24 🍽 £80
☺ Lunch 12.30-2, Dinner 7-9
☹ Sun & Mon, 2 wks Xmas, 2 wks Aug

Ignore the setting; this is a restaurant to be in, not to admire from outside, just 24 seats at the Blunos's fine restaurant at Stoke Bishop and not surprisingly they are usually full. Martin's fixed-price menu makes choice difficult, his now classic scrambled duck egg topped with Sevruga caviar served with featherlight blinis and iced vodka is hard to resist but pike tortellini with crayfish sauce, glazed pheasant with foie gras on sauerkraut or monkfish, saffron and watercress soup are also tempting. Just as difficult is the main course, should it be sea bass with salmon mousse and chive cream sauce, loin of venison with lentil crust served with juniper flavoured sauce, rump of roast lamb with garlic fritters and thyme leaf sauce or how about braised leg of rabbit stuffed with its loin in grain mustard sauce. Just when you thought you were winning the pudding needs to be chosen, a toss up between the vanilla and poppyseed parfait with macerated blueberries or a gratin of honey poached apple with hazlenuts and apple and calvados sorbet. Then coffee and delicious petits fours. There is one consolation – the lunch menu is shorter!

Bristol Markwicks

43 Corn Street, Bristol, Avon, BS1 1HT
☎ 0117-926 2658 📠 0117-926 2658
🪑 28 🍽 £65
☺ Lunch 12-2, Dinner 7-10.30
☹ Lunch Sat, all Sun, Bank Holidays, 1 wk Xmas, 1 wk Easter, 2 wks Aug

Stephen & Judy Markwick have been in this location since 1989, offering locally sourced, fine quality, fresh ingredients cooked simply and served in comfortable surroundings, found down the steps and with a black and white checked floor and bar. Set menus offer good value for money – as does the carte. Several vegetarian options are available; the cheeseboard is irresistible and puddings are a strength.

Bristol Michael's Restaurant

129 Hotwell Road, Bristol, Avon, BS8 4RU
☎ 0117-927 6190
🪑 55 🍽 £60
☺ Lunch Sun only 12-2.30, Dinner 7-11
☹ Dinner Sun, 26 Dec, 1 Jan, 4 days Aug

Michael McGowan has celebrated 21 years at his Clifton restaurant, decorated in Victorian style – very much part of the city scene. His menus have evolved with the times, and are now presented in a modern style though with traditional origins still very much in evidence. Set menus are excellent value for money.

England   133

Bristol Muset

16 Clifton Road, Bristol, Avon, BS8 1AF
☎ 0117-973 2920
🍴 120 🕑 £10

☺ Dinner 7-10.30   ☹ 25 Dec, 1 Jan

A labyrinthine cluster of dining rooms contributes to the great atmosphere at this Clifton restaurant, which always seems to be busy. Daily specials are chalked up on blackboards, and there are always 2 or 3 vegetarian options. There's no corkage charge if you want to bring your own wine. Service is by friendly, young staff who must be engaged according to agility as well as personality!

Bristol Neil's

112 Princess Victoria Street, Bristol, Avon, BS8 4DB
☎ 0117-973 3669
🍴 50 🕑 £55

☺ Dinner 7.30-11.30   ☹ Sun & Mon, 1 wk Xmas

Some of the best value in Bristol from the Ramsay family – Neil is now at front-of-house with wife Valerie while son Peter has taken over in the kitchen. Regularly changing menus offer bistro-style cooking prepared with flair and served with charm.

Bristol Swallow Royal Hotel

College Green, Bristol, Avon, BS1 5TE
☎ 0117-925 5100   📠 0117-925 1515
🛏 242 £120

Palm Court:
🍴 60 🕑 £70

☺ Dinner 7.30-10.30   ☹ Sun, Bank Holidays

A splendid Victorian hotel right in the heart of the city centre, next door to the Cathedral, which does good trade with the business community in the week, and with families at weekends. The bedrooms, many with super views over the harbour and the city, are luxuriously appointed and well maintained. The Roman-style basement leisure centre offers plenty of healthy opportunities, while the 2 restaurants which come under the guidance of head chef Michael Kitts – the Palm Court and the Terrace, both offer an international menu but with very individual twists, such as Michael's speciality which is an osso bucco of monkfish with squid noodles and orange oil. The Palm Court also offers the Concept of the Kitchen as a balanced meal which is also a sample of the brigade's creativity. Thus your taste-buds could be tantalised by pea and ham terrine with a mild mustard dressing; gratin of mushrooms with smoked duck breast and toasted pine nuts; a sorbet; then quail faggot with glazed parsnips and fruits of the forest or tournedos of arctic char with a lime and beetroot dressing and salsify; and finally peppered pineapple mille feuille with a bitter orange and vanilla sauce. This is priced for 2, 3 or 4 courses at £21, £24 and £27 respectively. The Terrace offers a simpler menu over longer hours.

Broadhembury Drewe Arms

Broadhembury, Devon, EX14 0NF
☎ (01404) 841267
⌂ 30 🍴 £50
☺ Lunch 12-2, Dinner 6-10 ☹ Dinner Sun

The Burges have been here since 1989 and are now definitely part of the local scene; English and Swedish cooking of predominantly fish and seafood is their speciality, and the style is unpretentious. Situated on the A373 Honiton to Cullompton road, just 5 miles from Junction 28 of the M5.

Broadway Collin House

Collin Lane, Broadway, Hereford & Worcester, WR12 7PB
☎ (01386) 858354
🛏 7 £ £87 ⌂ 24 🍴 £60
☺ Lunch 12-1.45, Dinner 7-9 ☹ 24-29 Dec

A mile north-west of Broadway via the A44 (turn right into Collin Lane), you'll find John Mills' intimate little country house hotel and restaurant, built of honey-coloured stone some 400 years ago for a wealthy wool merchant. It has been furnished with period charm and attention to detail, preserving all the best features: oak beams, inglenooks, mullion windows. The cooking is British with European influences.

Broadway Dormy House ❖

Willersey Hill, Broadway, Hereford & Worcester, WR12 7LF
☎ (01386) 852711 📠 (01386) 858636
🛏 49 £ £120 ⌂ 85 🍴 £90
☺ Lunch 12.30-2, Dinner 7.30-9.30 (Sat to 9)
☹ Lunch Sat, 25 & 26 Dec

Additional leisure facilities this year at this lovely Cotswolds hotel and restaurant. An air of elegance and gentle relaxation pervades the house, created by the decor and furnishings combined with friendly yet professional service. In the Roger Chant Dining Room, menus are a combination of English and French (including a separate card for vegetarians).

Broadway Lygon Arms

High Street, Broadway, Hereford & Worcester, WR12 7DU
☎ (01386) 852255 (01386) 858611
63 £195 120 £85
☺ Lunch 12.30-2, Dinner 7.30-9.15

Though to some it may seem rather twee and precious, Broadway is, perhaps, the epitome of how Britain is presented to the World. A delightful village of mellow, honey-coloured stone buildings set back from grass verges, sadly touristy but how could we keep this to ourselves? The Lygon Arms is the perfect place in which to enjoy the surrounding pleasures, a grand old coaching inn that is now owned by The Savoy Hotel Group and run very much in Savoy style. Lovely beamed bedchambers and a stunning Great Hall that serves as the dining room, a modern health spa that jars the senses, though splendid nevertheless. Roger Narbett is the young, very talented chef who creates an extensive carte alongside fixed price menus, fine produce is very well prepared giving a good selection of classic and modern dishes, which include a warm pithvier of smoked Cotswold game with peas and roasted tomato; spiced Cornish seabass with Dublin Bay prawn brochettes and tomato and basil salsa; and Dorset apple cake with Cornish clotted cream.

Brockenhurst Le Poussin

The Courtyard, Brookley Road, Brockenhurst, Hampshire, SO42 7RB
☎ (01590) 623063
24 £75
☺ Lunch 12-1.30, Dinner 7-9
☹ Dinner Sun, all Mon & Tue, 2 wks Jan

The Aitken family (chef/patron Alex, wife Caroline at front of house, son Justin in charge of the wine list) make you feel very much at home at their charming, elegant but friendly country restaurant, so much like the ones you come across so often in France but rarely do in England. Rest assured, they do exist, and this is a fine example. Menus change daily according to availability, and offer a couple of choices at each course, always well balanced. Try a salad of steamed, naturally-smoked haddock on a warm potato salad with olive oil, or freshly-made tagliatelle served in a light rosemary cream sauce with sautéed oyster mushrooms; a nage of seafood or the simpler fillet of salmon with orange butter sauce; crisply roasted breast of duck with mustard and honey or loin of free-range pork served with a muscat and prune sauce; and finish with cheeses, hot passion fruit soufflé or a terrine of white chocolate and strawberries. All dishes are equally inventive and successful, and are accompanied by a good list of wines by the glass.

Bromsgrove Grafton Manor

Grafton Lane, Bromsgrove, Hereford & Worcester, B61 7HA
☎ (01527) 579007 📠 (01527) 575221
▯ 9 £125 🪑 40 🍽 £75
☺ Lunch 12.30-1.30, Dinner 7.30-9 ☹ Sat

There was a manor on this site before Domesday, though the present building, set in its own extensive grounds, dates from 1567, rebuilt extensively in the early 18th Century. The atmosphere of those days emanates firstly from the dining room, and thence through lounges and bedrooms, equally. The Morris family describe the food style as modern British – with Indian influences! There's also a separate vegetarian menu.

Broughton Preston Marriott

418 Garstang Road, Broughton, Nr Preston, Lancashire, PR3 5JB
☎ (01772) 864087 📠 (01772) 861728
▯ 98 £96 🪑 110 🍽 £65
☺ Lunch 12-2, Dinner 7-9.45 ☹ Lunch Sat, Bank Holidays

Good leisure and business facilities at this hotel, (the former Broughton Park), set in a handsome, redbrick manor house. The Broughton Park Restaurant offers competent, modern, British cooking at reasonable prices. Less formal eating in the poolside restaurant.

Broxted Whitehall

Church End, Broxted, Essex, CM6 2BZ
☎ (01279) 850603 📠 (01279) 850385
▯ 25 £105 🪑 40 🍽 £80
☺ Lunch 12.30-2, Dinner 7.30-9.30

Small and friendly country house hotel run for over 10 years by the Keane family. Set menus show a modern European slant, but cooked with the individual flair of chef Stuart Townsend – the menu surprise shows his talent to the full. Comfort and relaxation are the watchwords for the hotel side.

Bruton Claire de Lune

2-4 High Street, Bruton, Somerset, BA10 0EQ
☎ (01749) 813395
▯ 3 £40 🪑 40 🍽 £55
☺ Lunch Sun only 12-2, Dinner 7-10
☹ Dinner Sun & Mon, Bank Holidays, 2 wks Jan

There's a mixture of options here: traditional styling in the brasserie/grill, while the bistro/pizzeria is more casual. The wine list has some helpful notes.

Bruton Truffles Restaurant

95 High Street, Bruton, Somerset, BA10 0AR
☎ (01749) 812255
🍴 20 🍽 £60

☺ Lunch 12-2, Dinner 7-10 ☹ Dinner Mon & Sun

Denise & Martin Bottrill have been here since 1986 and continue to operate their winning formula. Fixed-price, 3-course menus change monthly and, unusually, there's a separate well-planned vegetarian menu. Sunday lunch is deservedly popular. Good, modestly-priced wine list.

Buckland Buckland Manor

Buckland, Nr Broadway, Hereford & Worcester, WR12 7LY
☎ (01386) 852626 📠 (01386) 853557
🛏 14 £178 🍴 38 🍽 £95

☺ Lunch 12.30-1.45, Dinner 7.30-9

Buckland's elevation to Relais et Chateaux status in 1995 is well deserved, and a tribute to the Vaughans' dedication to their cause: providing an elegant and comfortable small hotel in a lovely location, rounded off with good food, impeccable service and an extensive list of fine wines. Cooking is English with French influences and takes good advantage of local produce. The surrounding 10 acres of flower, rose and water gardens are a joy to behold.

Burford The Angel

Witney Street, Burford, Oxfordshire, OX18 4SN
☎ (01993) 822438
🛏 3 £55 🍴 20 🍽 £55

Historic, high street setting for this pretty, small hotel. Intimate dining room with additional outside garden and patio seating in fine weather. Reasonably priced, fixed menus with some good choices.

Burford Bay Tree

Sheep Street, Burford, Oxfordshire, OX8 4LW
☎ (01993) 822791 📠 (01993) 823008
🛏 23 £110 🍴 65 🍽 £60

☺ Lunch 12.30-2.30, Dinner 7-10

Lovely setting in a quintessential Cotswold town for this creeper-clad hotel, with beautiful gardens in which to relax. Traditional comforts in lounges and bedrooms, and a fairly traditional menu is offered in the tented (modern-but-sympathetic) conservatory or the original flagstone dining room. The simpler dishes tend to be best.

England

Burford Lamb Inn

Sheep Street, Burford, Oxfordshire, OX18 4LR
☎ (01993) 823155 📠 (01993) 822228
🛏 16 £86 🪑 50 🍽 £70
☺ Lunch Sun only 12-1.45, Dinner 7.30-9 ☹ 25 & 26 Dec

15th-century, Cotswold hotel just off the main street. Atmospheric interior created by flag-stone floors, antiques and log fires; individually furnished bedrooms which vary in size but are all charming. Set and à la carte menus are offered in the non-smoking, pillared dining room – on fine days, lunch in the garden is a treat. There's a separate main-course menu for vegetarians.

Burgh le Marsh Windmill

46 High Street, Burgh-le-Marsh, Nr Skegness, Lincolnshire, PE24 5JT
☎ (01754) 810281
🪑 50 🍽 £550
☺ Lunch Sun only 12-2, Dinner 7-9.15
☹ Dinner Sun & Mon, 1 wk Xmas, 1 wk Jun

The main course determines the price of your meal at the Bosketts' attractive cottage restaurant, situated next to the mill from which it takes its name. There's also excellent value on the short wine list.

Burnham Market Fishes

Market Place, Burnham Market, Norfolk, PE31 8HE
☎ (01328) 738588
🪑 42 🍽 £40
☺ Lunch 12-2, Dinner 6.45-9.30
☹ Dinner Sun, all Mon, Xmas, 3 wks Jan

Friendly little local restaurant, ably run by chef Gillian Cape. Most dishes are fish-based, though carnivores are not ignored. Lunchtime sees a set menu, evenings offer the carte. Interesting flavour combinations abound.

**THE ACADEMY OF
FOOD & WINE SERVICE**
see page 22

England 139

Bury Normandie Hotel & Restaurant

Elbut Lane, Birtle, Nr Bury, Greater Manchester, BL9 6UT
☎ 0161-764 3869   0161-764 4866
23 £83 50 £80
☺ Lunch 12-2, Dinner 7-9.30
☹ Lunch Sat & Mon, all Sun, Bank Holidays, 1 wk Easter, 2 wks Xmas

A rather unexpected location in a very English part of Britain for such a typically French restaurant, where the food stars and the hotel understudies, yet this is one of the North's best Gallic representatives. Pascal Pommier has been at the stove for over 7 years now and seems to improve year by year, fine well judged cooking in classical style. There are modern touches too, Pascal is happy to use the likes of soya sauce and spring onions to enhance a steamed sea bass and to wrap goat's cheese in filo pastry to serve with a compote of red peppers. A fillet of beef with port sauce is garnished with wild mushrooms, grilled tuna with tomato vinaigrette, roast duck breast with blackcurrant sauce, not overdressed dishes but perfectly prepared. Gillian Moussa and her son, Max, run the hotel with great dedication, they are good hosts and make a visit to 'Normandie' a true pleasure.

Bury St Edmunds Angel Hotel

Angel Hill, Bury St Edmunds, Suffolk, IP33 1LT
☎ (01284) 753926   (01284) 750092
42 £85 40 £55
☺ Lunch 12.30-2, Dinner 7.30-10

An excellent base from which to explore the pleasures of East Anglia, the Angel has long been a focal point for the area since at least 1452; and it was immortalised by Dickens as Mr Pickwick's preferred hostelry. The Regency restaurant offers a modern international menu, supported by a carefully thought-out wine list.

Bury St Edmunds
Mortimer's Seafood Restaurant

31 Churchgate Street, Bury St Edmunds, Suffolk, IP33 1RG
☎ (01284) 760623   (01284) 752561
72 £45
☺ Lunch 12-2, Dinner 6.30-9 (Mon to 8.15)
☹ Lunch Sat, all Sun, Bank Holidays & following Tue, 23 Dec-1 Jan, 2 wks Aug

Fish, fish and more fish is what you come here for in this modest setting, and you won't be disappointed. So popular is this place that they have recently expanded. The puds are just what you need to round off a wholesome meal, and the wine list doesn't disappoint, either.

Calstock Danescombe Valley Hotel

Lower Kelly, Calstock, Cornwall, PL18 9RY
☎ (01822) 832414 📠 (01822) 832414
5 £120 12 £70
☺ Dinner at 8 ☹ Hotel Wed & Thu, Nov-Easter (open Xmas)

Small, Georgian building nestling in Cotehele woods where Martin & Anna Smith look after their few-at-a-time guests with great attention to detail. Anna's cooking shows some Italian influences, though local ingredients are also sourced. Her menus change seasonally, but she also ensures that no diner will eat the same menu twice. You might try the likes of goat cheese and pinenut tart with salad to start, followed by baked chicken breast stuffed with mushrooms and bacon and served with a mushroom sauce, rounding off your meal with pancake filled with custard and cointreau. The price is set for 4 no-choice courses plus coffee, and there's a 3% surcharge if you pay by credit card. No smoking in the dining room. The air of peace and well-being here can scarcely be done justice by mere words!

Cambridge 22 Chesterton Road

22 Chesterton Road, Cambridge, Cambridgeshire, CB4 3AX
☎ (01223) 351880
30 £55
☺ Lunch by arrangement, Dinner 7-10
☹ Dinner Sun & Mon, 1 wk Xmas

A busy place, popular with locals and visitors alike, where in either of the 2 dining rooms you can enjoy an imaginative, Mediterranean fixed-price menu. A worldwide wine list.

Campsea Ashe Old Rectory

Campsea Ashe, Nr Woodbridge, Suffolk, IP13 0PU
☎ (01728) 746524
9 £52 36 £55
☺ Lunch by arrangement, Dinner 7.30-8.45
☹ Dinner Sun, 2 wks Feb

Lovely Georgian former rectory (it's by the church), now an unpretentious restaurant with rooms run by Stewart Bassett in his own highly personal manner. Individually furnished and decorated rooms look out over the fine gardens at the back or the quiet village at the front. Lounges are friendly and relaxing. In the dining room the air is slightly more serious, reflecting Stewart's attitude to food. On set menus, freshly-prepared ingredients are used to good advantage, presented in modern British fashion.

Canterbury County Hotel

High Street, Canterbury, Kent, CT1 2RX
☎ (01227) 766266 📠 (01227) 451512
🪑 73 £100 🛏 50 🍽 £70
☺ Lunch 12.30-2.30, Dinner 7-10

City-centre hotel of Tudor origins with good business facilities (vehicular access, to the pedestrianised High Street, is via the Stour Street entrance to the car park). Ongoing refurbishments maintains standards throughout. In the '60s-style Sullys Restaurant, English food with a French slant is served.

Cartmel Uplands

Haggs Lane, Cartmel, Cumbria, LA11 6HD
☎ (01539) 536248 📠 (01539) 536248
🪑 5 £136 🛏 30 🍽 £65
☺ Lunch 12.30 for 1, Dinner 7.30 for 8 ☹ Mon, 1 Jan-24 Feb

Privately-owned and run by Tom & Diana Peter since 1985, Uplands is run very much in the Miller Howe tradition – they both worked with John Tovey before coming here. There's a warm, friendly atmosphere and the relaxing decor (pastel shades and modern art). Intricate menus challenge the taste buds, the extensive wine list challenges the legs!

Castle Cary Bond's

Ansford Hill, Castle Cary, Somerset, BA7 7JP
☎ (01963) 350464 📠 (01963) 350464
🪑 7 £64 🛏 20 🍽 £55
☺ Lunch 12-2, Dinner 7-9.30 (Sun & Mon to 7.30) ☹ 1 wk Xmas

400 yards past Castle Cary station, but still on the A371, you'll find Kevin & Yvonne Bond's friendly little hotel and restaurant, a listed late Georgian house known in its coaching days as the Half Moon Inn. Today's travellers are just as delighted to come across this oasis of peace and good food, cooked and served in modern English style. The Bonds are especially proud of their range of English farmhouse cheeses.

Castle Combe Manor House

Castle Combe, Nr Chippenham, Wiltshire, SN14 7HR
☎ (01249) 782206 (01249) 782159
40 £140 75 £95
☺ Lunch 12.30-2, Dinner 7.30-10

A charming country house hotel just outside one of Britain's most picturesque villages. Efficiently run by Martin Chubbe the hotel also boasts an 18 hole golf course for the energetic and splendid gardens with a river for more leisurely walks. Chef, Mark Taylor is a competant craftsman and his à la carte menu features some interesting dishes, soup of Cornish red mullet flavoured with saffron, a souffle of bacon, shallots and morels or terrine of quail wrapped in truffle pastry served with spiced pears and apple mayonnaise. His main courses might include a confit of turbot with boulangere potatoes, fine beans and a rosemary stock, a plump partridge stuffed with sweetbreads and foie gras or roast duck with vanilla and cinnamon sauce and sour cherries.

Chaddesley Corbett
Brockencote Hall

Chaddesley Corbett, Nr Kidderminster,
Hereford & Worcester, DY10 4PY
☎ (01562) 777876 (01562) 777872
17 £110 75 £80
☺ Lunch 12.30-1.30, Dinner 7-9.30 (Sun from 7.30) ☹ Lunch Sat

Didier Philipot has returned to the kitchen and offers a selection of fixed-price menus in true French style. You could choose from a ravioli of veal sweetbreads served with a light velouté scented with wild mushrooms; marinaded scallops flavoured with saffron served with seasonal salad; or roast breast of pigeon and pan-fried foie gras served in crunchy potato wafers with truffle-scented jus. To follow, the menu offers sole poached in champagne with compote of leeks; medallions of Aberdeen Angus fillet glazed with Madeira served with ragoût of cabbage and bacon; or venison fillet with green chartreuse-flavoured jus and a pithiviers surprise. While relishing the cooking, don't miss the view of the grounds with its lake and verdant fields. Hosts the Petitjeans will ensure that your stay is enjoyable.

BRITAIN'S TOP INDEPENDENT BUTCHERS
see page 9

Chagford Gidleigh Park

Chagford, Devon, TQ13 8HH

☎ (01647) 432367 📠 (01647) 432574

☐ 15 £ £290 🛏 40 🍽 £120

☺ Lunch 12.30-2, Dinner 7-9

The majestic Gidleigh Park enjoys a stunning setting amidst the flora and fauna of Dartmoor, wild country plays host to the most civilised of hotels. The Hendersons' home is a delight in every way, sumptuous bedrooms, comfortable panelled lounges and bar and of course a very serious dining room. Michael Caines' cooking is rapidly establishing him as one of the country's leading young chefs, mind you at £40 for lunch and £50 for dinner you do expect something rather special. It might come in the form of a first course of ravioli of crab with ginger and lemon grass or roast rabbit with tarragon flavoured hollandaise and salad. Try a dish of pan-fried sea bream with onion compote and olives, served with saffron sauce and anchovy oil or roast pigeon with potato galette, pan-fried foie gras and madeira sauce. A choice of 2 hot soufflées on the pudding list, a raspberry one with raspberry parfait or a pistachio one with pistachio ice cream. The cellar at Gidleigh must be the envy of many wine merchants, nothing is missing and there are plenty of top choices to drink by the glass.

Chapeltown Greenhead House

84 Burncross Road, Chapeltown, Nr Sheffield,
South Yorkshire, S30 4SF

☎ (0114) 2469004

🛏 32 🍽 £75

☺ Dinner 7-9

☹ Dinner Sun, Mon & Tue, Bank Holidays, 1 wk Xmas, 2 wks Easter, 2 wks Aug

Neil & Anne Allen's friendly restaurant just outside Sheffield continues to do good business. A combination of French and English influences on the menu is neatly worked out, with the meal priced according to the main course chosen. A network of local suppliers is used to maintain quality; and themed evenings (such as French Provincial) are popular.

**THE ACADEMY OF
FOOD & WINE SERVICE**
see page 22

Charingworth Charingworth Manor

Charingworth, Nr Chipping Camden,
Gloucestershire, GL55 6NS
☎ (01386) 593555 📠 (01386) 593353
⎕ 24 £110 🪑 48 🍽 £80
☺ Lunch 12.30-2, Dinner 7-10

A lovely Cotswold-stone manor house with flagstone floors and set in the heart of that countryside gives you the chance to sit back and imagine what life was like in those heady, country-house days. The well-kept gardens are part of a larger, 54-acre estate, but if you prefer your exercise and relaxation to be of a more modern kind, there's a very well-equipped leisure centre to pander to your every need. Lounges, function rooms and bedrooms are all furnished with great sympathy for the manor's origins as well as the needs of the modern traveller. The inner body is restored by some classic English and French cooking, served up with a modern flair by head chef Matthew Laughton, new in 1995. He offers fixed-price or à la carte lunches and dinners, with dishes like lightly spiced pheasant and red lentil broth, or grilled John Dory on a ratatouille crostini with an orange and black olive dressing; wild venison casserole with dried fruits in a port wine sauce, or pan-fried turbot with foie gras, smoked bacon and scallops in a sherry vinegar dressing; and to finish, chocolate and Grand Marnier bavarois with poached kumquats, or a warm almond and walnut pithiviers with armagnac and prune ice cream. There's a complete vegetarian menu – good to see at a place of this stature. There's an extensive New World section on a carefully compiled wine list. Under the same ownership as Bishopstrow House, Warminster.

Chartham Thruxted Oast

Mystole, Chartham, Nr Canterbury, Kent, CT4 7BX
☎ (01227) 730080
⎕ 3 £75
☹ Xmas, 25 Dec, 1 Jan

Set amongst idyllic countryside just outside Canterbury, this lovely home converted from oast houses is simply furnished, but guests are well looked after and given hearty breakfasts in the farmhouse kitchen.

Chedington Chedington Court

Chedington, Nr Beaminster, Dorset, DT8 3HY
☎ (01935) 891265 📠 (01935) 891442
⎕ 10 £115 🪑 26 🍽 £65
☹ Dinner 7-9 ☹ Jan

Hilary & Philip Chapman have run Chedington since 1981, as a hotel and golf club. Graceful proportions and honey-coloured stone set the scene as you approach, and the impression is heightened once indoors: lounges and bedrooms are spacious and comfortable. English and French menus change daily and ensure a continuation into the dining room of the air of hospitality and well-being.

Cheltenham Le Champignon Sauvage 🌸

24-26 Suffolk Road, Cheltenham, Gloucestershire, GL50 2AQ
☎ (01242) 573449
🍴 30 🍽 £75
☺ Lunch 12.30-1.30, Dinner 7.30-9.30
☹ Lunch Sat, all Sun, Bank Holidays, 24 Dec-3 Jan

Mushroom memorabilia from satisfied customers adorn the unpretentious bar and dining room of the Everitt-Mathias restaurant. David cooks and Helen hosts the front of house. The small menu always offers some interesting and unusual dishes, a fillet of smoked haddock served with cockle cous cous and a squid ink sauce, a duck sausage with chestnut polenta or perhaps a roast pigeon breast and boned chicken wings come with Alsace potato dumplings. To follow might be fillet of cod with leeks and a red wine butter sauce, a crepinette of mutton with purée of flageolet beans and caramelised carrots, stuffed leg of rabbit on turnip sauerkraut with black pudding or rump of Scotch beef with cumin flavoured aubergine and a tapenade sauce. A superb range of cheeses or puddings such as a Breton butter cake studded with prunes, pressed roasted apples, prune and armagnac ice cream and cider syrup (yes that's all together!), iced gingerbread souffle with orange and liquorice sorbet or layers of crunchy caramel and pistachio wafers with Catalan-spiced cream and caramel sauce. 3 courses of puds isn't a bad idea! The sound wine list has good tasting notes.

Cheltenham Epicurean

81 The Promenade, Cheltenham, Gloucestershire, GL51 1PJ
☎ (01242) 222466 📠 (01242) 222474
🍴 30 🍽 £100
☺ Lunch 12.30-2.30, Dinner 7.30-10
☹ Lunch Sat, all Sun, 2 wks Jan, 2 wks Aug

Cheltenham's loss is London's gain as Patrick Macdonald heads towards the capital, though life goes on at this lovely building with a first-floor restaurant and a ground-floor café/bar. Modern British cooking is offered on set menus and a carte which are not cheap; and the wine list is in keeping with the style of the place.

Cheltenham The Greenway 🍷

Shurdington, Cheltenham, Gloucestershire, GL51 5UG
☎ (01242) 862352 📠 (01242) 862780
🛏 19 £ £110 🍴 50 🍽 £85
☺ Lunch 12.30-2.30, Dinner 7.30-9.30

The Greenway takes its name from the pre-Roman path which runs alongside the hotel and on to the former burial site of Long Barrow – green way meant grove or sheep road, ie a safe path through the hillsides and marshland. Nowadays it means you can be assured of a warm welcome, comfortable accommodation, good food and fine wines in this Cotswold manor house.

Cheltenham On The Park

Evesham Road, Cheltenham, Gloucestershire, GL52 2AH
☎ (01242) 518898 (01242) 511526
12 £101 32 £70
☺ Lunch 12-1.45 (Sun to 2.15), Dinner 7.30-9.30 (Sat to 10)
☹ 1 wk Jan

Elegant town house hotel and restaurant, centrally located within this Regency town. Old-style standards of housekeeping and service combine with modern amenities, as well as the modern European cooking offered in the intimate restaurant, either as set or à la carte menus. The wine list includes a nod to the New World.

Cheltenham Staithes Restaurant

12 Suffolk Road, Cheltenham, Gloucestershire, GL50 2AQ
☎ (01242) 260666
30 £50
☺ Dinner 7.30-10 (Sat from 7)
☹ Dinner Sun, Bank Holidays, 1 wk Xmas, 2 wks summer

"Relaxed dining in elegant surroundings" is what Paul & Heather Lucas aim to provide, and they are concentrating their effort on the restaurant, rather than bistro, aspects of their talents. Carefully cooked and presented modern English food benefits from the occasional overseas influence. Short wine list with useful notes.

Chelwood Chelwood House

Chelwood, Bristol, Avon, BS18 4NH
☎ (01761) 490730 (01761) 490730
10 £75 30 £50
☺ Lunch Sun only 12.30-1.30, Dinner 7.30-9
☹ Dinner Sun, Hotel Xmas & 2 wks Jan

Standing between Bristol and Bath, listed Chelwood was built in 1681 and is fortunate to be in the caring hands of Jill & Rudi Birk, who have filled it with lovely antiques in keeping with the period. Rudi cooks a set menu of basically British design, though with influences of his native Bavaria. Modestly priced wine list with some good tasting notes and good-value house wines.

England   147

Chester Chester Grosvenor

Eastgate Street, Chester, Cheshire, CH1 1LT
☎ (01244) 324024 📠 (01244) 313246
🛏 86 [£] £220 🍴 45 |📷| £110
☺ Lunch 12-2.30, Dinner 7-9.30
☹ Lunch Mon, Dinner Sun, Hotel 25 & 26 Dec Restaurant Bank
  Holidays, 2 wks from 25 Dec

This majestic hotel ideally situated in the city centre keeps standards of the highest level both in its accomodation and in it's restaurants. Jonathan Slater's skilled staff run a smooth ship and Paul Reed has the kitchen brigade trained to the level of Arkle, the famous racehorse from which the restaurant takes it's name. Good skills on the dinner menu, a mousse of pike with braised chicory and chilled oysters, a globe artichoke with mousse of crab, roast Scottish lobster and gazpacho vinegar or soup of girolles with tiny leeks and truffle infusion. Beef fillet with shredded tongue and glazed goat's cheese, saddle of venison with with roasted vegetables and wild mushroom dumplings or guinea fowl with basil potatoes and tomato infusion. If you want a more casual lunch or dinner the brasserie has a true brasserie style menu which includes grills, braised dishes, pastas and plenty of imaginative starters, children are well looked after too. A really super hotel.

Chester Crabwall Manor

Parkgate Road, Mollington, Chester, Cheshire, CH1 6NE
☎ (01244) 851666 📠 (01244) 851400
🛏 48 [£] £125 🍴 120 |📷| £80
☺ Lunch 12.30-2, Dinner 7-9.30 (Sat to 10, Sun to 9)

2½ miles from the end of the M56 and also 2½ miles from Mollington, Crabwall Manor is on the A540 Chester to Hoylake road. It's a castellated manor in appearance, and a dwelling on this site is recorded in the Domesday book. Grand in appearance but friendly in atmosphere, it's a perfect place in which to unwind from the stresses of executive life. Michael Truelove turns out some splendid cooking for the Conservatory Restaurant, in modern British style. Favourite dishes include mille feuille of sautéed scallops, cabbage and Sauternes sauce, followed by galantine of suckling pig on a bed of potato purée served with a jus reduction, and ending with cold creamed rice pudding with rhubarb compote. Wine list of distinction.

Chester Francs

14 Cuppin Street, Chester, Cheshire, CH1 2BN
☎ (01244) 317952 📠 (01244) 661422
🍴 101 |📷| £40
☺ 12-11

Relaxed brasserie on 2 floors offering bistro fare with friendly service. A buzzy, fun place to go with a crowd – no pretentions whatsoever, and booking is advisable.

148   England

Chichester Comme Ça

67 Broyle Road, Chichester, West Sussex, PO19 4BD
☎ (01243) 788724
🍴 80 🍽 £55
☺ Lunch 11-2, Dinner 6-10.30 ☹ Dinner Sun, all Mon, Bank Holidays

A lovely private function room has been added to this delightful French restaurant, situated on the outskirts of Chichester (but very easily found). Cuisine bourgeoise is what Michel Navet produces, while wife Jane looks after front-of-house. There are pre- and post-theatre menus at exceptionally reasonable prices; and there's a surprisingly strong New World representation on the wine list for a traditionally French establishment.

Chilgrove White Horse Inn

Chilgrove, Nr Chichester, West Sussex, PO18 9HX
☎ (01243) 535219   📠 (01243) 535301
🛏 4 £70 🍴 70 🍽 £60
☺ Lunch 12-2, Dinner 7-9.30 (10.30 after Theatre)
☹ Dinner Sun, all Mon, 3 wks Feb, 1 wk Oct

Chef/partner Neil Rusbridger cooks up a storm at the White Horse, to the delight of owner/partners the Phillips and the regular clientele. English and French styles combine to great effect, seafood and game are used extensively. The pretty letting bedrooms and good value, extensive wine list make the experience complete: a useful stopover on the B2141 between Chichester and Petersfield.

Chipping Campden Cotswold House

The Square, Chipping Campden, Gloucestershire, GL55 6AN
☎ (01386) 840330   📠 (01386) 840310
🛏 15 £95 🍴 40 🍽 £70
☺ Lunch 12-2 Sun only, Dinner 7.15-9.30
   (Greenstocks: 9.30am-10pm) ☹ 24-28 Dec

A country house hotel with stylish furnishings, antiques and individually designed bedrooms. Greenstocks brasseries operates throughout the day and the Garden Room restaurants offers an eclectic mix of British and French cooking on a fixed-price menu.

Chipping Campden Seymour House

High Street, Chipping Campden, Gloucestershire, GL55 6AH
☎ (01386) 840429   📠 (01386) 840369
🛏 16 £90 🍴 70 🍽 £60
☺ Lunch 12-2.30, Dinner 7-10

Another lovely Cotswold stone hotel and restaurant, full of period charm and grace. The atrium in the restaurant (housing a 94-year-old vine) creates an airy atmosphere in which to enjoy some modern European cooking, often with a healthy bias. Smoking is not permitted.

Chobham Quails Restaurant

1 Bagshot Road, Chobham, Surrey, GU24 8BP
☎ (01276) 858491
🍴 40 🕐 £55
☺ Lunch 12.30-2, Dinner 7-10
☹ Lunch Sat, Dinner Sun, all Mon, 26 Dec

Chef/proprietor Christopher Wale cooks a modern English/French menu of carefully chosen flavours and textures, to good effect. His menu changes monthly and is offered as set-price or as a carte. The wine list, fairly priced, is mostly French but has one New World page.

Christchurch Splinters Restaurant

11/12 Church Street, Christchurch, Dorset, BH23 1BW
☎ (01202) 483454 📠 (01202) 483454
🍴 40 🕐 £55
☺ Lunch 10.30-2.30, Dinner 7-10.30 ☹ 2 wks Jan

Robert Wilson & Timothy Lloyd are busy at Splinters. There's the first-floor drawing room where guests can relax after lunch or dinner; a private dining room; and a less formal restaurant next door. Good use is made of both local and more exotic produce (kangaroo, alligator and bison to date) with the fresh, local fish also noteworthy.

Climping Bailiffscourt

Climping Street, Climping, Nr Littlehampton,
West Sussex, BN17 5RW
☎ (01903) 723511 📠 (01903) 723107
🛏 27 £ £125 🍴 50 🕐 £80
☺ Lunch 12.30-2, Dinner 7-9.30

The Goodmans' attractive small hotel and restaurant is a perfectly-preserved medieval manor set in 22 acres of meadow and gardens. Bedrooms, individually decorated, boast beams, 4-posters, open fires and lovely views. 6 new bedrooms came on stream for 1995; and more are planned in a converted thatched cottage with its own courtyard, within the hotel grounds. French/English menus (both fixed-price and à la carte) offer some competent cooking and a range of French cheeses.

Clitheroe Browns Bistro

10 York Street, Clitheroe, Lancashire, BB7 2DL
☎ (01200) 26928
🍴 66 🕐 £55
☺ Lunch 12-1.45, Dinner 7-10
☹ Lunch Sat, all Sun, 1 wk Xmas/New Year

Chef/proprietors David & Carole Brown pride themselves on the quality of their raw ingredients, and value the loyalty of their suppliers greatly. Fresh (some live!) fish comes in daily, Angus beef is hung to David's specification, chicken and ducks are local. Apart from his evident passion for food, another of David's hobbies is collecting ports.

Coatham Mundeville Hall Garth Golf & CC

Coatham Mundeville, Nr Darlington, Durham, DL1 3LU
☎ (01325) 300400 📠 (01325) 310083
🛏 41 £81 🍴 80 🍽 £60
☺ Lunch 12-2, Dinner 7-9.30
☹ Lunch Sat, Dinner Sun, 25 Dec evening

A hotel, golf, country club and pub just outside Darlington, celebrating a year in new ownership with Regal Hotels. Some bedrooms have been upgraded, as has the Stables Pub. Hugo's Restaurant offers a modern international menu, set-price at lunch time, set and à la carte in the evening.

Cockermouth Quince & Medlar

13 Castlegate, Cockermouth, Cumbria, CA13 9EU
☎ (01900) 823579
🍴 26 🍽 £30
☺ Dinner 7-9.30 ☹ Mon, Sun Xmas-Easter, 1 wk Nov, 2 wks Jan

A fine, totally vegetarian restaurant in this part of the country where such diners regularly seem at least to attract equal billing with their ominivorous companions. The panelled dining room is candle-lit at night, and completely non-smoking. Inventive dishes on the menu; farmhouse cheeses are well kept and well presented, and some wines on the short list are organic.

Coggeshall Baumann's Brasserie

4-6 Stoneham Street, Coggeshall, Essex, CO6 1TT
☎ (01376) 561453 📠 (01376) 563762
🍴 75 🍽 £65
☺ Lunch 12.30-2, Dinner 7.30-10
☹ Dinner Sun & Mon, Bank Holidays, 2 wks Jan

Mark Baumann is now part of the Essex scenery in his own right, having established his quirky menus presented with a modern interpretation, served in relaxed surroundings. Friendly, helpful service. A second branch, the North Hill Exchange Brasserie, has opened in Colchester.

Coggeshall White Hart Hotel

Market End, Coggeshall, Essex, CO6 1NH
☎ (01376) 561654 📠 (01376) 561789
🛏 18 £82 🍴 70 🍽 £60
☺ Lunch 12-2, Dinner 7-10 ☹ Dinner Sun, 25 & 26 Dec

An ongoing programme of refurbishment here at this former coaching inn full of old world charm. Traditional Italian cooking and a good list of Italian wines to accompany the menus.

Colerne Lucknam Park ❖ ❦ ✿

Colerne, Wiltshire, SN14 8AZ

☎ (01225) 742777 📠 (01225) 743536

🛏 42 £171 🪑 80 🍽 £100

☺ Lunch 12.30-2, Dinner 7.30-9.30 (Sat to 9.45)

A Palladian mansion built of Bath stone, approached via a superb avenue of beech trees and dating back to the early 18th century, that has been restored to its former glory with superb suites and bedrooms. The hotel is elegantly decorated and there are good value leisure facilities. Former sous chef, Alex Venables, is now in charge of the kitchens, and maintains the same level of excellence.

Corfe Castle Mortons House Hotel

45 East Street, Corfe Castle, Dorset, BH20 5EE

☎ (01929) 480988 📠 (01929) 480820

🛏 17 £80 🪑 45 🍽 £60

☺ Lunch 12-2, Dinner 7-8.30

David & Hilary Langford are resident owners here, at a 16th-century manor house linked by tunnels to Corfe Castle itself. Chris Button is now well into his second stint as head chef here, and in the non-smoking dining room he serves a simple set menu with a few choices at most of the 4 courses plus coffee. Lighter meals are also available at the bar.

Corse Lawn Corse Lawn House ❦ ✿

Corse Lawn, Nr Gloucester, Gloucestershire, GL19 4LZ

☎ (01452) 780771 📠 (01452) 780840

🛏 19 £90 🪑 50 🍽 £75

☺ Lunch 12-2, Dinner 7-10

The Hine family continue to provide high quality at reasonable prices in their delightful Queen Anne house overlooking the ornamental pond. Choose from the elegant dining room or the informal bistro, both present excellent, well prepared menus with Baba Hine presiding over the kitchen. The style is predominantly French though its modern interpretation sees the occasional use of soy and coriander and perhaps you might find colcannon potatoes with a lentil crusted best end of lamb. Cheeses come from the ubiquitous Neal's Yard and there are usually a dozen or so that show the best of British, and Irish unpasteurised varieties. An excellent wine list has plenty of variety too with lots by the glass. A friendly, welcoming establishment.

Cowan Bridge Cobwebs

Leck, Cowan Bridge, Nr Kirkby Lonsdale, Lancashire, LA6 2HZ
☎ (01524) 272141 📠 (01524) 272141
⬜ 5 £60 🛏 25 🍽 £60
☺ Dinner only 7.30 for 8 ☹ Dinner Sun, Jan-mid Mar

Friendly restaurant with rooms situated between the Lake District and the Yorkshire Dales (nearer the latter, despite the red-rose address), so well-located for holidaymakers. It was opened in 1987 by current owner Paul Kelly, and though he has a good loyal client base, there's always a warm welcome for first-timers, too. Good, modern British cooking is offered on a daily-changing set menu.

Crosby-on-Eden Crosby Lodge ❖ 🎯

High Crosby, Crosby-on-Eden, Nr Carlisle, Cumbria, CA6 4QZ
☎ (01228) 573618 📠 (01228) 573428
⬜ 11 £90 🛏 50 🍽 £65
☺ Lunch 12.15-1.30, Dinner 7.15-9
☹ Dinner Sun except residents, 3 wks Jan

Privately owned by the Sedgwicks since 1971, Crosby is a castellated country mansion that manages just to be south of the border. Lounges and bedrooms are comfortable and stylish. In the dining room, traditional British cooking benefits from the occasional French touch, and the wine list has plenty of useful tasting notes.

Cuckfield Murray's

Broad Street, Cuckfield, West Sussex, RH17 5LJ
☎ (01444) 455826
🛏 32 🍽 £66
☺ Lunch 12-1.30, Dinner 7.15-9.30
☹ Lunch Sat, all Sun, Bank Holidays

Sue & Peter Murray create an intimate cottage atmosphere at their restaurant in the 13th-century village of Cuckfield. Sue produces imaginative dishes in the kitchen, while Peter offers a warm welcome front-of-house.

Cuckfield Ockenden Manor

Ockenden Lane, Cuckfield, West Sussex, RH17 5LD
☎ (01444) 416111 📠 (01444) 415549
⬜ 22 £105 🛏 45 🍽 £80
☺ Lunch 12.30-2, Dinner 7.30-9.30

16th-century manor house set in beautiful grounds in a Tudor village. Tasteful furnishings are in keeping with the period of the place – some rooms have 4-posters. In the non-smoking Tudor dining room with its plaster ceiling, modern British cooking is presented and accompanied by a wine list of equal stature. Good dishes include Whitstable rock oysters served with shallot vinegar, lemon and buttered wholemeal bread and cutlet of monkfish roasted and served on saffron, tomato and caper sauce.

Darlington Sardis

196 Northgate, Darlington, Durham, DL1 1QU
☎ (01325) 461222
🪑 75 🍽 £50
☺ Lunch 12-2, Dinner 7-10.15
☹ Sun & Mon, Bank Holidays, 1 wk Jan, 1 wk Apr, 2 wks Aug

Sardinian, Italian, French, English: classic cuisine from those European traditions is what you'll find at the Obinus' friendly town-centre restaurant, although somewhat surprisingly for those cultures, there's also a complete vegetarian menu. The wine list starts with Italians, but then moves on to a world tour.

Darlington Victor's Restaurant

84 Victoria Road, Darlington, Durham, DL1 5JW
☎ (01325) 480818
🪑 30 🍽 £55
☺ Lunch 12-2, Dinner 7-10.30 ☹ Sun & Mon, 1 wk Xmas

Jayne & Peter Robinson are the stalwarts here, continuing their policy of offering good-value, set-price menus with some choice at most courses, not forgetting vegetarians. Courses are individually priced at lunchtime. Concise wine list, good value in the house selections.

Dartmouth Carved Angel ☘

2 South Embankment, Dartmouth, Devon, TQ6 9BH
☎ (01803) 832465 📠 (01803) 835141
🪑 45 🍽 £110
☺ Lunch 12.30-1.45, Dinner 7.30-9.30
☹ Dinner Sun, all Mon, Bank Holidays, 6 wks from Jan

If reading Elizabeth David's book `French Provincial Cookery' arouses your tastebuds come to the Carved Angel and Joyce Molyneux will demonstrate the art of serving such dishes – not that all the dishes are French, this is all about style. Only the finest produce finds its way into kitchen, much of it from local suppliers who have been delivering for many years, superb fish and shellfish, splendid game in the winter and always lovely vegetables. Salt cod with butter beans, parsley, garlic and virgin oil, a braised ox-tongue with beetroot, celeriac and piquant cream sauce or a brochette of venison with leek, juniper and potato cake are typical of main dishes. Puddings are surprisingly simple, a rhubarb cheesecake, Seville orange custard or a chocolate Pithivier with vanilla ice cream, it's the way that they are so skillfully prepared that makes the difference. The wine list is a joy to read but it needs time, 20 odd pages. Restaurant manager, David Shephard, is happy to help.

Dedham Fountain House & Dedham Hall ❖

Brook Street, Dedham, Nr Colchester, Essex, CO7 6AD
☎ (01206) 323027
⎕ 6 £ £57 🍴 32 🍽 £50
☺ Lunch Sun only 12.30-3, Dinner 7.30-9.30   ☹ Dinner Sun & Mon

James & Wendy Sarton are now well established in this pretty East Anglia setting, running a cosy restaurant with rooms. The emphasis is very much on comfort and tranquility for guests. Fine cooking with good raw ingredients. Clever and concise selection of pudding wines.

Dedham Maison Talbooth

Stratford Road, Dedham, Nr Colchester, Essex, CO7 6HN
☎ (01206) 322367 📠 (01206) 322752
⎕ 10 £ £120

The Milsoms' lovely small hotel in Constable country, built in Victorian times and offering just 10 luxurious suites, some of which overlook the pretty river valley. Dine at the award-winning Le Talbooth, 5 miles away.

Dedham Le Talbooth Restaurant ❖

Gunhill, Dedham, Nr Colchester, Essex, CO7 6HP
☎ (01206) 323150 📠 (01206) 322309
🍴 85 🍽 £100
☺ Lunch 12-2 (Sun to 5.30), Dinner 7-9

A lovely riverside setting with a delightful terrace makes this half timbered house an ever popular venue for locals and visitors. Gerald Milsom set this up over 40 years ago and still runs it with the help of his sons. The dining room is beamed and the epitome of a country hostelry, the food, ranging from traditional to modern dishes, is set in the right mould for the many regular customers. Try the warm marinated salmon topped with a poached egg and tomato salsa followed by venison tournedos with a broccoli crust and mashed potato. Quality is reliable and service attentive and friendly, wines are great value.

Denmead Barnard's

Hambledon Road, Denmead, Nr Portsmouth,
Hampshire, PO7 6NU
☎ (01705) 257788
🍴 38 🍽 £45
☺ Lunch 12-1.45, Dinner 7-9.45
☹ Lunch Tue & Sat, all Sun & Mon, Bank Holidays, 1 wk Xmas, 2 wks Aug

David & Sandie Barnard are now well established in their new location, to the delight of locals who seem to have taken the pair to their hearts. Gourmet evenings and wine tastings (held about every other month) have surely contributed to this status! David cooks the freshest possible ingredients in French style; soups and ice-creams are home made; and there's a choice of set or à la carte menus. All-French wine list.

Diss Weavers

Market Hill, Diss, Norfolk, IP22 3JZ
☎ (01379) 642411
🍴 80 🍽 £45
☺ Lunch 12-1.30, Dinner 7-9
☹ Lunch Sat, all Sun, 2 wk Xmas, 2 wks Aug

Wine bar and eating house under the auspices of William & Wilma Bavin since 1987. Cooking is based on the sound principles of traditional methods, so that a good depth of flavour is achieved with excellent raw materials. The other emphasis is on providing value for money, and thus set-priced menus are offered alongside the carte. Vegetarians are well catered for, too.

Dorchester Mock Turtle

34 High West Street, Dorchester, Dorset, DT1 1UP
☎ (01305) 264011
🍴 55 🍽 £54
☺ Lunch 12-2, Dinner 7-9.30
☹ Lunch Mon & Sat, all Sun, Dinner Bank Holidays, 26 Dec

Raymond & Vivien Hodder's popular local restaurant offers set-priced lunch and dinner menus with plenty of choice at each course, attractively presented in a relaxed setting. Additional daily specials are also available. Service is friendly, the concise wine list is helpfully laid out, so all in all, you get good value for money here.

Dorking Partners West Street

2-4 West Street, Dorking, Surrey, RH4 1BL
☎ (01306) 882826
🍴 45 🍽 £45
☺ Lunch 12-2, Dinner 7-9.30
☹ Lunch Sat, Dinner Sun, 25 & 26 Dec, 1 Jan

Intimate, twin-dining-roomed (ground and 1st floor), beamed restaurant owned by long-standing partners, Andrew Thomason & Tim McEntire. A la carte and fixed-price menus are imaginative and modern in style.

Dorrington Country Friends

Dorrington, Nr Shrewsbury, Shropshire, SY5 7JD
☎ (01743) 718707
🛏 3 £98 🍴 45 🍽 £65
☺ Lunch 12-2, Dinner 7-9 (Sat to 9.30)
☹ all Sun & Mon, Bank Holidays, 2 wks Jul, 1 wk Oct

Lunchtimes at the bar, evenings in the restaurant – this is the usual flow of activity at Country Friends, a delightful restaurant with rooms in the heart of England owned and run by Charles & Pauline Whittaker. Local produce is used in the kitchen when possible; the culinary calendar is marked by special meals; and there's a carefully compiled wine list.

Drewsteignton Hunts Tor House

Drewsteignton, Devon, EX6 6QW
☎ (01647) 281228
⎕ 4 £ £60 🪑 8 🍽 £55
☺ Dinner at 7.30 ☹ End Nov-start Mar

Tiny period restaurant with rooms in a lovely part of Devon with open fires in the sitting and dining rooms. A fixed-price, no-choice menu (notify any dietary constraints when booking) is carefully prepared by proprietor Sue Harrison.

Dulverton Ashwick House

Dulverton, Somerset, TA22 9QD
☎ (01398) 323868 📠 (01398) 323868
⎕ 6 £ £95 🪑 35 🍽 £60
☺ Lunch Sun only 12.30-1.45, Dinner 7.15-8.30

Lovely Exmoor National Park setting for Richard Sherwood's one-man-band approach to running a country house hotel. He checks you in, cooks and serves the meals, handwrites your menu personally – and even provides a weather forecast on the breakfast menu! His wine list contains something for most palates.

Duxford Duxford Lodge

Ickleton Road, Duxford, Nr Cambridge,
Cambridgeshire, CB2 4RU
☎ (01223) 836444 📠 (01223) 832271
⎕ 15 £ £88 🪑 46 🍽 £50
☺ Lunch 12-2, Dinner 7-9.30 ☹ Lunch Sat, 27-30 Dec

Privately owned and run by the Craddock family since 1991, this cosy and pretty hotel maintains high standards and is well suited to either business bookings or the tourist variety. French/English cooking is complemented by an off-beat wine list, arranged by style rather than area.

East Boldon Forsters

2 St Bedes, Station Road, East Boldon,
Tyne & Wear, NE36 0LE
☎ 0191-519 0929
🪑 28 🍽 £65
☺ Dinner 7-10
☹ all Sun & Mon, Bank Holidays, 1 wk Jun, 1 wk Aug, 1 wk Xmas

Barry & Sue Forster continue their team effort at this small, friendly local restaurant in the North-East. Affordable food in a relaxed atmosphere is their aim, of the type you just happen across in France. So happen across this little village and call in for some simply cooked French and English cooking, on either set-price or à la carte menus, accompanied by a concise wine list.

East Buckland Lower Pitt

East Buckland, Barnstaple, Devon, EX32 0TD
☎ (01598) 760243 📠 (01598) 760243
▯ 3 £60 🛏 32 🍽 £50

☺ Dinner 7-9   ☹ Dinner Sun & Mon, 2 days Xmas

At a pretty location just 2 miles north of the A361 you can enjoy the hospitality of Jerome & Suzanne Lyons in their small but very comfortable restaurant with rooms. Fresh local produce is used to good effect in the restaurant, for which Suzanne turns out an international-style menu. No smoking in the dining room or bedrooms.

East Grinstead Gravetye Manor ❖ 🐂 🌿 ❦

Vowels Lane, East Grinstead, West Sussex, RH19 4LJ
☎ (01342) 810567 📠 (01342) 810080
▯ 18 £200 🛏 42 🍽 £105

☺ Lunch 12.30-2, Dinner 7.30-9.30 (Sun to 9)

A delightful Elizabethan stone manor in the heart of the Sussex countryside, Gravetye owes its present appearance and reputation to the long custodianship of two men who have, at different times, loved it greatly. They were firstly, the great gardener William Robinson who between 1884 and 1935 laid out the splendid grounds as one of the first natural gardens of England. Then in 1958 the present incumbent, Peter Herbert, arrived to set the manor up for its crowning glory as one of the great country house hotels of England. Attention to detail is apparent in every aspect of a stay here; nothing is too much trouble and despite the sense of history, you can very quickly feel very much at home. There are surprisingly few bedrooms for the size of the building, but they are each individually appointed and spacious, hence deserving of the name "apartments". The return of head chef Mark Raffan guarantees consistency in the kitchen, which produces excellent menus that lean towards traditional British. Choices might include salad of braised ham hock and lentils with a mustard dressing and crisp croutons or Gravetye's rustic game terrine with Cumberland sauce and toast to start, followed by Gressingham duck – confit of the leg, roast breast and liquorice flavoured sauce or escalope of wild Scottish salmon with a sorrel butter sauce. The wine list has to be seen to be believed and is the result of Peter's lifelong dedication to the task of producing excellence.

Eastbourne Grand Hotel

King Edward's Parade, Eastbourne, East Sussex, BN21 4EQ
☎ (01323) 412345 📠 (01323) 412233
▯ 164 £140 🛏 50 🍽 £70

☺ Lunch 12.30-2.30, Dinner 7-10
☹ Sun & Mon, Bank Holidays, 2 wks Aug, 2 wks Jan

De Vere hotel on the seafront, most definitely in the grand manner. The formal Mirabelle restaurant is the setting for some international cooking, primarily in French and English styles. Elegant lounges offer good views.

Edburton Tottington Manor

Edburton, Nr Henfield, West Sussex, BN5 9LJ

☎ (01903) 815757 (01903) 879331

6 £60 50 £40

☺ Lunch 12-2, Dinner 7-9.15 ☹ Dinner Sun Jan-Easter, 25 & 26 Dec

Friendly hotel and restaurant on the South Downs, run by David & Kate Miller. The set dinner is amazing value at £38 per couple, including a bottle of house wine! Comfortable and pretty bedrooms allow an overnight stay and then exploration of the surrounding countryside.

Edenbridge Honours Mill Restaurant

87 High Street, Edenbridge, Kent, TN8 5AU

☎ (01732) 866757

38 £60

☺ Lunch 12.15-2, Dinner 7.15-10

☹ Lunch Sat, Dinner Sun, all Mon, 2 wks Xmas

Friendly local restaurant run by the Goodhew brothers since 1986. Cooking is modern English/French and the menu (table d'hote as well as à la carte) changes every couple of weeks or so. The origins of the mill are still apparent in the decor.

Elcot Jarvis Elcot Park

Elcot, Nr Newbury, Berkshire, RG16 8NJ

☎ (01488) 658100 (01488) 658288

75 £112 100 £45

☺ Lunch 12.30-2, Dinner 7.30-9.30

Comfortable hotel with health and leisure club and good conference and banqueting facilities.

Elton Loch Fyne Oyster Bar

The Old Dairy, Elton, Nr Peterborough, Cambridgeshire, PE8 6SH

☎ (01832) 280298 (01832) 280170

80 £40

☺ 9-9 (Fri & Sat to 10, Sun to 5) ☹ Dinner Sun, 25 & 26 Dec

UK branch of one of Scotland's finest: fresh and smoked fish and shellfish, served in unpretentious surroundings, accompanied by good-value wines.

England 159

Ely Fen House Restaurant

2 Lynn Road, Littleport, Ely, Cambridgeshire, CB6 1QG
☎ (01353) 860645
🍴 20 £70

☺ Lunch by arrangement, Dinner 7.30-9

☹ Dinner Sun & Mon, 25 & 26 Dec

David Warne cooks while wife Gaynor looks after front-of-house at this intimate little restaurant which offers plenty of choice on its 4-course (including cheese) menu. The restaurant is close to Littleport railway station, and the Warnes have been here since 1987.

Ely Old Fire Engine House

25 St Mary's Street, Ely, Cambridgeshire, CB7 4ER
☎ (01353) 662582
🍴 36 £50

☺ Lunch 12.30-2, Dinner 7.30-9

☹ Dinner Sun, Bank Holidays, 2 wks Xmas/New Year

A family-owned and run restaurant in the best traditions: over 25 years, and some key staff have been with them nearly as long. In the quaint dining room, enjoy some English farmhouse food that definitely has evolved over the years to display just enough modern touches to keep everyone – customers included! – on their toes.

Emsworth 36 On The Quay

The Quay, South Street, Emsworth, Hampshire, PO10 7EG
☎ (01243) 375592   📠 (01243) 374429
🍴 40 £80

☺ Lunch 12.30-2, Dinner 7-10

☹ Lunch Sat & Tue, Dinner Sun, Tue in winter, Sun in summer

News just in that Ramon Farthing, previously at Harvey's Restaurant in Bristol, has taken over here. Check next year's Guide for an update.

Erpingham The Ark

The Street, Erpingham, Norfolk, NR11 7QB
☎ (01263) 761535
🛏 3 £95   🍴 36 £55

☺ Lunch 12.30-2 (Sun Only), Dinner 7-9.30

☹ Dinner Sun, all Mon, 25-30 Dec

4 miles north of Aylsham, just off the A140, this tiny restaurant with rooms has built up a good reputation. Good-value set menus (priced for 2, 3 or 4 courses) have some choice at each course. A lovely place to stay and explore the area.

160   England

Eversley New Mill Restaurant

New Mill Road, Eversley, Hampshire, RG27 0RA
☎ (01734) 732277   📠 (01734) 328780
🪑 80 🍽 £80
☺ Lunch 12-2, Dinner 7-10 (Sun to 9), (Grill Room: Sun 12.30-9)
☹ Lunch Sat, all Mon, 26 Dec, 1 Jan

Pretty riverside location for the New Mill, which offers a mixture of set-price, à la carte and vegetarian menus with recommended wines by the glass and charming service. Choose between the larger restaurant and the smaller grill room – looking after both, new chef Simon Smith, who has settled in very well. Included on the wine list is a large range of options from the New World.

Evershot Summer Lodge

Evershot, Dorchester, Dorset, DT2 0JR
☎ (01935) 83424   📠 (01935) 83005
🛏 17 £ £125 🪑 50 🍽 £80
☺ Lunch 12.30-1.45, Dinner 7.30-9 ☹ 2 wks Jan

Nigel & Margaret Corbett have been at Summer Lodge since 1979, and during this time have created a loyal following of returnees as well as first-timers, who relax and revel in the graceful lines of the Georgian building and peaceful gardens. All the bedrooms have been individually decorated, and overlook either the gardens or the village rooftops and fields beyond. To maintain standards in the kitchen, the Corbetts supervise everything personally so that a change of head chef (this year Donna Horlock) has been absorbed smoothly. Modern British cooking is the order of the day: try diamonds of brill on a dark onion jam with a crisp potato rose, grilled loin of rabbit on roasted celeriac with a thyme jus, warm glazed pear tart with caramel sauce topped with hazelnut ice cream. The wine list is a fine accompaniment to the cooking.

Evesham Evesham Hotel

Cooper's Lane, off Waterside, Evesham,
Hereford & Worcester, WR11 6DA
☎ (01386) 765566   📠 (01386) 765443
🛏 40 £ £84 🪑 55 🍽 £60
☺ Lunch 12.30-2, Dinner 7-9.30 ☹ Hotel 25 & 26 Dec

Historic town and a historic building to go with it – ask for directions when booking, then relax once you get to this privately-owned and somewhat idiosyncratically run (by John & Margaret Jenkinson since 1975) establishment. Although there are jokes on the menu and on the drinks list, the cooking is actually seriously good, and in the Cedar Restaurant there's an extensive choice on an eclectic menu, which caters well for vegetarians, too.

Evesham Riverside Hotel

The Parks, Offenham Road, Evesham,
Hereford & Worcester, WR11 5JP
☎ (01386) 446200 📠 (01386) 40021
🛏 7 £ £80 🍴 45 🍽 £55

☺ Lunch 12-2 (Sun to 1.30), Dinner 7.30-9

☹ Dinner Sun, all Mon

Not too easy to find: turn off the B4510 Evesham to Offenham road, down a private drive called The Parks. Persevere to the end, and there's the Riverside (it's the Avon, by the way). Lovely views are to be enjoyed from bedrooms and lounges. Fixed-price menus at lunch and dinner (plus a carte at lunchtime) offer modern interpretations of English and French classics, using local produce when possible. The wine list has some useful tasting notes.

Exeter St Olaves Court

Mary Arches Street, Exeter, Devon, EX4 3AZ
☎ (01392) 217736 📠 (01392) 413054
🛏 17 £ £90 🍴 45 🍽 £90

☺ Lunch 12-2, Dinner 6.30-9.30

☹ Lunch Sat & Sun, Xmas/New Year

Set within its own walled garden with pond, fountain and well-established trees and shrubs, the hotel is now also able to offer the facility of Exeter's magnificent 900-year old St. Nicholas' Priory for private functions. Short but interesting menus feature fish and game strongly.

Eyton Marsh Country Hotel

Eyton, Leominster, Hereford & Worcester, HR6 0AG
☎ (01568) 613952
🛏 4 £ £110 🍴 24 🍽 £60

☺ Lunch Sun only 12.30-2, Dinner 7.30-9 ☹ 3 wks Jan

Pretty, timbered, originally 14th-century building which is carefully maintained and lovingly tended. Refurbishment has meant a reduction in bedroom numbers from 5 to 4. The garden is now sufficiently well established to supply most of the restaurant's fruit and vegetable requirements. In the non-smoking dining room, table d'hote and à la carte menus of modern British cooking are well presented, along with a concise but intelligent range of wines.

Falmouth Seafood Bar

Quay Street, Falmouth, Cornwall, TR11 3HH
☎ (01326) 315129
🍴 26 🍽 £45

☺ Dinner 7-10.30 ☹ Sun in winter, 2/3 wks Nov

Just what you'd expect, and just where you'd expect it, so go there and you won't be disappointed. 95% of the menu consists of various preparations of fresh local fish, and it's all served with charm in simple surroundings. Park just 100 yards away by the Customs House.

Faversham Read's

Painter's Forstal, Faversham, Kent, ME13 0EE
☎ (01795) 535344 📠 (01795) 591200
🪑 40 🍽 £75

☺ Lunch 12-2, Dinner 7-10   ☹ Sun & Mon, Bank Holidays

David & Rona Pitchford provide an oasis in the gastronomic desert of North Kent. David's cooking is finely judged and offers good variety. Excellent value at lunchtime when you can start with the likes of sautéed soft herring roes with parsley butter, chicken liver parfait with melba toast and winter leaves or a chicken and mushroom pancake with cheese sauce. Main dishes might include farmyard chicken on a bed of lentils with pancetta and onions, fillet of beef with black pudding, Lyonnaise onions and bacon or salmon on stir-fried vegetables with plum sauce. The extensive wine list is fairly priced too.

Felsted Rumbles Cottage

Braintree Road, Felsted, Essex, CM6 3DJ
☎ (01371) 820996
🪑 50 🍽 £55

☺ Lunch Sun only 12-2, Dinner 7-9   ☹ Dinner Sun & Mon, 2 wks Feb

Joy Hadley has made her mark on the 20th-century restaurant world by her concept of Guinea Pig menus, demonstrating her constant interest in improvement and discovery. Happy the people who have helped along the way! The wine list has some useful tasting notes, and a strong New World representation.

Fletching Griffin Inn

Fletching, East Sussex, TN22 3SS
☎ (01825) 722890
🛏 4 £75 🪑 110 🍽 £45

☺ Lunch 12-2.15 (Sat & Sun to 2.30), Dinner 7-9.30 (Fri & Sat to 10)
☹ 25 Dec

Welcoming staff at this characterful, 16th-century inn. Wide range of dishes on the frequently-changing menus and bags of variety on the wine list, too, with something for all tastes.

Flitwick Flitwick Manor

Church Road, Flitwick, Bedfordshire, MK45 1AE
☎ (01525) 712242 📠 (01525) 718753
🛏 15 £125 🪑 40 🍽 £100

☺ Lunch 12.30-2, Dinner 7-9.30

Major refurbishment of the public areas here during the last couple of years, to ensure standards are maintained at this Georgian country house. Menus are mostly set price, and are a mixture of classic and modern within an international theme; the seasons are acknowledged.

Folkestone Paul's

2a Bouverie Road West, Folkestone, Kent, CT20 2RX
☎ (01303) 259697 📠 (01303) 226647
🪑 120 🍽 £45

☺ Lunch 12-2.30, Dinner 7-9.30 (Sat from 7) ☹ 4 days Xmas

Booking is essential for the Sunday carvery at Paul Haggar's friendly and relaxing little restaurant. The main menu is changed bi-weekly but generally features modern English interpretations of some classic ideas. The speciality wine list reaches towards the top end of the market.

Fowey Food for Thought

Town Quay, Fowey, Cornwall, PL23 1AT
☎ (0172 683) 2221
🪑 38 🍽 £45

☺ Dinner 7-9.30 ☹ Sun

Friendly, family-run (by the Billingsleys) restaurant on the quayside, offering freshly-prepared dishes (lots of fish!) on fixed-price or à la carte menus. Relaxing atmosphere, lots of fun.

Frampton-on-Severn Saverys Restaurant

The Green, Frampton-on-Severn, Gloucestershire, GL2 7EA
☎ (01452) 740077
🪑 25 🍽 £60

☺ Dinner 7-9.15 ☹ Dinner Sun & Mon

Frampton boasts the longest village green in Britain, and after testing the claim, dinner at Saverys seems logical. 3-course set menus change periodically and offer modern British cooking in sensible quantities. Concise wine list.

Freshford Homewood Park

Hinton Charterhouse, Freshford, Bath, Avon, BA3 6BB
☎ (01225) 723731 📠 (01225) 723820
🛏 15 £ £135 🪑 60 🍽 £90

☺ Lunch 12.30-2, Dinner 7.15-9.45

Resident owners the Gueunings continue to supervise the day-to-day running of this friendly hotel, situated 6 miles from Bath on the A36 Warminster road. Lovely gardens and public areas ensure comfort as soon as you approach, borne out by the bedrooms – all with an individual charm. English/French cooking on the set and à la carte menus; chef Steve Morey in place since June 1995 is now well established.

Fressingfield Fox and Goose

Fressingfield, Nr Diss, Suffolk, IP21 5PB
☎ (01379) 586247 📠 (01379) 588107
🪑 50 🍽 £65
☺ Lunch 12-2.15, Dinner 7-9.30
☹ all Mon & Tue, 10 days Xmas (open New Year's Eve), 2 wks Jan

A fine example of how a country restaurant can be run with style, this black and white hostelry owes its inspiration to Ruth Watson, the lively patronne. A wide ranging menu includes a worldwide selection of dishes from snails with cafe de paris butter to griddled squid with coriander houmous, from chicken satay to Peking duck with pancakes. There's spiced rump of English lamb with celeriac and potato gratin, rabbit stew with saffron, chorizo and haricot beans, 'seized' fillet of local cod with parslied potato puree and sautéed calf's liver with sage and avocado. Puddings include the old classic, Poire Belle Helene which is a delicious concoction of poached pear with pear ice cream and hot chocolate sauce, cheeses are a super range from Neal's Yard and Ruth has composed an exciting menu for vegetarians and kids. All this in a tiny Suffolk village, brewers take note!

Gillingham Stock Hill House

Stock Hill, Gillingham, Dorset, SP8 5NR
☎ (01747) 823626 📠 (01747) 825628
🛏 9 £180 🪑 30 🍽 £80
☺ Lunch 12.30-1.45, Dinner 7.30-8.45 ☹ Lunch Sun

A lovingly-run country house hotel now in its tenth year in the skilled hands of Peter & Nita Hauser. The bedrooms each have their own character and the day rooms are full of antiques and objets d'art. Peter's cooking shows no signs of being dated, on the contrary he shows modern trends in dishes like cream of lovage soup with sweet water crayfish, breast of guinea fowl filled with mango and sauced with Noilly Prat and Cornish octopus braised in tomato sauce with green noodles. The Swiss flair with desserts is amply demonstrated to refuse them would be a sad mistake! Good wines are reasonably priced.

Gittisham Combe House

Gittisham, Nr Honiton, Devon, EX14 0AD
☎ (01404) 42756 📠 (01404) 46004
🛏 15 £97 🪑 58 🍽 £75
☺ Lunch 12-1.45, Dinner 7-9.30 ☹ Dinner Mon Jan & Feb, 25 Jan-8 Feb

John & Thérèse Boswell have run Combe House since 1970 and you feel very much that you are part of a family-run hotel when you stay here. Not only does Thérèse cook but she's also a talented artist and sculptress: she created the *Catey* statuette, much coveted in the hospitality industry. Friendly service adds to the appeal of a relaxing stay here.

Gloucester Hatton Court

Upton Hill, Upton St Leonards, Gloucester,
Gloucestershire, GL4 8DE

☎ (01452) 617412 📠 (01452) 612945

45 £95 70 £55

☺ Lunch 12.30-2 (Sun from 12), Dinner 7.30-10 (Sun to 9.30)

Situated on the B4073 Gloucester to Painswick road, on the edge of Upton St Leonards, Hatton Court is ideally located in the heart of the English countryside, and is especially popular during the Cheltenham Gold Cup race meeting. There are good leisure facilities, and medium-sized banquets and conferences can be accommodated.

Goring-on-Thames The Leatherne Bottel ✿

Riverside Inn & Restaurant, Goring-on-Thames,
Berkshire, RG8 0HS

☎ (01491) 872667

50 £70

☺ Lunch 12.15-2 (Sat & Sun to 2.30), Dinner 7.15-9
(Sat to 9.30, Sun to 8.30) ☹ 25 Dec

Keith Read cooks and Annie Bonnet looks after the rest of the detail at this charming restaurant housed in a row of cottages with a wonderful terrace dipping its feet into the Thames. The cooking is as fresh and imaginative as Annie's wonderful displays of flowers, a chilli pasta with nasturtium flowers, lemon balm and chives, local goat's cheese roasted with tarragon and fresh garlic leaves is served with fresh tomato ketchup, smoked halibut with smoked salmon and basil ice cream, fresh marinated anchovy fillet and prawn and coriander spring roll. Main dishes like lamb's tongues, sweetbreads and kidneys pan-fried with shallots and rosemary served with a black olive and rosemary pasta flavoured with garlic or perhaps, a knuckle of pork marinated with lemon leaves, cloves, herbs and red wine then braised with pumpkin chutney and baby savoy cabbage, boring it is not! A rice pudding ice cream with caramel and raspberry jam and a steamed marmalade and ginger pudding with custard defeat the dreary image of such dishes. The wine list is not massive though offers more than adequate variety at reasonable prices. You can charter the Edwardian launch for a short preprandial glass or two, what could be better?

Grasmere Michael's Nook

Grasmere, Nr Ambleside, Cumbria, LA22 9RP

☎ (01539) 435496 📠 (01539) 435645

14 £210 32 £100

☺ Lunch 12.30 for 1, Dinner 7-8.30

Reg Gifford demonstrates his ability to mix his interest in antiques and paintings with hospitality at this comfortable and elegant Victorian house; stylishly furnished, the dining room glistens and shines to welcome diners to the delights of new chef, Mark Treasure's kitchen. You might try seabass baked with truffle, asparagus and potato; Scotch beef fillet seasoned with tomato, rosemary and foie gras or confit of rabbit with artichokes and cepes. A well-balanced wine list has good value in French provincial areas.

Grasmere White Moss House

Rydal Water, Grasmere, Cumbria, LA22 9SE
☎ (01539) 435295 📠 (01539) 435516
6 £120 20 £60
☺ Dinner 7.30 for 8 ☹ Dinner Sun, mid Dec-mid Mar

Beautifully situated on Rydal Water, White Moss is the home of Sue & Peter Dixon and they are happy to welcome you to it. The first resident of note was Wordsworth's son, and as the Dixons say, the view indeed inspired poetry. Inspiration today comes from Peter Dixon's delicious menus, 5-course set dinners using local produce with a light touch, finished off with traditional puddings. An amazing wine list; and all home comforts.

Grasmere Wordsworth Hotel

Grasmere, Nr Ambleside, Cumbria, LA22 9SW
☎ (01539) 435592 📠 (01539) 435765
37 £105 65 £75
☺ Lunch 12.30-2, Dinner 7-9 (Fri & Sat to 9.30)

Reg Gifford, with Robin & Margaret Lees, continues to take good care of the poet's lakeland home, offering a warm welcome to a splendid setting, fine facilities for leisure and business visitors, and English/French dishes on set dinner menus. A list of fine wines includes plenty of New World representatives, and a pianist will serenade you on Saturday evenings.

Great Dunmow The Starr

Market Place, Great Dunmow, Essex, CM6 1AX
☎ (01371) 874321 📠 (01371) 876337
8 £85 50 £80
☺ Lunch 12-1.30, Dinner 7-9.30 (Sat to 10)
☹ Lunch Sat, Dinner Sun, 1 wk Jan

Just 7 miles from Junction 8 of the M11, this lovely old building houses a restaurant with rooms well worth a visit. Chef Mark Fisher offers English cooking with a French accent on a simply laid out menu which is accompanied by a fine wine list. The atmosphere is friendly yet professional.

L!VE TV: THE FACTS
see page 21

England 167

Great Gonerby Harry's Place

17 High Street, Great Gonerby, Nr Grantham,
Lincolnshire, NG31 8JS
☎ (01476) 61780
🍴 10 🕐 £95

☺ Lunch 12.30-2, Dinner 7-9.30

☹ Sun & Mon except by arrangement, Bank Holidays

Harry & Caroline Hallam run this as a husband-and-wife enterprise.
It's a tiny restaurant in a small village, north of Grantham on the B1174.
Local specialist suppliers provide fresh produce for a menu which changes
frequently, according to what is available and what diners ate on their
last visit! Try the soup of local celeriac and corn-fed chicken, followed
by fillet of cod lightly baked with herbs and coriander and served with
a sauce of red wine, shallots and lentils.

Great Milton
Le Manoir aux Quat'Saisons

Church Road, Great Milton, Oxfordshire, OX44 7PD
☎ (01844) 278881 📠 (01844) 278847
🛏 19 £ £195 🍴 110 🕐 £195

☺ Lunch 12.15-2.15, Dinner 7.15-10.15

What is there left unsaid about Le Manoir and Raymond Blanc? That
the brochure is in four languages (English, French, German and Japanese)...
That it offers some of the most sought-after rooms in which to sleep
and eat... That it's equally one of the most sought-after kitchens in which
to train... That it's acknowledged to be one of Britain's finest restaurants
and hotels. All this is true. And yet, there's still more. Raymond is one
of the most approachable of chefs and his enthusiasm for and knowledge
of his craft are unrivalled. Simply go there and experience Le Manoir
for yourself. The well-maintained rooms, the sheer extent of the herb
gardens and the professionalism of the kitchen brigade. (One of
Raymond's strengths is to acknowledge the value of team-work.) So after
the build-up, what of the food on the plate? He seems to have – and
to be able to instil into his brigade – a Midas touch that sets each dish
apart. How do you choose between trois bouchées gourmandes aux
parfums d'ailleurs (scallop tartare with shiso leaves, poached oyster in
a cucumber butter and croustillant of crab in seaweed); and petit paté
de canard confit et foie gras, salade Landaise (pressed duck confit and
foie gras masked with a truffle jelly, served with duck ham and winter
salad)? Or afterwards, between filet de daurade royale poêlé, jus de
bouillabaisse et fricassée de calamars (pan-fried fillet of royal sea bream
in a bouillabaisse jus with squid and garden herbs); and filet de chevreuil
poêlé, sauce au chocolat amer, fondue de marrons et légumes d'hiver
(pan-fried venison fillet with a bitter chocolate sauce, braised chestnuts
and winter vegetables)? Desserts – delicious – le fruit défendu. Or nature
morte hivernale (a frozen winter still life). A final note, which also
encapsulates Raymond Blanc's attitude to his restaurant. The menu states
clearly that "children of any age are not accepted: they are welcomed".

Great Missenden La Petite Auberge

107 High Street, Great Missenden,
Buckinghamshire, HP16 0BB
☎ (01494) 865370
🍴 28 🍽 £65
☺ Dinner 7.30-10
☹ Dinner Sun, Bank Holidays, 3 wks Xmas/New Year

The Martels run this very French restaurant and offer authentic cuisine at affordable prices, with an unpretentious wine list to accompany the food.

Great Yarmouth Seafood Restaurant

85 North Quay, Great Yarmouth, Norfolk, NR30 1JF
☎ (01493) 856009
🍴 40 🍽 £55
☺ Lunch 12-1.45, Dinner 7-10.45
☹ Lunch Sat, all Sun, Bank Holidays except Good Friday, 3 wks Xmas

The Kikis' super little fish restaurant set in a converted station building continues to attract regular custom. They have used the same source for produce for the past 15 years and this mutual loyalty is rewarded and rewarding. Some of the more unusual ingredients have created local press interest: a 76lb halibut, or a sturgeon!

Grimston Congham Hall   ❖ ♍ ✿

Lynn Road, Grimston, King's Lynn, Norfolk, PE32 1AH
☎ (01485) 600250 📠 (01485) 601191
🛏 14 £ £99 🍴 50 🍽 £70
☺ Lunch 12.30-2, Dinner 7.30-9.30 ☹ Lunch Sat

Trevor and Christine Forecast's charming hotel is just outside King's Lynn set amid acres of parkland. Relaxing and peaceful for a holiday or after a hectic business schedule the hosts and staff are most attentive and chef Jonathan Nicholson will satiate the tastebuds in The Orangery restaurant. Quite complex dishes appear on his menus, sautéed scallops on saffron risotto with buttered spinach and trompets de mort, Loch Fyne oysters travel down to be combined with tarragon and shallots in tortellini and are served with mushroom and champagne sauce back inside their shells. Main dishes receive equal attention, roast Gressingham duck with honey and Szechuan pepper glaze with celeriac purée and lentil sauce or perhaps pan-fried rib of beef served with sautéed polenta, grilled Mediterranean vegetables and a basil and tomato sauce. Some good wines on the varied list. A visit to the herb garden is a must.

England 169

Gulworthy The Horn of Plenty

Gulworthy, Tavistock, Devon, PL19 8JD
☎ (01822) 832528 📠 (01822) 832528
🛏 7 £108 🪑 50 🍽 £100
☺ Lunch 12-2, Dinner 7-9 ☹ Lunch Mon, Xmas

The welcoming home of Ian & Elaine Gatehouse in the foothills of Dartmoor with views of the Tamar Valley. There are comfortable bedrooms in the converted coach house for overnight stays. Peter Gorton is the chef and the fixed-price menus combine classic and modern trends, salt cod with lentils and shallot cream, salad of scallops with orange and lime vinaigrette or terrine of chicken and Parma ham on tomato compote to start. Roast Trelough duckling with red wine, orange and sage sauce, charred fillet of beef with roast, honeyed pearl onions, peppers and olives with port sauce or an unusual fillet of lemon sole coated with chopped prawns, scallops and coriander, cooked in a tempura batter served with white wine sauce to follow. There's a good selection of house wines available by the glass.

Hadley Wood West Lodge Park Hotel

Cockfosters Road, Hadley Wood, Nr Barnet, Hertfordshire, EN4 0PY
☎ 0181-440 8311 📠 0181-449 3698
🛏 45 £117 🪑 85 🍽 £65
☺ Lunch 12.30-2, Dinner 7.15-9.45

On the northern fringe of London – a mile from Cockfosters tube station or the same distance from Junction 24 of the M25 – this 19th-century house is set in 34 acres of parkland and gardens including a lake and arboretum. British food is presented in the modern fashion in the Cedar Restaurant.

Halford Sykes House

Queen Street, Halford, Shipston-on-Stour, Warwickshire, CV36 5BT
☎ (01789) 740976
🪑 24 🍽 £80
☺ Lunch by arrangement, Dinner 7.30-8.15 (booking essential)
☹ Dinner Sun-Tue, Xmas Eve-New Year's Eve

Booking is essential at this lovely Cotswold-stone house, for any of the 3 little dining rooms, each with a different character. The Inglenook is ideal for private parties, the Bailiff's Study has just 3 tables, and the Garden Room brings the outdoors indoors. Well-balanced set menus are cooked in modern style, and are complemented by a well-chosen wine list.

Halifax Design House Restaurant

Dean Clough, Halifax, West Yorkshire, HX3 SAX
☎ (01422) 383242 📠 (01422) 322732
🍴 70 £55
☺ Lunch 12-2, Dinner 6-10.30 ☹ Lunch Sat, all Sun, 25 & 26 Dec

Smart, ultra-modern restaurant where the cooking is done by David Watson, who moved here when Pool Court effectively moved into the centre of Leeds. The food is as modern as the decor, served à la carte in the evening, ditto plus set for 2 or 3 courses at lunchtime. In addition, a café menu offers light refreshments all day. Well-chosen, globe-trotting wine list.

Hambleton Hambleton Hall ❖ 🎯 ♣

Hambleton, Nr Oakham, Leicestershire, LE15 8TH
☎ (01572) 756991 📠 (01572) 724721
🛏 15 £152 🍴 60 £110
☺ Lunch 12-2, Dinner 7-9.30

A majestic Victorian house in a woodland setting that overlooks a spectacular lake. Tim & Stefa Hart maintain the standards that put Hambleton on the map, both in attention to detail in the house and in the kitchen under the guidance of Aaron Patterson. Bedrooms are impeccable, furnished with great flair and service lives up to the expected levels. Aaron's menus show great skill in combining ingredients and in the execution of the dishes, each dish is as tempting as another, choice is difficult. A terrine of lobster and monkfish with a salad of artichokes and lobster vinaigrette or ravioli of crab, ginger and coriander with soya roasted scallops and lemon grass scented juice are typical first courses. Noisettes of rabbit come with a small pie containing the braised leg meat, baby vegetables and mustard and tarragon juice, pot-roast calf's sweetbreads with a watercress and black truffle sauce and a 'simply' roasted loin of Spring lamb with mille feuille of aubergine, fondant potato, tapenade and rosemary scented jus. To choose a pudding is no simpler, croustade of apple with cinnamon ice cream and compote of blackberries, caramelised pear with ginger and caramel ice cream on a bed of brioche or perhaps a hot passion fruit souffle with its own ice. The wine list also shows care and judgement with wide ranging prices. A great place to get away from it all and enjoy yourself.

Handforth Belfry Hotel

Stanley Road, Handforth, Nr Wilmslow, Cheshire, SK9 3L
☎ 0161-437 0511 📠 0161-499 0597
🛏 80 £88 🍴 120 £88
☺ Lunch 12.30-2, Dinner 7-10

Owned and run by the Beech family since 1962, this is a modern and functional hotel which caters well to business visitors. 12 bedrooms are reserved for non-smokers; others are designated for lady guests. French/English menus, both set-price and à la carte, are offered by chef Mark Fletcher.

England

Harrogate Bettys Café & Tea Rooms

1 Parliament Street, Harrogate, North Yorkshire, HG1 2QU
☎ (01423) 502746 📠 (01423) 565191
🪑 156 🍽 £30
☺ 9-9 ☹ 25 & 26 Dec, 1 Jan

An institution in Harrogate and indeed throughout the north of England. Wonderful cakes and pastries, light dishes, hot meals, brunches, salads – all things to all people! The elegant Edwardian building is as reminiscent of a bygone age as is the institution of afternoon tea itself.

Harrogate The Bistro

1 Montpelier Mews, Harrogate, North Yorkshire, HG1 2TG
☎ (01423) 530708
🪑 40 🍽 £60
☺ Lunch 12-2, Dinner 7-10
☹ Sun & Mon, Bank Holidays, 10 days Xmas, 2 wks Aug

Town-centre restaurant created by Simon Gueller, and despite his imminent (as we went to press) reappearance at Rascasse in Leeds, modern Mediterranean cooking still keeps the loyal local clientele happy – outdoor eating in the cobbled courtyard is especially popular.

Harrogate Drum & Monkey

5 Montpellier Gardens, Harrogate, North Yorkshire, HG1 2TF
☎ (01423) 502650
🪑 50 🍽 £45
☺ Lunch 12-2.30, Dinner 6.45-10.15 ☹ Sun, 1 wk Xmas

Good quality food at reasonable prices: that's the secret of the success here at this almost exclusively seafood restaurant on two floors. Slightly different menus are offered at lunchtime and in the evening, together with a good range of mostly white wines.

Harrogate Old Swan Hotel

Swan Road, Harrogate, North Yorkshire, HG1 2SR
☎ (01423) 500055 📠 (01423) 501154
🛏 136 £132 🪑 40 🍽 £70
☺ Lunch 12.30-2, Dinner 7-10 (Sun to 9.30)

An ongoing programme of refurbishment ensures standards are maintained at the Old Swan, an elegant yet informal creeper-clad hotel in the centre of this spa town. The menus offered in the Library or the Wedgwood Room (according to numbers) are mainly British but with some international variations. Local, seasonal produce is used when possible.

Harvington The Mill at Harvington

Anchor Lane, Harvington, Nr Evesham,
Hereford & Worcester, WR11 5NR

☎ (01386) 870688   📠 (01386) 870688

🛏 15 £85   🍴 35 🍽 £60

☺ Lunch 11.45-1.45, Dinner 7-9   ☹ Sun, 1 wk Xmas

The mill (originally for malting, later for bread) stands on the banks of the River Avon in some very pretty countryside. Simon & Jane Greenhalgh have made of it a comfortable hotel and restaurant which strives to put the customers' needs first. Lots of places claim this: very few succeed, but this is one that does. Comfortable and relaxing, nourishing and refreshing: you'll want to return here.

Hastings Röser's Restaurant

64 Eversfield Place, St Leonards on Sea, Nr Hastings,
East Sussex, TN37 6DB

☎ (01424) 712218

🍴 30 🍽 £65

☺ Lunch 12-2, Dinner 7-10

☹ Lunch Sat, all Sun & Mon, Bank Holidays, 2 wks Jan, 2 wks Aug

Gerald & Jenny Röser have run their charming little restaurant since 1984, offering a modern style to classic French-based cuisine. They rate everything they do as specialities: this is not arrogance or even over-confidence: it simply reflects the attention to detail which they lavish on every aspect of the enterprise, and if they pay that much care, it deserves to turn out right – and it does! There are set-price menus as well as the carte, and the simple descriptions perhaps do not do justice to the food on the plate. Seafood salad, roast pork with red cabbage, pear salad with orange: it sounds simple – you might even assemble it yourself at home. But it wouldn't turn out quite like Gerald's version! More adventurous-sounding, yet just as delicious on the palate are cured wild goose with preserve of damsons, char-grilled venison fillets with bean and savory purée and juniper butter, or grilled seabass with coriander seeds, basil and tomato. A much-loved dessert is the chocolate mousse, made from fine Belgian chocolate and served with a coffee cream; another is apple mille feuille – layers of lightly poached Granny Smith apples and calvados-flavoured cream patissière served with a butterscotch sauce. The cheeseboard is offered with a selection of fresh fruit and nuts. This is definitely a favourite.

Hatfield Heath Down Hall

Hatfield Heath, Nr Bishop's Stortford,
Hertfordshire, CM22 7AS

☎ (01279) 731441   📠 (01279) 730416

🛏 103 £134   🍴 66 🍽 £50

☺ Lunch 12.30-2, Dinner 7-9.45

Italian-style mansion house with opulent decor and furniture, set in 100 acres of parkland. Popular conference venue with good leisure facilities.

England 173

Havant Cockle Warren Cottage Hotel

36 Seafront, Hayling Island, Havant, Hampshire, PO11 9HL
☎ (01705) 464961 📠 (01705) 464838
5 £84 10 £65
☺ Dinner 8, residents only ☹ 1 wk June

The Skeltons' attractive, family-run hotel on the seafront boasts a heated swimming pool in the walled garden and a smuggler's tunnel beneath the grounds! Dinner is a set menu affair, specialising in local produce enhanced by specialities – including flour for bread – brought over from France.

Haworth Weavers

15 West Lane, Haworth, Nr Bradford,
West Yorkshire, BD22 8DU
☎ (01535) 643822
4 £70 60 £50
☺ Lunch Sun in winter only 12-2, Dinner 7-9
☹ Dinner Sun & Mon, Bank Holidays, 2 wks Xmas, 2 wks July

Colin & Jane Rushworth's friendly little restaurant and bar with guest rooms has been going strong since 1978 – it's situated alongside the Brontë Parsonage Museum. Over the years, menus have become more British-oriented. Concise wine list has some interesting house selections.

Hayfield Bridge End Restaurant

7 Church Street, Hayfield, Derbyshire, SK12 5JE
☎ (01663) 747321 📠 (01663) 742121
4 £45 50 £65
☺ Lunch Sun only 12-2.30, Dinner 7-10
☹ Dinner Sun & Mon, 1 wk Jan

A guest house and restaurant housed in a 19th-century stone building in the heart of a conservation area. The restaurant offers British/French menus, occasionally arranged as gourmet evenings when live music is played. The wine list is well annotated.

Haytor Bel Alp House

Haytor, Nr Bovey Tracey, Devon, TQ13 9XX
☎ (01364) 661217 📠 (01364) 661292
9 £138 20 £85
☺ Dinner 7.30-8.30 ☹ Hotel Dec-Feb

Elegant Edwardian country house, owned and run by Roger & Sarah Curnock who bring their own touches of hospitality to bear in an area not under-endowed with hotels and restaurants. It's a tribute to their style that they retain a loyal clientele as well as the annual newcomers who discover these hidden delights on the edge of Dartmoor.

Hereford Steppes Country House Hotel

Ullingswick, Nr Hereford, Hereford & Worcester, HR1 3JG
☎ (01432) 820424 (01432) 820042
6 £76 12 £65

☺ Lunch 12.30-2, Dinner 7.30-9 (all day bar snacks)

☹ 2 wks before Xmas & 2 wks after New Year

A warm welcome and some good food await you at the Howlands' delightful house in the Wye Valley. Careful restoration of the listed period farmstead ensured a timeless elegance. Menus are worked out according to seasonal availability, and Tessa's expertise is best explored through the 5-course gourmet dinner menu. A modestly-priced wine list has lots of variety.

Herne Bay L'Escargot

22 High Street, Herne Bay, Kent, CT6 5LH
☎ (01227) 372876
40 £55

☺ Lunch 12.30-2, Dinner 7-9.30

☹ Lunch Sat & Mon, Thu in winter, 1 wk Jun, 1 wk Sep, 1 wk Jan

Alain & Joyce Bessemoulin have been here since 1984, serving up a French bistro-style menu on this side of the Channel: close your eyes, let your imagination go and you're over there. Daily specials are chalked up on a board and depend on market availability. Short, French wine list completes the picture.

Hersham The Dining Room

10 Queens Road, The Village Green, Hersham, Surrey, KT12 5LS
☎ (01932) 231686
90 £55

☺ Lunch 12-2 (Sun to 2.30), Dinner 7-10.30 (Sat from 6.30)

☹ Lunch Sat, Dinner Sun, Bank Holidays, 1 wk Xmas

5 dining rooms housed in what was originally 2 cottages, where open fires cheer winter days and the garden room is the ideal setting for relaxed summer evenings. Good, value-for-money, British cooking.

SCOTCH BEEF CLUB
see page 16

Herstmonceux Sundial Restaurant

Gardner Street, Herstmonceux, East Sussex, BN27 4LA
☎ (01323) 832217
🍴 60 🍽 £90
☺ Lunch 12-2, Sun 2.30, Dinner 7-9.30 (Sat to 10)
☹ Dinner Sun, all Mon, 2/3 wks Aug/Sep, Xmas-20 Jan

The sort of restaurant that you expect to find in every village in France or Italy but rarely do in England! Giuseppe & Laurette Bertoli set up their hostelry back in the '60s and have built a large regular clientele based on the philosophy that if you give people what they want they will come back time after time. The extensive menu is mainly French with a few Italian dishes and a fixed-price, 3-course option has at least half a dozen choices at each stage. Lunch comprises 2 fixed-price choices. Well worth a visit on a balmy summer's day when you can enjoy the garden and terraces and admire the Sussex countryside.

Hetton Angel Inn

Hetton, Nr Skipton, North Yorkshire, BD23 6LT
☎ (01756) 730263 📠 (01756) 730263
🍴 54 🍽 £70
☺ Lunch Sun only 12-2, Dinner 7-9.30,
   (Bar: 12-2, 7-10 (earlier in winter)) ☹ Dinner Sun, 1 wk Jan

A pub that offers rather more than the norm in pub food with a very busy restaurant and bar cum brasserie. John Topham's kitchen goes from strength to strength, the daily changing menu might include filo `moneybags' of seafood on lobster sauce, a terrine of Tuscan vegetables with tapenade crostini or chargrilled pigeon on a rissoto of cepes. Next you could try the confit of Barbary duck coked in it's own juices, served with onion marmelade, armagnac prunes and red wine thyme sauce, a breast of Goosnargh chicken filled with duxelle of prawns and bacon served with a crayfish sauce or calf's liver with sweetcure bacon on grilled polenta with marsala sauce. Lovely home baked breads and delicious puddings round off the treat, as does the excellent list of reasonably priced wines. Dennis Watkins can be justifiably proud of his well-deserved recognition. This is an excellent formula.

Higham The Knowle 👪

School Lane, Higham, Nr Rochester, Kent, ME3 7HP
☎ (01474) 822262
🍴 70 🍽 £68
☺ Lunch 12-1.30, Dinner 6.30-10 ☹ Dinner Sun, all Mon

The best sort of local restaurant: privately owned and sited within the Baragwanaths' home, so it can be endlessly flexible in accommodating customers' needs; and it is in response to demand that the vegetarian and bistro menus are expanding. Idiosyncratic combinations of ingredients can sometimes surprise.

Hintlesham Hintlesham Hall

Hintlesham, Nr Ipswich, Suffolk, IP8 3NS
☎ (01473) 652268 📠 (01473) 652463
🛏 33 £153 🪑 120 🍽 £70
☺ Lunch 12-2, Dinner 7-10 ☹ Lunch Sat

A lovely Georgian facade masks part of the house that dates back to Tudor times, all has been finely restored since Robert Carrier established the restaurant and cookery school back in the '70s. Now owned by David Allan, but still under the direction of Tim Sunderland. There are now over 30 suites and bedrooms and a golf course and leisure facilities have been added in recent years. The dining rooms have always been an essential part of Hintlesham's popularity and chef Alan Ford has done much to carry on the tradition of his predecessors. The 2 dining rooms are quite different in atmosphere one homely, one grander in style. Menus change seasonally and Alan uses fine produce in dishes such as a breast of pheasant on chestnut and sage farce with dark watercress sauce, medallions of venison topped with spinach and herbs with redcurrant jus or steamed turbot layered with lentils and a lemon grass butter sauce. Hintlesham is a wonderfully relaxing base from which to explore Constable country.

Hockley Heath Nuthurst Grange

Nuthurst Grange Lane, Hockley Heath, Warwickshire, B94 5NL
☎ (01564) 783972 📠 (01564) 783919
🛏 15 £125 🪑 50 🍽 £60
☺ Lunch 12-2, Dinner 7-9.30 ☹ Lunch Sat

David & Darryl Randolph run a homely hotel and restaurant about half a miles south of Hockley Heath set in well-maintained grounds. Bedrooms are individually furnished in country house style, and there are good facilities for business meetings (including heli-pad). English cooking from David for the formal-yet-friendly restaurant.

Holdenby Lynton House

Holdenby Road, Holdenby, Northamptonshire, NN6 8DJ
☎ (01604) 770777 📠 (01604) 770777
🛏 5 £55 🪑 45 🍽 £70
☺ Lunch 12.15-1.45, Dinner 7.30-9.45
☹ Lunch Sat & Mon, all Sun, Bank Holidays, 1 wk spring, 1 wk summer

Set in the heart of the English countryside, but featuring a menu of traditional Italian dishes: surprising only until you realise that the owners are Carlo & Carol Bertuzzi. Around 40 Italian wines on the list include some lesser-known ones, as well as a few clarets for traditionalists.

Holt Yetman's

37 Norwich Road, Holt, Norfolk, NR25 6SA
☎ (01263) 713320
🪑 32 🍽 £70
☺ Lunch 12.30-2, Dinner 7.30-9
☹ Lunch Mon-Fri, Dinner Mon, Tue in summer

Small, relaxed restaurant with crisp linen and a friendly atmosphere. Alison Yetman cooks, offering excellent local produce on good-value menus, priced according to the number of courses taken. A well-judged wine list has bags of New World selections.

Horley Langshott Manor

Langshott, Horley, Surrey, RH6 9LN
☎ (01293) 786680 📠 (01293) 783905
🛏 7 £106 🪑 14 🍽 £65
☺ Lunch by arrangement, Dinner 7.30-9.30
☹ Lunch Sun, 1 wk Xmas

A lovely Elizabeth manor house, Grade II listed and carefully restored, is now a small country house hotel and restaurant run by the Noble family. A courtesy car will meet you from Gatwick, just 10 minutes away, and transport you to another era. The cooking style, however, returns you to modern times: it is inventive yet uncomplicated, just like the concise wine list.

Horncastle Magpies Restaurant

73-75 East Street, Horncastle, Lincolnshire, LN9 6AA
☎ (01507) 527004
🪑 40 🍽 £55
☺ Lunch 12.30-2.30, Dinner 7.30-10
☹ Lunch Sat, Dinner Sun, all Mon, Bank Holidays, part of Jan

This converted row of cottages situated between Lincoln and Skegness is now home to the Lee family's restaurant. It's popular with the locals: small wonder, given the imaginative cooking at sensible prices. Wines are simply listed in price brackets (£8, £10, £12 etc) and only the finer bottles are individually priced. What a good idea!

Horndon-on-the-Hill
The Bell Inn & Hill House

High Road, Horndon-on-the-Hill, Essex, SS17 8LD

☎ (01375) 642463   (01375) 361611

14   £50

Hill House Restaurant:

30   £65

☺ Lunch 12.15-2, Dinner 7.15-10   ☹ Sun & Mon, 25-31 Dec

The Bell Restaurant:

40   £60

☺ Lunch 12-2, Dinner 6.30-10 (Sun from 7)   ☹ 25 & 26 Dec

John & Christine Vereker run this adjoining pair of establishments in rural Essex. The Bell is the older by a couple of centuries, but each has its own charm and attractions; and they operate in tandem to accommodate visitors and functions seamlessly. Predominantly modern English menus are the restaurant's attraction. Recommended dishes might include salt-cured salmon with dill mayonnaise, ragout of lamb kidneys with black pudding and mash followed by spotted dick with a caramel sauce.

Horton-cum-Studley Studley Priory

Horton-cum-Studley, Nr Oxford, Oxfordshire, OX33 1AZ

☎ (01865) 351203   (01865) 351613

19   £98   60   £65

☺ Lunch 12.30-1.45, Dinner 7.30-9.30   ☹ Bank Holidays

Originally a Benedictine nunnery, the Priory is a popular venue for small conferences, with elegant and well-furnished rooms. The kitchen offers modern English dishes on the à la carte menu.

Horton French Partridge

Horton, Nr Northampton, Northamptonshire, NN7 2AP

☎ (01604) 870033   (01604) 870032

40   £70

☺ Dinner only 7.30-9   ☹ Sun & Mon, 2 wks Xmas & Easter, 3 wks Aug

In the same hands for over 30 years, this restaurant continues to delight its long-standing clientele. David Partridge is at the helm, cooking 4-course menus that change seasonally. Dishes from the elegant dining room include smoked salmon parcels with cucumber salad, home-made game and mushroom pie and rum baba with an orange butter sauce. Good, reasonably-priced wine list.

England   179

Hull Le Bistro

400 Beverley Road, Hull, Humberside, HU5 1LW
☎ (01482) 43088
🍴 40 🍽 £45
☺ Dinner 7-9.30
☹ Dinner Sun, 26-28 Dec, 2 wks Aug, Bank Holidays

Choose from the blackboard menu and play games and quizzes while you wait for your meal. There's bags of choice at reasonable prices including good vegetarian options. House wine is only £9.90 a litre.

Hull Ceruttis

10 Nelson Street, Hull, Humberside, HU1 1XE
☎ (01482) 328501   📠 (01482) 587597
🍴 40 🍽 £60
☺ Lunch 12-2, Dinner 7-9.30
☹ Lunch Sat, all Sun, Bank Holidays, 1 wk Xmas

Ceruttis seems to have been here on the harbourside for ever – well, since 1974 at least: a seafood restaurant to take advantage of the North Sea location, run in a traditional family way. In addition to the carte there are weekly specials, together with wines of the month. Another branch, Cerutti 2, has been opened in Beverley.

Hunstrete Hunstrete House

Hunstrete, Chelwood, Nr Bath, Avon, BS18 4NS
☎ (01761) 490490   📠 (01761) 490732
🛏 23 £ £145 🍴 50 🍽 £100
☺ Lunch 12.30-2.30, Dinner 7.30-9.30

Lovely Georgian manor house, complete with its own deer park within 90 acres of beautiful parkland and gardens, half-way between Bristol and Bath. New owners Arcadian have definitely lifted Hunstrete back into the upper echelons of country house hotels. Chef Robert Clayton is lucky to have the walled garden which provides much produce for the kitchens. He turns out modern English dishes in well-balanced combinations, such as nage of sea fish, sautéed spinach and cèpe sauce; warm salad of duck with cassis and shallot dressing; breast of guinea-fowl with calvados and lime, its leg stuffed with a mushroom risotto; and to finish chocolate, coffee and hazelnut parfait with a warm apricot sauce and fruit tulip. The wine list matches the food in stature.

Huntingdon Old Bridge Hotel

1 High Street, Huntingdon, Cambridgeshire, PE18 6TQ
☎ (01480) 452681   📠 (01480) 411017
🛏 26 £ £95 🍴 44 🍽 £80
☺ Lunch 12-2.30, Dinner 6.30-10.30 (Terrace: 12-2.30, 6.30-10.30)

Attractive, 18th-century, 3-storey building overlooking the River Ouse, with individually designed and impeccably furnished rooms. Eat in the Terrace restaurant for a more relaxed atmosphere, or in the main restaurant for something more formal. As in all of John Hoskins' establishments, the wine list is quite exceptional and offers terrific value for money.

Huntsham Huntsham Court

Huntsham, Nr Bampton, Devon, EX16 7NA
☎ (01398) 361365 📠 (01398) 361456
🛏 14 £115 🪑 30 🍽 £75
🙂 Dinner 8-10 ☹ 2 wks winter

A somewhat eccentrically run hotel where you will feel delightfully at home amidst centuries of bric-à-brac. If you like teletext and videos forget it, there are, however some 3000 records to listen to and the console radio still crackles away or there's a piano and plenty of brass instruments on which to vent one's pent up energy. Dinner is a 5-course affair with candlelight and new found friends after wandering around the wine cellar to pick from the impressive offerings. It's amazing that there are not more hotels where the hosts do their thing rather than what they imagine the guests want.

Hurley Ye Olde Bell

High Street, Hurley, Nr Maidenhead, Berkshire, SL6 5LX
☎ (01628) 825881 📠 (01628) 825939
🛏 36 £114 🪑 70 🍽 £55
🙂 Lunch 12.30-2.30, Dinner 7.30-9.30, (Fri & Sat to 10)

Another claimant to the title of Oldest Inn in England, Ye Olde Bell, part of the Jarvis Hotel group, is certainly a pretty hotel and restaurant with a splendid shady garden in which to take afternoon tea. Set menus supplement the carte, and the wine list covers Europe thoroughly.

Hurstbourne Tarrant Esseborne Manor

Hurstbourne Tarrant, Nr Andover, Hampshire, SP11 0ER
☎ (01264) 736444 📠 (01264) 736473
🛏 10 £120 🪑 30 🍽 £80
🙂 Lunch 12-2, Dinner 7-9.30

Select, European-influenced, à la carte and set menus are on offer in the restaurant of this Victorian manor, set in the North Wessex Downs on a tributary of the River Test.

Ilkley Bettys

32-34 The Grove, Ilkley, West Yorkshire, LS29 9EE
☎ (01943) 608029 📠 (01943) 816723
🪑 110 🍽 £30
🙂 9-6 ☹ 25 & 26 Dec

A Wharfedale valley branch of Harrogate's famous tea shop. All the usual expectations are met, with the added benefit of some lovely views. Breakfast is popular here.

England   **181**

Ilkley Box Tree

37 Church Street, Ilkley, West Yorkshire, LS29 9DR
☎ (01943) 608484 📠 (01943) 607186
🪑 50 🕑 £85
🙂 Lunch 12-2.30, Dinner 7-10
☹ Dinner Sun, all Mon, Bank Holidays, 2 wks Jan, 1 wk Xmas

An institution in Yorkshire, indeed in England, since 1962, the Box Tree has now settled down well with its kitchens under the guardianship of Thierry Lepretre-Granet for the last couple of years. He has brought his own flair and style to a French and modern British menu, most ably demonstrated in his 4-course dinner menu. You might try rillette of salmon and smoked salmon with a dill and yoghurt sauce and toasted brioche to start, followed by confit of pork cheeks with honey, risotto of wild mushrooms and an aromatic sauce. There's an excellent range of coffees, leaf teas and fruit teas with which to complete your meal, which is served in one of the 3 intimate dining rooms, decorated in warm, dark colours, with gilt-framed pictures and china cabinets on the walls.

Ilkley Rombalds Hotel

West View, Wells Road, Ilkley, West Yorkshire, LS29 9JG
☎ (01943) 603201 📠 (01943) 816586
🛏 15 £ £84 🪑 35 🕑 £65
🙂 Lunch 12-2 (Sun brunch 9-2), Dinner 7-9.30 ☹ 27-31 Dec

Town centre hotel but with prompt access to some lovely countryside. Comfortable rooms, relaxed atmosphere, and British cooking featuring, on Sundays, both a brunch and a roast. Live piano is played on Saturday evenings.

Ipswich Mortimer's on the Quay

Wherry Quay, Ipswich, Suffolk, IP4 1AS
☎ (01473) 230225 📠 (01473) 752561
🪑 60 🕑 £55
🙂 Lunch 12-2, Dinner 7-9 (Mon 6.30-8.15)
☹ Lunch Sat, all Sun, Bank Holidays & following Tue, 2 wks Xmas/New Year, 2 wks Aug

The location (directly on the quay) ensures that the fish is fresh here, and also that there's a wide variety available. It's usually true to say that simplest is best, but the sauces here are equally reliable. The predominantly white list of wines is sensibly priced.

Ipswich Singing Chef

200 St Helen's Street, Ipswich, Suffolk, IP4 2LH
☎ (01473) 255236
🪑 36 🍽 £40

☺ Lunch by arrangement only, Dinner 7-11
☹ Dinner Sun & Mon

Chef/patron Ken Toye offers real value at his cheerful restaurant, where he bases his cooking on a French provincial style. And yes, he does sing to you. Mind you, if a couple can dine out for £20 (not Saturdays) on a fixed-price menu, that's surely something to shout about!

Ixworth Theobald's

68 High Street, Ixworth, Bury St Edmunds,
Suffolk, IP31 2HJ
☎ (01359) 231707
🪑 36 🍽 £72

☺ Lunch 12.15-1.30, Dinner 7-9.30
☹ Lunch Sat, Dinner Sun, all Mon, Bank Holidays, 1 wk Aug

Simon & Geraldine Theobald have been here since 1981, and so join the ranks of those recession-survivors who have stuck to their philosophy. In this case, it's to offer set menus priced according to the main course chosen, changed seasonally. A carte is also offered at lunchtime. The menu style is traditional, but with up-to-date touches.

Jevington Hungry Monk Restaurant

The Street, Jevington, Nr Polegate, East Sussex, BN26 5QF
☎ (01323) 482178 📠 (01323) 483989
🪑 44 🍽 £60

☺ Lunch Sun only 12-2.30 (Mon-Sat by arrangement), Dinner 7-10.30
☹ Bank Holidays, 3 days Xmas

The Mackenzies continue gently to expand their activities at this lovely old country restaurant. There's now a third private dining room for very small parties (the restaurant itself is a collection of interconnecting rooms) and another cook-book (on puddings) is due out. The basis of this success is everyday French and English cooking at affordable prices, with appropriate wines and friendly service in a charming restaurant.

Kendal The Moon

129 Highgate, Kendal, Cumbria, LA9 4EN
☎ (01539) 729254
🪑 38 🍽 £35

☺ Dinner 6.30-10 (Sat from 6)
☹ Lunch daily, 24, 25 & 31 Dec, 2 wks Jan

Cute little bistro near the Arts Centre with a blackboard menu of traditional favourites. Half the menu is devoted to vegetarian dishes, and the establishment is totally non-smoking. The Pudding Club is very popular, and meets regularly to indulge its collective sweet tooth.

Kenilworth Restaurant Bosquet

97a Warwick Road, Kenilworth, Warwickshire, CV8 1HP
☎ (01926) 852463
🍴 26 ⏱ £75
☺ Lunch 12-1.15, Dinner 7-9.15
☹ Sun & Mon, 1 wk Xmas, 3 wks Aug

Bernard & Jane Lignier have been here since 1981, serving traditional French menus in fixed-price and à la carte format. Some daily specials, too, principally fish, which Jane will tell you about when she takes your order. Bernard, in the kitchen, then delivers the goods – a combination which ensures a loyal, local clientele. Why not try wild mushroom soup served with truffle profiteroles to start, followed by terrine of duck foie gras with Muscat and served with salad and a spicy fig preserve.

Kenilworth Simpson's Restaurant

101-103 Warwick Road, Kenilworth,
Warwickshire, CV8 1HL
☎ (01926) 864567
🍴 80 ⏱ £50
☺ Lunch 12.30-2, Dinner 7-10 ☹ Lunch Sat, all Sun, Bank Holidays

Classic, modern British and Mediterranean influences combine to good effect at the Antonas' restaurant, easily located along the main road in Kenilworth. The aim is for customers to be able to relax in an informal ambience but to enjoy good quality food and wine at reasonable prices.

Keswick Brundholme Country House Hotel

Brundholme Road, Keswick, Cumbria, CA12 4NL
☎ (017687) 74495 📠 (017687) 73536
🛏 11 £80 🍴 50 ⏱ £65
☺ Lunch residents only, Dinner 7.30-8.45 ☹ Hotel Dec-mid Feb

In his brochure, chef/patron Ian Charlton makes an offer to his guests: join him for a run around the Fells. If running a bath is more your scene, do that instead (in one of the cosy bathrooms adjoining comfortable bedrooms) then go downstairs and enjoy dinner in the non-smoking dining room. Lovely setting overlooking the River Greta.

Keyston Pheasant Inn

Village Loop Road, Keyston, Nr Bythorn,
Cambridgeshire, PE18 0RE
☎ (01832) 710241 📠 (01832) 710340
🍴 100 ⏱ £50
☺ Lunch 12-2, Dinner 6.30-10 (Sun 7.15-9.45)
☹ Dinner 25 & 26 Dec & 1 Jan

Small, country pub with a good reputation in the area for fine food has recently undergone a change: Martin Lee joined from Whitechapel Manor just as we went to press. He has a good pedigree, so will not disappoint.

King's Lynn Rococo

11 Saturday Market Place, King's Lynn, Norfolk, PE30 5DQ
☎ (01553) 771483
🍴 40 🍷 £70

☺ Lunch 12-2, Dinner 7-10 ☹ Lunch Mon, all Sun, 26-30 Dec

Nick & Anne Anderson specialise in using local produce whenever possible to prepare carefully selected 2- or 3-course menus. An excellent wine list includes Nick's Personal Choices.

Kingham Mill House Hotel & Restaurant

Station Road, Kingham, Nr Chipping Norton,
Oxfordshire, OX7 6UH
☎ (01608) 658188 📠 (01608) 658492
🛏 23 £100 🍴 70 🍷 £60

☺ Lunch 12.15-1.45, Dinner 7-9.45

Cotswold hotel and restaurant on the outskirts of the village (take the B4450 into Kingham). The original mill dealt with flour, and two bread ovens are still in evidence. Individually decorated bedrooms are charming and peaceful, while fixed-price lunch and dinner menus supplement the full carte.

Kingston-upon-Thames
Restaurant Gravier

9 Station Road, Norbiton, Kingston-upon-Thames,
Surrey, KT2 7AA
☎ 0181-549 5557
🍴 40 🍷 £70

☺ Lunch 12.15-2, Dinner 7-10
☹ Lunch Sat, all Sun, Bank Holidays, 1 wk Xmas, 1 wk Aug

French-style seafood restaurant on the outskirts of town, run with panache by Jean-Philippe & Joanne Gravier (she cooks, he serves). An increasing range of meat dishes is also available. Good local restaurant.

Kington Penrhos Court

Penrhos, Kington, Hereford & Worcester, HR5 3LH
☎ (01544) 230720 📠 (01544) 230754
🛏 19 £70 🍴 70 🍷 £75

☺ Dinner 7.30-10 ☹ Sun, 2 wks Jan

Just one mile east of Kington on the A44, Penrhos is a fine example of a 13th-century timber-framed building. Daphne Lambert runs residential cookery courses, largely vegetarian or vegan (there are also jazz evenings, and wine or whisky tastings), following her philosophy of healthy eating.

England 185

Kintbury Dundas Arms

53 Station Road, Kintbury, Nr Hungerford,
Berkshire, RG17 9UT

☎ (01488) 658263 📠 (01488) 658568

5 £65 36 £65

☺ Lunch 12-2, Dinner 7.30-9.15

☹ Dinner Mon, all Sun, Xmas/New Year

A Home Counties institution: the Dundas Arms has been run by David Dalzell-Piper since 1967, to the delight of locals and travellers alike. An international-style menu combines classics with the occasional more unusual touch, and is always reasonably priced.

Knutsford Brasserie Belle Epoque

60 King Street, Knutsford, Cheshire, WA16 2DT

☎ (01565) 633060 📠 (01565) 634150

7 £60 80 £60

☺ Lunch 12-2, Dinner 7-10.30 ☹ Lunch Sat, all Sun, Bank Holidays

21 years at Cheshire's Edwardian Showpiece for Nerys & Keith Mooney. In intimate surroundings (there's even a canopied table for 2, for real romantics!) they serve some set menus and also a brasserie-style carte. Good size portions, with traditional dishes appearing for the most part, although the theming is happily not taken too far! The letting bedrooms are in similar style. A lively and fun restaurant.

Lacock At The Sign of The Angel

6 Church Street, Lacock, Nr Chippenham,
Wiltshire, SN15 2LB

☎ (01249) 730230 📠 (01249) 730527

6 £75 45 £70

☺ Lunch 12.30-2, Dinner 7.30-9 ☹ Lunch Mon, 1 wk Xmas

June 1995 saw the retirement of the senior Levis family from day-to-day running of the Angel – except that they are now just running the rooms in the cottage annexe as a semi-separate business (you can book through the main hotel). In the Angel itself, continuity is seamlessunder the junior Levis, as the whole family have been involved for such a long time. The lovely building (a 15th-century wool merchant's house) has seemed to have absorbed effortlessly such 20th-century amenities as ensuite bathrooms. The restaurant remains a favourite point of call for English traditionalists.

Land's End Land's End Hotel

Land's End, Sennen, Cornwall, TR19 7AA

☎ (01736) 871844 📠 (01736) 871599

34 £75 65 £60

☺ Lunch 12-2, Dinner 7-9.30 (Sun to 9)

The first or last hotel in England, depending on your direction of travel! Under the care of the experienced Ann Long there is an ongoing programme of complete refurbishment. Chef Alan Ward's contribution is a fine menu of modern international dishes, complemented by a concise, fairly priced wine list.

Langar Langar Hall

Langar, Nottinghamshire, NG13 9HG
☎ (01949) 860559 📠 (01949) 861045
12 £80 30 £70

☺ Lunch 12-2, Dinner 7-9.30 (7-10 Fri, Sat) ☹ Sun (except residents)

The hall is well hidden behind the village church, but to narrow it down: from the A46, it's half-way between Leicester and Newark; and from the A52, half-way between Grantham and Nottingham. All the bedrooms are non-smoking, thereby helping to preserve their period charm and grace while still offering modern amenities. The elegant pillared restaurant offers local ingredients cooked in the modern manner with Mediterranean influences, and the carefully-selected wine list is a good match.

Langho Northcote Manor

Northcote Road, Langho, Nr Blackburn,
Lancashire, BB6 8BE
☎ (01254) 240555 📠 (01254) 246568
14 £85 80 £90

☺ Lunch 12-1.30 (Sun to 2), Dinner 7-9.30 (Sat to 10)

A Victorian red brick house that has been transformed into a comfortable 14-bedroomed hotel by Craig Bancroft & Nigel Haworth. The latter is the chef who offers varied menus; his gourmet menu might start with a tartare of salmon with dill and a warm oyster salad followed by a pot au feu of smoked poultry and vegetables. After the sorbet of lemon, thyme and celery, loin of venison is garnished with grapes on a galette of celeriac, spinach and mushrooms and cocotte potatoes then a variety of British cheeses. Pudding is raspberry soufflé with vanilla ice cream and raspberries.

Lavenham Great House

Market Place, Lavenham, Suffolk, CO10 9QZ
☎ (01787) 247431 📠 (01787) 248007
4 £68 40 £45

☺ Lunch 12-2.30, Dinner 7-9.30 (Sat to 10.30)
☹ Dinner Sun, all Mon, 3 wks Jan

Restaurant with rooms which proprietor Régis Crépy describes as "a little corner of France in medieval England". Facing the market cross, it is steeped in history and the restaurant (which overflows into a paved courtyard) offers a mixture of set menus, snacks and the gourmet carte. Extensive list of French cheeses.

England 187

Lavenham The Swan

High Street, Lavenham, Nr Sudbury, Suffolk, CO10 9QA
☎ (01787) 247477 (01787) 248286
47 £128 70 £75
Lunch 12.30-2, Dinner 7-9.30, (coffee 10-12, tea 3-5.30)

Another East Anglia favourite – town-centre location; history in every beam, nook and cranny; vaulted dining room complete with minstrels' gallery; period furniture and 4-poster beds. Good business facilities; menus of traditional British dishes use local ingredients when possible.

Leamington Spa Mallory Court

Harbury Lane, Bishop's Tachbrook, Leamington Spa, Warwickshire, CV33 9QB
☎ (01926) 330214 (01926) 451714
10 £173 50 £120
Lunch 12.30-2, Dinner 9.30-9.45

Certainly Warwickshire's finest country house hotel in a superb location that is in deep country yet within easy reach of Birmingham, Stratford-upon Avon and the National Exhibition Centre. Allan Holland supervises the kitchen while partner, Jeremy Mort looks after the guests. Impeccable standards of housekeeping and good food are the things that bring people back to Mallory Court time after time. Light, modern cooking is Allan's forte, a pie of quail breasts with truffle dumplings and madeira sauce, roast scallops with sauce vierge or ravioli of lobster and fennel with light butter sauce to start. Turbot medallion with a timbale of mussels and thyme cream, a roast partridge with poached blueberries, cassis and rosti potatoes or sautéed calf's liver with glazed limes and walnuts are typical dishes. An excellent wine list shows fine clarets and burgundies but there is plenty of good value from other regions.

Ledbury Hope End

Hope End, Ledbury, Hereford & Worcester, HR8 1SQ
☎ (01531) 633613 (01531) 636366
9 £120 24 £70
Dinner 7.30-8.30 mid Dec-early Feb

The unpretentious yet very civilised home of the Hegarty family, elegant simplicity in decor and food has been the key to their success in this lovely setting between the cities of Hereford, Gloucester and Worcester. Patricia Hegarty is a natural cook, who prepares short fixed-price menus with usually a choice of 3 dishes at each course and uses produce that is almost still growing when it hits the pot! Soups like carrot and coriander seed, chilled lettuce and pea or tomato and rosemary are perfectly made. Spinach and pine nut pancakes, lovage soufflé, globe artichoke with prawn mayonnaise or cucumber roulade with spiced pepper sauce show skilled use of vegetable based dishes. A couple of the main dishes feature meat or fish, perhaps halibut with white wine and sage sauce, roast chicken with walnut and parsley crust or breast of guinea fowl with damson relish. The third dish is always vegetarian and never boring; chestnut soufflé with mushroom sauce or perhaps aubergine with rice and cashew nuts with peperonata sauce. Her choice of puddings shows equal care, a Winter Nellis pear with cardamom ice cream and caramel sauce, loganberry and redcurrant trifle or simple rhubarb and custard. A wonderful place to get away from it all and really enjoy what the country is all about.

Leeds Brasserie Forty Four

44 The Calls, Leeds, West Yorkshire, LS2 7EW
☎ 0113-234 3232 📠 0113-234 3332
🪑 112 🍽 £70
☺ Lunch 12-2, Dinner 6.30-10.30 (Sat 6-11)
☹ Lunch Sat, all Sun, Bank Holidays

Michael Gill & Jonathan Wix's original restaurant in this revitalised city-centre development area. Jeff Baker cooks an up-to-the-minute range of international ingredients in fascinating combinations at excellent prices. Certain dishes are highlighted as a "great vegetarian choice". The decor, too, is modern and relaxed – this is definitely the way restaurants are going these days.

Leeds Bryan's Fish Restaurant

9 Weetwood Lane, Headingley, Leeds,
West Yorkshire, LS16 5LT
☎ 0113-278 5679
🪑 100 🍽 £30
☺ 11.30-11.30 (Thu & Fri from 9, Sun 12-10) ☹ 25 & 26 Dec

A legend in the lifetime of many a student, Bryan's is an institution in itself. The large fish-and-chip shop is handy for the cricket and rugby grounds, and its soft heart is shown by the special deal for students on Sundays, on production of a current union card. No-nonsense, well-prepared fish and chips is what you come here for, although there are one or two healthy options, in case anyone's interested!

**THE ACADEMY OF
FOOD & WINE SERVICE**
see page 22

England 189

Leeds 42 The Calls

42 The Calls, Leeds, West Yorkshire, LS2 7EW
☎ 0113-244 0099 📠 0113-234 4100
🛏 41 £140
☹ Xmas week

Pool Court at 42
42-44 The Calls, Leeds, West Yorkshire, LS2 8AQ
☎ 0113-244 4242 📠 0113-234 3332
🍽 38 £80
☺ Lunch 12-2, Dinner 6-10.30 ☹ Sun, Bank Holidays

A beautifully designed hotel housed within the shell of an old grain mill down by the riverside. Stylish bedrooms offer extensive facilities for the business person and a choice of dining at the affiliated Brasserie 44 next door or at the newer Pool Court at 42. Yes, the Pool Court from Pool-in-Wharfdale owned by Michael Gill is now well established within the hotel and similar high standards prevail. Choose from the gourmet, 7 course menu or 2 or 3 courses on a fixed-price deal which has dishes such as an asparagus feuillete with wild mushrooms on a pinot grigio cream sauce, a potage of oysters and leeks with Beluga caviar amongst starters. A sauté of veal kidneys and sweetbreads with a timbale of spinach and garlic and Pommery mustard sauce, fillet of sea bass cooked on salt with a mousse of scallops and ginger and chive butter sauce or marinaded loin of venison on deep-fried polenta with melted onions and truffle sauce are typical main dishes. Well chosen wines have variety in origins and price, house champagne is under £30. Certainly the most distinctive hotel and restaurant in Leeds.

Leeds Haley's Hotel

Shire Oak Road, Headingley, Leeds,
West Yorkshire, LS6 2DE
☎ 0113-278 4446 📠 0113-275 3342
🛏 22 £112 🍽 45 £60
☺ Lunch Sun only in summer 12.15-2, Dinner residents only 7.15-9.45
☹ Hotel 25-30 Dec

Useful hotel and restaurant just 2 miles north of the city centre, in an area renowned for cricket, rugby and students! The house is Victorian and has been carefully modernised. A change of chef for 1995 but the cooking style is still modern English.

Leeds Leodis Brasserie

Victoria Mill, Sovereign Street, Leeds,
West Yorkshire, LS1 4BJ
☎ 0113-242 1010 📠 0113-243 0432
🍽 160 £80
☺ Lunch 12-2, Dinner 6-10 (Fri & Sat to 11) ☹ Lunch Sat, all Sun

Modern setting in a converted Victorian mill, where you can enjoy modern international cooking at very reasonable prices, served with a smile. There's a carte as well as fixed-price menus; and puddings are a strong point.

Leeds Olive Tree

Oaklands, Rodley Lane, Leeds, West Yorkshire, LS13 1NG
☎ 0113-256 9283
🍴 150 🍽 £55
☺ Lunch 12-2, Dinner 6-11 ☹ Lunch Sat, 25 Dec, 1 Jan

One of a kind: the Psarias' Greek restaurant spins you into a whirl of Mediterranean sounds and flavours: bouzouki music, Metaxa and meze. It takes very little imagination to believe you're on your favourite island and not on the outskirts of a busy Yorkshire city.

Leeds Sous le Nez en Ville

Basement, Quebec House, Quebec Street, Leeds, West Yorkshire, LS1 2HA
☎ 0113-244 0108 📠 0113-245 0240
🍴 86 🍽 £55
☺ Lunch 12-2.30, Dinner 6-10.30
☹ Lunch Sat, all Sun, Bank Holidays

Winebar and restaurant in a basement location in the city-centre. Printed menus are supplemented by blackboard specials and the style is modern international, served in relaxed and friendly surroundings.

Leicester Welford Place

9 Welford Place, Leicester, Leicestershire, LE1 6ZH
☎ 0116-247 0758 📠 0116-247 1843
🍴 60 🍽 £55
☺ 8am-11pm

The Hope family's Leicester branch (see also the original Wig & Mitre in Lincoln) opened in 1991, offering nourishment and refreshment all day long to grateful customers. As manager Sarah Hope says, "We aim to put our hearts and minds into every plate and into every glass, mug and cup." They succeed.

Lew Farmhouse Hotel & Restaurant

University Farm, Lew, Oxfordshire, OX18 2AU
☎ (01993) 850297 📠 (01993) 850965
🛏 6 £ £50 🍴 80 🍽 £45
☺ Dinner 7-7.30 (Fri & Sat to 9) ☹ Sun, 23 Dec-2 Jan

The Rouse family run this lovely establishment in the midst of a genuine working (University) farm – they have farmed here since 1959. Homely bedrooms are comfortable and characterful – plenty of beams to avoid – and a similar atmosphere prevails in the non-smoking dining room, where dinner, priced according to the number of courses taken, is a highlight of the day. Sensible wine list.

England 191

Lewdown Lewtrenchard Manor

Lewtrenchard, Lewdown, Nr Okehampton, Devon, EX20 4PN
☎ (01566) 783256 (01566) 783332
8 £98 35 £75
☺ Lunch Sun only 12.15-1.45, Dinner 7.15-9.30

Built around 1600 on the site of a dwelling recorded in the Domesday Book, Lewtrenchard has the atmosphere of a family home within a country house setting. There are elements of elegance and grandeur – oak panelling, carved ceilings, open fireplaces – but most of all there's the friendly atmosphere created by the Murray family. In the non-smoking dining room, French/British menus (set dinners, set and à la carte lunches) are served, accompanied by an extensive wine list.

Lifton Arundell Arms

Lifton, Devon, PL16 0AA
☎ (01566) 784666 (01566) 784494
29 £93 70 £75
☺ Lunch 12.30-2, Dinner 7.30-9.30 ☹ 2 days Xmas

Famous fishing hotel in the capable hands of Anne Voss-Bark since 1961: an institution in its own right, and very much part of the Devon countryside. Continuous upgrading of bedrooms ensures that standards are maintained; and the attractions of the dining room rest in the modern British menu with classic French influences, offered on set-price menus. Suppliers are credited (a neat way of ensuring quality and loyalty); and bar meals are becoming increasingly popular.

Lincoln The Jew's House

15 The Strait, Lincoln, Lincolnshire, LN2 1JD
☎ (01522) 524851
28 £58
☺ Lunch 12-1.30, Dinner 6.45-9.15
☹ Lunch Mon, all Sun, Bank Holidays except Good Friday

In one of the oldest recorded dwelling places in England (and situated on a very steep hill), Richard & Sally Gibbs now run a restaurant with some flair. Cooking style is modern French/English, menus set and à la carte, service friendly and welcoming. Reasonably priced wine list.

Lincoln Wig & Mitre

29 Steep Hill, Lincoln, Lincolnshire, LN2 1LU
☎ (01522) 535190 (01522) 532402
80 £60
☺ 8am-11pm ☹ 25 Dec

The Hope family's original branch (see also Welford Place in Leicester), close to the cathedral and castle. The former pub has been restored to its 14th-century glory utilising many original features. Flexibility is the essence of the operation here – providing customers with what they want, when they want it, and always with a cheerful disposition. England needs more places like this!

Linton Wood Hall

Tripp Lane, Linton, Nr Wetherby, West Yorkshire, LS22 4JA
☎ (01937) 587271 (01937) 584353
 43 £98 70 £85
☺ Lunch 12.30-2.30, Dinner 7-10 ☹ Lunch Sat

Lovely Georgian mansion set in over 100 acres of parkland, with views of Wharfedale. Comfortable lounges lead up to individually furnished bedrooms, while the dining room nourishes you with an modern international menu. There are good leisure and business facilities, with an increasingly diverse range of activities available, from jousting to off-road driving.

Liskeard Well House

St Keyne, Liskeard, Cornwall, PL14 4RN
☎ (01579) 342001
 7 £105 32 £65
☺ Lunch 12.30-2, Dinner 7-9

Near the coastal towns of Looe, Polperro and Fowey the Well House is a super retreat from the bustle of tourists but perfectly located to see the sights! Nick Wainford is a good host and has decorated his friendly house tastefully with comfortable bedrooms and gracious day rooms. The cooking is in modern style. From several choices on the 4 course dinner menu you could start with a terrine of Provencal vegetables with olive and basil vinaigrette and try the the grilled turbot with creamed spinach and chive beurre blanc. Next comes a variety of West Country cheeses with walnut bread which leaves just enough room for a tangy lemon tart with cassis sorbet.

Little Walsingham
Old Bakehouse Restaurant

33 High Street, Little Walsingham, Norfolk, NR22 6BZ
☎ (01328) 820454
 3 £40 36 £60
☺ Lunch 1 Sun a month 12.30, Dinner 7-9.30 (earlier in winter)
☹ 2 or 3 days – seasonally, 2 wks Jan/Feb

This was indeed formerly the local bakery, but it now provides the setting for Chris & Helen Padley's friendly restaurant with rooms. Food is cooked to order and the menu changes constantly. Modestly-priced wine list accompanies the cooking.

England 193

Liverpool Jenny's Seafood Restaurant

The Old Ropery, off Fenwick Street, Liverpool, Merseyside, L2 7NT
☎ 0151-236 0332
🪑 40 🍽 £50
☺ Lunch 12-2.15, Dinner 7-10
☹ Lunch Sat, Dinner Mon, all Sun, 23 Dec-5 Jan, last 2 wks Aug

Plenty of fish and shellfish on offer at this popular restaurant opposite the new law courts. Fixed-price menus still have choice, but the full range is available on the carte. There are also some meat dishes for dedicated carnivores.

Long Melford Chimneys

Hall Street, Long Melford, Sudbury, Suffolk, CO10 9JR
☎ (01787) 379806 📠 (01787) 312294
🪑 50 🍽 £80
☺ Lunch 12-2, Dinner 7-9.30 ☹ Dinner Sun, 1 wk Xmas

This lovely, 16th-century timbered building is home to a fine, country restaurant run by Sam & Zena Chalmers. Set menus offer an alternative to the carte, but both comprise modern European cooking at reasonable prices.

Longhorsley
Linden Hall Hotel & Health Spa

Longhorsley, Nr Morpeth, Northumberland, NE65 8XF
☎ (01670) 516611 📠 (01670) 788544
🛏 50 £125 🪑 80 🍽 £65
☺ Lunch 12-2, Dinner 6.30-9.45

Large, Georgian mansion set in 450 acres with health spa and conference facilities.

**BRITAIN'S TOP
INDEPENDENT BUTCHERS**
see page 9

Longridge Paul Heathcote's Restaurant ✤

104-106 Higher Road, Longridge, Nr Preston,
Lancashire, PR3 3SY
☎ (01772) 784969 📠 (01772) 785713
🪑 55 🍽 £90
☺ Lunch 12-2 (Sun to 2.30) (open 6 days in Dec), Dinner 7-9.30
☹ Lunch Tue-Thu & Sat, all Mon

The recent opening of Heathcote's Brasserie in Preston does not seem to have distracted Paul from his main venture – the saucepan of enthusiasm has certainly not gone off the boil! He's a man with a mission, and that's to bring quality food to more people, and if that means doing so in an otherwise rather gastronomically deserted part of the country, so be it. Those within hopping distance of Longridge or Preston must have to pinch themselves to believe their luck that this gifted chef's creations are available to them, in a superb restaurant that began life as the Quarryman's Arms in 1808. The current opulent (but not overpowering) surroundings enjoyed by diners are a far cry from those humble beginnings. Now, from menus that are a mixture of fixed-price only (at lunch) or fixed-price and à la carte (at dinner), those diners partake of some very fine cooking. To start with the best, Paul's signature menu (evenings only, £55) comprises 10 small but perfectly formed courses which really show his range (in itself an expansion on last year's 7-course gourmet menu). In your imagination (sadly, all that these mere paper pages allow), eat your way with me through this meal: wild mushroom and asparagus broth with truffle; black pudding with crushed potatoes; salad of foie gras and spiced chicken livers; lobster roasted with dried citrus fruit and herbs; wing of skate with tartare of mussels and parsley; a sorbet; Goosnargh duckling with buttered potatoes, prunes and jasmine-scented juices; tart of tomato and Welsh goat's cheese; layered terrine of dark and white chocolate with honey ice cream; bread and butter pudding with apricot coulis and clotted cream; and finally, coffee and sweetmeats. Sit back and sigh: perfection!

Louth Ferns

40 Northgate, Louth, Lincolnshire, LN11 0LY
☎ (01507) 603209 📠 (01507) 610828
🪑 34 🍽 £45
☺ Lunch 10-2, Dinner 7-9.30 ☹ Lunch Sat, all Sun & Mon

Good quality produce is the key to success at Nick & Kim Thompson's friendly little restaurant. There are set-price menus from Tuesday to Friday, and the carte operates on Saturday evenings. Luscious puddings are home made.

Lower Beeding Cisswood House Hotel

Sandygate Lane, Lower Beeding, Nr Horsham,
West Sussex, RH13 6NF
☎ (01403) 891216   (01403) 891621
32   £92   60   £55
Lunch 12-2.15, Dinner 7-9.15
all Sun, Bank Holidays, Xmas/New Year

Owned and run by Othmar & Elizabeth Illes, Cisswood was originally known as "Harrods in the country", as it was built in 1928 for the then Chairman and his wife, Sir Woodman and Lady Cissily Burbidge – hence also the current name. Othmar's Austrian origins are occasionally evident on the international menus.

Lower Beeding South Lodge

Brighton Road, Lower Beeding, West Sussex, RH13 6PS
☎ (01403) 891711   (01403) 891766
39   £154   40   £70
Lunch 12.30-2 (Sun to 2.30), Dinner 7.30-10 (Sat to 10.30)

Lovely Victorian house in the Sussex countryside, with its own carefully-maintained gardens and grounds – it was originally the home of botanist Frederick Ducane Godman. Plenty of outdoor leisure facilities, gracious yet comfortable bedrooms and lounges, and rather grand set dinner menus are appropriate for the formal, south-facing dining room.

Lower Slaughter
Lower Slaughter Manor

Lower Slaughter, Nr Bourton-on-the-Water,
Gloucestershire, GL54 2HP
☎ (01451) 820456   (01451) 822150
14   £190   26   £80
Lunch 12-2 (Sun 12.30-2.30), Dinner 7-9.30 (Fri & Sat to 10)
2 wks Jan

Recently purchased by the owners of Buckland Manor (qv), this is another delightfully relaxing Cotswold house where you can enjoy the English countryside at its best, excellent housekeeping, fine wines and fine food, too. Modern international cooking is the order of the day, but with some pretty unusual twists: try spring vegetable risotto flavoured with saffron, deep-fried garlic chips and parmesan; or terrine of duck foie gras with provençal vegetables and toasted honey bread. Follow perhaps with braised brill served with crab ravioli, deep-fried ginger and a lemon grass-flavoured sauce; or ragout of rabbit cooked in a truffle fumet with tarragon, dijon mustard and braised celery. Superb puddings might include a sorbet of mascarpone with chocolate-covered biscuits and banana cooked in rum, and a trio of apple desserts; but the cheeseboard is just as worthy of serious attention. No fewer than 8 well-kept cheeses are offered at any one time, categorised on a list according to milk source (cow's, ewe's, goat's) then as hard or soft. A strong wine list stands up well to the food and the surroundings.

Ludlow Feathers Hotel

Bull Ring, Ludlow, Shropshire, SY8 1AA
☎ (01584) 875261   (01584) 876030
 39 £98 60 £55
☺ Lunch 12-2, Dinner 7-9

Much-photographed and stunning frontage to this hotel in the centre of historic Ludlow. Plenty of business facilities, comfortable bedrooms, and the Housman Restaurant with its conservatory extension.

Ludlow The Merchant House

Lower Corve Street, Ludlow, Shropshire, SY8 1DU
☎ (01584) 875438
 20 £70
☺ Lunch 12.30-2, Dinner 7-10
☹ Lunch Tue-Thu, all Sun & Mon, 3 days Xmas

Anja & Shaun Hill's move up north from Devon to Shropshire has proved an instant success. Where once he cooked grandly to an expectant audience in an imposing country house, he now wows smaller crowds with a more down-to-earth approach and a fixed-price menu of market-fresh ingredients. His style is bold, yet light, his hand steady with judicious use of herbs and spices. Look out for dishes such as steamed bass with chinese spices, or open ravioli with chicken livers, lemon and garlic to start, followed by rack of lamb and sweetbreads with potato and olive cake or bourride of chicken (braised with red peppers and stock then thickened with garlic mayonnaise). For pudding you might try raspberry crème brûlée or caramel and apple tart with vanilla ice cream. Affordable wines, spot-on service – this is, indeed, a true restaurant for the people.

Lymington Gordleton Mill

Silver Street, Hordle, Nr Lymington, Hampshire, SO41 6DJ
☎ (01590) 682219   (01590) 683073
 7 £92 45 £105
☺ Lunch 12-2.30, Dinner 7-9.30 ☹ 2 wks Jan

Lovely, small hotel and French restaurant, just off the A337 Brockenhurst/Lymington road. Exquisite gardens (stretching for 5 acres and touching on to the River Avon) and a pretty interior; though the raison d'etre must be Le Provence restaurant. Currently under the auspices of former sous chef Toby Hill, the standards and style are maintained seamlessly.

Lymington Stanwell House Hotel

High Street, Lymington, Hampshire, SO41 9AA
☎ (01590) 677123   (01590) 677756
 35 £85 60 £45
☺ Lunch 12.30-2, Dinner 7-9.30

Stanwell dates back to the 18th Century and has been sympathetically extended over the years. Each bedroom is named after one of the great Bordeaux chateaux – so it will come as no surprise that the hotel is proud of its wine list. Accompanying menus are classic in origin but presented with a modern slant. Part of the Clipper group.

Lympstone River House

The Strand, Lympstone, Devon, EX8 5EY
☎ (01395) 265147
[] 4 [£] £87 🛏 34 🍽 £80
☺ Lunch 12-1.30, Dinner 7-9.30 (Sat to 10.30)
☹ Dinner Sun, all Mon, Bank Holidays, 26 & 27 Dec, 1 & 2 Jan

Art seminars are very popular at the River House, and the results – by both tutors and students – adorn the walls. Other activities on offer include cookery classes and gourmet events. A loyal local following return for the Wilkes' hospitality, based on anglo/continental cooking of good-quality ingredients. The New World is strongly represented on the wine list.

Lyndhurst Parkhill Hotel

Beaulieu Road, Lyndhurst, Hampshire, SO43 7FZ
☎ (01703) 282944 📠 (01703) 283268
[] 20 [£] £106 🛏 80 🍽 £70
☺ Lunch 12-2, Dinner 7-9

Rooms are tastefully furnished with a mix of antique and modern at this lovely, country house set amid the spectacular scenery of the New Forest. In the dining room you will find fixed-price lunch and dinner menus with plenty of variety. There's also a light lunch menu, if you are in a hurry to explore more of the local beauty spots!

Maidenhead Fredrick's

Shoppenhangers Road, Maidenhead, Berkshire, SL6 2PZ
☎ (01628) 35934 📠 (01628) 771054
[] 37 [£] £168 🛏 60 🍽 £100
☺ Lunch 12-2, Dinner 7-9.45 ☹ Lunch Sat, 24-30 Dec

Fredrick Losel has been here 20 years now, just off Junction 8/9 of the M4 and therefore handily situated for Heathrow. The red-brick building is well maintained, and ongoing refurbishment inside keeps standards high. A classic French/English menu is offered in the traditional dining room.

Maiden Newton Le Petit Canard

Dorchester Road, Maiden Newton, Dorset, DT2 0BE
☎ (01300) 320536
🛏 28 🍽 £55
☺ Dinner 7-9 ☹ Sun & Mon

Popular local restaurant in the centre of a pretty Dorset village some 9 miles north-west of Dorchester. Geoff & Lin Chapman are constantly refining their product, making improvements, learning yet more as they go; so there's a feeling of vibrancy about their establishment in general and the food in particular: international in style, but with strong Pacific Rim influences.

Malvern The Cottage in the Wood

Holywell Road, Malvern Wells,
Hereford & Worcester, WR14 4LG
☎ (01684) 575859 📠 (01684) 560662
🛏 20 £ £89 🍴 50 🍽 £65
🙂 Lunch 12.30-2, Dinner 7-9 (Sun-Thu to 8.30 in winter)

The hills inspired Elgar, the location inspired the Pattin family to offer their own brand of hospitality in this lovely setting. Well-maintained rooms provide every modern comfort while the sense of history is not disturbed; while in the restaurant an essentiall modern English menu is offered, set-priced at lunchtime but à la carte only in the evenings. Huge range of New World wines on the list.

Malvern Croque-en-Bouche

221 Wells Road, Malvern Wells,
Hereford & Worcester, WR14 4HF
☎ (01684) 565612
🍴 22 🍽 £90

🙂 Dinner 7.30-9 ☹ Sun-Tue (& Wed Oct-May), Xmas/New Year

How do they do it? Robin & Marion Jones make a living from their little restaurant being open only 4 nights a week in summer, 3 in winter. The answer must be: because they do so much themselves, and because they are passionate about what they do. When the restaurant isn't open there's the garden to tend – it produces all the herbs, salads, and most of the fruit and vegetables used in the kitchen. Then there's the wine retailing – Robin's pride and joy. (The restaurant's full wine list is so vast that it's actually been published, and copies are available for around £2!) But back to the food, and some changes this year. The midweek menu has been scaled to offer 5 courses for only £25 (a snip!), or 4 for £23, or even just 3 for £21. Rest assured that there is no lowering of standards of service or quality of ingredients: it is merely a bending to accommodate trends of smaller appetites; and also to encourage the belief that this need not be a "special occasions only" venue – though being there is certainly a celebration of food. There are usually 3 options at the principal courses, so that you can enjoy a meal comprising soup of butter bean, leek and celeriac flavoured with confit of duck; then a Japanese selection of salmon pickled with Sichuan peppercorns and ginger, tiger prawns with soba noodles, squid rolls with shiso leaves, asparagus and sweetcorn, all served with a traditional egg dressing; for the main course perhaps small steaks of home-smoked beef fillet, grilled and served with a Madeira sauce flavoured with porcini, the whole served with a mushroom, brown rice and marjoram pilaf. British cheeses (the famous Stinking Bishop is a local favourite), exquisite desserts, coffee, and wines selected to bring out the best in the food and in the wines themselves.

Manchester Market Restaurant

104 High Street, Manchester, Greater Manchester, M4 1HQ
☎ 0161-834 3743
🪑 42 🍽 £55

🙂 Dinner 6-9.30 (Sat from 7)

☹ Dinner Sun-Tue, 1 wk Xmas, 1 wk Easter, Aug

Home of a Pudding Club, and then a Starters Society, and already a bastion of interesting cooking: this is the O'Gradys' Market Restaurant! Recipe cards are available for some of the dishes on the international menu. I bet there are not too many restaurants which serve chocolate-covered Polish plums with coffee – they dare to be different here.

Manchester Victoria & Albert Hotel

Water Street, Manchester, Greater Manchester, M60 9EA
☎ 0161-832 1188 📠 0161-834 2484
🛏 132 £ £148 🪑 70 🍽 £75

🙂 Lunch 12-2 Weekdays, Dinner 7-10 (Café Maigret 7am-10.30pm daily)

☹ Lunch Sat, all Sun

Opposite Granada Television studios, this themed hotel offers the opportunity to absorb the atmosphere of television, with bedrooms (there's a new wing under construction) named after programmes. Then there's is the Sherlock Holmes restaurant and Café Maigret to choose between, the first offering British cooking with Oriental influences, the latter international.

Manchester Airport Moss Nook

Ringway Road, Moss Nook, Manchester, Greater Manchester, M22 5WD
☎ 0161-437 4778 📠 0161-498 8089
🛏 1 £ £140 🪑 65 🍽 £80

🙂 Lunch 12-1.30, Dinner 7-9.30

☹ Lunch Sat, all Sun & Mon, Bank Holidays, 2 wks Xmas

Useful restaurant with cottage accommodation adjoining, handy for but not in any way restricted to airport traffic. Seasonally changing menus are French in style, and game in season is very popular. Choose from the carte, or put yourself in the hands of chef Kevin Lofthouse with the 7-course tasting menu (whole tables only).

Manningtree Stour Bay Café

39-43 High Street, Manningtree, Nr Colchester,
Essex, CO11 1AH
☎ (01206) 396687 📠 (01206) 395462
🪑 70 🍽 £50
☺ Lunch 12-2.30, Dinner 7-9.30
☹ Lunch Tue-Fri, Dinner Sun, all Mon, Bank Holidays, 2 wks Jan,
   2 wks Sep

Sherri Singleton's menus offer some unusual treatment of basic ingredients, with plenty of Pacific Rim influences in evidence. The wine list is similarly imaginative, with some lesser-known bottles mainly from the New World.

Marlow Compleat Angler Hotel

Marlow Bridge, Marlow, Buckinghamshire, SL7 1RG
☎ (01628) 484444 📠 (01628) 486388
🛏 62 £ £169 🪑 96 🍽 £125
☺ Lunch 12.30-2.30, Dinner 7-10

A beautifully furnished and well-managed hotel overlooking the weir. After a glass of champagne on the river terrace, you can enjoy classic-style cooking with some modern interpretations in the Valaisan Restaurant. If you want to spoil yourself, or indeed someone else, there are few lovelier places on the river in which to do so!

Mary Tavy The Stannary

Mary Tavy, Nr Tavistock, Devon, PL19 9QB
☎ (01822) 810897 📠 (01822) 810898
🛏 3 £ £60 🪑 20 🍽 £75
☺ Dinner 7-9.30 ☹ Dinner Sun & Mon, Sun-Wed Jan-Easter

One of Britain's best vegetarian restaurants, also with letting bedrooms. Michael Cook & Alison Fife pay as much attention to detail as you would expect in any serious omnivore's restaurant, if not more. Set menus include home-made canapés, breads and petits fours; produce is free-range and/or organic as appropriate, salt and sugar are used sparingly or not at all, garlic and alcohol are always specified if they are used. Gluten-free and dairy-free diets can be accommodated with ease. All in all, a very special place.

Matlock Riber Hall

Matlock, Derbyshire, DE4 5JU
☎ (01629) 582795   📠 (01629) 580475
🛏 11   £98   🪑 50   🍽 £66
☺ Lunch 12-1.30, Dinner 7-9.30

Revamping the lounge and dining areas of Riber Hall has increased capacity, while the style of the lovely Hall has been sympathetically maintained. (It lay derelict until 1970 when it was rescued and transformed to present usage, and Alex Biggin put it firmly on the map.) English and French style combine well on the menus, and game in season is a speciality. There's a complete, separate, menu for vegetarians.

Mawnan Smith Meudon Hotel

Mawnan Smith, Nr Falmouth, Cornwall, TR11 5HT
☎ (01326) 250541   📠 (01326) 250543
🛏 30   £170   🪑 65   🍽 £65
☺ Lunch 12.30-2, Dinner 7.30-9   ☹ Dec-Jan

Friendly little hotel, located about 3 miles off the A39 Truro-Falmouth road, from the Hillhead roundabout. Sub-tropical hanging gardens lead down to the hotel's private beach. Indoors, standards of comfort are high and guests are well looked after.

Mawnan Smith Nansidwell

Mawnan, Nr Falmouth, Cornwall, TR11 5HU
☎ (01326) 250340   📠 (01326) 250440
🛏 12   £123   🪑 45   🍽 £66
☺ Lunch 12.30-1.30, Dinner 7-9   ☹ Jan

Nansidwell enjoys a splendid setting on National Trust land between the Helford River and the sea: from the air it appears totally surrounded by green fields. Close up, it's actually totally surrounded by lovely gardens which, because of the mild climate, seem to bloom all year round. Want to pick a banana in October? You can here! Individually decorated rooms are comfortable and well equipped; menus take advantage of local fish and dishes are carefully cooked.

Medmenham Danesfield House

Medmenham, Marlow, Buckinghamshire, SL7 3ES
☎ (01628) 891010   📠 (01628) 890408
🛏 88   £145   🪑 50   🍽 £100
☺ Lunch 12-1.45, Dinner 7-9.45

New owners since 1995 have brought a return to the creature comforts that a house of this stature demands: the tapestry-hung Great Hall makes an impressive conference venue; bedrooms are well-maintained and well-equipped. International menus.

Melbourn Pink Geranium

Station Road, Melbourn, Nr Royston,
Hertfordshire, SG8 6DX
☎ (01763) 260215 📠 (01763) 262110
🪑 65 🍽 £105
☺ Lunch 12-2.30, Dinner 7-10.30
☹ Dinner Sun, all Mon, 26 & 27 Dec

Pink it certainly is, from decor to menus, from upholstery to geraniums! The Saunders' pretty thatched cottage has plenty of beams and an attractive conservatory as part of the dining room. Paul Murfitt has now joined Steven Saunders as head chef and a winter menu featured some imaginative dishes such as warm marbled terrine of livers and foie gras with chargrilled brioche and marinated wild mushrooms, Provence gateau of crab with Thai ginger beurre blanc, breast of Barbary duck with its own confit and caramelised figs and armagnac jus and fillet of Scotch beef with forest mushrooms, black truffles and cepe scented jus. It's worth having a pudding as an excuse to order one of the excellent range of sweet wines that are offered, though the '85 Yquem merits a special occasion!

Melksham Toxique

187 Woodrow Road, Melksham, Wiltshire, SN12 7AY
☎ (01225) 702129
🛏 4 £ £84 🪑 30 🍽 £75
☺ Lunch 12.30-2, Dinner 7.30-10
☹ Lunch Wed-Sat, 2 wks Jan, 2 wks Aug/Sep

Helen Bartlett & Peter Jewkes run their friendly little restaurant with rooms with charm and aplomb, she from the kitchen, he more visibly. There's a themed evening at least once a month, which helps sustain local interest as well as draw those from further afield. Normally, the cooking is modern international, priced according to the number of courses taken. Decor in the rooms is highly individual and most attractive: this is definitely a pair with flair!

Melmerby Village Bakery

Melmerby, Penrith, Cumbria, CA10 1HE
☎ (01768) 881515 📠 (01768) 881848
🪑 45 🍽 £30
☺ 8.30-5 (Sun & Bank Holidays from 9.30, Jan & Feb to 2.30)

Andrew Whitley's superb restaurant and craft gallery has dealt with success very well indeed. From being just a secret destination well-kept by Lake District visitors, you can now find his products on the shelves of any decent food shop or deli right down south. Despite the expansion the philosophy remains true: organic ingredients baked in wood-fired brick ovens; or culled from the 5-acre organic smallholding and carefully cooked, home-style, into delicious light meals and snacks.

England 203

Melton Mowbray Olde Stocks Restaurant

Grimston, Nr Melton Mowbray, Leicestershire, LE14 3BZ
☎ (01664) 812255 📠 (01664) 813888
🪑 35 🍽 £60

☺ Dinner 7-9.30 ☹ Dinner Sun & Mon

Opened in 1962 as a private dining club, the restaurant now enjoys a strong local following, having dropped club status. The Harrison family organise themed evenings and special events for regular customers. Menus change as frequently as the weather and are thus written on boards, but there's always an interesting range of dishes using good produce. On Fridays, there's a special menu at £20 for 3 courses including canapés, coffee and petits fours.

Middle Wallop Fifehead Manor

Middle Wallop, Nr Stockbridge, Hampshire, SO20 8EG
☎ (01264) 781565 📠 (01264) 781400
🛏 16 £ £90 🪑 40 🍽 £65

☺ Lunch 12-2, Dinner 7.30-9.30, (tea 3-6) ☹ Xmas/New Year

The foundations at Fifehead date back to the 11th Century; and though the present building includes some quite modern, more spacious bedrooms, those in the older part of the house are smaller and more quirky. The dining room was probably the main hall in medieval times.

Midhurst Angel Hotel

North Street, Midhurst, West Sussex, GU29 9DN
☎ (01730) 812421 📠 (01730) 815928
🛏 21 £ £80 🪑 80 🍽 £60

☺ Lunch 12-2.30, Dinner 6.30-10 (Brasserie: 9-6)

16th-century former coaching inn which has been sympathetically restored to combine town-centre facilities within a country house ambience. Menus in the Cowdray Room are a mixture of English and French, modern and traditional, and the balancing act is very cleverly achieved by Peter Crawford-Rolt.

Midhurst Maxine's

Elizabeth House, Red Lion Street, Midhurst,
West Sussex, GU29 9PB
☎ (01730) 816271
🪑 26 🍽 £45

☺ Lunch 12-2, Dinner 7-11 ☹ Dinner Sun, all Mon & Tue, 2 wks Jan

A striking timbered building in this old market town on the River Rother: curfew is still rung at 8pm but you don't have to observe it – you might already be installed at the de Jagers' restaurant enjoying Robert's cooking and Marti's care at front-of-house. A good, neighbourhood restaurant.

Milford-on-Sea Rocher's

69-71 High Street, Milford-on-Sea, Hampshire, SO41 0QG
☎ (01590) 642340
🪑 30 🍽 £65

☺ Lunch 12.30-1.45, Dinner 7.15-9.45
☹ Lunch Mon-Sat, Dinner Sun-Tue, 2 wks Jun

Alain & Rebecca Rocher's charming little French restaurant offers a traditional menu priced for the number of courses taken. Alain grows his own herbs; Rebecca runs front-of-house. This is a fine example of good team work.

Minster Lovell Lovells at Windrush Farm

Minster Lovell, Oxfordshire, OX8 5RN
☎ (01993) 779802 📠 (01993) 779802
🛏 2 £ £95 🪑 18 🍽 £85

☺ Lunch 12.30-2 by arrangement, Dinner 7.45-9
☹ Dinner Sun & Mon, Jan

Famous Oxfordshire names combined here – the Lovell family, the River Windrush – in a small restaurant with rooms (fishing can be arranged). Marcus Ashenford produces French/English menus from fresh, local produce. Carefully structured no-choice set dinner menus with accompanying wines make for a leisurely and interesting evening.

Monkton Combe Combe Grove Manor

Brassknocker Hill, Monkton Combe, Nr Bath,
Avon, BA2 7HS
☎ (01225) 834644 📠 (01225) 834961
🛏 40 £ £175 🪑 50 🍽 £70

☺ Lunch 12.30-2, Dinner 7-9.30, (Manor Vaults: 10-11pm)

Good leisure/beauty/relaxing facilities are an additional attraction here – as if the lovely house in a pretty location offering carefully cooked food accompanied by fine wines were not enough in the first place! A new driveway has been carefully built, sympathetically created re-using local materials and preserving a wooded area as a wildlife sanctuary. This is typical of the attention to detail in all matters at Combe Grove.

Montacute Milk House

The Borough, Montacute, Nr Yeovil, Somerset, TA15 6XB
☎ (01935) 823823
🛏 2 £ £48 🪑 34 🍽 £65

☺ Lunch by arrangement, Dinner 7.30-9
☹ Sun, Mon & Tue, 2 wks Xmas, New Year

Attractive, 15th-century stone-built house, nowadays comprising a tiny restaurant and a couple of cosy bedrooms. Organic produce is used in the kitchen when possible, some from the Duttons' own garden. Well-chosen wine list has some useful tasting notes.

England 205

Moreton-in-Marsh Annie's

3 Oxford Street, Moreton-in-Marsh,
Gloucestershire, GL56 0LA
☎ (01608) 651981
🍴 30 🍽 £60
☺ Lunch Sun only 12-2, Dinner 7-10
☹ Dinner Sun, last wk Jan, 1st wk Feb

Anne & David Ellis continue their successful formula here, running a small, friendly, unpretentious and relaxing restaurant in the centre of town. David cooks (to order) in a mixture of English and French country styles, using local produce whenever possible and adapting with the seasons. He offers both set menus and a carte. House wine is very reasonably priced.

Moreton-in-Marsh Marsh Goose

High Street, Moreton-in-Marsh, Gloucestershire, GL56 0AX
☎ (01608) 652111
🍴 60 🍽 £65
☺ Lunch 12.15-2.30, Dinner 7.30-9.45
☹ Dinner Sun, all Mon, 26 Dec, 1 Jan

Low-key profile here: Sonia Kidney prefers to let her food speak for her, rather than seeking celebrity status. However, the word is getting around that there's something special at the Marsh Goose. The modern British menu sounds familiar, but the execution of the dish on the plate has a certain something. Go try it!

Morston Morston Hall

Morston, Holt, Norfolk, NR25 7AA
☎ (01263) 741041 📠 (01263) 740419
🛏 6 £140 🍴 40 🍽 £55
☺ Lunch Sun only 12.30 for 1, Dinner 7.30 for 8 ☹ Jan & Feb

The Hall dates back to the 17th Century but the young team of owners have 20th-century ideas when it comes to food, while respecting the history of the place and the beauty of the location – the Norfolk coast. Menus are accompanied by recommended wines each month. Special events like Bonfire Night are celebrated, and there are also cookery demonstrations.

Mottram St Andrew De Vere Mottram Hall

Mottram St Andrew, Prestbury, Cheshire, SK10 4QT
☎ (01625) 828135 📠 (01625) 829284
🛏 133 £140 🍴 160 🍽 £60
☺ Lunch 12.30-1.45, Dinner 7.30-9.45 (Sat 7-10)
☹ Lunch Sat

Situated on the A538 between Prestbury and Wilmslow, this gracious red-brick hotel is set in 270 acres of parkland, complete with lake. Lots of healthy outdoor pursuits are thus available, and there is also an indoor leisure complex complete with a palm-fringed pool.

Moulsford-on-Thames
Beetle & Wedge

Moulsford-on-Thames, Oxfordshire, OX10 9JF
☎ (01491) 651381 (01491) 651376
 10 £95

The Dining Room:
 30 £100
☺ Lunch 12.30-2, Dinner 7.30-10 ☹ Dinner Sun, all Mon, 25 Dec

The Boathouse:
 60 £70
☺ Lunch 12.30-2, Dinner 7.30-10 ☹ 25 Dec

A lovely riverside setting for a comfortable small hotel with a great pair of restaurants. Richard & Kate Smith are good hosts who make guests feel relaxed and welcome – for instance, there's no last order time for breakfast – they will accommodate a lie-in if that's what you need. (That said, it's also an ideal venue for small business conferences.) The heart of the welcome, though, lies in Richard's excellent cooking of good-quality raw ingredients, served up in a variety of styles. The Dining Room is a more elegant setting, the food more sophisticated; the Boathouse is more casual (exposed brickwork, rowing memorabilia) in its decor and in its menu structure, which is à la carte at lunch and dinner, while the Dining Room offers, in addition to the carte, set-price meals at lunch times, ranging from £17.50 for 2 courses and coffee in the week (£21.50 for 3) to £27.50 for 3 courses and coffee on Sundays. However, a common thread is the directness of Richard's approach to his ingredients, turning them into dishes which succeed in being robust yet delicate at the same time. In the Boathouse, try supreme of chicken with wild mushrooms and tarragon sauce; in the Dining Room supreme of Aylesbury duck with apples and cassis; in the Boathouse, sautéed spicy squid with beansprouts, tomato and spring onions; in the Dining Room steamed escalope of turbot with fresh brown shrimps, mussels and caviar or a simple, grilled steak. The distinction is less obvious when it comes to puds: beignets soufflées with warm lemon curd could appear on either menu, and there's always a good range of interesting and unusual cheeses. All in all, a great setting for great food.

Moulton Black Bull

Moulton, Nr Richmond, North Yorkshire, DL10 6QJ
☎ (01325) 377289 (01325) 377422
 100 £55
☺ Lunch 12-2, Dinner 6.45-10.15 ☹ all Sun, 23-27 Dec

Unusual setting in a pub-and-railway carriage for some well-cooked food: good quality ingredients, clever combinations, great sauces and a special fondness for seafood. Fairly-priced wine list.

Nantwich Churche's Mansion

Hospital Street, Nantwich, Cheshire, CW5 0RY
☎ (01270) 625933 📠 (01270) 74256
🪑 50 🍽 £70

☺ Lunch 12-2.30, Dinner 7-9.30   ☹ Dinner Sun, all Mon, 2nd wk Jan

Amanda Latham's popular and friendly restaurant offers a range of set-price lunch and dinner menus (which change monthly) in the non-smoking dining rooms, prepared from fresh local ingredients whenever possible. Morning coffee and afternoon tea are additionally available – book for the latter on Sundays. The lovely timbered building is full of charm, and they grow their own herbs in the garden.

Nantwich Rookery Hall

Worleston, Nr Nantwich, Cheshire, CW5 6DQ
☎ (01270) 610016 📠 (01270) 626027
🛏 45 £150 🪑 30 🍽 £85

☺ Lunch 12-2, Dinner 7-9.45

A member now of the Select group, Rookery Hall was built in the latter part of the 18th Century for a wealthy landowner. It is thus spacious and gracious, set in its own well-maintained 200 acres including a lake. Excellent business facilities include a heli-pad. Plenty of outdoor sporting pursuits are on offer, and Rookery is a much-sought-after venue for receptions. Modern European cooking is accompanied by a wine list of some stature.

Nether Langwith Goff's Restaurant

Langwith Mill House, Nether Langwith, Mansfield, Nottinghamshire, NG20 9JF
☎ (01623) 744538
🛏 2 £50 🪑 45 🍽 £65

☺ Lunch 12-1.30, Dinner 7-9.30

☹ Lunch Sat, Dinner Sun, all Mon, Bank Holiday Mon & Tue, 25-31 Dec

Graham & Lynne Goff have built their reputation on modern European food, prepared using as much fresh, local produce as possible, served up in a friendly environment. Retiring to one of the comfortably furnished bedrooms seems the most natural thing in the world. There's also a shorter bistro menu available (though in similar style), showing their versatility in our changing world.

New Alresford Hunters

32 Broad Street, New Alresford, Hampshire, SO24 9AQ
☎ (01962) 732468
🛏 3 £48 🪑 30 🍽 £55

☺ Lunch 12-2, Dinner 7-10   ☹ Dinner Sun, 1 wk Xmas

David & Martin Birmingham run Hunters as a friendly local restaurant with rooms offering a wide range of dishes in English/French style; and they have recently opened a branch in Winchester, too. Lunch menus change weekly, the table d'hote nightly, and the carte seasonally. Service is friendly yet professional.

New Barnet Mims Restaurant

63 East Barnet Road, New Barnet, Hertfordshire, EN4 8RN
☎ 0181-449 2974   📠 0181-447 1825
🪑 45 🍽 £75

☺ Lunch 12-2.30, Dinner 6.30-11, (Sun 12-10.30)
☹ Lunch Sat, all Mon, 1 wk Xmas, 2 wks Aug

Friendly, local restaurant in the northern suburbs of London, offering Mediterranean cooking in pleasant surroundings. Priced by the number of courses taken, the menus offer very good value for money. The wine list has aspirations beyond what you would expect in this setting.

New Milton Chewton Glen

Christchurch Road, New Milton, Hampshire, BH25 6QS
☎ (01425) 275341   📠 (01425) 272310
🛏 57 £ £214 🪑 120 🍽 £100

☺ Lunch 12.30-1.45 (Sun to 2.30), Dinner 7.30-9.30

More superlatives for this edge-of-the-New Forest gem. As a hotel and restaurant, health and country club it's second to none, and this is due to the dedication of Martin & Brigitte Skan, who set very high standards and are rewarded by grateful guests. The sport, health and beauty facilities are very comprehensive, and are geared equally to men and women. The house itself enjoys a beautiful setting in exquisite gardens, as well maintained as the rooms indoors which are, additionally, gracious and elegant. It's one of those places that manages to impress without overwhelming, a compliment also to the style of service. The food prepared by Pierre Chevillard for the non-smoking Marryat Room Restaurant does justice to the surroundings (as indeed does the vast cellar), being predominantly French with English influences, and presented on fixed-price and à la carte menus. Great care goes into the selection of ingredients, and just as much into the cooking and presentation, resulting in starters like escalope of hot foie gras served on a savoury wafer-thin apple tart, or filo gateau filled with layers of potato and raclette cheese. Main courses range from braised Hampshire hog served on a bed of crushed potatoes with a garlic and parsley butter, to crostinis of red mullet with a beurre blanc sauce, garnished with rocket salad. Irresistible desserts could include a chocolate tear filled with a passion fruit mousse served with a coconut sorbet, or Bramley apple pie served with home-made blackberry ice cream. This is an ideal place in which to relax, get fit and be very well nourished.

Newcastle-upon-Tyne
Blackgate Restaurant

Milburn House, The Side, Quayside, Newcastle-upon-Tyne, Tyne & Wear, NE1 3JE
☎ 0191-261 7356
🪑 43 🍽 £70

☺ Lunch 12.30-2, Dinner 6.30-10
☹ Lunch Sat, Dinner Mon, all Sun, Bank Holidays, 24-29 Dec

Chef/partner Douglas Jordan is the power behind the scenes at this smart, airy restaurant decorated in pastel shades, situated behind St Nicholas' Cathedral near the revived quayside. Quality British and (specifically) north-east regional produce is used to good effect and presented in modern style.

North Harrow Percy's Restaurant

66-68 Station Road, North Harrow, Middlesex, HA2 7SJ
☎ 0181-427 2021 📠 0181-427 8134
🍴 70 🍽 £70
🙂 Lunch 12-2.30, Dinner 6.30-10.30 🙁 all Sun & Mon, 1 wk Xmas

The Bricknell-Webbs have been here since 1988 ("here" is just opposite the underground station), and modern British is the style of their food. Seafood and game are specialities (in season). A concise wine list is an appropriate partner to the cooking.

Northallerton Bettys

188 High Street, Northallerton, North Yorkshire, DL7 8LF
☎ (01609) 775154 📠 (01609) 777552
🍴 58 🍽 £30
🙂 9-5.30 (Sun from 10) 🙁 25 & 26 Dec, 1 Jan

A Georgian home for this branch of Bettys, with all the familiar favourites in a High Street setting.

Northleach Old Woolhouse 🍀

Market Place, Northleach, Gloucestershire, GL54 3EE
☎ (01451) 860366
🍴 18 🍽 £90
🙂 Dinner only 8-9.30 🙁 Sun & Mon, 1 wk Xmas

A Cotswold stone, beamed cottage, a chef-patron from Lyon and 20 years dedication make this restaurant unique. It seats just 18 people, so you don't breeze in without a reservation, the menu is described by Jacques Astic's wife Jenny who also cooks some of the puddings. Classic French cuisine comes from Jacques' kitchen, generous portions and rich, intense sauces, many with cream. Always a delight to visit this charming restaurant that is consistently good.

Northleach Wickens

Market Place, Northleach, Gloucestershire, GL54 3EJ
☎ (01451) 860421
🍴 38 🍽 £55
🙂 Lunch 12.30-1.30, Dinner 7.20-8.45
🙁 all Sun & Mon, Lunch Nov-Apr

Christopher & Joanna Wickens' friendly local restaurant is a real find in the centre of Northleach. They offer modern English cooking on carefully constructed menus, priced according to the number of courses taken. Light lunches, a fairly recent innovation, have proved popular. The wine list has some very useful tasting notes.

England 209

Newcastle-upon-Tyne Courtney's

5-7 The Side, Quayside, Newcastle-upon-Tyne,
Tyne & Wear, NE1 3JE

☎ 0191-232 5537

🍴 28 🍽 £55

☺ Lunch 12-2, Dinner 7-10.30

☹ Lunch Sat, all Sun, Bank Holidays, 2 wks May, 1 wk Xmas

Michael & Kerensa Carr opened Courtney's in 1990 and have built up a loyal local following in this very down-to-earth city. Modern international cooking goes down well as the quality is very high, as is the value-for-money factor. The set menu is expanded by the carte; and on the short wine list, nearly everything is below £20 a bottle.

Newcastle-upon-Tyne
Fisherman's Lodge

7 Jesmond Dene, Jesmond, Newcastle-upon-Tyne,
Tyne & Wear, NE7 7BQ

☎ 0191-281 3281 📠 0191-281 6410

🍴 60 🍽 £85

☺ Lunch 12-2, Dinner 7-11 ☹ Lunch Sat, all Sun, Bank Holidays

Long-established (since 1979) seafood restaurant in the residential Jesmond district of Newcastle. In addition to fish, great store is set by the range of English farmhouse cheeses, which are local when possible. There is also a complete menu for vegetarians. The wine list has recently benefitted from an expanded range of half-bottles.

Newcastle-upon-Tyne
21 Queen Street

21 Queen Street, Princes Wharf, Quayside,
Newcastle-upon-Tyne, Tyne & Wear, NE1 3UG

☎ 0191-222 0755 📠 0191-230 5875

🍴 50 🍽 £95

☺ Lunch 12-2, Dinner 7-10.45

☹ Lunch Sat, all Sun, Bank Holidays, 2 wks Aug

Terry Laybourne has staying power, that's for sure, a determination to continue his chosen path of bringing fine food to the sometimes cynical but always refreshingly down-to-earth Geordies. This means that there's no leeway for him to sit back and simply take his profits: he works extremely hard here, his prices have to be reasonable, even affordable; but the rewards are enormous helpings of respect locally, a responsive clientele and the opening of a sister establishment, Café 21 in nearby Ponteland plus a bistro in Durham. So what can you expect? Perhaps Shanghai shellfish risotto with crispy ginger, or ham knuckle and foie gras terrine with pease pudding (a perfect combination of local staples with a touch of something special), or salad of crisply fried vegetables and herbs with a balsamic vinegar dressing. Main courses might be grilled snapper with chorizo, fennel and olive oil, rib-eye steak with Café de Paris butter and red wine sauce, or slow-cooked knuckle of veal with pasta and herbs: definitely something here for all palates.

Northwich Nunsmere Hall

Tarporley Road, Oakmere, Northwich, Cheshire, CW8 2ES
☎ (01606) 889100   (01606) 889055
32   £147   48   £70
☺ Lunch 12-2, Dinner 7-10

Turn-of-the-century hotel and restaurant (but built originally as a private home, for the Brocklebanks of shipping fame). Edwardian elegance prevails, for restorations were sympathetically carried out. The location is superb – the Hall is virtually surrounded by a 60-acre lake. Set-price menus are in the modern mould; and on Saturday evenings you can dine to the accompaniment of a harpist.

Norton Hundred House Hotel

Norton, Nr Shifnal, Shropshire, TF11 9EE
☎ (01952) 730353   (01952) 730353
10   £69   60   £65
☺ Lunch 12-2.30, Dinner 6.15-10 (Sun 7-9)

The Phillips family have been hosts here since 1986 and now have a world-wide clientele of satisfied customers, as their brochure testifies. Most seem particularly enamoured of the swing ..... the best way to explain it is to say: go and try it for yourself! In the Jacobean restaurant or bar, enjoy modern British cooking and a concise list of good-quality wines.

Norwich Adlard's

79 Upper St Giles Street, Norwich, Norfolk, NR2 1AB
☎ (01603) 633522
45   £85
☺ Lunch 12.30-1.45, Dinner 7.30-10.30   ☹ all Sun & Mon

A well established institution that is the place to eat in Norwich. The green walls are cheered by crisp, white tablecloths and skilful service is as accomplished as David Adlard's cooking. Turbot with fennel purée and tarragon with crisp spinach, vermicelli and a light chicken and aniseed stock or a mille feuille of Jerusalem artichokes and onion marmalade with warm basil and balsamic vinaigrette are examples of his complex dishes. Others are simpler, a fillet of beef with deep-fried onion rings and chips, a Mediterranean salad for vegetarians or navarin of lamb with parsnip and potato purée. A savarin of Yorkshire rhubarb and rhubarb sorbet and light lemon cheesecake with candied orange and orange syrup are typical puddings. Usually you can taste about a dozen wines by the glass from the well sourced list.

England

Norwich Brasted's

8-10 St Andrew's Hill, Norwich, Norfolk, NR2 1DS
☎ (01603) 625949
🍴 22 🍽 £70

☺ Lunch 12-2, Dinner 7-9.30 ☹ Lunch Sat, all Sun, Bank Holidays

City-centre location for a popular restaurant which recently underwent a facelift, painting a smarter backdrop for Adrian Clarke's evolving menus. Basically British in inspiration, each dish will have his own special touch: as a starter, warm salad of fish and chips? Very few chefs could get away with this, but Clarke is one. There's a fan club of dedicated diners who follow him around East Anglia whenever he makes a move.

Norwich Greens Seafood Restaurant

82 Upper St Giles Street, Norwich, Norfolk, NR2 1LT
☎ (01603) 623733 📠 (01603) 615268
🍴 48 🍽 £60

☺ Lunch 12.15-2.15, Dinner 7-10.30
☹ Lunch Sat, all Sun & Mon, Bank Holidays, 1 wk Xmas

Daily and seasonal specials ensure that you can never get tired of fish here. The atmosphere is relaxed and friendly; the wine list concise and well priced.

Norwich Marco's

17 Pottergate, Norwich, Norfolk, NR2 1DS
☎ (01603) 624044
🍴 22 🍽 £80

☺ Lunch 12-2, Dinner 7-10 ☹ all Sun & Mon, 3 wks Sept/Oct

Marco Vessalio has been here since 1970, offering traditional Italian cooking at very good prices in a friendly atmosphere. He specialises in seafood, pasta, and game in season. At lunchtime, a shorter set menu is available.

Norwich St Benedicts Restaurant

9 St Benedicts Street, Norwich, Norfolk, NR2 4PE
☎ (01603) 765377
🍴 42 🍽 £45

☺ Lunch 12-2, Dinner 7-10 (Fri & Sat to 10.30)
☹ Sun & Mon, 25 Dec, 1 Jan

A change of name here to reflect the broader appeal of the former Grill, but rest assured that Nigel & Jayne Raffles continue to provide hospitality and good value for money. A well-chosen wine list includes plenty of half bottles.

Nottingham Sonny's

3 Carlton Street, Hockley, Nottingham,
Nottinghamshire, NG1 1NL

☎ 0115-947 3041

🪑 80 🍽 £60

☺ Lunch 12-2.30, Dinner 7-10.30 (Fri & Sat to 11, Sun to 10),
(light meals in cafe Mon-Sat 11-3.30) ☹ Bank Holidays, 1 Jan

Relative of the branch in London SW13: modern English/eclectic cooking in cool surroundings and a relaxed, informal atmosphere. Concise list of wines; and a shorter, snappier café menu is available thoughout the day.

Oakham Whipper-In Hotel

Market Place, Oakham, Leicestershire, LE15 6DT

☎ (01572) 756971   📠 (01572) 757759

🛏 24 £ 67 🪑 50 🍽 £70

☺ Lunch 12.30-2, Dinner 7.30-9.30 (Sun to 9)

Cosy 17th-century hotel in the heart of England, the name giving a hint at one of the principle pursuits in the nearby Vale of Belvoir! Antiques, old prints and log fires supply the atmosphere, backed up by friendly service from the staff. The restaurant offers English country cooking using fresh, local produce whenever possible.

Old Burghclere Dew Pond

Old Burghclere, Newbury, Berkshire, RG15 9LH

☎ (01635) 278408

🪑 44 🍽 £70

☺ Dinner 7-9.30 ☹ Sun & Mon, 2 wks Jan, 2 wks Aug

Keith & Julie Marshall's friendly restaurant is building its reputation steadily, based on good treatment of good ingredients, presented in a modern European fashion. The dining room is non-smoking, and you can subscribe to their quarterly newsletter to keep up to date with changes.

Orford Butley-Orford Oysterage

Market Hill, Orford, Woodbridge, Suffolk, IP12 2LH

☎ (01394) 450277   📠 (01394) 450949

🪑 90 🍽 £40

☺ Lunch 12-2.15, Dinner 6.30-9 ☹ 25 & 26 Dec

Perennially popular seafood restaurant in a coastal setting. No frills or fuss in the first-floor dining room, just good quality fresh, local produce, cooked simply and served in a friendly manner. Short list of white wines.

Oswestry Restaurant Sebastian

45 Willow Street, Oswestry, Shropshire, SY11 1AQ

☎ (01691) 655444

🪑 35 🍽 £45

☺ Lunch 12-2, Dinner 6.30-10.30

☹ Lunch Sat-Tue, Dinner Sun & Mon, Bank Holidays

Mark & Michelle Fisher run an attractive restaurant in a pretty market town on the England/Wales border – so often an arena of conflict. Not so nowadays: Englishman Mark (his middle name is Sebastian, by the way!) happily cooks fresh fish from North Wales, often in classic French style.

Oxford Bath Place Hotel & Restaurant

4 & 5 Bath Place, Holywell Street, Oxford, Oxfordshire, OX1 3SU

☎ (01865) 791812   📠 (01865) 791834

🛏 10 £ £105 🪑 32 🍽 £80

☺ Lunch 12-2 (12.30-2.30 Sun), Dinner 7-10

(Fri & Sat to 10.30, Sun to 9.30)

Situated in a tiny, cobbled pedestrian lane, directly opposite the Holywell Music Rooms, this cosy little hotel and restaurant is really one of a kind. A relaxed atmosphere and high standards of maintenance ensure creature comforts, topped by French neo-classic and modern-with-med-and-English-influences menus. The menu surprise really puts chef Jeremy Blake O'Connor through his paces: an 8-course tasting menu served only to whole tables, at £49.50 per person!

Oxford Browns

5-11 Woodstock Road, Oxford, Oxfordshire, OX2 6HA

☎ (01865) 511995   📠 (01865) 52347

🪑 250 🍽 £45

☺ 11am-11.30pm (Sun from 12) ☹ 25 & 26 Dec

Browns heads for its 20th anniversary with an unchanged but successful formula, replicated in Cambridge, Brighton, Bristol and now London. Good food at reasonable prices in friendly surroundings, appealing to all age groups.

Oxford Cherwell Boathouse

Bardwell Road, Oxford, Oxfordshire, OX2 6SR

☎ (01865) 52746   📠 (01865) 52746

🪑 50 🍽 £50

☺ Lunch 12-2, Dinner 6-10.30

☹ Lunch Tue, Dinner Sun, all Mon, 1 wk Xmas

Right on the river (small car-park alongside), the Cherwell Boathouse is exactly what it says it is: a friendly, peaceful, unpretentious restaurant serving good food and great wines at value-for-money prices. Fresh, seasonal, local produce is used in imaginative combinations at set prices.

Oxford Restaurant Elizabeth

82 St Aldate's, Oxford, Oxfordshire, OX1 1RA
☎ (01865) 242230
🪑 40 🍽 £75
☺ Lunch 12.30-2.30, Dinner 6.30-11 (Sun 7-10.30)
☹ Mon, Good Friday, 24-30 Dec

Antonio Lopez, here since 1966, must have seen many a generation of students arrive and leave, and most of them at some time seem to have been customers at this friendly little French restaurant. Game in season and fish accordingly to market availability are the cornerstones of the carte and the lunchtime set menu all served in the panelled, first floor dining rooms. Mostly French wine list.

Oxford 15 North Parade

15 North Parade Avenue, Oxford, Oxfordshire, OX2 6LX
☎ (01865) 513773
🪑 60 🍽 £70
☺ Lunch 12-2, Dinner 7-10.30/11   ☹ Dinner Sun, all Mon, last 2 wks Aug

The Woods aim to offer inventive, interesting and delicious food at affordable prices, using quality craftsmanship. The returning regulars would indicate that they succeed, and this place has become an integral part of the Oxford eating scene. Influences are drawn from all over the world; and even a traditional Sunday lunch might have some unusual touches.

Oxford Gee's Restaurant

61a Banbury Road, Oxford, Oxfordshire, OX2 6PE
☎ (01865) 53540   📠 (01865) 310308
🪑 90 🍽 £55
☺ Lunch 12-3, Dinner 6-11   ☹ 25 & 26 Dec

Graham Corbett's cooking is in the modern style with a blend of Mediterranean influences. Served in the beautiful conservatory, you might try Piedmontese peppers, risotto with wild mushrooms, moules marinière and salad of duck confit and sautéed livers feature amongst first courses. Pasta can be chosen as a starter or main dish along with the likes of choucroute garnie, rack of lamb with braised lentils, mashed potatoes and port wine sauce, roast cod on a bed of fennel with herb vinaigrette and potatoes or roasted vegetables with polenta and minted yoghurt dressing. A good wine list sets off around the world starting at £9.50.

Oxford Old Parsonage

1 Banbury Road, Oxford, Oxfordshire, OX2 6NN
☎ (01865) 310210 📠 (01865) 311262
◻ 30 £ £140 🪑 60 🕰 £65

☺ Lunch 12-3, Dinner 6-11 (light meals in bar (seats 35) 7am-11pm)
☹ 25 & 26 Dec

Very much part of the city scene, the Old Parsonage succeeds in combining old world charm with modern conveniences. A fairly international menu is served in the Parsonage Bar – which is the restaurant. Jeremy Mogford's philosophy has been to create a small, individually run hotel with a distinct personality.

Padstow Seafood Restaurant

Riverside, Padstow, Cornwall, PL28 8BY
☎ (01841) 532485 📠 (01841) 533344
◻ 10 £ £98 🪑 70 🕰 £80

☺ Lunch 12.30-2.15, Dinner 7-10 ☹ Sun, 19 Dec-3 Feb, 1 May

Whilst St Petroc is rumoured to have founded a monastery here in the 6th century Rick Stein definitely founded the Seafood Restaurant in 1975 and seems to have packed in more people during his two decades of occupation than his revered rival! His market research was good, a fish restaurant in a pretty Cornish village overlooking the harbour full of bright, bobbing fishing boats, sounds right doesn't it? Others have tried but Rick's great advantage was that he got it absolutely spot on, fabulous fresh fish cooked in traditional and adventurous ways, a bustling atmosphere, and a light airy decor. Monkfish with garlic and fennel, turbot simply poached and served with hollandaise, Dover sole, grilled with sea salt and lime or chargrilled fillets of John Dory with coriander, saffron and kumquats. Usually shellfish as first courses, a mixture of oysters, crab, cockles, winkles, clams, scallops, langoustines and mussels are served hot with olive oil, garlic and lemon or perhaps a Goan dish of mussels, cockles and clams fried in hot, aromatic chilli, ginger, garlic and Masala spice paste. One meal here isn't enough, so stay overnight, either in the rooms above the restaurant or at St Petroc's, their more modest bistro with rooms, just up the hill.

Painswick Painswick Hotel

Kemps Lane, Painswick, Gloucestershire, GL6 6YB
☎ (01452) 812160 📠 (01452) 814059
◻ 20 £ £98 🪑 60 🕰 £65

☺ Lunch Sun only 12.30-2, Dinner 7.30-9.30 (Sun to 8.30)

Lovely Cotswold village which is home to an equally fine hotel and restaurant. Lounges and bedrooms are light and elegant. Modern international set and à la carte menus emphasise fish, reflecting the passion of owner Somerset Moore – he's also Chairman of the Gloucestershire Fish Club which meets here on the first Friday of each month.

Paulerspury Vine House

100 High Street, Paulerspury, Northamptonshire, NN12 7NA
☎ (01327) 811267 📠 (01327) 811309
🛏 6 £61 🍴 45 £55
☺ Lunch 12.30-1.45, Dinner 7-10.30
☹ Lunch Mon & Sat, all Sun, 24-30 Dec

Friendly little restaurant with rooms run by Marcus & Julie Springett, located just off the A5 about 2 miles south of Towcester. Fresh, local ingredients are used on daily-changing menus that tend to be modern English interpretations of French classics.

Penkridge William Harding's House

Mill Street, Penkridge, Stafford, Staffordshire, ST19 5AY
☎ (01785) 712955
🍴 30 £50
☺ Lunch first & last Sun in month only 12.30-2, Dinner 7.30-9.30
☹ Dinner Sun & Mon, Bank Holidays

The Bickleys have been here nearly 10 years now, running this beamed restaurant housed on the ground floor of their home, a listed 16th-century corner building. The supper club has proved a very successful venture. Seasonal dishes mean regular changes to the menu. There's just one sitting at lunch and at dinner.

Penzance Abbey Hotel

Abbey Street, Penzance, Cornwall, TR18 4AR
☎ (01736) 66906 📠 (01736) 51163
🛏 7 £85 🍴 18 £60
☺ Dinner 7.30-8.30 ☹ 1 wk Xmas

Small, cosy and friendly hotel, owned and run by the Cox family since 1979. Panelled baths, draped beds, log fires in the lounges and a sense of history set the scene, enhanced by some good cooking from the kitchen. Dinner is a set-price, 3-course affair with a few choices at each course. Concise, friendly wine list.

Plumtree Perkins Bar & Bistro

Old Railway Station, Station Road, Plumtree, Nottinghamshire, NG12 5NA
☎ (0115) 9373695 📠 (0115) 9376405
🍴 73 £50
☺ Lunch 12-2, Dinner 6.45-9.45 ☹ Sun & Mon, Bank Holidays

Tony & Wendy Perkins have been here since 1982 and have strengthened their position over the years, largely by moving with the times to an extent (there is now a much more modern approach to the cooking) but at the same time keeping to their original intention of serving honest, French/English bistro fare in a busy, bustling atmosphere.

Plymouth Chez Nous

13 Frankfort Gate, Plymouth, Devon, PL1 1QA
☎ (01752) 266793 📠 (01752) 660428
🪑 28 🍽 £80

☺ Lunch 12.30-2, Dinner 7-10.30

☹ Sun & Mon, Bank Holidays, 3 wks Feb, 3 wks Sep

It's in an unlikely spot, a shopping precinct; it has unpretentious, simple bistro decor and a blackboard menu; it's small, just about 30 seats; but it's the best thing to hit Plymouth since Sir Francis Drake! Husband and wife, Jacques & Suzanne Marchal's bistro is so typically French. He cooks in a tiny kitchen, authentic, homely cuisine, dishes are what they should be. Supreme of chicken with sweet peppers, grilled entrecote with oyster mushrooms, duck with lentils, medallion of venison with poivrade sauce or perhaps brill with saffron. Jacques doesn't need 20 or so Mediterranean ingredients to compose a dish and lose it's raison d'etre, he can cook. He knows about wine too, a fine list of French areas and lots of halves, some wines from autres pays seem very superfluous.

Plymouth Piermasters Restaurant

33 Southside Street, The Barbican, Plymouth, Devon, PL1 2LE
☎ (01752) 229345
🪑 60 🍽 £50

☺ Lunch 12-2, Dinner 7-10 (later for post-theatre suppers)

☹ all Sun, Xmas, Bank Holidays except Easter

Frenchman François Teissier cooks bistro-style food, making good use of fresh local fish. There's an extensive carte, or for £22.50 you can take a set menu which, again French-style, includes a half bottle of wine. Close your eyes and you're over in France...

Polperro Kitchen at Polperro

The Coombes, Polperro, Cornwall, PL13 2RQ
☎ (01503) 272780
🪑 24 🍽 £55

☺ Dinner 7-9.30 ☹ Dinner Sun & Mon in winter, Bank Holidays

Totally non-smoking restaurant offering eclectic menus and daily fish specials. There's a separate vegetarian menu, too; and all dishes are cooked to order. Concise wine list. Not suitable for children under 10; opening times vary considerably according to season.

Poole Haven Hotel

Banks Road, Sandbanks, Poole, Dorset, BH13 7QL
☎ (01202) 707333 📠 (01202) 708796
🛏 96 £120 🍽 150 🍴 £55
☺ Lunch 12.30-2, Dinner 7-9.30 (Terrace Conservatory: 10.30am-6pm)

Useful seaside hotel with 2 restaurants, popular primarily with holiday-makers who can also take advantage of the excellent leisure facilities, though business needs are also well-catered. French-style menus offer good variety; and there's also a conservatory brasserie for less formal eating.

Poole Mansion House

11 Thames Street, Poole, Dorset, BH15 1JN
☎ (01202) 685666 📠 (01202) 665709
🛏 28 £110 🍽 40 🍴 £65
☺ Lunch 12-2, Dinner 7-9.30 (Sat from 7)
☹ Lunch Sat, Dinner Sun, Bank Holidays

Hotel and dining club, where non-members pay a 15% supplement. Food is modern British with European and Oriental influences. Different menus are offered, including a Slimmers' Choice for £10, a 50-minute Luncheon for those short of time (priced with or without unlimited house wine up to the end of the main course), and Benjamin's Choice, again with or without wine. Some excellent ideas here, well executed and appreciated by the loyal clientele.

Porlock Oaks Hotel

Porlock, Somerset, TA24 8ES
☎ (01643) 862265 📠 (01643) 862265
🛏 10 £80 🍽 24 🍴 £45
☺ Dinner 7-8.30 ☹ Hotel Jan-Feb

Pretty setting on the north Somerset coast for the Rileys' comfortable small hotel. Edwardian in origin and style. Comfortable lounges offer good views; while in the dining room British cooking allows for some choice at each course.

Powburn Breamish Country House Hotel

Powburn, Alnwick, Northumberland, NE66 4LL
☎ (01665) 578266 📠 (01665) 578500
🛏 11 £116 🍽 30 🍴 £60
☺ Lunch Sun only 12.30-1, Dinner 7.30-8 ☹ 1 Jan-14 Feb

First a 17th-century farmhouse, then a hunting lodge, now a country house hotel in a splendid part of the North East. Traditional English cooking goes with the setting – game is popular in season.

Prestbury White House Manor

New Road, The Village, Prestbury, Cheshire, SK10 4HP
☎ (01625) 829376 📠 (01625) 828627
▯ 9 £ £112 ⏚ 70 ⓘ £65
☺ Lunch 12-2, Dinner 7-10 ☹ Lunch Mon, Dinner Sun

Small and friendly hotel and restaurant, owned and run by Ryland & Judith Wakeham. There are function facilities too, which have recently been refurbished. British cooking from Ryland is offered on set and à la carte menus in the dining room, and duck is a speciality.

Preston Heathcotes Brasserie

23 Winckley Square, Preston, Lancashire, PR1 3JJ
☎ (01772) 252732 📠 (01772) 203433
⏚ 65 ⓘ £55
☺ Lunch Sun 12-3, Dinner Sun 7-9 (light meals 12-9)

Paul Heathcote's second venture (in line with trends of one serious restaurant then a more relaxed younger sister) makes his interpretations of modern British cooking, executed through new head chef James Ginghill, (he replaces Max Gnoyke who will open Heathcotes new restaurant in Manchester later this year), more accessible to a greater number of customers. It's much more a case of giving people what they want, having previously accustomed them to wanting what you can best provide! Paul seems to have managed this sleight of hand with great aplomb. Good-quality ingredients are sensitively handled and served in a bright, modern setting; wine list is very reasonably priced.

Puckrup Puckrup Hall

Puckrup, Tewkesbury, Gloucestershire, GL20 6EL
☎ (01684) 296200 📠 (01684) 850788
▯ 84 £ £98 ⏚ 34 ⓘ £55
☺ Dinner 7-9.30 (Brasserie: 12.30-2.30, 6.30-10) ☹ Dinner Sun-Tue

Hotel and golf club with a gracious yet welcoming reception area, good business and conference facilities (one of the most popular corporate hospitality venues in the country), and spacious, well-equipped bedrooms. Generations Leisure Club bridges that gap!

L!VE TV: THE FACTS
see page 21

Pulborough Stane Street Hollow

Codmore Hill, Pulborough, West Sussex, RH20 1BG
☎ (01798) 872819
🍴 32 🍽 £60
☺ Lunch 12.30-1.30, Dinner 7.15-9.15
☹ Lunch Sat, Dinner Sun, all Mon & Tue, 25 Dec-5 Jan, 2 wks May,
2 wks Oct

The cottage home and restaurant of René & Ann Kaiser that has now completed two decades of service to the local community and countless visitors. They keep chickens and ducks for eggs, smoke hams, fish and chickens and grow lots of the delicious fruit and vegetables in their own garden. The menu changes monthly to take in all this fine produce that Rene transforms into dishes such as a fried pancake of home-smoked fish in a cheese sauce with quail eggs, a vegetarian pancake filled with stir-fried fresh vegetables flavoured with garlic, chilli and fresh ginger topped with yoghurt cream and smoked ham with mushrooms and herbs baked in puff-pastry. The wine list is terribly reasonable and lunch, either during the week or on Sunday is tremendous value for money.

Purton Pear Tree

Church End, Purton, Nr Swindon, Wiltshire, SN5 9ED
☎ (01793) 772100 📠 (01793) 772369
🛏 18 £ £75 🍴 50 🍽 £70
☺ Lunch 12-2, Dinner 7-9.30 ☹ Lunch Sat, 1 wk Xmas

Very comfortable hotel run by Francis & Anne Young, who pay great attention to the small details which make all the difference. The refurbishment of this former vicarage uses lots of pink, and the U-shaped conservatory restaurant means you can wave to fellow guests (assuming you know them!) across the paved courtyard! Useful place to stay for exploring a pretty area of England.

Quorn Quorn Grange

88 Wood Lane, Quorn, Leicestershire, LE12 8DB
☎ (01509) 412167 📠 (01509) 415621
🛏 18 £ £102 🍴 50 🍽 £65
☺ Lunch 11.30-2.30, Dinner 7-9.30 (Sat to 10, Sun to 9)
☹ Lunch Sat, 26 Dec, 1 Jan

Family-owned and run, Quorn Grange is an oasis of tranquility in the heart of England. The original 18th-century building has modern additions and landscaped gardens. Good business and conference facilities; international menu, substantial wine list.

Ramsbottom Village Restaurant

Ramsbottom Victuallers Co Ltd, 16-18 Market Place, Ramsbottom, Bury, Lancashire, BL0 9HT
☎ (01706) 825070
🪑 40 🍽 £45

☺ Lunch 12-2.30 (Sun at 1.30), Dinner 7.30 for 8
☹ Dinner Sun, all Mon & Tue

Ros Hunter & Chris Johnson have reverted to their former no-choice-till-pudding evening option at their eclectic restaurant. There's now an additional dining room, as well as a shop in the basement. Organic produce is used when possible, conservation grade is the next choice. Lunch menus are on a blackboard, dinner ones are printed. This is still one of the best restaurants in the area.

Reigate La Barbe

71 Bell Street, Reigate, Surrey, RH2 7AN
☎ (01737) 241966 📠 (01737) 226387
🪑 65 🍽 £65

☺ Lunch 12-2, Dinner 7.15-9.45
☹ Lunch Sat, all Sun, Bank Holidays, 25-29 Dec

Friendly, neighbourhood restaurant with a menu which changes every 8 weeks or so and offers wine recommendations to accompany each dish. The style is French and there's live accordian music on Friday nights!

Reigate The Dining Room

59a High Street, Reigate, Surrey, RH2 9AE
☎ (01737) 226650
🪑 50 🍽 £65

☺ Lunch 12-2.30, Dinner 7-10
☹ Lunch Sat, all Sun, Bank Holidays, 1 wk Easter, 2 wks Xmas, 1 wk Aug

Modern English cooking, with seafood and game as specialities, is on offer at this friendly local restaurant. Set menus and a carte are both offered, with plenty of choice throughout. Chef Tony Tobin is now well established, having joined proprietor Paul Montalto in June 1994.

Remenham The Little Angel

Remenham Lane, Henley-on-Thames, Oxfordshire, RG9 2LS
☎ (01491) 574165 📠 (01491) 411879
🪑 90 🍽 £45

☺ Lunch 12.30-2.30, Dinner 7.30-10

Popular pub just outside Henley which comes into its own during the Regatta and Festival. Riverside setting, plenty of outdoor eating and some good food served in the extended Conservatory restaurant make this a destination as well as a useful venue for locals.

Richmond Burnt Chair

5 Duke Street, Richmond, Surrey, TW9 1HP
☎ 0181-940 9488
🍴 31 🍽 £55

☺ Dinner 6-11 (Sat 5.30) ☹ all Sun, 1 wk Xmas, 1 wk Aug

Modern European cooking at a quaint little town-centre restaurant, under the auspices of chef/proprietor Weenson Andrew Oo. Interesting flavours are married together on the set and à la carte menus, while the well-annotated wine list is very reasonably priced. Booking is advisable.

Richmond Café Flo

149 Kew Road, Richmond, Surrey, TW9 2PN
☎ 0181-940 8298 📠 0181-332 2598
🍴 70 🍽 £50

☺ Lunch 12-4 (Sat to 5), Dinner 6-11.30 (Sat from 6.30, Sun from 7)
☹ 25 & 26 Dec

The winning formula at this friendly chain of London-based restaurants is that there's generally something for everyone on the varied menu. 2 courses and coffee for under £7 is still a force to be reckoned with. Friendly service, and a few outside tables for those balmy summer days...

Richmond Petersham Hotel

Nightingale Lane, Richmond, Surrey, TW10 6UZ
☎ 0181-940 7471 📠 0181-940 9998
🛏 54 £130 🍴 70 🍽 £65

☺ Lunch 12.15-2.15, Dinner 7-9.45 (Sun to 8.45)

Petersham Road is one-way and steep, but the care taken to access the hotel is rewarded by some stunning views over the meandering Thames and the water meadows alongside, grazed by cattle – yes, you are just 6 miles from Hyde Park Corner! Traditional hospitality prevails once inside, and in Nightingales Restaurant (a newer extension which takes best advantage of the setting) you can enjoy traditional English and French cooking. The hotel's red-brick tower is a local landmark.

Richmond King's Head

Market Place, Richmond, North Yorkshire, DL10 4HS
☎ (01748) 850220 📠 (01748) 850635
🛏 28 £82 🍴 50 🍽 £55

☺ Lunch Sun only 12-2, Dinner 7-9.15

Popular hotel in a much-loved market town – it's no surprise to learn that this elegant Georgian building was once a coaching inn. Comfort for travellers is still of paramount importance, with good food at reasonable prices to emphasise the hospitality.

Ridgeway Old Vicarage

Ridgeway Moor, Ridgeway, Nr Sheffield,
Derbyshire, S12 3XW
☎ (0114) 2475814   (0114) 2477079
50   £90
☺ Lunch 12.15-2.30, Dinner 7-10.45
☹ Dinner Sun, all Mon, Bank Holidays, 10 days in Jan

Tessa Bramley and her son Andrew have turned this particular former vicarage into something of a shrine to good cooking: it's certainly no longer a mere local restaurant (though it continues also to serve that purpose par excellence) and has become a destination on the gastronomic tour of England. Tessa cooks instinctively, in a kind of modern, British, country way, using the best possible ingredients (from local sources when possible) and turning them into something rather special. In keeping also with current trends of making excellent food more accessible, the conservatory bistro (where the same attention to detail is observed, but in a more relaxed format) enjoys continued success. Additionally, there's always an excellent choice for vegetarians. In the bistro you can enjoy 3 courses for only £18.50, whereas the a full 4 courses in the restaurant is worth every penny of its £35. A typical bistro meal could comprise warm salad of chicken livers with pine kernels and a raspberry vinegar dressing, followed by baked fillet of turbot with saffron tagliatelle and pesto, with Tessa's famous baked chocolate pudding with chocolate fudge sauce and English custard to finish. By contrast, the restaurant could tempt you with quail, roasted over lavender with a stuffing of spinach and ceps; then English sea bass steamed with 5-spice and ginger, served with a soy butter sauce; a crisp praline layered dessert of English strawberries (what do you mean, I can't have the chocolate pudding every time I go?); and to finish, portions of Celtic romise (an intensely flavoured, soft, cow's milk cheese from Wales) and Flower Marie (a fragrant, Sussex goat's cheese). This is definitely a favourite!

Ripley Michels'

13 High Street, Ripley, Surrey, GU23 6AQ
☎ (01483) 224777
50   £90
☺ Lunch 12.30-1.30, Dinner 7.30-9 (Sat 7-9.30)
☹ Lunch Sat, Dinner Sun, all Mon, 1st wk Jan

Friendly local restaurant which offers stylish food in many menu combinations: a 4-course surprise menu at £21, a 4-course gourmet menu (not Saturdays) at £28 including a glass of wine with each course, and the carte itself. Erik Michel cooks with a sure touch; Karen looks after front-of-house. There's a strong New World section on the wine list.

Ripponden Over the Bridge Restaurant

Millfold, Ripponden, Sowerby Bridge,
West Yorkshire, HX6 4DL
☎ (01422) 823722 📠 (01422) 824810
🪑 50 🍽 £60

☺ Dinner 7.30-9.30   ☹ Dinner Sun, Bank Holidays

A monthly-changing menu operates at Ian Beaumont & Sue Tyer's friendly little restaurant. Ingredients are local when possible, home-cooked with care, and accompanied by an interesting wine list.

Roade Roadhouse Restaurant

16 High Street, Roade, Northamptonshire, NN7 2NW
☎ (01604) 863372
🪑 40 🍽 £55

☺ Lunch 12.15-1.45, Dinner 7-9.30 ☹ Dinner Sun, all Mon

The Kewleys' philosophy remains to offer an affordable, informal setting where the emphasis is on conscientiously prepared food using fresh and, where practicable, local ingredients. A modern European slant is brought to the presentation (as well as to the ingredients) and both carte and set menus are, indeed, very reasonably priced, as is the concise wine list.

Rochford Hotel Renouf & Renoufs Restaurant

Bradley Way, Rochford, Essex, SS4 1BU
☎ (01702) 541334 📠 (01702) 549563
🛏 24 £78 🪑 60 🍽 £60

☺ Lunch 12-1.45, Dinner 7-9.30
☹ Lunch Bank Holidays, Sun residents only, 26-30 Dec

The next generation of the Renouf family now holds the reins since Melvin took over the kitchens from his father, Derek, though the whole family is very much involved in all aspects of this establishment. Extensive wine list to accmpany the ambitious menu.

Romaldkirk Rose and Crown

Romaldkirk, Durham, DL12 9EB
☎ (01833) 650213 📠 (01833) 650828
🛏 12 £75 🪑 24 🍽 £65

☺ Lunch Sun only 12-1.30, Dinner 7.30-9
☹ Dinner Sun (residents only), 25 & 26 Dec

Christopher & Alison Davy, chef/proprietors here since 1989, continue the tradition of hospitality which has held good here since the Rose & Crown began life as a coaching inn. Nowadays it makes a splendid base from which to explore the Tees valley, and to which to return and enjoy set menus of regional English cooking. Wine appreciation weekends are a recent innovation.

Romsey Old Manor House

21 Palmerston Street, Romsey, Hampshire, SO51 8GF
☎ (01794) 517353
⊟ 45 🍴 £90
☺ Lunch 12-2, Dinner 7-9.30 ☹ Dinner Sun, all Mon, 1 wk Xmas

Exciting and original dishes emanate from the kitchen of Mauro Bregoli in his attractive, beamed manor house opposite the Broadlands Estate. A home-made cotechino salami is served warm with lentils, skate sits on broccoli flavoured with just lemon juice and extra virgin olive oil, tagliatelle with Parma ham and dandelion leaves or home-made bresaola smoked in the Manor House chimney. A breast of chicken comes with a creamy sauce of mushrooms and saffron, a boned pig's head stuffed with morels is served with borlotti beans and red onion marmalade, fish is usually simply grilled with herbs or served with a light sauce. An unusual crème brulée has fennel and fresh herbs to flavour it, a warm pear and hazlenut tart has a more intense flavour than the normal almond one and try the delicious combination of vanilla ice cream with rich Pedro Ximenez sherry that would warm a Jerezano's heart. Wines are chosen with consummate skill, all will please either the beginner or the master. Service is also worthy of mention.

Ross-on-Wye Pheasants

52 Edde Cross Street, Ross-on-Wye,
Hereford & Worcester, HR9 7BZ
☎ (01989) 565751
⎿ 2 £ £45 ⊟ 22 🍴 £70
☺ Lunch 12.30-2 (bookings only Nov-Mar), Dinner 7-10
☹ Sun & Mon, Bank Holidays, 1 wk Xmas

Revamped table settings this year at Pheasants, a friendly little restaurant with rooms in border country. Chef/proprietor Eileen Brunnarius changes her menus every 4-6 weeks, but the constant theme is English, both ancient and modern. Good local produce is sourced when possible. Fine range of wines by the glass from an exellent list.

Rotherwick Tylney Hall

Rotherwick, Nr Hook, Hampshire, RG27 9AZ
☎ (01256) 764881 📠 (01256) 768141
⎿ 91 £ £122 ⊟ 100 🍴 £95
☺ Lunch 12.30-1.45, Dinner 7.30-9.30 (Fri & Sat to 10)

Privately owned, Grade II listed mansion which was sympathetically restored in 1985. Professional service and good leisure facilities are added attractions while in the Oak Room restaurant, fine English and classic continental cuisine happily rub shoulders. The grand Tylney conference suite was recently refurbished.

England 227

Rowde George & Dragon

High Street, Rowde, Wiltshire, SN10 2PN
☎ (01380) 723053
🍴 35 🍽 £60

☺ Lunch 12-2, Dinner 7-10 ☹ all Sun & Mon, 25 & 26 Dec, 1 Jan

Friendly and welcoming pub run by Tom & Helen Withers since 1989, offering some imaginative and well-cooked dishes. They specialise in fresh fish, delivered direct from Cornwall twice-weekly. A fully annotated wine list is very reasonably priced.

Rushlake Green Stone House

Rushlake Green, Heathfield, East Sussex, TN21 9QJ
☎ (01435) 830553   📠 (01435) 830726
🛏 8 £ £95 🍴 16 🍽 £80

☺ Dinner residents only 7.30-9 ☹ 24 Dec, 9 Jan

On the borders of East Sussex and Kent, Jane & Peter Dunn run this friendly little hotel and restaurant. Lunches are for pre-booked parties only, but dinner is a set-price affair of 3 courses with plenty of choice. There's even more choice on the wine list, so allow plenty of time to relax and peruse it – it repays the effort!

Rye Landgate Bistro

5/6 Landgate, Rye, East Sussex, TN31 7LH
☎ (01797) 222829
🍴 30 🍽 £60

☺ Dinner 7-9.30 (Sat to 10)
☹ Dinner Sun & Mon, 1 wk Xmas, 1 wk Jun, 1 wk Autumn

In the quaint town of Rye, a useful little bistro which makes good use of local seafood in its modern British menus. Dinner is set-priced during the week, à la carte at weekends, and changes seasonally. Concise wine list is very reasonably priced.

Rye Mermaid Inn

Mermaid Street, Rye, East Sussex, TN31 7EU
☎ (01797) 223065   📠 (01797) 225069
🛏 28 £ £117 🍴 60 🍽 £60

☺ Lunch 12-2, Dinner 7-9.15

Steeped in history (former haunt of smugglers), quintessentially English (timbered exterior, set on a sloping cobbled street), the Mermaid is a "must" on the tourist circuit. It's just as popular with locals, however, who pop in for a pint; or with nearer visitors who want a light lunch after checking out some antiquity or other.

St Austell Boscundle Manor

Tregrehan, St Austell, Cornwall, PL25 3RL
☎ (01726) 813557   📠 (01726) 814997
🛏 10 £ £110   🍴 16 🍽 £60

🙂 Dinner 7.30-8.30   ☹ Sun (except residents), Nov-Mar

Continual maintenance ensure high standards are maintained and subtle improvements made at this small hotel which is really more like a luxurious private house, thanks to the good offices of Andrew & Mary Flint. Some accommodation is in the main house, some in converted cottages. Mary offers a short set-price dinner menu with some choice at each course.

St Ives Pig'n'Fish

Norway Lane, St Ives, Cornwall, TR26 1LZ
☎ (01736) 794204
🍴 30 🍽 £45

🙂 Lunch 12.30-1.30, Dinner 7-9.30   ☹ Sun & Mon, Nov-mid Feb

Established in 1991, the Sellars' primarily fish and seafood restaurant is proving popular. French and Italian influences infiltrate Paul's cooking, sitting comfortably on the prime local ingredients. Service, led by Debby, is friendly and welcoming. Concise wine list.

St Margaret's Wallett's Court

West Cliffe, St Margaret's, Dover, Kent, CT15 6EW
☎ (01304) 852424   📠 (01304) 853430
🛏 10 £ £60   🍴 60 🍽 £60

🙂 Dinner 7-9   ☹ Dinner Sun (except residents), 1 wk Xmas

Lovely country house on the Kent coast, run as a family concern by the Oakleys. The history of the building (it goes back to Domesday times) is well documented within its walls, or even within its atmospheric beams! Set menus offer good value for money, with some choice at each course. Interesting wine list; great breakfasts.

St Mawes Idle Rocks Hotel

Harbourside, St Mawes, Cornwall, TR2 5AN
☎ (01326) 270771   📠 (01326) 270062
🛏 24 £ £118   🍴 65 🍽 £65

🙂 Lunch 12-2.30, Dinner 7-9.15 (light meals 8.30am-9.15pm)
☹ Lunch Mon-Sat in winter

Archetypal English hotel in a consummate Cornish fishing village. Lovely views over the sea – but they've sold the ketch now. Menus change frequently to take best advantage of local produce (especially, of course, fish!) and are presented in the modern style. Refurbished Terrace restaurant also has good views; and the wine list is usefully laid out.

Salcombe Spinnakers

Fore Street, Salcombe, Devon, TQ8 8JG

☎ (01548) 843408

🪑 60 🍽 £50

☺ Lunch 12-2, Dinner 7-9.30

☹ Dinner Sun, all Mon & Tue in winter, mid Nov-mid Feb

David & Sandra May have been at Spinnakers since 1987 and their style has developed over the years into its current modern British mode. Naturally, spanking fresh fish is the backbone of their menu (daily specials are chalked on a board), though plenty of other ingredients find their way to the dining table, too, via set and à la carte menus.

Scarisbrick Master McGrath's

535 Southport Road, Scarisbrick, Lancashire, L40 9RF

☎ (01704) 880050   📠 (01704) 880227

🪑 120 🍽 £55

☺ Lunch 12-2 (Sun to 2.30), Dinner 5.30-10

Situated on the A570 between Ormskirk and Southport, this is a pub-based restaurant, but one of charm and wit. John Nelson (Highmoor at Wrightington) and Jim Sines combine their talents to produce lunches in the bar or on the terrace, and evening bar and restaurant meals (fixed price with limited choice). Dinner dances on Saturdays, themed nights on some Fridays, traditional lunch on Sundays.

Seaford Quincy's

42 High Street, Seaford, East Sussex, BN25 1PL

☎ (01323) 895490

🪑 32 🍽 £60

☺ Lunch Sun only 12-2, Dinner 7-10

☹ Dinner Sun & Mon, 25 & 26 Dec

Dawn & Ian Dowding have run this friendly little restaurant since 1988. Menus change regularly, are always seasonal, and usually include a couple of choices for vegetarians. Food is imaginative and well prepared. The wine list benefits from a good range of half-bottles.

Seahouses Olde Ship Hotel

9 Main Street, Seahouses, Northumberland, NE68 7RD

☎ (01665) 720200   📠 (01665) 721383

🛏 16 £68   🪑 30 🍽 £45

☺ Lunch 12-2, Dinner 7-8.30   ☹ Dec & Jan

Harbourside setting for an atmospheric hotel and restaurant which also does a roaring trade in bar lunches. Basic accommodation is clean and cheerful, and a couple of rooms have 4-posters. Seafaring memorabilia make up the decor.

Seaton Burn Horton Grange

Seaton Burn, Nr Newcastle-upon-Tyne,
Tyne & Wear, NE13 6BU
☎ (01661) 860686 📠 (01661) 860308
🛏 9 £ £80 🪑 30 🍽 £80
☺ Dinner 7-8.30 ☹ Dinner Sun (except residents), 25 & 26 Dec

On the edge of a large farm complex, Horton Grange was originally the family home and the make-over ensured good standards of housekeeping in a friendly atmosphere. English country cooking with a modern slant is enjoyed in the non-smoking dining room.

Seaview Seaview Hotel

High Street, Seaview, Isle of Wight, PO34 5EX
☎ (01983) 612711 📠 (01983) 613729
🛏 16 £ £60 🪑 30 🍽 £50
☺ Lunch 12-2, Dinner 7-9.30 ☹ Dinner Sun (except Bank Holidays)

A new extension at the rear of the hotel has meant additional car parking as well as extra rooms at the Seaview, home of owner/managers Nick & Nicky Hayward since 1980. A friendly, relaxing atmosphere prevails here, aided by some sound cooking for the restaurant. Local fish and shellfish, island vegetables including the now famous garlic and asparagus, are used when possible, to the delight of returning and new guests of all ages.

Sevenoaks Royal Oak

5 Upper High Street, Sevenoaks, Kent, TN13 1HY
☎ (01732) 451109 📠 (01732) 740187
🛏 39 £ £70 🪑 60 🍽 £65
☺ Lunch 12.30-2, Dinner 7.30-9.45 ☹ Lunch Sat

Town-centre hotel within the garden of England. Smartly-decorated lounges and bedrooms, and there's a conservatory where you can take morning coffee or afternoon tea. In the main restaurant, menus offer a mix of the classic and the modern, but usually with a French influence.

Shaftesbury La Fleur de Lys

25 Salisbury Street, Shaftesbury, Dorset, SP7 8EL
☎ (01747) 853717
🪑 36 🍽 £60
☺ Lunch 12-3, Dinner 7-10 ☹ Dinner Sun, Lunch Mon

Small, first-floor dining room where set menus and a carte, all using fine ingredients are offered in a relaxed setting.

Shanklin Old Village The Cottage

8 Eastcliff Road, Shanklin Old Village,
Isle of Wight, PO37 6AA

☎ (01983) 862504 📠 (01983) 867512

🍴 32 🍽 £60

☺ Lunch 12-1.45, Dinner 7.30-9.45 ☹ Sun & Mon, Oct & Mar

Alan Priddle & Neil Graham have run the Cottage since 1973, so are dab hands at knowing what their customers want. This means fairly traditional menus, with inspiration from the classics of England and France. A short wine list is very reasonably priced. A separate small lounge for smokers has recently been added.

Sheffield The Harley

334 Glossop Road, Sheffield, South Yorkshire, S10 2HW

☎ 0114-275 2288 📠 0114-272 2383

🛏 23 £75 🍴 55 🍽 £50

☺ Lunch 12-2.30, Dinner 7.30-9.45 ☹ Sun, 25 & 26 Dec, 1 Jan

Small, comfortable hotel usefully located near the city centre and the university. It was originally opened as lodgings for visiting Harley Street doctors visiting the city.

Shepton Mallet Blostin's Restaurant

29 Waterloo Road, Shepton Mallet, Somerset, BA4 5HH

☎ (01749) 343648

🍴 32 🍽 £50

☺ Dinner 7-9 ☹ Sun & Mon, 2 wks Jan, 2 wks Jun

Nick & Lynne Reed have kept to their successful formula and pegged price rises to a minimum as an incentive to their loyal local following. This policy also ensures that new guests are likely to return, for there is sufficient change to the menu (at least monthly) to keep even the most jaded palate lively. The style is British, fresh fish come from Cornwall, game in season comes from local shoots.

Shere Kinghams Restaurant

Gomshall Lane, Shere, Surrey, GU5 9HB

☎ (01483) 202168

🍴 44 🍽 £60

☺ Lunch 12-2.30, Dinner 7-9.30

☹ Dinner Sun, all Mon, Bank Holidays, 25 & 26 Dec

In the pretty English village of Shere, Kinghams serves modern English food in a charming setting (it used to be a very popular tea-room) and the Bakers also offer an outside catering service. The garden is available for fine-weather dining.

Shifnal Weston Park

Weston Park, Shifnal, Shropshire, TF11 8LE

☎ (01952) 850201   📠 (01952) 850430

⎕ 19   🍴 120   🍽 £70

☺ Lunch & Dinner by arrangement only   ☹ 25 & 26 Dec

The magnificent, 17th century home of the Earl of Bradford is open only for corporate entertaining or private parties, though there is also an extensive programme of special events such as the Music Festival in July, and various gourmet dinners throughout the year.

Shinfield L'Ortolan

Old Vicarage, Church Lane, Shinfield, Nr Reading, Berkshire, RG2 9BY

☎ (01734) 883783   📠 (01734) 885391

🍴 60   🍽 £140

☺ Lunch 12.15-2.15, Dinner 7.15-10

☹ Dinner Sun, all Mon, last 2 wks Aug, last 2 wks Feb

The old rectory of Shinfield has been elevated to great heights under the leadership of John & Christine Burton-Race. Exceptional, well-judged cooking from John's kitchen sees dishes such as an artichoke heart salad dressed with truffle oil vinaigrette garnished with roast scallops, a terrine of foie gras layered with savoy cabbage between layers of Parma ham served with a warm, creamed mustard vinaigrette or a light oyster flan masked with herb butter garnished with warm oysters. A roast fillet of lamb topped with crab is served with a light curried cream sauce, sea bass and langoustine tails are grilled and masked with a rosemary-scented chicken jus and leg and saddle of rabbit filled with sauerkraut are pot-roasted dressed on onion cream and served with white wine sauce. Great care is evident in each dish with fine produce being used in imaginative and often unusual ways. Christine pays equal attention to guests, leading her brigade of young ladies with a firm guiding hand.

Sissinghurst Rankins

The Street, Sissinghurst, Kent, TN17 2JH

☎ (01580) 713964

🍴 30   🍽 £65

☺ Lunch Sun only 12.30-2, Dinner 7.30-9

☹ Dinner Sun-Tue, Bank Holidays

Hugh & Leonora Rankin opened their pretty little restaurant in 1986 and have built up a loyal, local following (to the extent that they will now also do dinner parties on request!). "Cross-cultural" is the description of the cooking style, and it's a good one. Menus are priced for 2, 3 or 4 courses, and the admirably short wine list includes some good halves.

England 233

Six Mile Bottom Swynford Paddocks

Six Mile Bottom, Nr Newmarket, Cambridgeshire, CB8 0UE
☎ (01638) 570234 (01638) 570283
15 £107 34 £60
☺ Lunch 12-2, Dinner 6.30-9.30 ☹ 1 wk Xmas/New Year

A country hotel since 1976, Swynford before that played an important role in the life of Lord Byron. Nowadays, Patricia Evans runs it in such a way that she hopes it will play an important role in the lives of its new and returning guests, who come to enjoy set and à la carte menus of modern international cooking, served in traditional surroundings.

Slough Tummies Bistro

5 Station Road, Cippenham, Slough, Berkshire, SL1 6JJ
☎ (01628) 668486 (01628) 663106
55 £40
☺ Lunch 11.30-3, Dinner 5.30-12 ☹ Lunch Sat, 25 & 26 Dec, 1 Jan

Good value for money is the order of the day at this family-friendly bistro just off Junction 7 of the M4. Popular also for group bookings. The Mariaux family now also have 2 other outlets: a sandwich shop/ outside catering venture based called Yummies (also based in Cippenham) and a pasta bar called Spaggo's in Slough.

Solihull Jarvis International Hotel

The Square, Solihull, West Midlands, B91 3RF
☎ 0121-711 2121 0121-711 3374
127 £105 120 £60
☺ Lunch 12-1.45, Dinner 7-9.45 (Sun to 9)

Renamed (George, then Jarvis George) town-centre hotel, handy for the Exhibition Centre – there are good business and conference facilities, and there's free use of the nearby leisure centre for residents. About half of the rooms are reserved for non-smokers.

South Molton Whitechapel Manor

South Molton, Devon, EX36 3EG
☎ (01769) 573377 (01769) 573797
10 £125 24 £80
☺ Lunch 12-1.45, Dinner 7-8.45

A rather fine Elizabethan manor house with more history attached to it than we could tell you about here, thus a visit is strongly recommended so that you can update yourselves! What is of more immediate relevance is the superb way that the Shapland family run the 10 bedroomed house set in lovely terraced gardens on the lower slopes of Exmoor. The interior has lovely features, William and Mary plasterwork and panelling, an exquisite Jacobean oak screen and antiques abound in every room. Patricia Shapland is in charge of the kitchen, and the fixed-price menu has local produce at the fore cooked in modern style. Sea bass, brill, turbot and scallops from the sea, Devon beef and lamb or game in season for the meat eater, local cheeses are served with home-made walnut and raisin bread. Wines are from further afield, a good selection at fair prices, many at well under £10.

Southsea Bistro Montparnasse

103 Palmerston Road, Southsea, Hampshire, PO5 3PS
☎ (01705) 816754
🍴 40 🍽 £55

🙂 Dinner 7-10 ☹ Dinner Sun & Mon, Bank Holidays, 2 wks Jan

Gillian & Peter Scott (she cooks, he serves) run a small restaurant which is especially popular with people catching ferries to France or Spain. There's a fixed 3-course dinner menu available on weekdays, in addition to the carte. The style of food is modern international.

Southwold The Crown

90 High Street, Southwold, Suffolk, IP18 6DP
☎ (01502) 722275 📠 (01502) 724805
🛏 12 £ £69 🍴 22 🍽 £50

🙂 Lunch 12.30-1.30, Dinner 7.30-9.30 ☹ 1 wk Jan

Another famous Adnams house in this lovely Suffolk coastal town. Period charm galore, and a very friendly atmosphere. In the restaurant and bar, daily-changing menus are eclectic but with New World influences with the odd touch of Old England thrown in for good measure – not that you are likely to forget where you are unless you really go overboard on Adnams' amazing lists!

Southwold The Swan

Market Place, Southwold, Suffolk, IP18 6EG
☎ (01502) 722186 📠 (01502) 724800
🛏 45 £ £91 🍴 86 🍽 £65

🙂 Lunch 12-1.45, Dinner 7-9.30 ☹ Lunch Mon-Fri, Jan-Easter

In this popular seaside town, a historic hotel backing on to and owned by Adnams, who restored and refurbished it in 1989. A sense of history pervades the public rooms, while comfort is the keynote in the characterful bedrooms. Set menus of classic English food are served in the non-smoking dining room, and the extensive wine list is all that you would expect.

SCOTCH BEEF CLUB
see page 16

Speen
Old Plow Bistro & Restaurant at Speen

Flowers Bottom Lane, Speen, Nr Princes Risborough, Buckinghamshire, HP27 0PZ

☎ (01494) 488300 📠 (01494) 488702

⌇ 45 🍽 £60

☺ Lunch 12-1.45, Dinner 7.30-8.45

☹ Dinner Sun, all Mon, some Bank Holidays, 1 wk Xmas

Two distinct markets are satisfied here – those needing a light bistro snack for around £8, and those preferring a 3-course restaurant meal at around £25. Although the Old Plow's origins as an inn are evident in the style of the building, the style of the Cowans' operation is as far removed as you could imagine. Right in the middle of lush countryside you'll find a level of cooking which would do credit to any city-centre venue. The Bistro menu might offer home-made venison terrine with cranberry and orange relish and a tossed salad, or a platter of giant prawns, smoked salmon, mussels, squid, artichoke and sun-dried tomatoes as starters. Sample main courses could be Toulouse cassoulet with sausage, duck, smoked pork, garlic, wine and haricot beans; or a steaming bowl of Thai noodles with beef, prawns, mussels and crispy vegetables. Chocolate rum truffle cake with fresh raspberry sauce brings the menu back home. In the Restaurant, 2- or 3-course set-price menus are available at lunch and dinner, and show Malcolm Cowan's expertise in an even broader spectrum. Try French smoked duck with sweet mustard fruits and seasonal leaves, then grilled salmon with artichoke, sweet peppers and a lemon butter sauce, and an iced Drambuie parfait with brandied candied fruits to finish. Definitely worth a day trip from miles around!

Staddlebridge McCoy's

The Cleveland Tontine, Staddlebridge, Nr Northallerton, North Yorkshire, DL6 3JB

☎ (01609) 882671 📠 (01609) 882660

⌇ 6 £ £99 ⌇ 50 🍽 £85

☺ Dinner 7-9.30 (Bistro: 12-2, 7-10 daily)

☹ all Sun & Mon, 25 & 26 Dec, 1 Jan

A delightfully eccentric restaurant with rooms run by the equally delightful McCoy brothers who have great style and a relaxed approach to their task. Strong statements are made in all that they do, the decor is not average country house hotel, the staff are not regimented like those at a grand hotel and the food has powerful flavours. These are the reasons for its success as all combine harmoniously to create a quite unique experience and are executed with great care and skill. Try the scallops with caviar beurre rouge, curried parsnip and apple soup or fried polenta with mushrooms and asparagus to start. Halibut with mixed shellfish and lime butter, sea bass with deep-fried vegetables and plum vinaigrette, a pigeon de Bresse with mixed pulses and foie gras sauce or good char-grilled steaks to follow. Puddings are not for the weak at heart, Cointreau ice cream with prunes, sticky toffee pudding or a pancake with vanilla cream, amaretti and Grand Marnier. Wines are not totally run of the mill either, some good value, some top of the range necessarily expensive. Downstairs is a cheaper bistro with food of equal standard in an informal setting. If you can't find Staddlebridge on the map (because it doesn't exist!) McCoys is at the junction of the A19 and the A172.

Stamford The George of Stamford

71 St Martins, Stamford, Lincolnshire, PE9 2LB
☎ (01780) 55171 📠 (01780) 57070
🛏 47 £ £105 🍴 67 🍽 £85
☺ Lunch 12.30-2.30, Dinner 7.15-10.30 (Garden Lounge: 7am-10.30pm)

Famous coaching inn, just a mile from the A1 and about half-way between London and York; part of the Huntsbridge Group that also owns several good restaurant pubs in the area. Lovely, creeper-clad exterior and atmospheric, olde worlde interior (4-posters, antiques). The garden lounge is a light, airy alternative in which to enjoy a light meal or snack, while the main restaurant offers a classic European menu. Exceptional wine list.

Stapleford Stapleford Park

Stapleford, Nr Melton Mowbray, Leicestershire, LE14 2EF
☎ (01572) 787522 📠 (01572) 787651
🛏 43 £ £155 🍴 70 🍽 £90
☺ Lunch 12-2.30, Dinner 7-9.30 (Fri & Sat to 10), (light meals 9am-11pm)

A visit to Stapleford could be described as "a very upmarket Ideal Homes Exhibition meets the Design Museum of the 20th century", a legacy of the shrewd marketing know-how of the late, sadly missed, Bob Payton. That the inheritance continues to yield dividends is demonstrated in the recent refurbishment of the former gardener's cottage to provide an additional 4 signature rooms, sponsored by MGM, Coca Cola, IBM and Range Rover. These now rank alongside the David Hicks room, the Crabtree & Evelyn room, the Osborne & Little room – not to mention the Anton Mosimann kitchen, from whence comes good food to be enjoyed in the Grinling Gibbons dining room, flamboyantly adorned with the great man's carvings. Chef Malcolm Jessop lives up to the style of Stapleford, offering a carte of interesting choices (and a set-price lunch on Sundays). Try peppered duck breast salad with fresh berries and a black cherry jus, or Stapleford quesadillos with chorizo, black beans, Red Leicester cheese, pico de gallo and soured cream to start. Move on to grilled swordfish served with roasted corn relish and spicy fried black pasta, or fillet of beef topped with a horseradish cream, served with a herb potato cake, oyster mushrooms and port wine sauce. Finish with pumpkin cheesecake with lime syrup, or crème brulée with seasonal berries. And to think, this was the house which Victoria forbade Edward, Prince of Wales, to purchase lest he be corrupted by local Leicestershire hunting society! It is also the English Outpost of the Carnegie Club, belonging to new owner Peter de Savary.

England 237

Stoke-by-Nayland Angel Inn

Stoke-by-Nayland, Suffolk, CO6 4SA
☎ (01206) 263245   (01206) 263373
6   £60   40   £45
☺ Lunch 12-2, Dinner 6.30-9 (all day bar meals)
☹ Lunch Tue, Dinner Sun, all Mon, 25 & 26 Dec, 1 Jan

Take pot luck and eat in the bar, or reserve a table in the Well Room restaurant – the well was the source for the water which was used to brew beer. The Angel has been a hostelry for centuries, looking after travellers to the lovely Dedham Vale. The menu is chalked up on a board, and offers an extensive range of well-cooked dishes accompanied by a concise wine list.

Stokesley Chapters

27 High Street, Stokesley, North Yorkshire, TS9 5AD
☎ (01642) 711888   (01642) 713387
13   £60   45   £40
☺ Dinner 7-9.30   ☹ Sun, Xmas & New Year's Day

Menus change according to availability, especially of fish supplies, and the blackboard in the bistro shows the range at the Thompsons' friendly little hotel and restaurant. The non-smoking area of the bistro has recently been extended, in response to current trends! Two of the bedrooms are also reserved for non-smokers.

Ston Easton Ston Easton Park

Ston Easton, Nr Bath, Avon, BA3 4DF
☎ (01761) 241631   (01761) 241377
21   £169   40   £95
☺ Lunch 12.30-2, Dinner 7.30-9.30 (Fri & Sat to 10)

A classic, 18th-century, Palladian mansion owned by Peter & Christine Smedley that is an absolute delight with exquisite decorative and architectural features. The gardens are as well maintained as the house with many features designed by Humphrey Repton. Mark Harrington is also a well established feature of Ston Easton having presided over its kitchens for 10 years; he has done much to further its reputation during this time. His imaginative cooking might include dishes such as a soup of oysters with mushrooms and thyme, a panaché of Cornish seafood on creamed leeks with deep-fried won ton of lobster, a charcoal grilled breast of mallard on root vegetable spaghetti flavoured with truffle oil and puddings like a baked banana and clotted cream clafoutis with rum and raisin ice cream. Impeccable service and a classic range of wines, a memorable experience.

Stonham Mr Underhill's

Stonham, Nr Stowmarket, Suffolk, IP14 5DW
☎ (01449) 711206
🍴 24 🕐 £75

😊 Lunch Sun only 12.30-1.45, Dinner 7.30-9

☹ Dinner Sun & Mon, Bank Holidays (open 25 Dec)

The Bradleys have survived the recession, to the delight of East Anglians, and now go from strength to strength. Their small, comfortable country restaurant presents serious food but in a relaxed setting. If forced to use a label, they would say modern British; but blanket terms rarely do justice to what individual chefs are trying to achieve, and this is true here. Good raw ingredients used in ways to display the full flavour and potential are the backbone of Mr Underhill's success.

Stonor Stonor Arms

Stonor, Nr Henley-on-Thames, Oxfordshire, RG9 6HE
☎ (01491) 638345 📠 (01491) 638863
🛏 9 £ £93 🍴 20 🕐 £80

😊 Lunch 12-2, Dinner 7-9.30 (light meals Blades: 12-2, 7-9.30)

☹ Bank Holidays

Former village pub dating from the 18th Century which now houses a serious restaurant with rooms. The Stonor restaurant offers formal dining while there's a more relaxed approach in Blades – the name presumably a tribute to the Thames valley location.

Storrington Little Thakeham

Merrywood Lane, Storrington, West Sussex, RH20 3HE
☎ (01903) 744416 📠 (01903) 745022
🛏 9 £ £150 🍴 30 🕐 £90

😊 Lunch 12.30-2, Dinner 7-9

☹ Lunch Mon, Dinner Sun, Xmas/New Year

Fine Lutyens manor house with gardens in the style of Gertrude Jekyll, now owned and run by Tim & Pauline Ractliff. English country house cooking uses plenty of game in season on the set-price menus (some choice at each course). The wine list is of a stature appropriate to the setting.

England 239

Storrington Manleys

Manleys Hill, Storrington, West Sussex, RH20 4BT
☎ (01903) 742331
☐ 1 £85 ☐ 48 ⊚ £102
☺ Lunch 12-1.45, Dinner 7-9.15 (Sat to 10)
☹ Dinner Sun, all Mon, Bank Holidays, 10 days Jan

An attractive stone built cottage with low beams creates a warm atmosphere at the Löderers' restaurant. Karl cooks substantial French and Austrian dishes, calf's liver with apple slices and crispy onions, breast of duck with oriental spices on cabbage with ginger, fillets of sole cooked with riesling and langoustines or terrine of home smoked chicken and guinea fowl served with potato and cucumber salad. His puddings are also a tour de force.

Storrington The Old Forge

6 Church Street, Storrington, West Sussex, RH20 4LA
☎ (01903) 743402 📠 (01903) 742540
☐ 36 ⊚ £60
☺ Lunch 12.30-1.30, Dinner 7.15-9
☹ Lunch Sat & Tue, Dinner Sun, all Mon, 1 wk spring, 3 wks autumn

Recent acquisition of the adjacent premises means that even more people can enjoy the Roberts' hospitality and excellent cooking. Seasonal produce is used in imaginative, modern style, and the wine list has plenty of New World representations.

Stourbridge Bon Appetit

38 Market Street, Stourbridge, West Midlands, DY8 1AG
☎ (01384) 375372
☐ 60 ⊚ £55
☺ Lunch 12.30-2, Dinner 7.30-10 ☹ all Sun & Mon, 1st wk Jan

Andrew Allchurch & Simon Rudge's friendly local restaurant is set on 2 floors; but in either room you can enjoy modern English cooking with plenty of choice at each course. Prices are set according to the number of courses taken. Some quite adventurous combinations work surprisingly well.

Stow Bridge Swinton House

Stow Bridge, King's Lynn, Norfolk, PE34 3PP
☎ (01366) 383151 📠 (01366) 383151
☐ 18 ⊚ £45
☺ Lunch Sun only 12.15-2, Dinner Fri & Sat only 7-9 ☹ 1 wk Xmas

The sensation here is that you are a house guest rather than a customer, but whatever your status, you can be assured of local produce, carefully cooked and charmingly served in country-house-style surroundings. The short wine list is very modestly priced.

Stow-on-the-Wold Fosse Manor Hotel

Fosse Way, Stow-on-the-Wold, Gloucestershire, GL54 1JX
☎ (01451) 830354 (01451) 832486
20 £98 72 £50
☺ Lunch 12.30-2, Dinner 7.30-9.30 (Fri & Sat to 10) ☹ 22-30 Dec

Just a mile south of Stow, on the A429 Warwick to Cirencester road, Bob & Yvonne Johnston's Fosse Manor is a lovely Cotswold stone building. Some bedrooms, and the residents' lounge, have recently been refurbished to keep them in line with the generally high standards throughout. Set and à la carte menus available in the restaurant.

Stow-on-the-Wold Grapevine Hotel

Sheep Street, Stow-on-the-Wold, Gloucestershire, GL54 1AU
☎ (01451) 830344 (01451) 832278
21 £108 60 £50
☺ Lunch 12-2.30, Dinner 7-9.30 ☹ Hotel Bank Holidays, 24 Dec-10 Jan

Cotswold-stone hotel right at the heart of one of the most pretty and famous Cotswold towns. Bedrooms are individually decorated and well equipped. Extended business facilities since Spring 1995. Chef Dean Collins promises a continuation of the Vine Restaurant's reputation for good food.

Stow-on-the-Wold Wyck Hill House

Burford Road, Stow-on-the-Wold, Gloucestershire, GL54 1HY
☎ (01451) 831936 (01451) 832243
31 £108 70 £95
☺ Lunch 12-2, Dinner 7.30-9.30 (Sat to 10)

Just 2 miles outside Stow on the A424, this lovely Cotswold-stone house combines the tranquility and quaintness of bygone days with 20th-century amenities. The panelled library and galleried staircase set the scene, while in the elegant dining room, international cooking rounds off a day in the heart of England.

Stratford-upon-Avon Ettington Park

Alderminster, Stratford-upon-Avon, Warwickshire, CV37 8BS
☎ (01789) 450123 (01789) 450472
48 £145 45 £80
☺ Lunch 12-1.45, Dinner 7-9.30 (Fri & Sat to 10) ☹ Xmas

All of the bedrooms at Ettington underwent refurbishment during 1995, maintaining the high standards to which visitors here have become accustomed over the years. The Gothic-style building stands in its own grounds and has fine views over the surrounding countryside. Leisure facilities include an indoor swimming pool, with dining in the panelled Oak Room restaurant.

England 241

Stratford-upon-Avon Liaison

1 Shakespeare Street, Stratford-upon-Avon,
Warwickshire, CV37 6RN
☎ (01789) 293400 (01789) 297863
58 £65

☺ Lunch 12-2.30, Dinner 6-10.30 ☹ Lunch Sat, all Sun, 2 wks Jan

"The quintessential ingredient to the success of Liaison must be its simple elegance, by day or by night." So say Patricia Plunkett & Ank van der Tuin and we wouldn't argue with them! Modern British cooking with interesting, clean flavours is the cornerstone of their style, and there's a separate menu for vegetarians. This is a "must" when you're in Stratford.

Streatley-on-Thames Swan Diplomat

High Street, Streatley-on-Thames, Berkshire, RG8 9HR
☎ (01491) 873737 (01491) 872554
46 £134 75 £85

☺ Lunch 12-2, Dinner 7.30-9.30 (Sat from 7 in summer),
(tea 3.30-5.30) ☹ Lunch Sat

Riverside setting for this hotel and restaurant, well-equipped with leisure facilities. For business or private parties, hire the Magdalen College Barge which is permanently moored alongside. The formal Riverside Restaurant takes full advantage of the setting, and offers classic French menus; while the less formal Duck Room brasserie is a good choice for a light meal (it's not open on Sunday lunchtimes).

Stretton Dovecliffe Hall

Dovecliffe Road, Stretton, Nr Burton-on-Trent,
Staffordshire, DE13 0DJ
☎ (01283) 531818 (01283) 516546
7 £95 90 £65

☺ Lunch 12-1.45, Dinner 7-9.30

☹ Lunch Mon & Sat, Dinner Sun, 1 wk Xmas, 2 wks summer, 2 wks spring

Just ¾ mile from the A38, between the villages of Stretton and Rolleston-on-Dove, Dovecliffe is a Grade II listed Georgian building which dates from around 1790 with its own 7-acre garden overlooking the River Dove. Conferences are accommodated with ease, though the location also makes it ideal for tourists to the area. All guests enjoy the modern English cooking which specialises in seafood. The New World is well-represented on the wine list.

Stretton Ram Jam Inn

Great North Road, Stretton, Nr Oakham, Rutland, Leicestershire, LE15 7QX
☎ (01780) 410776   (01780) 410361
7   £61   30 £40
☺ Lunch 12-2.30, Dinner 7-10, (light meals 7am-11pm) ☹ 25 Dec

Tim Hart's roadside retreat, despite celebrating 10 years here to great acclaim, has still not been imitated despite his having identified and filled a market niche: high-grade food and accommodation for weary travellers who care about quality. Expanded facilities now also allow for business meetings. The menu is simply laid out, reasonably priced, there's no pressure on you to overeat.

Stuckton Three Lions

Stuckton, Nr Fordingbridge, Hampshire, SP6 2HF
☎ (01425) 652489   (01425) 656144
60 £65
☺ Lunch 12.15-2, Dinner 7.15-9.45 (Sat to 10)
☹ all Mon & Dinner Sun, Bank Holidays, last 2 wks Jan & last wk Feb

After many years, the Wadsacks have gone; in situ now are Mike & Jayne Womersley – a fine chef, he made his mark at Lucknam Park near Bath. One to watch! I look forward to my next visit.

Sturminster Newton Plumber Manor

Hazelbury Bryan Road, Sturminster Newton, Dorset, DT10 2AF
☎ (01258) 472507   (01258) 473370
16   £115   60 £55
☺ Lunch Sun only 12.30-1.30, Dinner 7.30-9.30 ☹ Hotel Feb

Charles Brune built Plumber Manor in the early 17th Century, and in 1973 the Prideaux-Brunes, constant residents, took the plunge of turning it into a restaurant with rooms: they haven't looked back. Comfortable and individually decorated bedrooms are a haven, while English/French menus in the restaurant are structured as 3 or 4 courses with plenty of choice.

Sudbury Mabey's Brasserie

47 Gainsborough Street, Sudbury, Suffolk, CO10 7SS
☎ (01787) 374298
50 £55
☺ Lunch 12-2, Dinner 7-10 ☹ Sun & Mon, 5 days Xmas

Robert & Johanna Mabey run this friendly brasserie as well as Regatta in Aldeburgh and St Peters in Ipswich. Here you can enjoy good home cooking with an eclectic touch. Daily specials augment the seasonally-changing menus. Good local restaurant.

Sutton Coldfield New Hall

Walmley Road, Sutton Coldfield, West Midlands, B76 1QX
☎ 0121-378 2442   📠 0121-378 4637
🛏 60 £ £134 🪑 60 🍽 £95
☺ Lunch 12.30-2 (Sun to 2.15), Dinner 7-10 (Sun 7.30-9.30)
☹ Lunch Sat

Ian & Caroline Parkes go to great lengths to satisfy the requests of guests at New Hall; and since they've secured return visits from Pavarotti, they reckon they're doing it right! New chef Valentine Rodriguez offers seasonal menus with intricate combinations of ingredients; and the wine list is of stature appropriate to the surroundings.

Sutton Partners Brasserie   ❖

23 Stonecot Hill, Sutton, Surrey, SM3 9HB
☎ 0181-644 7743
🪑 32 🍽 £50
☺ Lunch 12-2, Dinner 7-9.30
☹ Lunch Sat, all Sun & Mon, Bank Holidays, 1 wk Xmas

Modern British cooking from the partners here – or more specifically, from new chef Rebecca Jones who joined at the turn of the year. A very reasonably priced carte is supplemented by a monthly-changing set menu. Short and excellent value wine list, with nothing over £20.

Swaffham Strattons Hotel

4 Ash Close, Swaffham, Norfolk, PE37 7NH
☎ (01760) 23845   📠 (01760) 720458
🛏 7 £ £78 🪑 20 🍽 £60
☺ Dinner 7-9 (Sun 6.30-9)   ☹ 25 & 26 Dec

Set in a lovely Queen Anne country house (which was previously called The Villa, and described by one James Ackerman – no relation – as "a building in the country designed for its owners enjoyment and relaxation"), this is now a friendly little restaurant with rooms run by Les & Vanessa Scott. Set-price dinner menus use some interesting ingredients in inspired ways (shades of Gunn Eriksen in the nettle and herb soup?).

Swanage Galley

9 High Street, Swanage, Dorset, BH19 2LN
☎ (01929) 427299
🪑 30 🍽 £45
☺ Dinner 7-9.30   ☹ 2 wks Nov, 31 Dec-14 Feb

An attractive corner site down by the old stone quay – so it's no surprise to find plenty of fish on the menu, as well as some meat dishes. The wine list has some unusual selections, grouped by fruitiness, at reasonable prices.

Tadworth Gemini Restaurant

28 Station Approach, Tadworth, Surrey, KT20 5AH
☎ (01737) 812179
🍴 40 🍽 £55
☺ Lunch 12-2, Dinner 7-9.30
☹ Lunch Sat, Dinner Sun, all Mon, 2 wks Xmas, 2 wks Jun

Small, friendly local restaurant run by the Fosters since 1991, offering frequently-changing menus in French style: pasta, seafood and game are specialities. 2-course variations are available from Tuesday to Thursday. Concise wine list has a few halves, and some useful tasting notes.

Taplow Cliveden

Taplow, Nr Maidenhead, Berkshire, SL6 0JF
☎ (01628) 668561 📠 (01628) 661837
🛏 37 £ £266 🍴 65 🍽 £140
☺ Lunch 12.30-2.30, Dinner 7-10.30

The ultimate luxury, a hotel where standards are set for all others to be judged by. The setting, of course, helps – an exquisite house now owned by The National Trust that has seen a formidable list of previous owners, most notably the Astors. Amidst 400 acres of beautifully maintained gardens that overlook the Thames, the house retains its majesty with stunning grandeur and from the moment that you arrive you are pampered in appropriate style. Needless to say there is everything that you could wish for at Cliveden: pools, indoor and outdoor tennis, air-conditioned gym, boats on the river for summer picnics and 2 dining rooms in which to indulge even further. Waldo's is where chef Ron Maxwell really shows his art with dishes such as risotto of foie gras and langoustines, turbot with roast baby artichokes, tomatoes and olives on citrus and ginger butter sauce or venison with blackberries, caramelised apples and black pudding with game sauce. A hot mirabelle soufflé with liquorice ice cream is the ultimate undulgence! The Terrace Dining Room looks out on the formal gardens, a breathtaking vista where you can enjoy an imaginative range of dishes from a simple mixed grill or chateaubrand to pot-roast scallops with spring cabbage, pancetta and Périgord truffles or braised ham hock with sauerkraut served with rocket leaves and warm potato and chive salad. When you want to spoil yourself for whatever reason, there is no better place in which to be spoilt!

**THE ACADEMY OF
FOOD & WINE SERVICE**
see page 22

Taunton Castle Hotel

Castle Green, Taunton, Somerset, TA1 1NF
☎ (01823) 272671 📠 (01823) 336066
▯ 35 £ £110 🛏 80 🍽 £90
☺ Lunch 12.30-2, Dinner 7.30-9

Where better to enjoy modern British cooking than with Kit Chapman, plus the help of various chefs. He has pioneered the advancement of the new approach to our national dishes and Phil Vickery continues with the campaign. A salad of braised ham hocks is spiced with English mustard, shallots and herbs, a rich oyster and smoked haddock broth has pearl barley and root vegetables, potted game comes with spiced pears. Main dishes such as braised shoulder of pork with apples and cider, roast monkfish with braised vegetables and mashed potatoes or roast baby chicken with tarragon, garlic and artichokes are perfectly prepared. The puddings are also based on English classics, warm bread and butter pudding, rhubarb crumble with custard, baked egg custard tart with nutmeg ice cream or a hot chocolate pudding with chocolate sauce and vanilla ice cream, delicious.

Taunton Nightingales Restaurant

Bath House Farm, Lower West Hatch, Nr Taunton, Somerset, TA3 5RH
☎ (01823) 480806
🛏 40 🍽 £55
☺ Lunch Sun only 12.30-2.30, Dinner 7.15-9.30
☹ Dinner Sun, 25 Dec

Jeremy & Margaret Barlow, together with Sally Edwards, have now returned to Nightingales after an 18-month migration – they created it in 1987 and ran it themselves for 4 years or so. Fixed-price menus offer a choice of 4 or 5 dishes at each course. West country cheeses are a difficult choice against some very good puds. Great value lunch on Sundays in this pretty village setting on the outskirts of Taunton.

Taunton Porters

49 East Reach, Taunton, Somerset, TA1 3EX
☎ (01823) 256688
🛏 50 🍽 £40
☺ Lunch 12-2, Dinner 7-9.45
☹ Lunch Sat, all Sun, Bank Holidays, 1 wk Xmas

Murray & Joanna Porter have been running this wine bar and restaurant since 1985, and chef Clive Arthur has been with them since 1992. So there's an air of confidence about the place, apparent both in the service and in the multi-national menu which changes daily and is chalked up on a blackboard. There are some dishes for vegetarians, and most wines are available by the bottle or the glass.

Teddington Spaghetti Junction

20 High Street, Teddington, Middlesex, TW11 8EW
☎ 0181-977 6756   📠 0181-977 9199
🍴 70 🕑 £50

☺ Lunch 12-2.30, Dinner 6-11.15 (Sun to 10.30) ☹ Mon, Bank Holidays

Smart but fun and friendly Italian restaurant near the Thames. You can't book in advance on Friday or Saturday night, but you can place your order from the bar while you wait for a table. Excellent selection of predominantly Italian wines.

Teffont Evias Howard's House

Teffont Evias, Nr Salisbury, Wiltshire, SP3 5RJ
☎ (01722) 716392   📠 (01722) 716820
🛏 9 £ 111   🍴 35 🕑 £75

☺ Lunch Sun only 12.30-2, Dinner 7.30-10

Interesting architectural features here: the original 17th-century building was extended 100-odd years later in Swiss style, as required by the then owner. Most recent restoration was completed in 1989, resulting in a small and friendly country houses set in lovely gardens in a quiet location. Sustenance comes in the form of modern British cooking using fresh fish daily and game in season.

Teignmouth Thomas Luny House

Teign Street, Teignmouth, Devon, TQ14 8EG
☎ (01626) 772976
🛏 4 £ 60
🍴 1 large table for residents & guests seating 8 🕑 £50

☺ Dinner 7.30 for 8   ☹ Hotel mid Dec-end Jan

Thomas Luny was a marine artist, and this graceful home was built for him in the later 18th Century to take advantage of the lovely harbour views. Modern visitors do likewise, though the house is also home (since 1988) to the Allan family. The room rate not only includes early morning tea but also afternoon tea. A simple, no-choice dinner is served in the non-smoking dining room.

Tetbury Calcot Manor

Tetbury, Gloucestershire, GL8 8YJ
☎ (01666) 890391   📠 (01666) 890394
🛏 20 £ 115   🍴 50 🕑 £65

☺ Lunch 12.30-2, Dinner 7.30-9.30

Pretty and rambling collection of Cotswold buildings that can by turn be the main house of the hotel, bedrooms in the stable block, or the Gumstool Inn. On a recent visit, an as yet unused barn was spotted – we're opening a book as to what ideas manager Richard Ball has in mind for it! Comfort and relaxation are the watch-words throughout. In the restaurant, the former sous-chef is now in charge so the style remains similar: modern British though with individual touches. Fairly priced wine list.

Tetbury The Close

8 Long Street, Tetbury, Gloucestershire, GL8 8AQ

☎ (01666) 502272   📠 (01666) 504401

15 £95   36 £75

Lunch 12-2, Dinner 7.15-9.45

Now part of the Virgin hotel group, the Close is undergoing gradual improvements and upgrades to the public areas while manager Sean Spencer and chef Paul Welch guarantee continuity. A fairly international menu has a definitely modern slant to it. This historic building is well worth a visit and has both historic and modern style.

Thame Spread Eagle

Cornmarket, Thame, Oxfordshire, OX9 2BW

☎ (01844) 213661   📠 (01844) 261380

33 £90   65 £50

Lunch 12.30-2 (Sun to 2.30), Dinner 7-10 (Sat from 7.30, Sun to 9)

3 days Xmas/New Year

English landmark hostelry which dates back to the 16th Century. Perhaps its most famous landlord (before the present incumbent, of course!) was John Fothergill in the 1920s, in whose honour the restaurant and bar are named. Banqueting and conferences provide much custom, as do such attractions as the local antiques fair and the Thame Show.

Thornbury Thornbury Castle

Thornbury, Nr Bristol, Avon, BS12 1HH

☎ (01454) 281182   📠 (01454) 416188

18 £105   50 £85

Lunch 12-2, Dinner 7-9.30 (Sun to 9)   2 days Jan

A 16th-century castle once appropriated by Henry VIII that has for many years been run as a hotel. A must for all American and visiting gourmets, it has 18 bed chambers, some with splendid Tudor fireplaces and oriel windows, all with phone and colour television, a sign of the times. The kitchen offers a variety of classic and modern dishes which can be enjoyed in the octagonal tower room. Walled gardens and its own vineyard make Thornbury something rather special.

Thornton-le-Fylde River House

Skippool Creek, Thornton-le-Fylde, Nr Blackpool, Lancashire, FY5 5LF

☎ (01253) 883497   📠 (01253) 892083

5 £80   40 £85

Lunch by arrangement (Sun 12.30 for 1), Dinner by arrangement 7.30-9.30   Dinner Sun, some Bank Holidays

Small and friendly restaurant with rooms – each room has its own feature such as a hooded bath or a half-four-poster, though all benefit from the warm welcome proffered by Bill Scott. Concise set menus or the carte take you through his repertoire of dishes – game is a speciality. Extensive and interesting wine list.

Thornton Cleveleys Victorian House

Trunnah Road, Thornton Cleveleys, Lancashire, FY5 4HF
☎ (01253) 860619 📠 (01253) 865350
3 £94 44 £55
☺ Lunch 12-1.30, Dinner 7-9.30 ☹ Sun, 1st wk Feb

Louise & Didier Guerin have been here since 1987 and have built up a loyal, local following for their very French restaurant in a very English Victorian setting. A classic menu has some modern touches, and the predominantly French wine list is distinctly affordable.

Thundridge Hanbury Manor

Thundridge, Nr Ware, Hertfordshire, SG12 0SD
☎ (01920) 487722 📠 (01920) 487692
96 £161 48 £130
☺ Lunch 12-2.30, Dinner 7-9.45 (Fri & Sat 7-9.45)
☹ Dinner Sun, Bank Holidays

A sumptious, Jacobean-styled mansion built at the end of the last century set in 200 acres of Hertfordshire some 25 miles South of London. Principally a country house estate and golf club with health club catering for conferences and functions as well as functioning as a normal hotel. Two restaurants; The Vardon has a varied menu with everything from burgers to sandwiches and grilled meats and fish to pasta whilst the Zodiac Restaurant is overseen by chef Rory Kennedy. Elegant rooms are well furnished and there is lovely panelling and fine tapestries in the Oak Hall.

Tintagel Trebrea Lodge

Trenale, Nr Tintagel, Cornwall, PL34 0HR
☎ (01840) 770410
7 £64 14 £40
☺ Dinner at 8 ☹ 8-31 Jan

Set on a wooded hillside overlooking the north Cornish coast, Trebrea Lodge dates largely from the late 18th Century, when the formal Georgian facade was added, resulting in the present Grade II listed building which is now a small but very comfortable hotel. Set-price no-choice 4-course dinner menus are in English/French style and very reasonably priced, as is the wine list.

Torquay Mulberry House

1 Scarborough Road, Torquay, Devon, TQ2 5UJ
☎ (01803) 213639 📠 (01803) 213639
3 £43 30 £50
☺ Lunch 12-2, Dinner 7.30-9.30 ☹ Mon & Tue

Lesley Cooper's one-woman show is a testament to her passions for food and for quality. Her daily-changing menu is written up on a blackboard, and meals are enjoyed either in the elegant, light and spacious or on the front patio, if weather permits. Lighter lunches and snacks are also available.

England

Torquay Remy's Restaurant Français

3 Croft Road, Torquay, Devon, TQ2 5UF
☎ (01803) 292359
🪑 36 🍽 £40
☺ Dinner 7.30-9.30 ☹ Dinner Sun & Mon

Remy offers good value with his fixed-price menus and well-judged wine list. Start with cream of quail soup with mushrooms, home-smoked salmon, rillettes of pork or snails en croute with garlic. Then you can choose from around 10 main courses; lamb's kidneys in cream and mustard sauce, sirloin steak in red wine sauce, salmon in pastry with Pernod sauce or choose from the blackboard for daily specials or vegetarian dishes. Poached pear with hot chocolate sauce, iced soufflé flavoured with cognac on raspberry coulis or tarte au chocolat are typical puddings.

Tunbridge Wells Downstairs at Thackeray's

85 London Road, Tunbridge Wells, Kent, TN1 1EA
☎ (01892) 537559 📠 (01892) 511921
🪑 30 🍽 £45
☺ Lunch 12.30-2.30, Dinner 7-10 ☹ Sun & Mon, 5 days Xmas

Downstairs (separate entrance) is the little sister of Bruce Wass's main restaurant (see below). There's a more relaxed approach to the menu here, with several dishes available as starters/mains, or starters/light meals. The surroundings, too, are less formal, encouraging more folk to enjoy this gem in Kent. Garden patio in summer.

Tunbridge Wells Thackeray's House

85 London Road, Tunbridge Wells, Kent, TN11 1EA
☎ (01892) 511921 📠 (01892) 511921
🪑 50 🍽 £90
☺ Lunch 12.30-2.30, Dinner 7-10
☹ Dinner Sun, all Mon, Bank Holidays, 5 days Xmas

Thackeray would probably turn in his grave with pleasant surprise if he could see the multi-faceted operation that Bruce Wass has created within his home. Choose from fixed-price or carte in the main restaurant, a mix of classic and modern dishes, hot turbot pate with langoustine sauce, crispy fried sardine fillet salad with scallops and rouille, saddle of hare with apples and green peppercorns or guinea fowl with morels.

Turners Hill Alexander House

East Street, Turners Hill, West Sussex, RH10 4QD
☎ (01342) 714914   (01342) 717328
15   £150   55   £120
☺ Lunch 12.30-2, Dinner 7-9.30 (Sun to 9)

A rare Sussex mansion where you can be treated like a house guest at the home of Earl & Countess Alexander of Tunis. There are excellent business and leisure facilities, and the house is also highly desirable for social events: arrive in a limousine under the porte cochère, or by heli on the pad. In the elegant and formal dining room, enjoy classic English and French cooking from a carte which changes seasonally or a table d'hote which changes twice daily. Wine list of some stature, as you would expect in this grand setting.

Twickenham Hamiltons

43 Crown Road, St Margarets, Twickenham, Middlesex, TW1 3EJ
☎ 0181-892 3949
50   £50
☺ Lunch 12-2, Dinner 7-10.30 (Fri & Sat to 11)
☹ Lunch Sat, Dinner Sun, all Mon, Bank Holidays, 1 wk New Year

Eye-catching red-and-gold awnings herald the approach to Hamiltons, which specialises in fine Anglo-French food served in stylish surroundings in a unique atmosphere. Live jazz plays at Sunday lunchtimes. A concise wine list is very user-friendly.

Twickenham McClements

2 Whitton Road, Twickenham, Middlesex, TW1 1BJ
☎ 0181-744 9610   (01784) 240593
35   £65
☺ Lunch 12-2.30, Dinner 7-10.30
☹ Sun, 10 days from 26 Dec

John McClements is now concentrating all his efforts on this delightful little restaurant, with an art-deco style interior and a warm welcome from friendly staff. Excellent cooking, too, from the kitchen, bringing classic southern French cooking up to date with starters such as salad gourmand – lobster, quail and foie gras; or oyster fritters seved with celeriac and sauce tartare. Followed by breast of guinea fowl with artichokes and wild mushrooms or perhaps roast fillet of monkfish served with a ratatouille jus and little crispy squids. For those of you with a sweet tooth there are some delicious puds, too, on the fortnightly-changing menus. With the added benefit of air-conditioning, there's no excuse not to visit – go there and enjoy!

England 251

Uckfield Hooke Hall

250 High Street, Uckfield, East Sussex, TN22 1EN
☎ (01825) 761578 (01825) 768025
9 £85 36 £65
☺ Lunch 12-2, Dinner 7.30-9 ☹ Lunch Sat, all Sun, 1 wk Feb

An elegant Queen Anne house now offers hospitality to weary passers-by, tourists to this pretty part of the country, and business events. Cooking is northern Italian in origin, and the wine list is also predominantly Italian. Rooms are named after famous lovers and mistresses!

Uckfield
Horsted Place Sporting Estate & Hotel

Little Horsted, Uckfield, East Sussex, TN22 5TS
☎ (01825) 750581 (01825) 750459
20 £136 40 £95
☺ Lunch 12-2, Dinner 7.30-9.30

This splendid, neo-Gothic house, built in 1850 for a wealthy merchant, was converted in 1986 into a splendid country house hotel. Surrounded by the 1,100-acre Horsted Estate, it offers plenty of outdoor sporting pursuits, while indoors, the Pugin dining room (named after Augustus Pugin who designed much of the detail in the house) provides a perfect backdrop for Allan Garth's cooking. Choose from fixed-price, à la carte or vegetarian menus, but whichever, be sure of a mix of classic and modern dishes prepared to a high standard.

Ullswater Leeming House

Watermillock, Ullswater, Cumbria, CA11 0JJ
☎ (01768) 486622 (01768) 486443
40 £142 80 £80
☺ Lunch 12.30-1.45, Dinner 7.30-8.45

Just a 10-minute drive from Junction 40 of the M6 will bring you to Leeming House, with its fine views of Lake Ullswater from its landscaped grounds. Ongoing bedroom refurbishment ensures high standards are maintained, and matched by the housekeeping. Set dinners offer British cooking in traditional style.

Ullswater Old Church Hotel

Watermillock, Ullswater, Cumbria, CA11 0JN
☎ (01768) 486204 (01768) 486368
9 £120 24 £60
☺ Dinner 7.30-8.30 ☹ Hotel Nov-Mar

Small, family-run hotel which is a haven of peace and quiet. Children are well catered for, both in terms of facilities and food. Breakfasts are splendid, and set you up for a day's activity on the lake.

Ullswater
Rampsbeck Country House Hotel

Watermillock, Ullswater, Cumbria, CA11 0LP
☎ (01768) 486442   (01768) 486688
 21 £80 40 £55
☺ Lunch 12-1.15, Dinner 7-8.30   6 wks Jan/Feb

Lovely, 18th-century country house set in its own gardens and parkland, privately owned and run. The white-washed exterior sets the scene for the elegant and airy interior, with large windows, carved ceilings and open fires. Set-price menus use local ingredients when possible, and are carefully compiled.

Ullswater Sharrow Bay

Howtown, Ullswater, Cumbria, CA10 2LZ
☎ (01768) 486301   (01768) 486349
 28 £260 65 £95
☺ Lunch 1-1.45, Dinner 8-8.45, (tea 4-4.45)   Hotel Dec-Feb

Every year we wonder whether those grandees of the country house scene, Francis Coulson & Brian Sack, will yet surrender the reins to their capable protégés, Nigels Lawrence & Lightburn, and kitchen brigade headed up by Johnnie Martin (who have also notched up a good few years between them). But like the great stars, indomitable and ever-smiling, there they are, year after year, modestly accepting the accolades of their numerous well-wishers. The epitome, nay the original example, of what became the country house hotel genre is superbly located amid breathtaking scenery; there's clean fresh air with which to fill your lungs, wonderful Fells in which to stretch your muscles, and either side of these healthy outdoor pursuits, a feel to the interior of the house which makes you feel like you're sinking into clouds of cotton wool, and some top-hole cooking to feed the inner man and woman. The fixed-price menus offer a staggering range of choices at the principal courses, and the sheer exuberance of flavours and textures is enough to take your breath away. Try to choose between starters like terrine of duck, venison, grouse and pistachios served with spicy oranges, toasted brioche and Cumberland sauce; ravioli of lobster mousseline in lemon pasta, served with fried julienne of vegetables and lobster sauce; or smoked chicken consommé served with chicken and herb quenelles from the dozen or so on offer. The fish course (no choice) could be fillet of halibut served with a marinière sauce and soufflé suissesse, after which comes a sorbet. On to the main courses: honey-glazed roast Lunesdale duckling served with glazed apples, blueberries, and gravy made from the duck juices with honey and thyme; medallion of local venison served with Sharrow noodles, chestnuts and a gravy (not sauce, note!) enriched by juniper berries and a dash of brandy; or fried fillet of monkfish served with grilled salmon and 2 sauces: one a saffron, cream and herb sauce, the other a beurre blanc. No fewer than 6 vegetables accompany the 7 or 8 main dishes. At least 8 puddings jostle for attention: La Stupenda is an apricot bavarois laced with apricot brandy, created by Francis for Dame Joan Sutherland; the chocolate and rum pye has its origins in the 18th century. An all-British cheeseboard (shepherd's purse, smoked cherrywood, pencarreg, lanark blue for instance) precedes coffee and petits fours. You'll appreciate a good night's sleep! Then the next morning, a legendary Sharrow breakfast will set you up for the day ahead...

England 253

Ulverston Bay Horse Inn

Canal Foot, Ulverston, Cumbria, LA12 9EL
☎ (01229) 583972 📠 (01229) 580502
🛏 7 £ £150 🍴 50 🍽 £65

🙂 Lunch 12.30-2, Dinner 7.30 for 8   ☹ Lunch Sun & Mon, Jan

1½ miles from Ulverston is where you'll find the Bay Horse, run by Robert Lyons who's a product of the John Tovey school. The atmosphere is friendly and informal, rooms are cosy and comfortable, and in the restaurant modern English cooking uses local produce whenever possible to produce a carte with plenty of choices.

Upper Slaughter Lords of the Manor

Upper Slaughter, Nr Bourton-on-the-Water, Gloucestershire, GL54 2JD
☎ (01451) 820243 📠 (01451) 820696
🛏 27 £ £115 🍴 65 🍽 £90

🙂 Lunch 12.30-2 (Sun to 2.30), Dinner 7.30-9.30 (Fri & Sat from 7)
☹ Hotel 2-11 Jan

Originally built around 1650 and much extended in Victorian times, the Lords in question were the Witts (rectors of the parish). Set in parkland and with a lake, it's now a lovely retreat in the Cotswold, furnished with quiet comfort and attention to detail, topped by chef Clive Dixon's country cooking with a modern influence and a thoroughly researched wine list.

Uppingham The Lake Isle

16 High Street East, Uppingham, Leicestershire, LE15 9PZ
☎ (01572) 822951 📠 (01572) 822951
🛏 12 £ £66 🍴 40 🍽 £62

🙂 Lunch 12.30-1.45 (Sun 12-2), Dinner 7.30-9.30 (7-10 Sat)
☹ Lunch Mon, Dinner Sun (except residents)

David & Claire Whitfield, chef/proprietors here since 1982, run a comfortable and charming hotel and restaurant, both of which receive constant attention to detail to ensure that their high standards are maintained. Modern European menus are accompanied by some fine wines.

Veryan Nare Hotel

Carne Beach, Veryan, Nr Truro, Cornwall, TR2 5PF
☎ (01872) 501279 📠 (01872) 501856
🛏 35 £ £160 🍴 70 🍽 £70

🙂 Lunch 12-2, Dinner 7.15-9.30   ☹ 3 Jan-15 Feb

The sea is so close that you might think the outdoor pool is superfluous – but remember that the weather on this part of the Roseland peninsula can be very – well, British! So, too, is the cooking which features plenty of local seafood, and home-made pudding specialities.

Walkington Manor House

Northlands, Walkington, Beverley, Humberside, HU17 8RT
☎ (01482) 881645 📠 (01482) 866501
🛏 7 £ £97 🍴 60 🍽 £75
☺ Dinner 7.30-9.15 ☹ Dinner Sun

Just outside Walkington on the Beverley to Newbald road, Derek & Lee Baugh's Manor House is a lovely small hotel and restaurant. An elegant drawing room, spacious bedrooms and a conservatory dining room all pave the way for some modern international menus with some intriguing combinations, on either set-price or à la carte menus.

Walterstone Allt-Yr-Ynys Hotel

Walterstone, Hereford & Worcester, HK2 0DU
☎ (01873) 890307 📠 (01873) 890539
🛏 11 £ £85 🍴 30 🍽 £60
☺ Dinner 7pm ☹ Sun, first 2 wks Jan

Located between Hereford and Abergavenny, this originally 16th-century house is set in well-established gardens which reach down to the banks of the River Monmow. The clay-pigeon centre is popular with businesses for corporate entertaining.

Wansford-in-England The Haycock

Wansford-in-England, Peterborough, Cambridgeshire, PE8 6JA
☎ (01780) 782223 📠 (01780) 783031
🛏 51 £ £98 🍴 90 🍽 £75
☺ Lunch 12-2, Dinner 7-10, (Orchard Room: 7.30am-11pm)

A recent addition to the Arcadian group, the Haycock was originally a 17th-century coaching inn, and continues to offer rest and refreshment to travellers, just off the A1. The menu is designed for relaxed eating so you can have as many or as few courses as you like, with wines by the bottle or the glass. Definitely worth breaking your journey here.

Wareham Priory Hotel

Church Green, Wareham, Dorset, BH20 4ND
☎ (01929) 551666 📠 (01929) 554519
🛏 19 £ £110 🍴 66 🍽 £75
☺ Lunch by arrangement only 12.30-2, Dinner 7.30-10, (Tea 3.30-5.30)

An ongoing programme of refurbishment ensures constancy of standards at this former priory, sympathetically converted to an extremely comfortable country hotel. Its boathouse, created from a 16th-century barn, is right on the River Frome, and there are views also of the Purbeck Hills. In the restaurant, modern English cooking takes advantage of local shellfish, and game in season. Excellent range of English farmhouse cheeses.

England 255

Warminster Bishopstrow House

Boreham Road, Warminster, Wiltshire, BA12 9HH
☎ (01985) 212312 📠 (01985) 216769
30 £125 65 £80
☺ Lunch 12.30-2, Dinner 7.30-9.30

Bishopstrow was built in 1817 by one John Pinch of Bath, but no expense was spared during its conversion to elegant country house hotel with superb leisure facilities (that famously curvy pillared swimming pool, tennis, fishing). In the public and private rooms there's a homely feel which combines well with the elegant Georgian proportions. Great attention to detail is lavished on appointing the bedrooms as well as maintaining them: some suites have a jacuzzi bath. Chef Chris Suter has hit the right note in pitching his cooking to suit his clientele: an up-to-date English style has just enough classical heritage to please both purists and modernists. Try a warm salad of honey-glazed duck confit with Puy lentils and a shallot and cassis dressing, or baked natural smoked haddock with Welsh rarebit, plum tomato and chive salad; then pan-fried saddle of local venison with wild mushrooms Agen prunes and vanilla bean sauce or baked fillet of brill, mushroom duxelle, tomato fondue and a soft herb crust. Tempting puddings might be toffee apple crumble with butterscotch sauce and cinnamon ice cream, or tart of chocolate with orange sauce and chocolate sauce – there are usually 5 or 6 choices at each course, and the meal is priced at £33 for 3 courses or £38 for 4 (ie the addition of a fine selection of farmhouse cheeses). Live piano music is played at weekends.

Waterhouses Old Beams

Leek Road, Waterhouses, Staffordshire, ST10 3HW
☎ (01538) 308254 📠 (01538) 308157
5 £80 40 £80
☺ Lunch 12-2, Dinner 7-9.30 ☹ Lunch Sat, Dinner Sun, all Mon

A friendly, comfortable inn that provides a welcome haven in this semi-wilderness for gastronomes. The Wallis' hospitality is generous and Nigel's cooking makes a visit well worthwhile. A fixed-price menu at under £20 is tremendous value but if you really want the works try the gourmet menu when you could try tartare of salmon, crab and avocado on a tomato coulis with sevruga caviar or scallops wrapped in dry cure bacon on a ginger beurre blanc. Main courses might be a tart of pigeon, foie gras and wild mushrooms with madeira sauce, a lightly cooked fillet of lamb on a bed of spinach with roast baby onions and garlic or a glazed pig's trotter with sweetbreads and morels on truffle sauce. Soufflés are popular as puddings, hot raspberry with eau-de-vie de framboise sauce or a chocolate soufflé pudding on a guanaja chocolate sauce. Excellent bedrooms are located in an annexe just across the road so take care when retiring!

Wath-in-Nidderdale Sportsman's Arms

Wath-in-Nidderdale, Pateley Bridge, Nr Harrogate,
North Yorkshire, HG3 5PP
☎ (01423) 711306   (01423) 712524
7 £58   50 £60
☺ Lunch Sun only 12-2, Dinner 7-9.30   ☹ 25 Dec

Former 16th-century inn that is now a fine restaurant in a lovely location.
Ray Carter offers a fixed-price menu using good-quality raw ingredients,
cooked to show best their true flavours. Letting bedrooms enhance the
appeal of this delightful retreat.

Wells-Next-The-Sea The Moorings

6 Freeman Street, Wells-Next-The-Sea, Norfolk, NR23 1BA
☎ (01328) 710949
40 £50
☺ Lunch 12.30-2, Dinner 7.30-9   ☹ Lunch Tue-Thu, 2 wks Dec, 2 wks Jun

Bernard & Carla Phillips have been running this little coastal restaurant
since 1986, offering a good choice of home-cooked international-style
dishes in friendly surroundings. The wine list is laid out in user-friendly
fashion, and has a depth not always appreciated at first glance.

Wells Ritchers Restaurant

5 Sadler Street, Wells, Somerset, BA5 2RR
☎ (01749) 679085
14 £55
☺ Lunch 12-2 (reservations only), Dinner 7-9.30 (Sat to 9.30),
   (Bistro: 12-2, 7-9, 7 days, 18 seats)
☹ Sun & Mon, 26 Dec, 1 Jan

Nick Hart & Kate Ritcher offer classic French cooking with a modern
approach at their friendly little restaurant, presented on very reasonably
priced set menus. A concise, fairly-priced wine list has useful tasting
notes.

West Didsbury Lime Tree

8 Lapwing Lane, West Didsbury, Manchester,
Greater Manchester, M20 8WS
☎ 0161-445 1217
80 £45
☺ Lunch 12-2.30, Dinner 6-10.30   ☹ Lunch Mon & Sat, Bank Holidays

Friendly little bistro on the outskirts of Manchester, offering modern
international-style cooking in a relaxed atmosphere. The same people
run café/wine bars in Chorlton and Rusholme, so they are obviously
successfully meeting a local demand for good-quality food (set-price and
à la carte menus) and wine.

West Mersea Le Champenois Restaurant

Blackwater Hotel, 20-22 Church Road, West Mersea, Essex, CO5 8QH

☎ (01206) 383038   📠 (01206) 383338

🛏 8 £ £62 🍴 40 🍽 £60

☺ Lunch 12-2, Dinner 7-10   ☹ Lunch Tue, Dinner Sun, 3 wks Jan

Very French restaurant in a typically English coastal setting. Bright and cheerful atmosphere created by oak beams, gingham napery and shiny copper pans. Traditional French cooking throughout – except for Sunday lunch, which reverts to British roasts and is good value.

Weymouth Perry's

4 Trinity Road, Old Harbour, Weymouth, Dorset, DT4 8TJ

☎ (01305) 785799

🍴 54 🍽 £60

☺ Lunch 12-2, Dinner 7-9.30 (Sat to 10)

☹ Lunch Mon & Sat, Dinner Sun winter

The Hodders run this quayside restaurant with an individual touch which makes it popular with locals as well as holidaymakers. Fish is, naturally, a speciality, and very good it is, too, being locally caught and quickly cooked to best effect: the day's catches are chalked up on the board which supplements the printed menu. Predominantly French wine list, but the occasional excursion to other countries also.

Whimple Woodhayes

Whimple, Nr Exeter, Devon, EX5 2TD

☎ (01404) 822237

🛏 6 £ £90 🍴 16 🍽 £65

☺ Lunch by arrangement for residents, Dinner 7.30 for 8

A pretty, small, Georgian country house set in 4 acres of gardens just 8 miles west of Exeter. The Rendles have been here since 1988 and make their guests feel very much at home. A set-price dinner menu runs to 5 courses plus coffee and is excellent value, making good use of local produce in a mainly English style. There's good value on the wine list, too.

Whitby Magpie Café

14 Pier Road, Whitby, North Yorkshire, YO21 3PU

☎ (01947) 602058

🍴 80 🍽 £40

☺ 11.30-6.30   ☹ Jan-Feb

In Whitby, you ought to be able to eat sea-fresh fish and here's where you can. All the traditional favourites are on offer, either plain or sauced. In for a penny, in for a pound: round off the meal with a wicked home-made pudding. If your conscience is stronger than your appetite, choose from the Weight Watchers Menu: an excellent idea, even though you probably won't find me sharing it with you! Seriously, some of the best fish'n'chips in the country!

Whitby Trenchers

New Quay Road, Whitby, North Yorkshire, YO21 1DH
☎ (01947) 603212   📠 (01947) 821025
🍴 200   💷 £50
🙂 11am-9pm   🙁 mid Nov-mid Mar

Seaside fish restaurant, popular with locals and visitors alike. Good quality catch, freshly cooked and served in a cheerful manner – what more could you ask? And just in case, good puds and wines as well.

Whitstable Whitstable Oyster Fishery Co

Royal Native Oyster Stores, Horse Bridge Beach, Whitstable, Kent, CT5 1BU
☎ (01227) 276856   📠 (01227) 770666
🛏 8   £ £50   🍴 130   💷 £45
🙂 Lunch 12-2 (Sun 12-3), Dinner 7-9
🙁 Dinner Sun, all Mon, Bank Holidays

A complete refurbishment of the kitchens and the addition of extra outdoor seating has made the spanking fresh fish on offer here available to an even greater number of happy customers. Clean and simple letting bedrooms are an added bonus. Some of the best oysters in Britain.

Wickham Old House Hotel

The Square, Wickham, Hampshire, PO17 5JG
☎ (01329) 833049   📠 (01329) 833672
🛏 12   £ £87   🍴 40   💷 £75
🙂 Lunch 12-1.45, Dinner 7.30-9.30
🙁 Lunch Sat & Mon, all Sun, Bank Holidays, 2 wks Xmas, 2 wks Aug, 1 wk Easter

A Grade II listed, early Georgian house in the centre of an historic old town. Richard & Annie Skipwith converted it from a private residence to hotel and restaurant in 1970 and thus approach their 25th anniversary with an ever-growing reputation. A modern French slant to the cooking (such as local game in season) makes the best of available produce and talent. Concise wine list is reasonably priced.

Williton White House

Williton, Somerset, TA4 4QW
☎ (01984) 632306
🛏 12   £ £70   🍴 26   💷 £70
🙂 Dinner 7 for 7.30 & 8.30   🙁 Nov-May

A well established small hotel that has been successfully run by Dick & Kay Smith for over 25 years. Bedrooms in the main, Georgian house and the converted coach house are an ideal base from which to explore the lovely local countryside and enjoy some excellent cooking by Kay.

Wilmslow Stanneylands

Stanneylands Road, Wilmslow, Cheshire, SK9 4EY
☎ (01625) 525225 📠 (01625) 537282
▫ 32 £87 🪑 80 🍽 £80
☺ Lunch 12.30-2, Dinner 7-10
☹ Dinner Sun, Good Friday, 26 Dec, 1 Jan

Red-brick 1920s house in its own mature gardens, and sister to the Belfry at Handforth. The richly-furnished and decorated interior does not, however, overpower guests who can still be very relaxed here. It is also popular as a business venue. Contemporary English and European cooking in the restaurant. Live music occasionally; lots of New World wines on the list.

Winchester Lainston House

Sparsholt, Winchester, Hampshire, SO21 2LT
☎ (01962) 863588 📠 (01962) 772672
▫ 37 £145 🪑 60 🍽 £85
☺ Lunch 12-2.30, Dinner 7-10.30

Graceful, William & Mary, 17th-century house with a history dating back to the Domesday Book. A careful combination of period charm and modern amenities works well, and extends to the restaurant where modern interpretations of the classics attract a regular local following.

Winchester Old Chesil Rectory

Chesil Street, Winchester, Hampshire, SO23 8HU
☎ (01962) 851555
🪑 55 🍽 £50
☺ Lunch 12-2.30, Dinner 7-9.30 (late bookings by arrangement)
☹ all Sun & Mon, Bank Holidays, 1 wk Xmas, 1 wk Jul, 1 wk Aug

Popular local restaurant which has built up a regular clientele as well as a continual stream of new faces. The modern international menu is now only available à la carte, and there are also themed evenings. Loyal suppliers are greatly valued by the Ruthven-Stuarts, a policy which pays dividends.

Winchester Hotel du Vin & Bistro ❖ 🎀

14 Southgate Street, Winchester, Hampshire, SO23 9EF
☎ (01962) 841414 📠 (01962) 842458
⎕ 19 £ £100 🪑 45 🕐 £65
☺ Lunch 12-2.30, Dinner 7-9.30

The two main protagonists here – Robin Hutson and Gerard Bassett – both worked at Chewton Glen for many years. Since opening their very individual and innovative hotel and bistro a couple of years ago, the plaudits have been raining in, and rightly so. A wine theme permeates throughout the hotel with drinks companies sponsoring classy bedrooms and a cellar that is Gerard's pride and joy. James Martin in the kitchen produces outstanding food at sensible prices – nothing too elaborate, perhaps a risotto milanaise, roast rump of lamb with bubble and squeak and a bitter chocolate tart with crème anglaise. The accompanying wine list is, of course, rather special and fairly priced, the service spot-on from enthusiastic staff. This is *the* place to visit when in town with the added benefits of easy parking and a secluded garden.

Windermere Holbeck Ghyll 🦌

Holbeck Lane, Windermere, Cumbria, LA23 1LU
☎ (01539) 432375 📠 (01539) 434743
⎕ 14 £ £130 🪑 36 🕐 £55
☺ Dinner 7-8.45

Situated between Windermere and Ambleside, Holbeck is a friendly, creeper-clad country house offering individually decorated bedrooms, comfortable lounges and in the restaurant, traditional English menus with European influences, priced for 4 or 5 courses. Extensive ranges of farmhouse cheeses and of New World wines.

**BRITAIN'S TOP
INDEPENDENT BUTCHERS**
see page 9

Windermere Miller Howe

Rayrigg Road, Windermere, Cumbria, LA23 1EY
☎ (01539) 442536 📠 (01539) 445664
🛏 12 £ £150 🍴 70 🍽 £75

☺ Light Lunch at 12.30, Dinner only at 8.30, (tea 3.30-5)
☹ Hotel early Dec-early Mar

Another long-established, lakeland country house hotel, this time coming up to its silver anniversary of being under the guidance of John Tovey – chef, restaurateur, author, TV presenter. The highly individual decor is very representative of John's style, and his hospitality is boundless, from the complimentary glass of buck's fizz which starts off the daily breakfast, to the wonderful views at sunset which seem to have been laid on especially for you. John has trained many a chef who has gone on to his or her own venture, often investing more than just his experience and generous spirit in their futures. The instantly recognisable Miller Howe style of food is currently, at its home, in the capable hands of head chef Chris Blaydes. A recent, summer, set-price dinner menu (a mere £26, with choices only at the pudding stage) offered the following explosion of delights: pre-dinner canapés of parmesan sablés, stuffed cherry tomatoes and puff pastry rounds (a good indicator of the care lavished on the smallest detail), while the freshly-made bread rolls contained leek and diced mushroom. The first course was pan-fried aubergine, red pepper and cumin terrine served with virgin olive oil ratatouille; and the fish course a delicate lemon-crusted lemon sole fillet, served on a warm caper, lemon and anchovy vinaigrette with aïoli and garden marjoram. A short pause preceded the main course of roast sirloin of Aberdeen Angus beef with caramelised onion marmelade, horseradish cream, Yorkshire pudding and gravy made from beef stock and red wine, which was accompanied by broccoli florets in toasted sesame oil, sliced courgettes in marsala, glazed carrots with rosemary and cumin, spiced red cabbage with orange, and crispy roast potato. Another pause was needed before trying to choose between shortbread galettes layered with fresh raspberries and duo of chocolate mousses with rich chocolate sauce; lemon and vanilla cream iced cheesecake with sweet lemon sauce; the famous Miller Howe summer pudding served with fresh strawberry purée and Jersey cream from a local herd. An alternative is the Miller Howe simple cheese platter, but don't be fooled by the "simple": it's as intricate and inventive as everything which precedes! Coffee and home-made truffles complete the experience, which you really should try for yourself.

THE ACADEMY OF FOOD & WINE SERVICE
see page 22

Windermere Roger's Restaurant

4 High Street, Windermere, Cumbria, LA23 1AF
☎ (01539) 444954
🍴 22 🍽 £55

☺ Dinner 7-9.30   ☹ Sun (except Bank Holidays)

Having seen 15 years elapse since the Pergl-Wilsons opened their restaurant in up-town Windermere they maintain their simple formula of good food and service in comfortable surroundings at sensible prices. The result is that more and more customers return year after year for Roger's competent cooking and Alena's charming welcome. Choose from the limited fixed-price menu or short carte, you won't find better value in the Lake District. Warm French onion tart followed by cream of celery soup then a breast of chicken with Parma ham and Gruyère and marsala. Pudding was Austrian style apple crumble cake then coffee with petits fours, all this at under £16. No wonder it's busy!

Windsor Oakley Court

Windsor Road, Water Oakley, Nr Windsor,
Berkshire, SL4 5UR
☎ (01628) 74141   📠 (01628) 37011
🛏 92 £ £183 🍴 70 🍽 £100

☺ Lunch 12.30-2, Dinner 7.30-10

Haunt of rowers during Henley, *Dracula* during Hammer filming, visitors to Olde Englande in summer, and tourists at any time, Oakley Court is again one of a kind. The atmosphere is of a castle but within a country house, with oak furniture and heavy drapes. Cooking is fairly classic, with the occasional nod towards modern trends. The wine list is grand rather than modest.

Winkleigh Pophams

Castle Street, Winkleigh, Devon, EX19 8HQ
☎ (01837) 83767
🍴 10 🍽 £30

☺ Lunch 12-3   ☹ Sun, 25 Dec, Feb

Unusual little restaurant in the heart of Devon, unlicensed and no corkage on bring-your-own! Daily menus are chalked up on a blackboard and are English in inspiration. All dishes are home made and cooked to order. A fun place.

England 263

Winteringham Winteringham Fields ❖ 🐄 🌼

Winteringham, North Lincolnshire, DN15 9PF
☎ (01724) 733096 📠 (01724) 733898
🛏 7 £ £94 🍴 28 🍽 £115
☺ Lunch 12-1.30, Dinner 7.30-9.30
☹ Lunch Sat & Mon, all Sun, Bank Holidays, 2 wks Xmas, 1 wk Aug

An oasis in a somewhat drab hinterland which offers a touch of perfection from its cosy interior to the attractively presented menus. Germain Schwab is chef patron and creates exciting dishes to show his skills and imagination. A charlotte of ox tongue with sautéed potatoes and warm spinach salad dressed with a vinaigrette of it's own juices or a pressed confit of duckling with foie gras covered with port and truffle jelly on a salad of rocket might feature as starters. Hake with black ink noodles is served with a ravioli of clams, a gateau of quail with duck liver and asparagus in juices of poultry and Marc de Champagne or a rack of goat is charcoal grilled and served with rosti and juniper berries. Puddings follow in the same appealing way, a rich, dark chocolate tart served warm with honey ice cream, crème brulée with a hint of violets with fresh berries or the hot Winteringham corn tart with butterscotch and fresh cream. Mouthwatering! The wine list is not massive but has been carefully chosen and perfectly complements the food. 7 tastefully furnished rooms enable you to stay to enjoy more of Germain's cooking for breakfast, as if you'd need persuasion.

Witherslack Old Vicarage 🐄 🌼

Church Road, Witherslack, Cumbria, LA11 6RS
☎ (01539) 552381 📠 (01539) 552373
🛏 14 £ £98 🍴 40 🍽 £60
☺ Lunch Sun only 12.30 for 1, Dinner 7.30 for 8

If you only eat breakfast at this hospitable Victorian vicarage you will certainly survive the day without any pangs of hunger! Home-cured bacon and Cumberland sausages fit for the Queen are served along with the home-baked, toasted Cumberland molasses bread, simply wonderful. Dinner is worth walking the fells for, a choice of first courses then a traditional roast with excellent vegetables, a couple of puddings and fine, Northern British cheeses. Friendly service from the owners, the Reeves and Burrington-Brown families.

Wiveliscombe Langley House

Langley Marsh, Wiveliscombe, Nr Taunton, Somerset, TA4 2UF
☎ (01984) 623318 📠 (01984) 624573
🛏 8 £ £85 🍴 20 🍽 £75
☺ Dinner 7.30-8.30

Set in the peaceful Brendon hills, Langley House dates from the 16th Century but it is the Georgian extensions that set the tone of elegance at this unpretentious hotel and restaurant. Run by Anne & Peter Wilson for the past 10 years, the house benefits from their attention to detail in all departments – housekeeping, garden, kitchen. A fixed-price 4-course dinner menu of modern English cooking uses local produce but served with Mediterranean touches.

Woburn Paris House

Woburn Park, Woburn, Bedfordshire, MK17 9QP
☎ (01525) 290692   📠 (01525) 290471
🍴 44 🍽 £90

☺ Lunch 12-2, Dinner 7-9.30   ☹ Dinner Sun, all Mon, Bank Holidays, Feb

Nothing you read really prepares you for the sight of this place: the huge expanse of Woburn Park (encompassing both the abbey and wildlife as well as the House) surrounded by miles of red-brick wall (miss the gateway and it'll be a good half-hour before you come around again!) and then a long, sweeping drive dividing the grazing grounds of a herd of deer. Although imposing from a distance, the House is actually quite small once you come closer: it's a rather grand 2-up, 2-down, the former being the plush cloakrooms, the latter the restaurant and lounge areas, with the kitchen housed in a side addition. It's thus obvious that the reputation of the place will stand or fall by the cooking of chef Peter Chandler, and his style definitely seems to suit his clientele. Home-made canapés (perhaps smoked salmon mousse barquettes, cheese and sesame straws) and warm, home-baked bread precede a starter such as cajun prawn salad (a skewer of king prawns, grilled with cajun spices and set on a bed of mixed leaves); moving on to a fish course of baked monkfish in a champagne and herb sauce, then rack of English lamb in a basil sauce, with ratatouille and rösti potatoes. A platter of French cheeses follows then for dessert, raspberry surprise: a hot raspberry soufflé, raspberry ice-cream and a raspberry meringue. Coffee and petits fours round off the meal. This is a particularly delightful venue for summer Sunday lunch on the terrace. If you want to know why it's called Paris House, read an earlier edition of this Guide, or go and ask Peter!

Woodstock Bear Hotel

Park Street, Woodstock, Oxfordshire, OX20 1SZ
☎ (01993) 811511   📠 (01993) 813380
🛏 44 £133 🍴 80 🍽 £60

☺ Lunch 12.30-2.30, Dinner 7-10

Former coaching inn on the edge of the Cotswolds, still providing hospitality and comfort to passing or destination travellers. English cooking, as befits the setting, and there's a separate menu for vegetarians. Good British cheeses, too.

L!VE TV: THE FACTS
see page 21

England   265

Woodstock Feathers Hotel

Market Street, Woodstock, Oxfordshire, OX20 1SX
☎ (01993) 812291 📠 (01993) 813158
🛏 17 £119 🍴 60 🍽 £75
☺ Lunch 12.30-2.15 (Sun to 2.30), Dinner 7.30-9.30
(Whinchat Bar: 12.30-2.15, 7.30-9.30)

A very comfortable hotel in the lovely village of Woodstock, the very epitome of the Cotswolds. Behind the Cotswold stone exterior is a labyrinth of small rooms all furnished with style, bar, study, drawing room, dining room and a charming courtyard. David Lewis continues to preside over the kitchen and his menus show skill in their simplicity, marinated queen scallops with shallot and chilli dressing, mushroom fritter with black olive oil, or perhaps a trio of smoked salmon items on one plate, a tartare, a mousse and a slice that has been chargrilled. Norfolk duckling also shows 2 methods of cooking, the breast is roast, the leg as a confit, a fillet of red mullet is served with roasted aubergine with garlic and pan-fried fillet of monkfish comes with sweet peppers and olive oil.

Woolton Hill Hollington House Hotel

Woolton Hill, Nr Newbury, Berkshire, RG20 9XA
☎ (01635) 255100 📠 (01635) 255075
🛏 20 £130 🍴 50 🍽 £90
☺ Lunch 12-2.30, Dinner 7-9.30

Standing in 24 acres of beautifully-maintained grounds, this is a lovely country house, splendidly converted into a relaxing hotel *par excellence*. Huge bedrooms are models of good taste, all individually designed, with sumptuous bathrooms. Every conceivable luxury has been considered, including an indoor swimmimng pool from September 1996. It was opened by John & Penny Guy in 1992, previously proprietors of a fine hotel just outside Melbourne, Australia, which explains the plethora of Australian wines on the exceptional list. The Oak Room restaurant offers modern English cooking with French overtones, typically dishes such as "plate from the land and the sea" – oak-smoked Scottish Salmon, roasted scollops and fresh Cornish crab with an émincé of leeks, grain mustard and orange sauce to start; main course of marinated and roasted loin fillet of kangaroo with crispy pak choi, ginger, beanshoots and sweet soy sauce and the house speciality is Hollington bread and butter pudding with home-made ice cream. John himself is usually on hand to carve the Sunday roast.

SCOTCH BEEF CLUB
see page 16

Worcester Brown's

24 Quay Street, Worcester,
Hereford & Worcester, WR1 2JJ
☎ (01905) 26263
🍴 100 🕐 £75

☺ Lunch 12.30-1.45, Dinner 7.30-9.45

☹ Lunch Sat, Dinner Sun, Bank Holidays, 1 wk Xmas

An attractive, converted warehouse overlooks the River Severn in this busy County town famed for it's sauce, the Cathedral and one of the loveliest cricket grounds in Britain. Brown's has been going strong for some fifteen years and is deservedly popular with locals and vistors. Fixed-price menus at lunch and dinner vary more in price than content, lunch is a bargain when you could perhaps kick off with a risotto of mixed mushrooms or devilled herring roes on brioche toast before roast duck with Seville oranges, charcoal grilled fillet of beef or chicken with sweet peppers in white wine. Rhubarb crumble with vanilla ice cream or parfait of coffee and rum are perfect puddings before sloping off to watch the afternoons cricket and perhaps a siesta in the sun. The lengthy wine list majors on France and has plenty of half bottles.

Worfield Old Vicarage

Worfield, Bridgnorth, Shropshire, WV15 5JZ
☎ (01746) 716497 📠 (01746) 716552
🛏 14 £ £90 🍴 50 🕐 £72

☺ Lunch Sun only 12-2, Dinner 7-9

Lovely red-brick Edwardian house and adjoining conservatory which is home to Peter & Christine Iles as well as to their guests, who come for English country house cooking in an English country house setting. Ideal for business or leisure travellers alike, as it's located just a mile off the A454, or 2 miles from the A442, to the east of Bridgnorth.

Wrightington High Moor

High Moor Lane, Wrightington, Nr Wigan,
Lancashire, WN6 9QA
☎ (01257) 252364 📠 (01257) 255120
🍴 95 🕐 £55

☺ Lunch 12-2, Dinner 5.30-10

John Nelson & Jim Sine's other outlet, which is very different in style to Scarisbrick. Enjoy the relaxed, stylish atmosphere in this cleverly converted building, with flagstone floors, a friendly bar area and cosy restaurant. Dishes worth trying include country terrine with Cumberland sauce and 'doorstep' toast, followed by roasted cod topped with a herb brioche crust or char-grilled rumpsteak with a green peppercorn and brandy sauce. Particularly good value 'Early Doors' menu served 5.30 - 7pm.

Wych Cross Ashdown Park Hotel

Wych Cross, Nr East Grinstead, East Sussex, RH18 5JR
☎ (01342) 824988   (01342) 826206
95   £115   150   £80
☺ Lunch 12.30-2, Dinner 7.30-9.30 (Fri & Sat to 10)

Victorian Gothic building set in its own grounds in the heart of the Ashdown Forest, this well-restored and well-maintained hotel is popular for business and private functions, as well as recreational travellers, guaranteed by the golf and country club facilities. An international menu is offered in the Anderida Restaurant, in either set menus or the carte.

Wymondham Number Twenty Four

24 Middleton Street, Wymondham, Norfolk, NR18 0BH
☎ (01953) 607750
65   £45
☺ Lunch 11-2.30, Dinner 7.30-9.30
☹ Dinner Tue, all Sun & Mon, 24-31 Dec

The smaller dining room has now been converted into a lounge as part of the constant programme of upgrading (chairs, linen, kitchen!) here. Richard Hughes' aim is quality dining at sensible prices, and this he achieves with such success that his partner Sue and their sous-chef Nigel have opened another branch, Wilsons in Norwich.

Yattendon Royal Oak

The Square, Yattendon, Nr Newbury, Berkshire, RG16 0UF
☎ (01635) 201325   (01635) 201926
5   £85   24   £85
☺ Lunch 12-2.30, Dinner 7-10 (Sun to 10.30)

Well-known and much-loved 16th-century inn, very accessible from London, Oxford, Reading and Heathrow. Oak-beamed bar; garden room for private parties; comfortable bedrooms and modern English cooking.

Yeovil Little Barwick House

Barwick Village, Nr Yeovil, Somerset, BA22 9TD
☎ (01935) 23902   (01935) 20908
6   £76   40   £70
☺ Dinner 7-9 (Sat to 9.30)
☹ Dinner Sun (except residents), Hotel 2 wks Jan

A listed Georgian dower house set in its own gardens is now a country house restaurant with rooms, owned and run by the Colleys. English cooking uses local produce whenever possible to good effect on set menus with some choice at each course, served in the non-smoking dining room.

York Bettys

6 St Helens Square, York, North Yorkshire, YO1 2QP
☎ (01904) 659142 📠 (01904) 627050
🪑 174 🍽 £30
☺ 9-9   ☹ 25 & 26 Dec, 1 Jan

The Swiss founder of Bettys was certainly on to a good thing, creating an archetypically English tea room which rapidly became an institution throughout the north of England. In addition to tea-time treats there are seasonal specialities within the hot menu section, and these might tip a nod back to Swiss origins.

York Grange Hotel

Clifton, York, North Yorkshire, YO3 6AA
☎ (01904) 644744 📠 (01904) 612453
🛏 30 £98 🪑 55 🍽 £60
☺ Lunch 12-2, Dinner 7-10 (Brasserie: 12-3, 6.30-10.30)
☹ Lunch Sat

Choose between the Ivy Restaurant or the less formal brick-vaulted Brasserie (formerly the cellars) when you dine at this classical Regency town house. Well-equipped bedrooms and good business facilities are other attractions, as is its location just outside the old walls of this most historic city. Somehow, it cleverly combines the atmosphere of a country house with its urban setting.

York Melton's

7 Scarcroft Road, York, North Yorkshire, YO2 1ND
☎ (01904) 634341
🪑 42 🍽 £50
☺ Lunch 12-2, Dinner 5.30-10
☹ Lunch Mon, 3 wks Xmas, 1 wk Aug, Easter Sun

The exterior of the Hjorts' unpretentious restaurant in a Victorian terrace belies the excellent fare which is proffered within. Michael's menu changes monthly but is kept sensibly short to ensure freshness, February might have a ragout of oysters and leeks, rillettes of goose with green peppercorns or a coconut and aubergine loaf with hot pepper sauce amongst first courses. Pan-fried fillet of cod with parsley puree comes with saffron mashed potatoes and a gratin of courgettes and fennel, breast of pheasant with spring onions and ginger with stir fried vegetables or a vegetarian spinach and ricotta turnover with sundried tomato dressing to follow. A rich walnut tart has armagnac icing, a poached pear in red wine comes with cinnamon ice cream or there's a hot apple and calvados souffle for pudding. Lunchtime and early evening diners are offered great value on a fixed-price menu and they continue to give free mineral water and coffee and include service in the prices. Wines are keenly priced.

York Middlethorpe Hall

Bishopthorpe Road, York, North Yorkshire, YO2 1QB
☎ (01904) 641241   (01904) 620176
30   £141   60   £100
Lunch 12.30-1.45, Dinner 7.30-9.45

A stunning William III house that maintains its former elegance with fine antiques and furniture and well manicured gardens. The 30 bedrooms are equally stylish having good bathrooms and are the perfect place to rest during the races at nearby York. Chef Andrew Wood continues in the tradition of Middlethorpe with fixed-price menus at lunch and dinner. Cooking is modern in style, with the likes of a terrine of foie gras and leeks with warm hazelnut dressing, fillet of codling with tapenade crust and ratatouille dresssing, braised shoulder of lamb set on a bed of spring vegetables. The grill room is rather less formal than the oak panelled dining room. A comprehensive wine list has plenty of choice under £20 and some fine wines for a bit more.

York 19 Grape Lane

19 Grape Lane, York, North Yorkshire, YO1 2HU
☎ (01904) 636366
34   £75
Lunch 12-1.45, Dinner 6-9 (Sat to 10)
Sun & Mon, Xmas, 2 wks Jan/Feb, 2 wks Sep

Contemporary English cooking is on offer at this friendly restaurant near the Minster, suggesting light lunches (salads and sandwiches as well as main courses) with a more formally structured menu in the evening. Concise wine list.

York Ristorante Bari

15 The Shambles, York, North Yorkshire, YO1 2LZ
☎ (01904) 633807
80   £45
Lunch 10.30-2.30, Dinner 6-11   25 & 26 Dec, 1 Jan

In the heart of this picturesque old city, Bari is the longest established Italian restaurant. Pasta and pizzas, seafood and steaks are the backbone of the menu. Apart from champagne, the wine list is all-Italian and very reasonably priced.

York Taylor's

46 Stonegate, York, North Yorkshire, YO1 2AS
☎ (01904) 622865   (01904) 640348
65   £30
9-5.30   25 & 26 Dec, 1 Jan

Another branch of Bettys though with its own name, located near the Minster. The elegant building has low ceilings, oak beams and open fires in winter. Rare and exotic blends of tea are still very much to the fore.

Scotland

Aberdeen The Marcliffe at Pitfodels

North Deeside Road, Pitfodels, Aberdeen, Grampian, AB1 9YA
☎ (01224) 861000 📠 (01224) 868860
🛏 42 £120 🍴 32 🍽 £90
☺ Dinner 7-10 (light meals Conservatory 12-2.30 & 6.30-10)
☹ Sun & Mon

Now definitely part of the Aberdeen scenery, the Spences' Marcliffe goes from strength to strength. Dine in style in the Invery Room or more informally in the Conservatory. Excellent business facilities.

Aberfeldy Farleyer House

Weem, Aberfeldy, Tayside, PH15 2JE
☎ (01887) 820332 📠 (01887) 829430
🛏 11 £130 🍴 22 🍽 £75
☺ Dinner 8pm (Bistro 10-2 & 6-9.30)

Hidden away in the Tay valley but still easily accessible, Farleyer was originally a 16th-century croft, then expanded a couple of hundred years later to become the bailiff's residence, then the main residence of the Clan Menzies – hence the name of the restaurant. Here you can enjoy local produce, especially seafood and game, cooked with a modern touch.

Aberfoyle Braeval

By Aberfoyle, Central, FK8 3UY
☎ (01877) 382711
🍴 34 🍽 £75
☺ Lunch Sun only, 12.30-1.30, Dinner 7-9.30
☹ Dinner Sun, all Mon, Bank Holidays, 1 wk Feb, 1 wk May/Jun, 1 wk Nov

Nick & Fiona Nairn are well established at Braeval, offering modern Scottish produce, carefully prepared and cooked with interesting international flavours, on a daily-changing basis according to what is available. Dinner is 4 courses with a choice only at the pudding stage, but dietary needs can always be accommodated, so advise when booking.

Achiltibuie Summer Isles

Achiltibuie, by Ullapool, Highland, IV26 2YG
☎ (01854) 622282 📠 (01854) 622251
🛏 12 £95 🍴 26 🍽 £75
☺ Lunch 12.30-2.30 (light lunches), Dinner at 8 (Café 10.30am-9pm)
☹ mid Oct-April

Stunning location for the Irvines' 60s-style hotel, a relaxing place with "a marvellous amount of nothing to do". 3 of the 12 bedrooms are in Norwegian pine-log cabins a few steps from the main building. To keep you fit for such intense activity, a set-price, 5-course dinner is served using as many home-grown or home-produced ingredients as possible. The restaurant is now also open for light lunches.

Alexandria Cameron House

Loch Lomond, Alexandria, Strathclyde, G83 8QZ
☎ (01389) 755565 📠 (01389) 759522
68 £150 42 £80
☺ Lunch 12-1.45, Dinner 7-10 ☹ Lunch Sat

Lovely stately home on the banks of Loch Lomond, with its own 100-acres of gardens and woodland. Excellent leisure facilities, indoors and out. Choose from 3 dining rooms: the Georgian Room is luxurious and elegant with a classic menu; the Grill Room (peak seasons only) offers West Coast and freshwater seafood and local beef; and the Brasserie makes an ideal venue for informal family dining.

Alyth Drumnacree House

St Ninians Road, Alyth, Tayside, PH11 8AP
☎ (01828) 632194 📠 (01828) 632194
6 £65 30 £55
☺ Dinner 7-9.30 ☹ Dinner Sun & Mon, 15 Dec-1 April

Privately-owned and run, Drumnacree is situated at the foot of Glenisla and is a good base from which to explore Deeside. Enjoy a set-price dinner menu with plenty of choice at each course, using local produce (including organically-grown herbs and vegetables from the garden).

Anstruther Cellar

24 East Green, Anstruther, Fife, KY10 3AA
☎ (01333) 310378 📠 (01333) 312544
30 £75
☺ Lunch 12.30-1.30, Dinner 7.30-9 ☹ Sun & Mon, 10 days Xmas

Stone walls, log fires in winter, right near the harbour: a true original cellar where the wine list does justice to the setting. So, too, does the attitude and cooking of chef/patron Peter Jukes. Seafood is the main thing, and turbot, scallops and monkfish are invariably available, cooked to perfection and a sure touch to the flavourings. It's tiny and popular, so book well ahead.

Appin Invercreran Country House Hotel

Appin, by Oban, Highland, PA38 4BJ
☎ (01631) 730414 📠 (01631) 730532
9 £126 18 £65
☺ Lunch 12.30-1.45, Dinner 7-8.15 ☹ Hotel Nov-Feb

A mountain setting overlooking Glen Creran surrounded by mountains and with easy access to Fort William and Oban. The Kersley family all participate in the running and are attentive hosts, fixed-price menus offer good variety in the dining room.

Scotland 273

Arisaig Arisaig House

Beasdale, Arisaig, Highland, PH39 4NR
☎ (01687) 450622 📠 (01687) 450626
🛏 14 £160 🍴 36 🍽 £85
😊 Lunch 12.30-2, Dinner 7.30-8.30 ☹ Nov-Mar

A grey, stone exterior conceals an extremely warm welcome and endless hospitality from the Smither family. Comfortable rooms are impeccably furnished, and the gardens are as well groomed as the house (at their peak when the azaleas and rhododendrons are in bloom). David Wilkinson's cooking is the other attraction: his set-price, 4-course menus are British with French influence, and make the most of good Scottish ingredients. Excellent cheeseboard, good wines too.

Auchencairn Balcary Bay Hotel

The Shore Road, Auchencairn, Dumfries & Galloway, DG7 1QZ
☎ (01556) 640217 📠 (01556) 640272
🛏 17 £88 🍴 50 🍽 £60
😊 Lunch 12-1.45 by arrangement only, except on Sun, Dinner 7-8.30 (summer to 9) ☹ mid Nov-Feb

An idyllic location on the shores of Balcary Bay for this small, family-run hotel. Wonderful sea views from some of the bedrooms and lounges. Franco-Scottish cooking forms the base of the set-price dinner menu.

Auchencairn Collin House

Auchencairn, Castle Douglas, Dumfries & Galloway, DG7 1QN
☎ (01556) 640292 📠 (01556) 640276
🛏 6 £78 🍴 16 🍽 £68
😊 Dinner 7.30 for 8 ☹ 3-4 wks Jan/Feb

Galloway coastal setting for this small, pretty, pink-washed house in its own grounds. The set-price dinner menu offers some choice; and the wine list has some excellent bottles of good vintage and pedigree.

Auchterarder Auchterarder House

Auchterarder, Tayside, PH3 1DZ
☎ (01764) 663646 📠 (01764) 662939
🛏 15 £130 🍴 23 🍽 £90
😊 Lunch 12-2.30, Dinner 6-9.30

An imposing Victorian mansion set in lovely gardens with no fewer than 400 different species of tree and shrub! Inside, the house is full of attractive features: oak panelling, open fireplaces, a conservatory winter garden, beamed billiard room and fine library. Good business and sporting facilities. Formal menus match the ambience in the dining room, though food is presented in modern style. An excellent wine list is strong on clarets.

Auchterarder Gleneagles Hotel

Auchterarder, Tayside, PH3 1NF
☎ (01764) 662231 📠 (01764) 662022
🛏 234 £230 🍴 160 🕐 £110
☺ Lunch 12.30-2.30, Dinner 7.30-10

Whatever you are looking for in a hotel you will certainly find at Gleneagles, and probably more! A sporting dream with no fewer than 3 championship golf courses, riding, shooting, fishing, falconry and a health spa. Over 230 bedrooms and as many staff as guests to ensure that you are pampered in grand style. A choice of restaurants from formal to casual and an impressive shopping arcade which even includes a bank!

Auchterhouse Old Mansion House

Auchterhouse, By Dundee, Tayside, DD3 0QN
☎ (01382) 320366 📠 (01382) 320466
🛏 6 £120 🍴 50 🕐 £75
☺ Lunch 12.30-1.45, Dinner 7-9.30 (Sun to 8.30)
☹ 25 & 26 Dec, 1st wk Jan

A sparkling, white-painted 16th-century baronial house is home to Nigel & Eva Bell, and their friendly attitude ensures that their guests feel equally at home. Set in 10 acres of gardens with a squash court, tennis and croquet lawns and outdoor (heated) pool, the house is just 7 miles from Dundee. Menus offer plenty of variety, not forgetting vegetarians, and there's bags of choice on the wine list, too, with some exciting bin-ends.

Ayr Fouters Bistro

2a Academy Street, Ayr, Strathclyde, KA7 1HS
☎ (01292) 261391 📠 (01292) 619323
🍴 38 🕐 £50
☺ Lunch 12-2, Dinner 6.30-10.30
☹ Lunch Sun, all Mon, 4 days Xmas, 4 days New Year

The building began life as bank vaults but has been a restaurant since 1973, when Laurie & Fran Black acquired it. Proximity to Ayr's fish market means the main thrust of the menus comes as no surprise, though the treatments are individual. There's a bistro menu as well as the carte, but either will give you a good meal. Wines from neighbours Whighams of Ayr. If you're not familiar with it, ask Laurie for details of his Taste of Scotland Guide.

Ayr The Stables

Queen's Court, 41 Sandgate, Ayr, Strathclyde, KA7 1BD
☎ (01292) 283704
🍴 52 🕐 £30
☺ 10-4.45 ☹ Sun in winter, 25 & 26 Dec, 1 & 2 Jan

Restaurant and coffee house offering excellent value for money in friendly surroundings. They claim to be the only restaurant specialising in "ethnic" Scottish dishes in the south-west of Scotland, and they certainly also have a good range of malts!

Ballater Balgonie Country House

Braemar Place, Ballater, Grampian, AB35 5RQ
☎ (01397) 75582 ✉ (01397) 755482
9 £88 28 £60
☺ Lunch 12-2 (residents only), Dinner 7-9 ☹ mid Jan-mid Feb

Edwardian-style country house, whose rooms are named after fishing pools on the River Dee! Most have views across the Ballater golf course toward Glen Muick. Fixed-price lunch and dinner menus usually offer choices at each course except fish. After your meal, relax in the pretty garden.

Ballater Craigendarroch Hotel

Braemar Road, Ballater, Grampian, AB35 5XA
☎ (01339) 755858 ✉ (01339) 755447
44 £125 45 £65
☺ Lunch Sun only 12-1.30, Dinner 7-9.45

Luxurious hotel and country club on the banks of the Dee with excellent leisure facilities. Eat formally in the Oaks Restaurant, or in the Clubhouse (12 noon to 10pm) which offers a more relaxed setting.

Ballater Tullich Lodge

Ballater, Grampian, AB35 5SB
☎ (01339) 755406 ✉ (01339) 755397
10 £190 26 £60
☺ Lunch only at 1, Dinner 7.30-9

Overlooking the River Dee and built in Scottish baronial style, Tullich has been in the same loving hands since the late '60s. Lovely views from the first-floor drawing room; Tower Bedroom for those with a head for heights. No-choice dinner menus are, however, well balanced; and light lunches are also available.

Banchory Raemoir House

Raemoir, Banchory, Grampian, AB31 4ED
☎ (01330) 824884 ✉ (01330) 822171
25 £95 70 £75
☺ Lunch 12.30-2, Dinner 7.30-9 ☹ 1st 2 wks Jan

Just 2½ miles north of Banchory on the A980 in a lovely Dee-side setting. An 18th-century building, it now houses individually furnished bedrooms, and lounges with log fires. Menus feature the best of local produce such as Dee salmon and Aberdeen Angus beef.

Bearsden Fifty Five BC

128 Drymen Road, Bearsden, Glasgow, Strathclyde, G61 3RB
☎ 0141-942 7272 📠 0141-942 9650
🪑 25 🍽 £50

🙂 Lunch 12-3 (Sun 12.30-4), Dinner 7-10 ☹ New Year's Day

Bar and restaurant offering some imaginative cooking, including a vast range of Scottish cheeses and plenty of variety for vegetarians. Chic and stylish interior, though the atmosphere is informal.

Blairgowrie Kinloch House

Kinloch, by Blairgowrie, Tayside, PH10 6SG
☎ (01250) 884237 📠 (01250) 884333
🛏 21 £ £152 🪑 55 🍽 £75

🙂 Lunch 12.30-2, Dinner 7-9.15 ☹ 16-30 Dec

An early Victorian house with Edwardian extensions, Kinloch has been in the same careful hands since 1981. Both history and care are evident in the style and maintenance of the interior (four-poster and half-tester beds, oak panelling, galleries); while the grounds and parkland are home to Highland cattle. Modern Scottish cooking is the backbone of the menu.

Cairndow Loch Fyne Oyster Bar

Clachan Farm, Cairndow, Strathclyde, PA26 8BH
☎ (01499) 600236 📠 (01499) 600234
🪑 80 🍽 £50

🙂 9-9 (Nov-Mar 9-6) ☹ 25 Dec-3 Jan

John Noble & Andrew Lane teamed up in 1978 to develop oyster beds in Loch Fyne, following on from which it seemed logical to revive the 18th-century custom of offering oysters and wine at reasonable prices in simple surroundings. If you can't subsist on a diet of pure oysters, there are other kinds of seafood, too. Definitely a "must" if you're remotely in the area!

Callander Roman Camp Hotel

off Main Street, Callander, Tayside, FK17 8BG
☎ (01877) 330003 📠 (01877) 331533
🛏 14 £ £95 🪑 45 🍽 £129

🙂 Lunch 12-2, Dinner 7-9.30

Originally (in 1625) the hunting lodge for the Dukes of Perth, Roman Camp has been a hotel since 1939, and in the capable hands of the Brown family since 1989. 20 acres of garden surround the house, and include a walled kitchen garden. Views over the River Teith from the drawing room; the panelled library, the tapestry-hung dining room: all add to the charm of the place. Carefully constructed residents' tasting dinners are offered in the non-smoking restaurant, candle-lit at night.

Canonbie Riverside Inn

Canonbie, Dumfries & Galloway, DG14 0UX
☎ (01387) 371512
▯ 6 £ £72 🛏 24 🕐 £55
☺ Dinner 7.30-8.30
☹ Dinner Sun, 25 & 26 Dec, 1 Jan, 2 wks Feb, 2 wks Nov

Small and friendly inn – the river in question is the Esk, and the area is very popular with scenery-lovers seeking a peaceful retreat. Robust breakfasts to set you up; dinner features fresh, local, seasonal produce, lovingly prepared. Home-made organic breads, unpasteurised cheeses.

Colbost Three Chimneys Restaurant

Colbost, By Dunvegan, Isle of Skye, Highland, IV55 8ZT
☎ (01470) 511258
🛏 30 🕐 £60
☺ Lunch 12.30-2, Dinner 7-9
☹ Sun (open Sun pre Bank Holidays), Nov-Mar

Super little restaurant in a remote but beautiful setting, housed in a former croft. Shirley & Eddie Spear use speciality Scottish produce to excellent effect, and offer refreshment at lunch, dinner, afternoon tea/light meals, and from their Wee Shop next door. Set dinner (booking essential) is much sought-after, and vegetarians are fully and intelligently accommodated.

Contin Coul House

Contin, By Strathpeffer, Highland, IV14 9EY
☎ (01997) 421487 📠 (01997) 421945
▯ 21 £ £90 🛏 40 🕐 £65
☺ Lunch 12-2 (bar lunches), Dinner 7-9

Secluded country mansion with views over forests and mountains – bliss! Explore on horseback, or go fishing or golfing instead. A hearty breakfast will set you up well for a strenuous day out; then replenish your energy banks with a fixed-price candle-lit dinner using local produce. Retire in style to an elegant and well-equipped bedroom.

**BRITAIN'S TOP
INDEPENDENT BUTCHERS**
see page 9

Crinan Crinan Hotel

Crinan, By Lochgilphead, Strathclyde, PA31 8SR
☎ (01546) 830261 📠 (01546) 830292
🛏 22 £115 🪑 20 🍽 £95
🙂 Dinner at 8   🙁 Dinner Sun & Mon, October-1 May

The Crinan Hotel is Crinan, there is little else in the tiny village situated at the North of the canal that connects Loch Fyne to the mighty Atlantic. The talented Ryan family have established a deservedly popular hostelry over the last 25 years welcoming yachtsmen, travellers and gourmets to this lovely location on Argyll's rugged coast. If the catch has been landed the Lock 16 restaurant on the roof of the hotel offers a real chance to taste fish at its best. A typical menu might include Loch Craignish mussels cooked marinière, charcoal grilled king clams from the Sound of Jura, smoked wild salmon and Loch Crinan jumbo prawns (landed at 6.45.p.m – you can't get fresher than that!). The Gallery Roof Bar has been refurbished creating a light, plant filled area with superb views of the Canal and Basin. An art gallery has been created around the central bar where you can enjoy paintings by the owners, if you're really lucky you might hear daughter Julia sing. The Westward Restaurant also features seafood alongside some meat dishes of local produce and the Caledonian weather forecast included on the menu will keep you informed of impending storms!

Cumbernauld Westerwood Hotel

St Andrews Drive, Westerwood, Cumbernauld, Strathclyde, G68 0EW
☎ (01236) 457171 📠 (01236) 738478
🛏 49 £100 🪑 75 🍽 £70
🙂 Lunch 12-2.45, Dinner 7-10   🙁 Dinner Sun, all Mon & Tue, 1-3 Jan

Country club and hotel with its own golf course in the range of sporting facilities. Eat in either the circular, tented Old Masters or the informal Tipsy Laird restaurants. On Sundays, you can have a Swim-and-Lunch.

Cupar Ostlers Close

25 Bonnygate, Cupar, Fife, KY15 4BU
☎ (01334) 655574
🪑 28 🍽 £60
🙂 Lunch 12.15-2, Dinner 7-9.30   🙁 Sun & Mon, 25 & 26 Dec

Small, friendly restaurant run by the Grahams since 1981. Daily-changing menus are based on fresh, local supplies, especially seafood, free-range ducks, wild mushrooms, venison and home-grown vegetables.

Scotland 279

Drumnadrochit Polmaily House

Drumnadrochit, Highland, IV3 6XT
☎ (01456) 450343
12 £90 40 £45
☺ Lunch by arrangement, Dinner 7.30-9.30 ☹ Mid Nov-Mid Dec

Small and informal retreat near Glen Urquart, airily and elegantly furnished. Set dinner menus include some choice at each course, with healthy eating very much in mind. The carte offers more choice but is just as well balanced. Reasonably priced wine list.

Drybridge Old Monastery Restaurant

Drybridge, Buckie, Grampian, AB56 2JB
☎ (01542) 832660
45 £55
☺ Lunch 12.15-1.30, Dinner 7-9.30
☹ all Sun & Mon, Bank Holidays, 3 wks Jan, 2 wks Nov

Perched high up above the fishing village of Buckie on the Moray Firth, the Grays' monastic retreat is a delightful place to unwind and enjoy this unusual setting. The monks are long gone, but their heritage of hospitality remains. Maureen looks after the guests while Douglas cooks some fine local produce with individual style and flair – he's very strong on sauces. A fine range of wines has been carefully chosen to complement the food.

Dryburgh Dryburgh Abbey Hotel

St Boswells, Dryburgh, Melrose, Borders, TD6 0RQ
☎ (01835) 822261 📠 (01835) 823945
26 £110 50 £55
☺ Lunch 12.15-2.15, Dinner 7.30-9.15

Comfortable, well-run hotel in the heart of Scottish Border country, ideally located for devotees of fishing and golf. Good standards of housekeeping and business facilities.

Dulnain Bridge Auchendean Lodge

Dulnain Bridge, Grantown-on-Spey, Highland, PH26 3LU
☎ (01479) 851 347 📠 (01479) 851 347
8 £69 18 £55
☺ Dinner only 7.30-9 ☹ 4 wks before or after Xmas

Small and friendly holiday destination, in the same hands since 1988, ideally located for leisure activities. Cooking is Scottish/French using local ingredients, and they are especially proud of their wild fungi; New Zealand wines feature strongly on the list. Note that if you pay by credit card, commission is charged.

Dunblane Cromlix House

Kinbuck, by Dunblane, Central, FK15 9JT
☎ (01786) 822125 📠 (01786) 825450
🛏 14 £140 🍴 40 🍽 £90
☺ Lunch 12.30-1.15, Dinner 6.45-8.30 ☹ Jan

Guests at Cromlix have access to the 3,000 acre estate with 3 trout lochs and miles of walks, while the house itself has over a century's worth of fine furniture, paintings and porcelain. The lovely private chapel is in great demand for weddings and christenings. Bedrooms and suites are individually furnished and full of little extras. Modern British food from the kitchen is served in either the light and airy dining room or the Scots Victorian shooting lodge-style room. Breakfasts are taken in the conservatory. Fine wine list of stature.

Dunkeld Kinnaird

Kinnaird Estate, Dalguise, By Dunkeld, Tayside, PH8 0LB
☎ (01796) 482440 📠 (01796) 482289
🛏 9 £185 🍴 35 🍽 £90
☺ Lunch 12.30-1.45, Dinner 7.15-9.30
☹ Mon, Tue & Wed during Jan, Feb & Mar

Privately owned and run, and with a wonderful Tayside setting, Kinnaird is part of a 9,000-acre estate which therefore offers plenty of outdoor pursuits. There's still the atmosphere of gracious Edwardian house-party, underlined by some good cooking from John Webber's kitchens, served in the formal elegance of the non-smoking dining room. You might start with shellfish minestrone flavoured with lemon grass and herbs, followed by breast of Gressingham duck with a sauce of red wine, honey and orange and finish with apple and currant crumble tart. Value-for-money wine list, with an extensive selection of half bottles.

Dunoon Chatters

58 John Street, Dunoon, Strathclyde, PA23 8BJ
☎ (01369) 706402
🍴 35 🍽 £50
☺ Lunch 12-2.30, Dinner 6-10 ☹ Sun, Jan

Fresh local produce cooked and served in the French manner. As much as possible is made on the premises – breads; desserts, ices and sorbets; and petits fours. Lighter meals also available in the bar. Well annotated wine list.

Scotland 281

Edinburgh Alp-Horn

167 Rose Street, Edinburgh, Lothian, EH2 4LS
☎ 0131-225 4787 📠 0131-225 1546
🍴 66 🍽 £45
☺ Lunch 12-2, Dinner 6.30-10 ☹ Sun, 4 days Xmas/New Year

A little touch of Switzerland in Scotland, and very well they sit together.
Cosy interior of wood panels and red painted walls. Menus are extensive
and interesting, written in French but often including Italian touches.
Rösti and spätzli are specialities.

Edinburgh The Atrium

Saltire Court, 10 Cambridge Street, Edinburgh,
Lothian, EH1 2ED
☎ 0131-228 8882
🍴 70 🍽 £60
☺ Lunch 12-2.30, Dinner 6-10.30 (later for Residents of Festival)
☹ Lunch Sat, all Sun, 10 days Xmas

Excellent Scottish ingredients prepared and presented in eclectic style
at this award-winning, ground-floor restaurant adjacent to the Traverse
theatre. Unusual decor throughout includes wrought-iron sculptures,
railway sleeper tables and torch lighting. The kitchen, headed up by Glyn
Stevens and overseen by chef/proprietor Andrew Radford, produces the
likes of chicken liver parfait, fillet of salmon with courgettes, fine herbs
and aïoli and chocolate coffee pot with crème fraiche. Service, under the
watchful eye of Lisa Radford, is friendly and efficient and together with
an excellent wine list, make this well worth a visit.

Edinburgh L'Auberge

56 St Mary Street, Edinburgh, Lothian, EH1 1SX
☎ 0131-556 5888 📠 0131-556 2588
🍴 65 🍽 £75
☺ Lunch 12.15-2, Dinner 6.15-9.30

A little bit of France in Scotland – Scottish produce served in French
bistro style on fixed-price menus. Chef/proprietor Daniel Wencker is
from Alsace, so regional trends tend to veer in that direction.

Edinburgh The Balmoral Hotel

Princes Street, Edinburgh, Lothian, EH2 2EQ
☎ 0131-556 2414 📠 0131-557 3747
🛏 189 £167 🍴 45 🍽 £110
☺ Lunch 12-2.30, Dinner 7-10.30 ☹ Lunch Sat & Sun

Grand and luxurious city-centre hotel with all the elegance of by-gone
days. Excellent leisure facilities, in-house cashmere and crystal shops.
Dine in style at the Grill Room, or more informally in the brasserie.
Local ingredients are prepared in classic French style.

Edinburgh Caledonian Hotel

Princes Street, Edinburgh, Lothian, EH1 2AB
☎ 0131-459 9988   0131-225 6632
236   £280

Carriages:
130   £60
☺ Lunch 12-2.30, Dinner 6.30-10   ☹ Lunch Sat, all Sun

La Pompadour:
60   £105
☺ Lunch 12.30-2.15, Dinner 7.30-10.15
☹ Lunch Sat & Sun, Dinner Sun in winter

The Caley is an institution in its own right (just as famous as the Castle!), and seems to have been looking after weary travellers since the dawn of time. There's a choice of 2 restaurants, Carriages and the attractive Pompadour Room, which offers a good range of classic dishes such as Borders duckling terrine layered with preserved duck liver and marinated walnuts brushed with lime syrup, followed by pan-fried supreme of young pigeon on a confit of red cabbage, or calf's liver with creamed truffle potato and baked quince. Wine list of appropriate stature.

Edinburgh Channings

South Learmonth Gardens, Edinburgh, Lothian, EH4 1EZ
☎ 0131-315 2226   0131-332 9631
48   £135   60   £50
☺ Lunch 12.30-2, Dinner 6.30-9.30
☹ Lunch Sat, 25-28 Dec, 3 days Xmas

Five Edwardian townhouses have been combined to create this comfortable, privately owned and run hotel. Decor and furnishings are atmospheric, and business facilities here are good. Lovely views from some rooms, and it's handily located for airport and station.

Edinburgh Denzlers 121

121 Constitution Street, Leith, Edinburgh, Lothian, EH6 7AE
☎ 0131-554 3268
65   £50
☺ Lunch 12-2, Dinner 6.30-10
☹ Lunch Sat, all Sun & Mon, 2 days Xmas, 2 wks July, 1 wk Jan

Sister restaurant to the Alp-Horn (qv), with a lighter, brighter decor but a similar menu. The premises were formerly a bank. Unusually, here you can drink Swiss wines with your fondue.

Edinburgh Kelly's

46 West Richmond Street, Edinburgh, Lothian, EH8 9DZ
☎ 0131-668 3847   📠 0131-668 3847
🪑 34 🍽 £60
☺ Dinner 6-10   ☹ Dinner Sun, Mon & Tue, Oct & 1st wk Jan

Jeff & Jacquie Kelly offer simple dinner set menus with plenty of choice at each course (though individual items can also be selected on an à la carte basis – minimum charge £10 per person). The style is modern Scottish, and there's always a vegetarian option. No smoking before 9.30pm in the dining room.

Edinburgh Malmaison Edinburgh

1 Tower Place, Leith, Edinburgh, Lothian, EH6 7DB
☎ 0131-555 6868   📠 0131-555 6999
🛏 25 [£] £90 🪑 74 🍽 £60
☺ Lunch 12-2.30, Dinner 6-11 (light meals 7-11)

The Edinburgh outlet of Ken McCulloch's recent venture is proving very successful – a small, contemporary hotel which includes a French café/brasserie. All mod cons within the accommodation, which is well above the ordinary, illustrating Ken's wife Amanda's keen eye for style. Fun atmosphere when you eat. Chef Roy Brett has settled in well and the citizenry is well contented.

Edinburgh Le Marché Noir

2 Eyre Place, Edinburgh, Lothian, EH3 5EP
☎ 0131-558 1608   📠 0131-556 0798
🪑 35 🍽 £60
☺ Lunch 12-2.30, Dinner 7-10 (Fri & Sat to 10.30, Sun 6.30-9.30)
☹ Lunch Sat, Sun, 25 & 26 Dec, 1 & 2 Jan

Prix-fixe menus at both lunch and diner offer a choice of prices as well as dishes, though whatever your needs, you can be assured of good food, a lively atmosphere and great wines. There are 2 lists in fact: a shorter one for speedy choosing starting at around £8.50, and the full monte, which goes up to a Chateau Petrus '66 at £685!

L!VE TV: THE FACTS
see page 21

Edinburgh Martin's

70 Rose Street, North Lane, Edinburgh, Lothian, EH2 3DX

☎ 0131-225 3106

🍴 28 🍽 £75

☺ Lunch 12-2, Dinner 7-10 (Fri & Sat to 10.30)

☹ Lunch Sat, all Sun & Mon, 4 wks Dec/Jan, 1 wk Jun, 1 wk Oct

A small, stylish restaurant tucked away behind the cobbled North Lane, Martin's is a real discovery once located. Forbes Stott prepares short menus making choice simple and satisfaction guaranteed with his well executed cooking of the likes of a crayfish bisque with langoustine tails and sweet pepper, sautéed chicken livers with spring onion mashed potato and caramelised onion as starters. You could follow with braised breast and leg of duck with root vegetables and star anise, grilled halibut with fennel and mustard or perhaps a fillet of sea bass with sun-dried tomatoes, basil vinaigrette and leeks. A rhubarb compote is served with ginger ice cream and tuile biscuits, a chocolate truffle torte with pecan, espresso and praline ice cream or there are always some superb unpasteurised Scottish and Irish cheeses. Lunch menus offer less choice at much less money but are equally well prepared; wines are well chosen and sensibly priced.

Edinburgh Round Table

31 Jeffrey Street, Edinburgh, Lothian, EH2 3DX

☎ 0131-557 3032

🍴 50 🍽 £40

☺ 10-10 ☹ all Sun & Mon, some Bank Holidays

Bistro-style setting and menu in a useful Edinburgh location. Fixed-price lunches offer excellent value; a shorter afternoon menu is just the thing to refresh weary tourists; while a relaxing dinner rounds off the day perfectly. Choose from the carte if you prefer to compile your own meal – do try one of the specials which use top quality Scottish meats (lamb, beef or venison). Concise and fairly-priced wine list.

Edinburgh The Shore Bar & Restaurant

3/4 Shore, Leith, Edinburgh, Lothian, EH6 6QW

☎ 0131-553 5080   📠 0131-553 5080

🍴 32 🍽 £50

☺ Lunch 12-2.30, Dinner 6.30-10.15 ☹ 25 & 26 Dec, 1 & 2 Jan

Popular bar-cum-restaurant with daily-changing blackboard menus. Seafood a speciality; excellent value on the lunch menu and bargains on the wine list, too.

Scotland 285

Edinburgh Vintners Room

The Vaults, 87 Giles Street, Leith, Edinburgh, Lothian, EH6 6BZ
☎ 0131-554 6767 📠 0131-554 8423
🪑 60 🍽 £55
🙂 Lunch 12-2.30, Dinner 6.30-10.30 ☹ Sun, 2 wks Xmas

Tim & Sue Cummings' delightful, atmospheric restaurant and wine bar pays close attention to detail and uses good, local ingredients in a modern French style. Cheeses are carefully chosen and well kept; and there's a separate menu for vegetarians.

Edinburgh The Witchery by the Castle 🌼

352 Castlehill, Edinburgh, Lothian, EH1 2NF
☎ 0131-225 5613 📠 0131-220 4392
🪑 100 🍽 £90
🙂 Lunch 12-4, Dinner 5.30-10.30 ☹ 25 & 26 Dec

Historic location, tucked away in the castle, The Witchery has 2 separate dining rooms, each with a distinct atmosphere. Candle-lit at night with elegant, traditional fittings and the occasional modern touch. Professional yet friendly and attentive service. Starters range from simple tomato and black olive salad with a basil dressing to warm salad of quail with fois gras and truffle dressing; main courses from an excellent fillet of sea bass served with couscous and tapenade dressing to grilled fillet of Scotch beef cooked with thyme and served on a horseradish and celeriac rosti. Good value, set-price dinner menu.

Eriska Isle of Eriska

Eriska, Ledaig, by Oban, Strathclyde, PA37 1SD
☎ (01631) 720371 📠 (01631) 720531
🛏 17 £165 🪑 40 🍽 £85
🙂 Dinner 8-9 ☹ Jan-Feb

Perennially popular island retreat, owned and run by the Buchanan-Smith family since 1973. The baronial mansion is in the middle of 100 hectares of unspoilt countryside in which you can build an appetite for a substantial set-price dinner which offers two or three choices per course.

Fairlie Fins Restaurant

Fencefoot Farm, Fairlie, Nr Largs, Strathclyde, KA29 0EG
☎ (01475) 568989
🪑 30 🍽 £60
🙂 Lunch 12-2, Dinner 6.30-9.30
☹ Dinner Sun, all Mon, 25-27 Dec, 1-3 Jan

The philosophy here is "the freshest fish, simply prepared", and as much as possible goes into the pan straight out of the water (farmed and fished). Fins is part of a working farm (which also offers B&B) and smokehouse. If you subscribe to the ideas but haven't much time to spare, buy their produce from the farm shop instead.

Fort William
Crannog Seafood Restaurant

Town Pier, Fort William, Highland, PS33 7NG
☎ (01397) 705589
⌂ 70 🍽 £50

☺ Lunch 12-2.30, Dinner 6-9.30 (May-Sep to 10) ☹ 25 Dec, 1 Jan

Locally-caught then home-prepared: if this is how you like your fish, this is where to come and eat it. A blackboard complements the printed menu. The simply-furnished restaurant has views over Loch Linnhe; and there's now also a branch in Edinburgh.

Fort William Inverlochy Castle

Torlundy, Fort William, Highland, PH33 6SN
☎ (01397) 702177 📠 (01397) 702953
⌂ 17 £276 ⌂ 34 🍽 £100

☺ Lunch 12.30-1.45, Dinner 7.15-9.15 ☹ Dec-Feb

A Victorian fortress set in the foothills of Ben Nevis surrounded by some five hundred acres of woodland and landscaped gardens is one of Scotland's most impressive and well-loved hotels. Spacious and elegant rooms are high ceilinged and handsomely decorated and furnished in classic Victorian style. Housekeeping is of a very high standard and there is great attention to detail, staff endorse the feeling of an almost bygone age. 2 dining rooms offer similar high standards of produce and service with Simon Haigh creating fine menus with skill and imagination. Pan-fried fillet of red mullet is accompanied by a filo pastry tart of Roma tomatoes with basil, a slice of halibut with sauce of orange and star anise, pot-roast breast of farm chicken with morels and wild rice or a mille feuille of confit of duck with crispy potatoes are typical offerings. Simpler dishes are always available and puddings are irresistible. A gargantuan wine list satisfies all palates. Inverlochy is a wonderful place in which to spoil oneself for a few days living in a style to which one can easily become accustomed.

Gairloch Creag Mor

Charleston, Gairloch, Highland, IV21 2AH
☎ (01445) 712068 📠 (01445) 712044
⌂ 19 £80 ⌂ 60 🍽 £60

☺ Dinner 6.30-9.30 ☹ Nov-Feb

Cheerful, small hotel efficiently run by owners Larry & Elizabeth Nieto since 1988. Lovely views of bays, islands and beaches. Eat in the Mackenzie restaurant, or in the Buttery (open all day from 8am to 10pm).

Glamis Castleton House

Glamis, By Forfar, Angus, Tayside, DD8 1SJ
☎ (01307) 840340 📠 (01307) 840506
🛏 6 £90 🍴 28 🍽 £55
☺ Lunch 12-2.30, Dinner 7-9.30 (light meals Conservatory: 12-10)

Small, country house hotel run in friendly fashion by William & Maureen Little. Fresh local produce is carefully cooked and presented on both set menus and a carte. Concise wine list has useful tasting notes.

Glasgow Brasserie on West Regent Street

176 West Regent Street, Glasgow, Strathclyde, G2 4NL
☎ 0141-248 3801 📠 0141-248 8197
🍴 100 🍽 £45
☺ 12-11 ☹ all Sun & Sat 3-5, Bank Holidays

French food in friendly surroundings at a city-centre venue. Under the same ownership as the Rogano and the Buttery (qv).

Glasgow Buttery

652 Argyle Street, Glasgow, Strathclyde, G3 8UF
☎ 0141-221 8188 📠 0141-204 4639
🍴 50 🍽 £75
☺ Lunch 12-2.30, Dinner 7-10.30 ☹ Lunch Sat, all Sun, Bank Holidays

One of the livliest spots in town: a bustling atmosphere in an almost art nouveau decor within a converted Victorian pub! The food, however, is bang up to date, with a separate menu for vegetarian menu and a good-value table d'hote at lunchtimes.

Glasgow D'Arcy's

Basement Courtyard, Princes Square, Glasgow, Strathclyde, G1 3JN
☎ 0141-226 4309
🍴 72 🍽 £40
☺ 9am-10.30pm (Mon, Tue & Wed to 9.30) ☹ Dinner Sun

3 courses including coffee for under a tenner must offer some of the best value in town. The fixed-price menu changes every 2 weeks, the carte of international dishes seasonally. Light snacks available throughout the day.

Glasgow Glasgow Hilton

1 William Street, Glasgow, Strathclyde, G3 8HT
☎ 0141-204 5555 📠 0141-204 5004
🛏 319 £140 🍴 55 🕑 £95
☺ Lunch 12-2.30, Dinner 7-10.30
☹ Lunch Sat, all Sun, Bank Holiday Mondays

Conveniently situated between Bothwell and Waterloo Streets, this large, city-centre hotel offers reliable accommodation and amenities, as well as Minsky's New York style Deli and Restaurant, Raffles Bar and more formal dining in Camerons.

Glasgow Malmaison Hotel et Brasserie

278 West George Street, Glasgow, Strathclyde, G2 4LL
☎ 0141-221 6400 📠 0141-221 6411
🛏 21 £90 🍴 80 🕑 £60
☺ Lunch 12-2.30, Dinner 6-11 ☹ Xmas Day

The Glasgow outlet of Ken McCulloch's recent venture is just as successful as its Edinburgh sister. The concept is the same – "independent hotels for individual people". All-day eating in the informal café/wine bar/brasserie – the mood is spot on.

Glasgow One Devonshire Gardens

1 Devonshire Gardens, Glasgow, Strathclyde, G12 0UX
☎ 0141-339 2001 📠 0141-337 1663
🛏 27 £145 🍴 50 🕑 £95
☺ Lunch 12.30-2, Dinner 7-10.30 ☹ Lunch Sat

Impeccably designed, furnished and run, this converted Victorian terrace recalls the style of the period during which it was built. Rich colours add to the warmth of mahogany furniture, and rich fabrics are used in the bedrooms and public areas: attention to detail is obvious in every corner. Staff, ably managed by Beverley Payne, attend to needs in true "downstairs" style: nothing is too much trouble. Menus are equally sophisticated: pressed sautéed foie gras comes with a nage of vegetables set in Sauternes jelly with toasted orange brioche; roasted king scallops with beansprouts and crisply fried vegetables in a Thai spiced sauce; pan-fried fillet of venison with a potato and turnip gratin and pickled red cabbage. Appropriate wine list. Without doubt, this is the place to stay in Glasgow.

Glasgow Puppet Theatre

11 Ruthven Lane, Glasgow, Strathclyde, G12 9BQ
☎ 0141-339 8444 📠 0141-339 7666
🪑 65 🍽 £75

☺ Lunch 12-2.30, Dinner 7-11
☹ Lunch Sat, all Mon, 25 & 26 Dec, 1 & 2 Jan

Fresh Scottish produce served with a European/Mediterranean twist is the thing here, and the short lunch menu (3 choices per course) is well priced. More choices on the dinner carte; concise wine list.

Glasgow Rogano

11 Exchange Place, Glasgow, Strathclyde, G1 3AN
☎ 0141-248 4055 📠 0141-248 2608
🪑 50 🍽 £75

☺ Lunch 12-2.30, Dinner 7-10.30 (Sun till 10), (café 12-11, Fri & Sat 12-12, Sun 6-10) ☹ Lunch Sun, Bank Holidays, 26 Dec

Ground floor restaurant and basement café, a showcase for 1930's decor. Good food, too, with seafood a speciality. The style is modern, the ingredients local, the customers happy.

Glasgow Two Fat Ladies

88 Dumbarton Road, Glasgow, Strathclyde, G11 6NX
☎ 0141-339 1944
🪑 30 🍽 £55

☺ Lunch 12.15-2, Dinner 5.45-10.15 ☹ Sun, 1st wk Jan

Modern Scottish cooking at a quaintly-named restaurant; concise, very reasonably priced wine list.

Glasgow Ubiquitous Chip

12 Ashton Lane, Glasgow, Strathclyde, G12 8SJ
☎ 0141-334 5007 📠 0141-337 1302
🪑 140 🍽 £75

☺ Lunch 12-2.30, Dinner 5.30-11 ☹ 25 Dec, 31 Dec-2 Jan

Ron Clydesdale's long-running show, known locally as The Chip, never fails its packed houses. Whether in the slightly more formal downstairs restaurant, or the more relaxed café/bistro, Upstairs at the Chip, you can be assured of the good cooking of fine ingredients, served at the right price in friendly surroundings. Imagination and flair are the watchwords here.

Glenelg Glenelg Inn

Glenelg, by Kyle of Lochalsh, Highland, IV40 8JR
☎ (01599) 522273 📠 (01599) 522273
6 £76 20 £55
☺ Dinner 7.30-9 ☹ Hotel Nov-Mar

Christopher Main's home-from-home overlooks the Sound of Sleat and the Isle of Skye, so from your bedroom you might be lucky enough to see basking seals and sea otters. If you want to get closer, hire the Swallow of Glenelg, the hotel's own boat. Local produce appears frequently on the menus, cooked and presented in Scottish/French style in the non-smoking dining room.

Gullane Greywalls Hotel

Muirfield, Gullane, Lothian, EH31 2EG
☎ (01620) 842144 📠 (01620) 842241
22 £170 50 £85
☺ Lunch 12.30-2, Dinner 7.30-9.30 ☹ Hotel Nov-Mar

House by Lutyens, gardens by Jekyll – lucky indeed are the Weaver family, the current generation of whom have been running Greywalls (and thus sharing their home with guests) since 1977. Bright bedrooms and a stylish library and bar set the scene for some serious food and wine.

Gullane La Potinière

Main Street, Gullane, Lothian, EH31 2AA
☎ (01620) 843214
30 £75
☺ Lunch at 1, Dinner at 8
☹ Lunch Wed, Fri & Sat, Dinner Sun-Thur, 1 wk Jun, all Oct, 25 Dec, 1 Jan

Hilary Brown cooks and David Brown serves, booking is essential, cooking is first class and wines are sensational. Lunch is at 1pm, dinner is at 8pm and there's no choice on the menu. You normally start with a soup then a fish or a vegetable dish before perhaps Barbary duck, guinea fowl or a humble chicken are elevated to the realm of exquisite. The atmosphere is that of dining in a friend's cottage not that of a trendy restaurant, the accent is on the plate and the glass rather than the scale of the menu and number of staff. A perfect place to dine with true friends and enjoy real food.

Ingliston Norton House

Ingliston, Nr Edinburgh, Lothian, EH28 8LX
☎ 0131-333 1275   📠 0131-333 5305
🛏 47   £120   🍴 80   🍽 £65
☺ Lunch 12-2, Dinner 7-9.30   ☹ Lunch Sat

An ornate, Victorian mansion just outside Edinburgh and very handy for the airport. Well restored and maintained, it features fine panelling and rich marble, while the dining room is housed in the conservatory. A converted stable block is now a tavern with walled garden, barbecue and children's play area.

Inverness Culloden House

Inverness, Highland, IV1 2NZ
☎ (01463) 790461   📠 (01463) 792181
🛏 23   £175   🍴 50   🍽 £85
☺ Lunch 12.30-2, Dinner 7-9

A well-proportioned Georgian mansion, steeped in history and retaining an elegant air thanks to the hospitality of resident owners, the McKenzies. There are comfortably furnished rooms, some with four-posters, as well as suites in the Garden Mansion. Set-price dinner menus include plenty of choice; and the wide variety on the wine list ranges from good value to good heavens!

Inverness Dunain Park

Inverness, Highland, IV3 6JN
☎ (01463) 230512   📠 (01463) 224532
🛏 14   £130   🍴 45   🍽 £65
☺ Lunch 12.30-1.30, Dinner 7-9

A converted hunting lodge in extensive gardens, including an area devoted to produce for the kitchen, appearing in Franco-Scottish format. Accommodation ranges from spacious suites in the main house to a garden cottage with its own sitting room.

Inverurie Thainstone House Hotel

Inverurie Road, Inverurie, Grampian, AB51 9NT
☎ (01467) 621643   📠 (01467) 625084
🛏 48   £126   🍴 42   🍽 £60
☺ Lunch 12-2, Dinner 7-9.30

14 miles north-west of Aberdeen lies Thainstone House, set in 40 acres of grassland. The creeper-clad Georgian house is inviting and friendly, and the atmosphere inside is one of gracious living, typified by the galleried reception area. Bedrooms are cosy and comfortable, and there are good leisure facilities. Modern Scottish food is served with some international flavours.

Kentallen of Appin Ardsheal House

Kentallen of Appin, Highland, PA38 4BX
☎ (01631) 740227 📠 (01631) 740342
🛏 13 £ £160 🪑 45 🍽 £80
☺ Lunch 12-1.45, Dinner 8-8.30

Since the Sutherlands bought Ardsheal in November 1994, they have undertaken a major refurbishment, of bedrooms and public areas; and also of the gardens. Continuity, however, is provided by the Kelso family, resident chef/managers since 1992. Local produce is used in the kitchen, supplemented by home-made items like pasta and petits fours.

Kilchrenan Ardanaiseig

Kilchrenan, By Taynuilt, Strathclyde, PA35 1HG
☎ (01866) 833333 📠 (01866) 833222
🛏 14 £ £142 🪑 30 🍽 £80
☺ Lunch 12.30-2, Dinner 7.30-9 ☹ Oct-Apr

On the shores of Loch Awe and thus with splendid views, Ardanaiseig has been a hotel since 1980 (it was a private house previously). In Scottish baronial style, the imposing aspect of the house is softened by the lovely gardens and trees. Set menus of modern Scottish cooking are served in formal yet relaxed surroundings.

Kilchrenan Taychreggan Hotel

Kilchrenan, By Taynuilt, Strathclyde, PA35 1HQ
☎ (01866) 833211 📠 (01866) 833244
🛏 20 £ £80 🪑 60 🍽 £70
☺ Lunch 12-2.30, Dinner 7.30-9

A lovely inn on a beautiful loch where a small and dedicated team provide fine wines, a relaxing atmosphere and good food on a 5-course table d'hote menu which takes the best of available local produce, and serves it with a modern interpretation. The hotel is not suitable for children under 12.

Kildrummy Kildrummy Castle Hotel

Kildrummy, Alford, Grampian, AB33 8RA
☎ (0197 55) 71288 📠 (0197 55) 71345
🛏 16 £ £130 🪑 42 🍽 £70
☺ Lunch 12.30-1.45, Dinner 7-9 ☹ Hotel 3 Jan-10 Feb

By the River Don, set in lovely gardens. Small, friendly hotel in the same hands since 1978. Set-price dinner menu has some choice at each course – dining room is non-smoking.

Kilfinan Kilfinan Hotel

Kilfinan, By Tighnabruaich, Strathclyde, PA21 2EP
☎ (01700) 821201 (01700) 821205
11 £72 22 £70
☺ Lunch 12-2 Sun only, Dinner 7.30-9.30 (light meals 12-9.30)

Wonderfully isolated setting in the west of Scotland, and a very friendly welcome from the Muellers. Short but well-balanced menus use Scottish produce presented modern fashion, and the wine list is very reasonably priced. A haven.

Killiecrankie Killiecrankie Hotel

Killiecrankie, By Pitlochry, Tayside, PH16 5LG
☎ (01796) 473220 (01796) 472451
10 £145 34 £70
☺ Dinner 7-8.30 ☹ Hotel Jan & Feb

Clearly signposted from the A9 between Pitlochry and Blair Atholl, Killiecrankie has been in the capable hands of the Andersons since 1988. It's a cosy rather than imposing place, set in 4 acres of grounds and gardens. Take light meals in the bar, or dine more formally in the restaurant on good Scottish produce presented in a modern manner, with Mediterranean and oriental influences.

Kilmore Glenfeochan House

Kilmore, Oban, Strathclyde, PA34 4QR
☎ (01631) 770273 (01631) 770624
3 £128 10 £70
☺ Dinner at 8 ☹ 1 Nov-1 Mar

5 miles south of Oban at the head of Loch Feochan is where you'll find this tiny, friendly hotel – more of a private home, really. Fairy-tale turrets, gorgeous gardens (they grow their own vegetables), attentive furnishings and good housekeeping enhance the feeling of well-being and relaxation. Well-balanced, limited choice set dinner menus are a delight.

Kilmun The Bistro at Fern Grove

Kilmun, Strathclyde, PA23 8SB
☎ (01369) 840334 (01369) 840334
3 £40 24 £50
☺ 11-9 ☹ Nov, weekdays Jan-Mar

Serious food at affordable prices in the philosophy here, and no-nonsense blackboard menus, which change daily, bear it out. Modern touches to the repertoire. The location is unmissable: on the edge of the Holy Loch, just 50 yards from the pier.

Kinclaven by Stanley
Ballathie House

Kinclaven by Stanley, Tayside, PH1 4QN
☎ (01250) 883268 (01250) 883396
39 £155 80 £70
☺ Lunch 12.30-2, Dinner 7-9 ☹ 4 days Jan

A baronial mansion on the banks of the tay, with graceful and stylishly-decorated public rooms. There's plenty of golf available in the area, to build up an appetite for set-price dinner menus with a modern Scottish slant.

Kingussie The Cross

Tweed Mill Brae, Ardbroilach Road, Kingussie,
Highland, PH21 1TC
☎ (01540) 661166 (01540) 661080
9 £170 28 £70
☺ Lunch 12.30-2, Dinner 7-9 ☹ Tue, 1st Dec-28 Feb (open New Year)

The enthusiasm of Tony & Ruth Hadley seems to increase rather than diminish and The Cross goes from strength to strength. Ruth's enthusiasm manifests itself in the kitchen where she prepares daily fixed-price menus which may offer a choice at 1 or 2 of the 5 courses (7 on Saturdays). A platter of salmon that includes gravadlax, ceviche and rillettes or a roast breast of pigeon with onion confit and salad then a capsicum soup with a touch of orange is followed by a pike 'sausage' with leek and lemongrass sauce. The main dish could be a choice of roast breast of duck with a sauce of sherry, soy and spices or Aberdeen Angus fillet with shallots and madeira then either pear and almond tart topped with frangipane, chocolate roulade with hazlenut ice cream or cheeses to finish. Tony is a great host and knows a thing or two about his wines. He will discuss the impressive list in detail with you and always has recommendations of appropriate wines to accompany Ruth's dishes on the menu. His comments add fun to the experience, Jackson Estate's Sauvignon is 'like sticking your nose into a gooseberry bush'. Stay in one of the nine comfortable bedrooms.

Kirknewton
Dalmahoy Hotel, Golf & CC

Kirknewton, Lothian, EH27 8EB
☎ 0131-333 1845 0131-335 3203
151 £127 120 £70
☺ Lunch 12.30-2, Dinner 7-9.30 (From 7.30 on Sundays) ☹ L Sat

Very much the country club on the fringes of Edinburgh. Conferences are big business here, and the facilities are due to be expanded. Dine formally in the Pentland restaurant, or more casually in the Terrace. Cooking is Scottish/French with a modern slant to some ambitious combinations.

Linlithgow Champany Inn

Champany, Linlithgow, Lothian, EH49 7LU
☎ (01506) 834532 📠 (01506) 834302
🍴 50 🍽 £100
☺ Lunch 12.30-2, Dinner 7-10
☹ Lunch Sat, all Sun, 25 & 26 Dec, 1 & 2 Jan

Eat a steak at Champany Inn, and wherever else you eat one subsequently will probably be a lesser experience. Aberdeen Angus beef is treated with due reverence and hung in optimum conditions until ready for the table. You can choose from steaks cut on or off the bone and have them with or without sauces (the meat really doesn't need them). Choose some tender young vegetables to accompany them from the basket proffered when you order and perhaps start with some oysters, prawns or home-smoked salmon. Excellent Scottish lamb and lobsters from a tank are worthwhile additions to the menu. The wine list is a serious tome with bags of house wines and one of the largest ranges of South African wines available in a restaurant. The Chop and Ale house next door (see below), is a cheaper place to eat similar steaks together with burgers and other dishes in a less formal setting.

Linlithgow Champany Inn Chop & Ale House

Champany, Linlithgow, Lothian, EH49 7LU
☎ (01506) 834532 📠 (01506) 834302
🍴 38 🍽 £50
☺ Lunch 12-2 (Sun 12.30-2.30), Dinner 6.30-10 (Sat from 6)
☹ 25 & 26 Dec, 1 & 2 Jan

The Davidsons rightly pride themselves on the quality of their beef and the standards of cooking here; and no less praiseworthy is the friendly but professional service and the careful selection of wines. In addition to the printed menu, there's a regularly-changing blackboard choice.

Markinch Balbirnie House

Balbirnie Park, Markinch, by Glenrothes, Fife, KY7 6NE
☎ (01592) 610066 📠 (01592) 610629
🛏 30 £ £125 🍴 100 🍽 £65
☺ Lunch 12-2.30, Dinner 7-9.30

An elegant, Georgian, country house set in landscaped gardens and parkland. Spacious, well-proportioned rooms have delightful features and are well maintained. Extensive, fixed-price menu offers local produce, and a mammoth wine list has bottles from just about everywhere.

Maryculter Maryculter House

South Deeside Road, Maryculter, Grampian, AB1 0BB
☎ (01224) 732124 📠 (01224) 733510
🛏 23 £ £115 🍴 36 🍽 £75
☺ Lunch 12-2.15, Dinner 7-9.30   ☹ Dinner Sun

Comfortable hotel just outside Aberdeen on the banks of the Dee. Good business facilities. Plenty of choice on the fixed-price menu.

Maybole Ladyburn

Maybole, Strathclyde, KA19 7SG
☎ (01655) 740585 📠 (01655) 740580
🛏 8 £ £140 🪑 25 🍽 £60
☺ Dinner only 7.30-8.30

Small and friendly hotel and restaurant run by the Hepburns. Some recipes are traditional family favourites, all are carefully cooked.

Melrose Burts Hotel

Market Square, Melrose, Borders, TD6 9PN
☎ (01896) 822285 📠 (01896) 822870
🛏 21 £ £74 🪑 50 🍽 £55
☺ Lunch 12-2, Dinner 7-9.30, Sun 7-9   🚫 24-26 Dec

Owned and run by the Henderson family since 1970, Burts enjoys a central location in the border district, A68, a position it has commanded since 1722. Set lunches and dinners, a carte and lighter daytime meals all help satisfy the range of customers. Usefully, this town-centre hotel has its own car park.

Moffat Well View Hotel ❖

Ballplay Road, Moffat, Dumfries & Galloway, DG10 9JU
☎ (01683) 20184
🛏 6 £ £70 🪑 24 🍽 £60
☺ Lunch 12.30-1.15, Dinner 6.30-8.30   🚫 Lunch Sat

Moffat has been popular as a spa town since the 17th Century, when the curative powers of its waters were first identified; and the Well View is named after one of the sulphurous wells which contributed to its fame – it's on the hills, outside town. Imaginative menus accompanied by a good selection of wines.

Muir-of-Ord Dower House

Highfield, Muir-of-Ord, Highland, IV6 7XN
☎ (01463) 870090 📠 (01463) 870090
🛏 5 £ £100 🪑 28 🍽 £70
☺ Lunch 12.30-2, Dinner 7.30-9   🚫 Xmas, 1 wk Oct, 2 wks Mar

Tiny restaurant with rooms where the kitchen specialises in seafood, venison and local beef. No-choice, set price dinner menus are well balanced, and there's no smoking in the dining room.

Nairn Clifton House Hotel

Viewfield Street, Nairn, Highland, IV12 4HW
☎ (01667) 453119 📠 (01667) 452836
🛏 12 £ £96 🍽 35 🍽 £60
☺ Lunch 12.30-1, Dinner 7-9.30 ☹ Hotel Dec-Feb, Restaurant Dec-Jan

Long-established and lovingly cared for (by J Gordon Macintyre since 1952). Creeper clad exterior, while the interior cleverly combines the imposing with the cosy. Raw ingredients for the kitchen are of the highest possible quality, cooked and served with a nod to French style.

Newton Stewart Kirroughtree Hotel

Newton Stewart, Dumfries & Galloway, DG8 6AN
☎ (01671) 402141 📠 (01671) 402425
🛏 17 £ £96 🍽 40 🍽 £65
☺ Lunch by arrangement only, Dinner 7-9.30
☹ 3 Jan-mid Feb

Luxurious hotel set in 8 acres of gardens in a beautiful part of Scotland. Classic French food is served in 2 dining rooms, both of which are now completely non-smoking. Piano music plays nightly.

North Middleton Borthwick Castle Hotel

North Middleton, Nr Gorebridge, Lothian, EH23 4QY
☎ (01875) 820514 📠 (01875) 821702
🛏 10 £ £120 🍽 25 🍽 £75
☺ Dinner 7-9 ☹ Lunch daily, Jan & Feb

Just 12 miles from Edinburgh, Borthwick is an imposing yet romantic castle, once the home to Mary, Queen of Scots. 45,000 acres of surrounding land include fishing and shooting. In the Great Hall, dine formally from a set 4-course menu.

Oban Knipoch Hotel

by Oban, Strathclyde, PA34 4QT
☎ (01852) 316251 📠 (01852) 316249
🛏 17 £ £130 🍽 44 🍽 £80
☺ Lunch by arrangement, Dinner 7.30-9 ☹ mid Nov-mid Feb

Owned and run (as a hotel) by the Craig family since 1981; friendly atmosphere, stunning location. Daily changing gourmet menu specialises in local produce: they smoke their own salmon; feature unusual cheeses and – though it's not local! – even the blend of coffee shows attention to detail.

Onich Allt-Nan-Ros Hotel

Onich, by Fort William, Highland, PH33 6RY
☎ (01855) 821210 (01855) 821462
21 £95 50 £55
☺ Lunch 12.30-2, Dinner 7-9 ☹ mid Nov-Xmas

The name means "burn of the roses" in Gaelic, and the hotel takes advantage of its south-facing aspect as much as possible. Decor is equally light and airy in lounges, bedrooms and dining room, where you can enjoy set-price dinner menus which take advantage of local produce.

Peat Inn The Peat Inn

Peat Inn, By Cupar, Fife, KY15 5LH
☎ (01334) 840206 (01334) 840530
8 £135 48 £85
☺ Lunch 12.30 for 1, Dinner 7-9.30
☹ Sun & Mon, Restaurant 25 Dec, 1 Jan

David Wilson has been delighting the public at his remote, stone built Inn for over 20 years and maintains high standards in his kitchen. Take the problem out of choosing what to eat with his tasting menu that might offer lobster cake with scallops, smoked fish fillet with potato, leek and chive sauce, a julienne of pigeon breast on a confit of spiced pork, roast rack of lamb with stewed shoulder in thyme flavoured sauce, cheeses and a selection of puddings. The wine list is excellently composed with good bargains even at the top of the range. An overnight in one of the 8 bedrooms will make your stay complete.

Peebles Cringletie House

Peebles, Borders, EH45 8PL
☎ (01721) 730233 (01721) 730244
13 £98 56 £65
☺ Lunch 1-1.45, Dinner 7.30-8.30 ☹ 2 Jan-8 Mar

Just north of Peebles on the A703 Edinburgh road, Cringletie is a fine stone house complete with turrets, and most of the rooms enjoy lovely views of the surrounding countryside as well as their own 28 acres of gardens. Inside, traditional furnishings set the scene, while there is a magnificent painted ceiling in one of the lounges. Set menus of 4 courses plus coffee offer some choice at each course: their most requested speciality is roast duckling.

Perth Number Thirty Three

33 George Street, Perth, Tayside, PH1 5LA
☎ (01738) 633771
45 £55
☺ Lunch 12.30-2.30, Dinner 6.30-9.30 ☹ Sun & Mon, 1st 3 wks Feb

Art deco is the interior style, seafood is the main ingredient, relaxed options the menu style. Naturally, local ingredients are used when possible by chef/patron Mary Billinghurst, and you can eat either in the more formal dining room or the more speedy oyster bar.

Port Appin Airds Hotel

Port Appin, Appin, Strathclyde, PA38 4DF
☎ (01631) 730236 (01631) 730535
12 £266 34 £80
☺ Lunch 12.30-2, Dinner at 8

The Allen family have created something rather special at this old ferry inn on the banks of Loch Linnhe: welcoming and comfortable, it is utterly unpretentious. Bedrooms are well furnished, and the dining room is a delight in every way. Betty and son Graeme Allen run the kitchen and produce some superb, light dishes with a few choices at each course except for the soup. Salad of roast quail with smoked salmon and champagne jelly, fillet of halibut on a bed of honeyed aubergines with champagne and chive sauce, roast saddle of roe deer on a potato cake with thyme and juniper sauce, mousse of mango with walnut shortbread, or prune and armagnac ice-cream show off their skills to fine effect. Eric Allen's wine list is something of a treasure trove, too.

Port Appin
The Pierhouse & Seafood Restaurant

Port Appin Pier, Nr Appin, Strathclyde, PA38 4DE
☎ (01631) 730302 (01631) 730213
11 £70 40 £55
☺ Lunch 12-3, Dinner 6.30-9.30 ☹ Lunch Dec 25

Lovely location on the edge of Loch Linnhe: small and friendly hotel and restaurant which takes full advantage of its setting, in terms of activities offered and produce used. Excellent seafood (some kept in creels till required) and also good meat dishes. Family run and proud of it.

Portpatrick Knockinaam Lodge

Portpatrick, Nr Stranraer, Dumfries & Galloway, DG9 9AD
☎ (01776) 810471 (01776) 810435
10 £104 32 £80
☺ Lunch 12-2, Dinner 7.30-9.30 (Tea 3-6)

Ask for directions when booking to make sure you don't miss out on this friendly, well sited small hotel. A change of ownership in Autumn 1994 resulted in a face-lift for the decor, but the kitchen remains in the capable hands of Stuart Muir so regulars are reassured by his familiar menus, using fresh, local ingredients to their best potential.

Quothquan Shieldhill

Quothquan, Biggar, Strathclyde, ML12 6NA
☎ (01899) 20035 (01899) 21092
11 £104 30 £70
☺ Lunch 12-1.30, Dinner 7-9 (booking essential)

Part castle, part country house, Shieldhill's bedrooms bear the names of battles from Scottish history. 5 acres of lawn and woodland surround the house, which has a relaxing ambience. Set-price dinner menus (3 or 4 courses) and 2-course lunches are offered.

St Andrews Grange Inn

Grange Road, St Andrews, Fife, KY16 8LJ
☎ (01334) 472670 📠 (01334) 478703
🪑 76 🍽 £45
🙂 Lunch 12.30-2.15, Dinner 6.30-9.15 ☹ Mon & Tue (Nov-Mar)

Tending to be more of a restaurant and less of a bar nowadays, the Grange is still a very useful place to know about in the area. Golf is, unsurprisingly, an integral part of the decor! Homely food makes good use of local produce, especially fish, and puds are a strong point.

St Andrews St Andrews Old Course Hotel

St Andrews, Fife, KY16 9SP
☎ (01334) 474371 📠 (01334) 477668
🛏 125 £ £245 🪑 90 🍽 £85
🙂 Dinner 7-10

The Home of Golf, in grand hotel style. Guaranteed to put your game right – or console failure with the amazing range of malts! Luxury throughout public rooms, with attention to detail in bedrooms and bathrooms. Full range of health and beauty treatments in the indoor spa, based around the glass-covered, pillared and frescoed pool area. Traditional cooking in the formal restaurant.

Scarista Scarista House

Scarista, Isle of Harris, Highland, H53 3HX
☎ (01859) 550238 📠 (01859) 550277
🛏 8 £ £89 🪑 16 🍽 £55
🙂 Lunch by arrangement, Dinner at 8.15 ☹ mid Sep-Mid May

Surely one of the most remote hotels in Britain, with just the Atlantic between its shell-sand shore and the States. The Georgian house was once a manse, and rooms enjoy splendid views and an absence of TV, radio and newspapers. Candle-lit no-choice dinners (let them know of any dietary requirements when booking) are a delight.

Scone Murrayshall House

Scone, Tayside, PH2 7PH
☎ (01738) 551171 📠 (01738) 552595
🛏 19 £ £125 🪑 80 🍽 £60
🙂 Lunch 12-2, Dinner 7-9.30, (light meals Clubhouse 12-10, closed Mon-Fri winter)

Lovely country house set in its own grounds which include a golf course, facilities for clay-pigeon shooting, an indoor golf school and any number of other outdoor sporting pursuits. To fuel all this activity, enjoy a set menu taking the best of Scottish produce and serving it up in modern style. Impressive wine list.

Sleat Kinloch Lodge

Sleat, Isle of Skye, Highland, IV43 8QY
☎ (01471) 833214 (01471) 833277
10 £130 28 £75
☺ Dinner only at 8 by arrangement ☹ 1 Dec-29 Feb

The Lord and Lady Macdonald are your gracious hosts in their family home, now a comfortable, small hotel and restaurant in a beautiful setting. Set price dinner menus are well balanced and usually offer a few choices, based on the finest available ingredients.

Spean Bridge Old Station Restaurant

Station Road, Spean Bridge, Highland, PH34 4EP
☎ (01397) 712535
30 £45
☺ Lunch by arrangement only, Dinner 6.30-9
☹ Dinner Mon-Wed in winter, 25 Dec, 1 Jan

You can fit in dinner here with a railway journey to and from Fort William, so reliable is the timetable and so reliable, also, the cooking at Richard & Helen Bunney's restaurant located – you've guessed – in the old station building. The dining rooms were formerly the ticket hall and waiting rooms, and offer good local ingredients cooked with modern touches. The wine list repays plenty of attention!

Stewarton Chapeltoun House

Stewarton-Irvine Road, Stewarton, Strathclyde, KA3 3ED
☎ (01560) 482696 (01560) 485100
8 £99 55 £65
☺ Lunch 12-2, Dinner 7-9 ☹ 1st 2 wks Jan

Comfortable hotel, built in 1900 for a wealthy merchant, in an attractive setting just south of Glasgow, ideally situated for golfers. Several bedrooms have recently undergone refurbishment. Good business facilities. The hotel is not really suitable for children under 12.

Strachur Creggans Inn

Strachur, Strathclyde, PA27 8BX
☎ (0136 986) 279 (0136 986) 637
21 £98 30 £55
☺ Lunch 12-2.30, Dinner 7-9 (Café:12.30-2.30, 5.30-9)

A lovely old inn on Loch Fyne. As well as superb fish, it offers the home-brewed MacPhunn malt whisky. Menus are a mixture of Scottish country house and French styles.

Troon Highgrove House

Old Loans Road, Loans, Troon, Strathclyde, KA10 7HL
☎ (01292) 312511   📠 (01292) 318228
🛏 9   £95   🍴 80   🍽 £55
☺ Lunch 12-2.30, Dinner 6-9.30

Built by a retired sea captain who obviously wanted to keep in touch with the love of his life: there are superb views over the Ayrshire coast to the Isle of Arran and the Mull of Kintyre. Comfortable bedrooms and lounges; good value fixed-price lunch and dinner menus.

Turnberry Turnberry Hotel

Turnberry, Strathclyde, KA26 9LT
☎ (01655) 331000   📠 (01655) 331706
🛏 132   £210   🍴 180   🍽 £130
☺ Lunch Sun only 1-2.30, Dinner 7.30-10 (tea 2.30-5.30)

A truly grand hotel that was built as a grand hotel and maintains very high standards in all aspects of its management. As well as retaining period grace and charm, it also offers every modern amenity, including two championship golf courses and a health spa. There are several restaurants to cater for all appetites and needs, and one – The Bay – is particularly dedicated to producing light dishes.

Ullapool Altnaharrie Inn

Ullapool, Highland, IV26 2SS
☎ (01854) 633230
🛏 8   £280   🍴 18   🍽 £150
☺ Light lunches for residents only, Dinner at 8   ☹ Nov-Easter

There is nowhere quite like Altnaharrie. It has some magical charm that continues to draw visitors to the remote shore of Loch Broom opposite Ullapool where a launch has to pick up guests for the 10 minute trip across the water. Much of the charm lies in the unexpected sophistication that awaits you in the converted drover's cottage – perhaps the isolation from the rest of the world helps, and simplicity is the keynote, a tribute to the skills of Fred Brown & Gunn Eriksen, the hosts. You have the feeling of being house guests and there is little to do except walk, study wild life, relax and eat and imbibe. The latter pastimes are more than well catered for, and the food that emanates from Gunn's kitchen would justify swimming across the Loch, never mind the launch! A typical menu might start with a warm salad of scallops on a bed of spinach with green lentils, morel and champagne vinegar sauce, then a soup of crab, followed by a fillet of sika on a bed of Spanish onions, red onions and juniper berries with a little ravioli of mushrooms and grapes and two sauces, one of the juices of the venison with red burgundy, the other of juniper and cream. Next a selection of cheeses and the puddings where you are offered a choice between vanilla ice cream, caramel ice cream with caramelised apples and pineapple sauce, a banana baked in a thin shell of pastry with sauce of orange, cream and Cointreau or warm chocolate cake with a soft runny centre and chocolate ice cream – the good news is that you can usually try all of them! Fred has an excellent wine list that makes island life even more enjoyable.

Ullapool Ceilidh Place

14 West Argyle Street, Ullapool, Highland, IV26 2TY
☎ (01854) 612103 📠 (01854) 612886
🛏 13 £100 🍴 50 🍽 £60
☺ Dinner 6.30-10 (light meals 8am-9.30pm) ☹ 2 wks Jan

Coffee shop, restaurant and rooms in the hotel or bunkhouse. Short menu of traditional favourites, friendly service and atmosphere.

Whitebridge Knockie Lodge

Whitebridge, Highland, IV1 2UP
☎ (01456) 486276 📠 (01456) 486389
🛏 10 £90 🍴 20 🍽 £70
☺ Dinner only at 8 ☹ Nov-Apr

Small but comfortable, beautifully sited hotel and restaurant which takes full advantage of its location both in terms of leisure pursuits offered, decor and furnishings, and even ingredients for the kitchen. Set price dinner menu has no choice, but special requests can be catered for in advance.

SCOTCH BEEF CLUB
see page 16

Wales

Wales 305

Abercynon Llechwen Hall

Abercynon, Nr LLanfabon, Mid Glamorgan, CF37 4HP
☎ (01443) 742050 📠 (01443) 742189
🛏 11 £70 🍴 35 £50
☺ Lunch 12-2, Dinner 7-9.30 ☹ Dinner Sun

Converted farm and house, conveniently situated between Abercynon and Llanfabon. The name probably means "a place of shelter or refuge". Characterful old buidings make up the hotel, and the restaurant, St Cynons, is located in the original farmhouse kitchen.

Abergavenny Walnut Tree Inn

Llandewi Skirrid, Abergavenny, Gwent, NP7 8AW
☎ (01873) 852797 📠 (01873) 859764
🍴 46 £80
☺ Lunch 12.15-3.15, Dinner 7.15-10.15 ☹ Sun & Mon, Xmas, 2 wks Feb

Rather than try to re-invent Mediterranean cooking Franco Taruschio cooks real Italian food. Sometimes he adopts alien flavours – a Thai dip with goujons of sole, kumquats with duck or rhubarb and ginger with salmon – but in the main the cooking is the real thing. Try his bresaola, bruschetta with cannellini beans and pancetta, brodetto or fillets of red mullet with sage and Parma ham and you could equally be in Franco's native Marches. The setting is an old inn, not pretentious in decor, this place is for eating and enjoying, not for being seen! The menu doesn't change too much, as after 30 years the regulars won't allow too many changes and always return for their favourite dishes. New customers will find that there is no lack of variety, for example as many as 24 puddings; the wine list is simply superb and Italian wines the essential highlight. Worth driving miles for, and everybody does!

Abersoch Porth Tocyn Hotel

Bwlchtocyn, Abersoch, Gwynedd, LL53 7BU
☎ (01758) 713303 📠 (01758) 713538
🛏 17 £94 🍴 50 £60
☺ Lunch 12.30-2, Dinner 7.30-9.30 ☹ Hotel mid Nov-wk before Easter

Built as a row of miners' cottages but lovingly transformed into a hotel in 1948 by the Fletcher-Brewer family, Porth Tocyn is now in the capable hands of that family's third generation. Splendid location, taking in Cardigan Bay as well as Snowdonia, and surrounded by its own pretty grounds which include an outdoor pool. Comfortable and relaxing interior, international daily-changing menu in the dining room.

Abersoch Riverside Hotel

Abersoch, Gwynedd, LL53 7HW
☎ (01758) 712419 📠 (01758) 712671
🛏 12 £70 🍴 30 £60
☺ Lunch 12-2 (bar only), Dinner 7.30-9 ☹ mid Nov-Feb

Long-established, prettily-located hotel run by the Bakewells since 1967. Fixed-price set dinner menu changes daily.

Aberystwyth Conrah Country Hotel

Chancery, Aberystwyth, Dyfed, SY23 4DF
☎ (01970) 617941 (01970) 624546
20 £93 50 £60
☺ Lunch 12-2, Dinner 7-9 ☹ 1 wk Xmas

Just to the south of the town, Conrah is accessed by a rhododendron-lined drive. Fine views of the surrounding countryside, close to the coast – an ideal base from which to explore this part of Wales. Set-price and à la carte menus.

Beaumaris Ye Olde Bulls Head Inn

Castle Street, Beaumaris, Anglesey, Gwynedd, LL58 8AP
☎ (01248) 810329 (01248) 811294
15 £73 70 £60
☺ Lunch 12-2.30 (Sun to 1.30), Dinner 7.30-9.30 ☹ 25 & 26 Dec, 1 Jan

This is one of those places where you might be tempted to choose the wine first, and fit your meal around it, such is the depth of the list offered by Keith Rothwell & David Robertson – it's certainly a fitting testament to one of Wales' oldest (1472) inns, and can only make the lovely views across the Menai Straits even more enjoyable! Keith cooks up a storm with local ingredients when possible, presented in a fairly international way – all the more reason to sip your way around the world!

Cardiff Armless Dragon

97 Wyeverne Road, Cathays, Cardiff, South Glamorgan, CF2 4BG
☎ (01222) 382357
45 £50
☺ Lunch 12.15-2.15, Dinner 7.15-10.15
☹ Lunch Sat, all Sun & Mon, 1 wk Xmas

Good value, busy bistro where an inventive menu offers modern interpretations of international dishes but with Welsh overtones. Reasonably priced wines – plenty under £10.

Cardiff Le Cassoulet

5 Romilly Crescent, Canton, Cardiff, South Glamorgan, CF1 9NP
☎ (01222) 221905
40 £65
☺ Lunch 12-2, Dinner 7-10
☹ Lunch Sat, all Sun & Mon, 2 wks Xmas, Aug

Toulouse cuisine – of course! – at Gilbert Viader's friendly little restaurant, and the dish from which it takes its name has pride of place. Wines are classics, but at reasonable prices.

Cardiff Champers

61 St Mary Street, Cardiff, South Glamorgan, CF1 1FE
☎ (01222) 373363
180 £40
☺ Lunch 12-2.30, Dinner 7-12   ☹ Lunch Sun

High on atmosphere, low on price: this Spanish-style bodega offers a range of tapas as well as main meals. Large selection of mature Riojas on the wine list.

Cardiff Le Monde

60 St Mary Street, Cardiff, South Glamorgan, CF1 1FE
☎ (01222) 387376
180 £40
☺ Lunch 12-2.30, Dinner 7-12.15   ☹ Sun, 25, 26 Dec

Lively, bustling wine bar and restaurant within an oval ball's punt of the Arms Park. Fish, steaks, and good-value wines.

Cardiff New House Country Hotel

Thornhill Road, Cardiff, South Glamorgan, CF4 5UA
☎ (01222) 520280   (01222) 520324
33 £80 40 £45
☺ Lunch 12-2, Dinner 7-9.45

Substantial, well-furnished hotel on the outskirts of the city but set in its own grounds. Ideally situated and equipped for conferences and training courses.

Colwyn Bay Café Niçoise

124 Abergele Road, Colwyn Bay, Clwyd, LL29 7PS
☎ (01492) 531555
32 £45
☺ Lunch 12-2, Dinner 7-10
☹ Lunch Mon-Wed, all Sun, 1 wk Jun, 3 days Xmas

Carl & Lynne Swift's intimate little restaurant provides welcome relief from the fast food ghetto that this north Wales resort has threatened to become. Great value on the fixed-price menu, and there's also a carte so you can put together a Mediterranean-style meal based on good ingredients like Welsh lamb and cheeses. Interesting wine list.

Coychurch Coed-y-Mwstwr Hotel

Coychurch, Nr Bridgend, Mid Glamorgan, CF35 6AF
☎ (01656) 860621 📠 (01656) 863122
🛏 23 £140 🍴 60 🍽 £60
☺ Lunch 12-2, Dinner 7-10

Now managed by the Virgin group, "Whispering Trees" is a gracious red-brick building, set on a wooded hillside, not far from the sea, from Cardiff and from the M4. Indoors, elegant proportions, wood panelling and crystal chandeliers enhance the feeling of well-being. Most of the bedrooms enjoy splendid views. In the vaulted Eliot Restaurant, traditional dishes are presented with a modern touch.

Crickhowell Bear Hotel

High Street, Crickhowell, Powys, NP8 1BW
☎ (01873) 810408 📠 (01873) 811696
🛏 29 £54 🍴 60 🍽 £55
☺ Lunch 11-2 (Sun 12-2), Dinner 7-9.30 ☹ Dinner Sun

Popular old hotel with comfortable rooms and cosy bars, atmospheric with beamed ceilings and open fires in winter: an ideal base for exploring this part of Wales. Set-price lunches, à la carte dinners.

Crickhowell Gliffaes Country House Hotel

Crickhowell, Powys, NP8 1RH
☎ (01874) 730371 📠 (01874) 730463
🛏 22 £85 🍴 85 🍽 £55
☺ Dinner 7.30-9.15 ☹ 5 Jan-23 Feb

Just a mile from the A40, 2 miles west of Crickhowell, is where you'll find this lovely south-facing hotel. Comfortably furnished and decorated, the conservatory Sun Room is one attraction. The main one, however, is probably the fishing – Gliffaes has its own stretches of the Usk in an area famous for wild brownies as well as salmon. Plenty of other activities, too, for fishing widows.

Dolgellau Dolmelynllyn Hall

Ganllwyd, Dolgellau, Gwynedd, LL40 2HP
☎ (01341) 40273 📠 (01341) 40273
🛏 11 £90 🍴 24 🍽 £60
☺ Light lunches only 12-2, Dinner 7.30-8.30 ☹ Dec-Feb

Follow the River Mawddach from Dolgellau, go along a beech-lined drive and come to this imposing house set in 3 acres of terraced gardens. Bedrooms are individually furnished and very comfortable. Imaginative use of prime local produce in the set menus (dinner and light lunches); superb wine list. The hotel and restaurant are entirely non-smoking.

Dolgellau Dylanwad Da

2 Smithfield Street, Dolgellau, Gwynedd, LL40 1BS
☎ (01341) 422870
⌨ 30 🍽 £55
☺ Dinner 7-9 ☹ Lunch daily, (Sun-Wed Winter), Feb

Picturesque town of dark slate buildings in which Dylan Rowlands' friendly little restaurant also stands out. Sound cooking at reasonable prices, excellent value on the wine list: only champagne costs more than £15!

Eglwysfach Ynyshir Hall

Eglwysfach, Machynlleth, Powys, SY20 8TA
☎ (01654) 781209 📠 (01654) 781366
🛏 8 £120 ⌨ 40 🍽 £60
☺ Lunch 12.30-1.30, Dinner 7-8.30 ☹ Lunch Mon-Sat

The Reens have worked hard over the last 18 months, carrying out an extensive refurbishment of their lovely Georgian home, adorned with the fruits of Rob's "other" life as an artist. Changes, too, in the kitchen where duties are split between 2 new young chefs who cook in the modern style using local produce when possible. In all, great strides forward for Ynyshir.

Ewloe St David's Park Hotel

St David's Park, Ewloe, Clwyd, CH5 3YB
☎ (01244) 520800 📠 (01244) 520930
🛏 121 £107 ⌨ 140 (after refurbishment) 🍽 £50
☺ Lunch 12.30-2, Dinner 7-10

Purpose-built, modern hotel with Georgian facade and well-maintained gardens. There are good business and leisure facilities. Bedrooms are carefully designed and equipped.

Fishguard Three Main Street

3 Main Street, Fishguard, Dyfed, SA65 9HG
☎ (01348) 874275
🛏 3 £50 ⌨ 24 🍽 £65
☺ Lunch 12-2, Dinner 7-9.30 ☹ Sun (& Mon in winter), Feb

Georgian house containing a restaurant, coffee shop and letting bedrooms. The decor comprises vibrant colours, natural woods and a profusion of fresh flowers, all adding up to a warm and hospitable atmosphere. Local ingredients are used on the menu, but are served with a Mediterranean slant. Wines are well described and moderately priced.

Llandrillo Tyddyn Llan

Llandrillo, Nr Corwen, Clwyd, LL21 0ST
☎ (01490) 440264 📠 (01490) 440414
🛏 10 £88 🍴 60 🍽 £60
☺ Lunch 12.30-2, Dinner 7-9.30 (Sun 7-8.30) ☹ 3 wks Jan

Elegant Georgian house with later sympathetic additions, set in lovely grounds. Relaxing rather than overpowering interior, high standards of comfort throughout, and a constant programme of discreet maintenance. Good cooking in the kitchen: local ingredients used in modern British style; Welsh cheeses a speciality.

Llandudno Bodysgallen Hall

Llandudno, Gwynedd, LL30 1RS
☎ (01492) 584466 📠 (01492) 582519
🛏 29 £140 🍴 60 🍽 £75
☺ Lunch 12.30-2, Dinner 7.30-9.45

An imposing 17th-century house in gorgeous gardens and parkland with the bonus of overlooking Snowdonia. Oak panelling and mullioned windows feature in the main house and there are cottages grouped around a garden courtyard where guests have their own sitting rooms. The surrounding area abounds with sights to see, the castles of Beaumaris, Caernarfon, Conwy and Harlech the Isle of Anglesey and don't miss a ride on the Ffestiniog railway. Mike Penny is the chef and his cooking shows good combinations of ingredients, seabass on a compote of smoked bacon, broad beans and garlic, a hot ratatouille souffle served on a ragout of peppers and globe artichoke or Dublin Bay prawns risotto with a scallop tortellini and chive sauce are typical. Many special events are planned throughout the year, wine tastings, piano recitals and garden days in conjunction with nearby Bodnant Gardens.

Llandudno Richard's Bistro Restaurant

7 Church Walks, Llandudno, Gwynedd, LL30 2HD
☎ (01492) 875315 📠 (01492) 877924
🍴 24 🍽 £55
☺ Dinner 6-10

Richard Hendey is the one-man-band in question, and he offers a wide range of bistro-style dishes on a fairly international menu. A good variety of wines is modestly priced. Richard aims to entertain customers as much as possible, and the word is: he succeeds!

Llandudno St Tudno Hotel

The Promenade, Llandudno, Gwynedd, LL30 2LP
☎ (01492) 877544 📠 (01492) 877788
🛏 21 £110 🍴 55 🍽 £70
☺ Lunch 12.30-1.45, Dinner 7-9.30 (Sun to 8.30)

You can't really miss the St Tudno: it's right opposite the pier, just 100 yards from the cenotaph. Individually furnished bedrooms are comfortable and well equipped, and there's a non-smoking sitting room with sea views. In the restaurant, traditional menus are served with an extensive range of Welsh cheeses, complete with accompanying range of ports!

Llangammarch Wells
Lake Country House Hotel
Llangammarch Wells, Powys, LD4 4BS
☎ (01591) 620202 📠 (01591) 620457
🛏 19 £115 🍽 50 🍴 £65
☺ Lunch 12.15-2, Dinner 7.30-8.45

There's a collect-from-train service to take you to this lovely, well-maintained country house set in 50 acres of gardens, including its own trout lake (if you prefer river fishing, it's handy for the Wye, Irfon and the Chewfru). Indoors the house is richly and stylishly furnished. Modern French/British menus are served in the elegant dining room, and the wine list matches the surroundings.

Llangybi Cwrt Bleddyn Hotel
Llangybi, Tredunnock, Nr Usk, Gwent, NP5 1PG
☎ (01633) 450521 📠 (01633) 450220
🛏 36 £102 🍽 60 🍴 £60
☺ Lunch 12-3, Dinner 7-10

That increasingly popular pastime, Murder Weekends, is one of the attractions at Cwrt Bleddyn (now managed by the Virgin group). History is another: its origins go back to the 14th Century though the house is now mostly Victorian in appearance. The beamed and draped Nicholls dining room is the venue for a traditional international menu; while business and leisure facilities are also good.

Llanrug Seiont Manor
Llanrug, Caernarfon, Gwynedd, LL55 2AQ
☎ (01286) 673366 📠 (01286) 672840
🛏 28 £100 🍽 65 🍴 £65
☺ Lunch 12-2.30, Dinner 7-10

Lovely parkland setting for this stone-built hotel with excellent leisure facilities. The restaurant is housed in a stylish conservatory, and offers Welsh-influenced French cuisine. One of the Virgin group of hotels.

Llansanffraid Glan Conwy Old Rectory
Llanrwst Road, Llansanffraid Glan Conwy, nr Conwy, Gwynedd, LL28 5LF
☎ (01492) 580611 📠 (01492) 584555
🛏 6 £84 🍽 16 🍴 £70
☺ Dinner 7.30 for 8   ☹ Hotel: 20 Dec-1 Feb

A haven of peace near the north Wales coast and home to the Vaughans, who have been dispensing hospitality here for over 10 years now. Wendy's kitchen takes pride of place: as much as possible is home made; ingredients are carefully sourced (only Welsh black beef and Welsh mountain lamb, for example); and the set dinners are well balanced.

Llanwyddyn Lake Vyrnwy Hotel

Lake Vyrnwy, (via Oswestry), Llanwyddyn, Powys, SY10 0LY
☎ (01691) 870692 📠 (01691) 870259
🛏 35   £77   🪑 70   🍽 £65
☺ Lunch 12.30-1.45, Dinner 7.30-9.15

Purpose-built, but with a twist: from local stone at the end of the last century (when a huge dam, then the biggest in Europe, was created to provide water for Liverpool), the hotel provided accommodation to tourists and visiting dignitaries. The lake was stocked shortly afterwards, so this sporting country hotel was set for a century of continuing the original vision. Nowadays it is further enhanced by some good and very careful cooking, using fresh local ingredients and making as much as possible (including canapés, breads, petits fours) on the premises.

Llyswen Llangoed Hall

Llyswen, Brecon, Powys, LD3 0YP
☎ (01874) 754525 📠 (01874) 754545
🛏 23   £155   🪑 40   🍽 £155
☺ Lunch 12.30-2.15, Dinner 7.15-9.30

A delightful country house rebuilt by the legendary Sir Clough Williams-Ellis and converted to a hotel by Sir Bernard Ashley. The decor is impeccable, rooms are spacious and not unnaturally feature many Laura Ashley fabrics and there is a fascinating collection of Edwardian paintings and drawings, including some by Whistler. Ben Davies has now taken over as head chef, offering fixed-price menus at lunch, carte or a set menu in the evening. Cooking is in modern idiom using good produce, many of the vegetables and herbs coming from their own garden. A superb range of wines has been amassed with some high pedigrees from around the World.

Miskin Miskin Manor

Miskin, Pontyclun, Mid Glamorgan, CF7 8ND
☎ (01443) 224204 📠 (01443) 237606
🛏 32   £95   🪑 60   🍽 £60
☺ Lunch 12-2, Dinner 7-9.45

A large, well-propotioned manor house about 8 miles west of Cardiff. Spacious, panelled lounges, comfortable bedrooms and good conference facilities. Leisure club in the hotel grounds.

Mumbles Norton House

17 Norton Road, Mumbles, Swansea,
West Glamorgan, SA3 5TQ
☎ (01792) 404891 📠 (01792) 403210
🛏 15 £65 🍴 30 🕐 £65

☺ Lunch Sun only 12.30-2.30, Dinner 7-9.30

Originally home to a master mariner, this bright, white 18th-century building now houses John & Jan Power's comfortable hotel, just a (longish) pebble's throw from Swansea Bay. Lovely walks in this part of the Gower peninsular – rise early to watch the cockle-gatherers at work. The menu is written in Welsh but translated into English – presentation is traditional. The extensive wine list has been well sourced and is reasonably priced.

Newport Celtic Manor

The Coldra, Newport, Gwent, NP6 2YA
☎ (01633) 413000 📠 (01633) 412910
🛏 73 £120 🍴 60 🕐 £65

☺ Lunch 12-2.30, Dinner 7-10.30 ☹ Lunch Sat, all Sun

19th-century house in 300 acres of its own grounds and woodlands, just minutes from the M4 (Junction 24). The planned golf course duly opened in 1995, the tennis club is on the way. In addition to leisure facilities, popular with holiday-makers, there are also good business facilities, thus ensuring year-round interest.

Newport Cnapan Restaurant

East Street, Newport, Dyfed, SA42 0SY
☎ (01239) 820575 📠 (01239) 820878
🛏 5 £46 🍴 48 🕐 £50

☺ Lunch 12-2, Dinner 7-9 ☹ Tue, Feb, 25 & 26 Dec

Attractive listed building housing restaurant with rooms run with care by the Coopers and the Lloyds. Light lunches and more substantial dishes emanate from the kitchen, but all with the homeliness that typifies the whole enterprise, which they call a Country House for Guests. There's a good range of Welsh cheeses, and there's even a Welsh wine on the list.

Northop Soughton Hall

Northop, Nr Mold, Clwyd, CH7 6AB
☎ (01352) 840811 📠 (01352) 840382
🛏 14 £99 🍴 50 🕐 £65

☺ Lunch 12-2.30, Dinner 7.30-9.30 (Sat to 10, Sun to 8)

Lovely house in its own beautifully maintained gardens – it was a bishop's palace originally. The Rodenhurst family turned it into a country house hotel in 1987 with all due courtesy to to its roots, and their attention to detail is still apparent. There are 2 dining rooms: the first floor gourmet à la carte restaurant serving classic British fare; and the more relaxed and informal room where plainer fresh food (fish, steaks) is served. A wine list of stature.

Penally Penally Abbey

Penally, Nr Tenby, Dyfed, SA70 7PY
☎ (01834) 843033 📠 (01834) 844714
🛏 12 £ £90 🍴 46 🍽 £50
☺ Lunch 12.30-2, Dinner 7.30-9.30

Historic associations at an elegant country house hotel set in 5 acres of wooded gardens with views over Carmarthen Bay. Elegant dining room serving Anglo-Franco-Welsh food!

Porthkerry Egerton Grey

Porthkerry, Nr Cardiff, South Glamorgan, CF6 9BZ
☎ (01446) 711666 📠 (01446) 711690
🛏 10 £ £85 🍴 30 🍽 £65
☺ Lunch 12-2, Dinner 6.30-9.30

The Pitkins have been here since 1989 and have put their own mark on this elegant country house, which was a rectory in the 19th Century. It's set in a peaceful wooded valley away from main roads, but is still only 10 miles from Cardiff. The dining room, formerly the billiard room, offers a daily-changing menu with an international flavour.

Portmeirion Hotel Portmeirion

Portmeirion, Gwynedd, LL48 6ER
☎ (01766) 770228 📠 (01766) 771331
🛏 37 £ £132 🍴 100 🍽 £65
☺ Lunch 12.30-2, Dinner 7-9.30 ☹ Lunch Mon, 7 Jan-4 Feb

Actually a village that was created by Sir Clough Williams-Ellis, Portmeirion is quite unique, a Portofino of the Northern hemisphere that remains a tribute to the dream of its architect founder. Bright painted cottages dotted around a central piazza serve as accommodation in addition to rooms in the main hotel building. All are furbished to high standards and there are 5 suites that overlook a swimming pool. Chef Craig Hindley finds inspiration in local produce, Welsh lamb, venison and fish being popular on fixed-price menus.

Pwllheli Plas Bodegroes

Nefyn Road, Pwllheli, Gwynedd, LL53 5TH
☎ (01758) 612363 📠 (01758) 701247
🛏 8 £ £140 🍴 35 🍽 £75
☺ Dinner 7-9.30 (Sun to 9) ☹ Mon, Hotel Nov-Feb

Standards remain high at Chris & Gunna Chown's Plas Bodegroes, although they divide their time between here and their establishment in Bath. Visitors are still assured of good hospitality, good food and fine wines. Try the likes of scallop and smoked haddock fishcake with tartare sauce, followed by roast Hereford duck with lentils, bacon and a Madeira sauce, finishing with barabrith (Welsh tea bread) and butter pudding with apricot sauce. Diverse wine list has helpful sweet/dry indicators.

Reynoldston Fairyhill

Reynoldston, Gower, Swansea, West Glamorgan, SA3 1BS
☎ (01792) 390139 (01792) 391358
9 £85 68 £70
☺ Lunch Sun only 12.30-1.15, Dinner 7.30-9.15

Comfortable mansion dating back to 1720, set in 20 or so acres of woodland with trout stream and lake, in the heart of the Gower peninsula. Traditional Welsh produce is presented with a modern touch, with wines recommended to accompany each course. Good range, too, of farmhouse cheeses.

Rossett Llyndir Hall

Llyndir Lane, Rossett, Nr Wrexham, Clwyd, LL12 0AY
☎ (01244) 571648 (01244) 571258
38 £110 50 £55
☺ Lunch 12-2, Dinner 7-10

Graceful hall set in its own well-maintained gardens, undergoing constant improvement. Additional bedrooms are planned, and this year the restaurant was extended by the addition of a conservatory. Half of the bedrooms are reserved for non-smokers.

Swansea Annie's Restaurant

56 St Helen's Road, Swansea, West Glamorgan, SA1 4BE
☎ (01792) 655603
34 £55
☺ Dinner 7-10 ☹ Dinner Sun, Mon in winter, 1st 2 wks June

Annie Gwilym's fixed-price menus concentrate on producing strong flavours with a Mediterranean twang, often in gutsy combinations. The short wine list with concise tasting notes is very refreshing!

Swansea Number One

1 Wind Street, Swansea, West Glamorgan, SA1 1DE
☎ (01792) 456996
40 £55
☺ Lunch 12-2.30, Dinner 7-9.30
☹ Dinner Mon & Tue, all Sun, Bank Holidays, Xmas-New Year

Friendly, local bistro serving unpretentious modern British and provincial French fare; plenty of seafood, Welsh produce when possible. Easy-going, relaxed atmosphere – booking advisable.

Talsarnau Maes-y-Neuadd

Talsarnau, Nr Harlech, Gwynedd, LL47 6YA
☎ (01766) 780200 📠 (01766) 780211
🛏 16 £107 🪑 50 🍽 £70
☺ Lunch 12.15-1.45, Dinner 7-9

Lovely location within some of Britain's most breathtaking scenery (Snowdonia) for the Horsfall & Slatter families' home from home and country house hotel. Flower-bedecked without, beamed and stone-walled within, the atmosphere is one of relaxation and friendliness. Standards are high, and the kitchen produces carefully constructed set menus, using local produce when possible and always for any lamb dish. No smoking in the dining room.

Tintern Abbey Royal George

Tintern Abbey, Nr Chepstow, Gwent, NP6 6SF
☎ (01291) 689205 📠 (01291) 689448
🛏 19 £72 🪑 60 🍽 £50
☺ Lunch 12-2, Dinner 7-9.30 (Fri & Sat to 10)

Formerly a coaching inn, now the Royal George offers 20th-century travellers and visitors just as warm a welcome as in bygone days. Comfortable rooms, pretty garden.

Trellech Village Green

Trellech, Nr Monmouth, Gwent, NP5 4PA
☎ (01600) 860119
🛏 2 £45 🪑 70 🍽 £45
☺ Lunch 11.45-2, Dinner 7-10 ☹ Dinner Sun, all Mon, 1 wk Jan

Known as the Crown until Bob & Jane Evans arrived 10 years ago and transformed it into the popular restaurant and brasserie with rooms that it is today – though you can still pop in for a pint! Careful cooking on the international-style menu (main courses chalked up on the board) is accompanied by an interesting wine list with useful tasting notes. There's even a Welsh wine – the Tintern Parva Rosé at under £10! Lovely setting on the Wye. Go on, try it!

Welsh Hook Stone Hall

Welsh Hook, Wolfscastle, Nr Haverfordwest, Dyfed, SA62 5NS
☎ (01348) 840212 📠 (01348) 840815
🛏 5 £60 🪑 34 🍽 £63
☺ Lunch by arrangement, Dinner 7-9.30 ☹ 2 wks Jan

14th-century origins, secluded location for this tiny hotel; French menus change daily (table d'hote) or quarterly (carte).

Whitebrook Crown at Whitebrook

Whitebrook, Nr Monmouth, Gwent, NP5 4TX
☎ (01600) 860254 📠 (01600) 860607
🚪 12 £ £65 🛏 32 🍽 £80
☺ Lunch 12-2, Dinner 7-9.30)
☹ Lunch Mon, Dinner Sun to non-residents, 25 & 26 Dec, 2 wks Jan, 2 wks Aug

French-style auberge in the lovely Wye valley, combining French cooking in the restaurant and Welsh hospitality in the rooms, all co-ordinated by Roger & Sandra Bates. Lighter lunches and more formal dinners each display carefully chosen and combined ingredients; and local cheeses are a speciality.

**THE ACADEMY OF
FOOD & WINE SERVICE**
see page 22

Channel Islands & Isle of Man

ALDERNEY

St Anne Georgian House

Victoria Street, St Anne, Alderney
☎ (01481) 822471
🍴 48 🍽 £45

☺ Lunch 12-2.30 Dinner 7.15-9.30 ☹ Dinner Tue

Bedrooms once more available at the Georgian House, call for details; outdoor eating in The Garden Beyond a popular destination.

St Anne Inchalla Hotel

The Val, St Anne, Alderney
☎ (01481) 823220 📠 (01481) 824045
🛏 9 £73 🍴 30 🍽 £55

☺ Lunch Sunday only 1-2 Dinner 7-8.45 ☹ 2 wks Xmas/New Year

Small, comfortable, family-run hotel in a peaceful setting; seafood (local of course!) is the thing to eat here.

GUERNSEY

Castel La Grande Mare Hotel

Vazon Bay, Castel, Guernsey
☎ (01481) 56576 📠 (01481) 56532
🛏 34 £113 🍴 75 🍽 £70

☺ Lunch 12-2 Dinner 7-9.30

Modern hotel and country club with wide variety of rooms and suites – golf is the main interest here! Traditional, formal French cooking, huge wine list.

St Peter Port Absolute End

St George's Esplanade, St Peter Port, Guernsey
☎ (01481) 723822 📠 (01481) 729129
🍴 60 🍽 £60

☺ Lunch 12-2 Dinner 7-10 ☹ Sun, Jan

At the far end of St Peter Port, with lovely views of the bay, Absolute End makes a good setting for seafood, often presented in traditional French or Italian style.

St Peter Port La Frégate

Les Cotils, St Peter Port, Guernsey
☎ (01481) 724624 📠 (01481) 720443
🛏 13 £95 🍴 80 🍽 £55

☺ Lunch 12.30-1.30 Dinner 7-9.30

Town-centre hotel, traditional decor and cooking. By night, great floodlit harbour views.

GUERNSEY (contd)

St Peter Port Le Nautique

The Quay Steps, St Peter Port, Guernsey
☎ (01481) 721714 📠 (01481) 721786
🍴 68 🍽 £55

☺ Lunch 12-2 Dinner 7-10   ☹ Sun, 25 Dec–10 Jan

Traditional-style French seafood offered in old-style surroundings with old-style hospitality and service.

St Peter Port Old Government House

Ann's Place, St Peter Port, Guernsey
☎ (01481) 724921 📠 (01481) 724429
🛏 72 £92 🍴 120 🍽 £55

☺ Lunch 12-2 Dinner 7-9.30

Former Governor's residence, now a comfortable hotel. Traditional menus in the Regency Room restaurant.

St Peter Port St Pierre Park

Rohais, St Peter Port, Guernsey
☎ (01481) 728282 📠 (01481) 712041
🛏 135 £135 🍴 77 🍽 £50

☺ Lunch 12-2.30 Dinner 7-10.30   ☹ Lunch Sat, Dinner Sun

Luxurious, modern, international standard hotel with excellent sporting facilities. Well-equipped bedrooms and well-served public rooms. Eat in formal Victor Hugo restaurant or more informal Café Renoir.

HERM

Herm White House

Herm, GY1 3HR
☎ (01481) 722159 📠 (01481) 710066
🛏 38 £110 🍴 118 🍽 £40

☺ Lunch 12.30-2 Dinner 7-9.30   ☹ Oct-Mar

Peaceful location, comfortable accommodation; plenty of local seafood (especially oysters) in the restaurant and adjoining Ship Inn.

JERSEY

Gorey Jersey Pottery Garden Restaurant

Gorey, Jersey, JE3 9EP
☎ (01534) 851119 📠 (01534) 856403
🍴 250 🍽 £60

☺ 12-4.30   ☹ Sun (& Sat in winter), 1 wk Xmas

Local produce, especially seafood, served in relaxed, friendly surroundings.

JERSEY (contd)

Rozel Bay Chateau la Chaire

Rozel Valley, Rozel, Jersey, JE3 6AJ
☎ (01534) 863354 📠 (01534) 865137
▯ 14 £118 🍴 65 🍽 £70
☺ Lunch 12-2 Dinner 7-10 (Sun 9.30)

Small but grand-style hotel; traditional menus, extensive wine list.

St Aubin Old Court House Inn

St Aubin, Jersey
☎ (01534) 46433 📠 (01534) 45103
▯ 9 £80 🍴 60 🍽 £60
☺ Lunch 12.30-2.30 Dinner 7.30-10.30 ☹ Wed in winter, 25 & 26 Dec

Indeed the original courthouse, now a popular small hotel and restaurant – excellent seafood dishes a speciality.

St Brelade Hotel Chateau Valeuse

Rue de la Valeuse, St Brelade, Jersey, JE3 8EE
☎ (01534) 46281 📠 (01534) 47110
▯ 33 £84 🍴 70 🍽 £50
☺ Lunch 12.45-1.45 Dinner 8-9

Medium-sized seashore hotel set in landscaped gardens; à la carte and set menus.

St Brelade Sea Crest

Petit Port, St Brelade, Jersey, JE3 8HH
☎ (01534) 46353 📠 (01534) 47316
▯ 7 £92 🍴 60 🍽 £70
☺ Lunch 12.30-2 (Sun to 3) Dinner 7.30-10
☹ all Mon, Dinner Sun in winter, mid Jan-Feb

Tiny, comfortable, owner-run hotel; French and Italian cooking.

St Brelade's Bay Hotel L'Horizon

St Brelade's Bay, Jersey, JE3 8EF
☎ (01534) 43101 📠 (01534) 46269
▯ 107 £170 🍴 260 🍽 £55
☺ Lunch 12.30-2.15, Dinner 7.30-9.30

The house dates back to 1850 but now has modern amenities for business travellers and holiday-makers alike. In the Crystal Restaurant and the Star Grill, chef Peter Marek offers an extensive range of modern English dishes.

JERSEY (contd)

St Helier De Vere Grand

Esplanade, St Helier, Jersey, JE4 8WD

☎ (01534) 22301 📠 (01534) 37815

🛏 115 £ £115 🪑 160 (Victoria's) 250 (Regency) 🕙 £75

☺ Lunch 2.30-2.15 (Victoria's only) Dinner 7-10 (Victoria's)
7.30-9.30 (Regency) ☹ Dinner Sun, Bank Holidays

Seafront location, ideal for families or business visitors. Modern French cooking in the Victoria and Regency restaurants.

St Ouen The Lobster Pot

L'Etacq, St Ouen, Jersey, JE3 2FB

☎ (01534) 482888 📠 (01534) 481574

🛏 13 £ £70 🪑 90 🕙 £70

☺ Lunch 12.30-2 Dinner 7.30-10, (Set menu 12-6)

17th century granite farmhouse, now a comfortable hotel overlooking the bay. International menus, seafood a speciality.

St Saviour Longueville Manor 🍷 ❀

St Saviour, Jersey, JE2 7SA

☎ (01534) 25501 📠 (01534) 31613

🛏 32 £ £160 🪑 65 🕙 £90

☺ Lunch 12.30-2 Dinner 7.30-9.30

Jersey's premier hotel continues to maintain its high standards, in public rooms, bedrooms and restaurant alike. Originally a 13th-century manor house, its elegant proportions are now graced with fine antiques and furnishings, backed up with smooth and professional service. The manor is set in 15 acres of wooded valley, complete with sports facilities, stream and lake. Bedrooms, each named after a rose, are excellently equipped and maintained – two suites even have private patios. Andrew Baird has been in charge of the kitchens since 1990 and his assured touch guarantees success with new guests and those returning to the non-smoking, oak-panelled dining room. The Tasting Menu (served only to complete tables – £50 per head) gives his imagination full rein over nine well-balanced dishes, some of which might also available on the carte. Try gateau of Jersey crab and plum tomatoes with a salad of roasted sweet peppers, or poached scallops with vegetable noodles and roast lobster, followed by noisettes of lamb with an artichoke mousseline and a thyme-flavoured jus or grilled fillet of Jersey seabass on a terrine of aubergine with a tomato and olive sauce, accompanied in each case by appropriate, lightly-cooked vegetables. Excellent farmhouse cheeses vie for your attention with desserts such as warm feuilleté of fruits with a Grand Marnier sabayon. The sommelier's recommendations are well worth considering, though the full wine list is also a delight to read.

SARK

Sark Aval Du Creux

Sark, GY9 0SB

☎ (01481) 832036 (01481) 832368

12 £70 40 £55

☺ Lunch 12-3 Dinner 5.30-9 ☹ 1 Oct-1 May

Family-run, small and friendly hotel. The Lobster Restaurant and Oyster Bar offer traditional French cooking with the occasional ethnic touch.

Sark Dixcart Hotel

Sark, GY9 0SD

☎ (01481) 832015 (01481) 832164

15 £70 60 £40

☺ Lunch 12-1.30 Dinner 7-9

Cosy, family-run hotel in a former 16th-century Sark longhouse – quaint beamed bedrooms, sunny outdoor eating, local seafood a speciality.

Sark La Sablonnerie Hotel

Sark, GY9 0SD

☎ (01481) 832061 (01481) 832408

22 £70 40 £55

☺ Lunch 12-2.30 Dinner 7-9.30 ☹ mid Oct-Easter

Well-established, owner-run hotel housed in a former 400-year-old farmhouse – charming and relaxed setting. International menu with a French flavour, lots of seafood.

Sark Stocks Hotel

Sark, GY9 0SD

☎ (01481) 832001 (01481) 832130

24 £70 60 £50

☺ Lunch 12-2.30 Dinner 7-9 ☹ Oct-Apr

Friendly, family-run hotel; modern British cooking in the Cider Press restaurant.

ISLE OF MAN

Ballasalla Rosa's Place

Main Road, Ballasalla, Isle of Man
☎ (01624) 822940 (01624) 822702
⌨ 45 🍽 £70
☺ Lunch 12-3 Dinner 7-10 ☹ 1st 2 wks Jan

Straightforward but extensive menus here – formerly known as La Rosette. Still offers well-cooked fish and classic meat dishes.

Ramsey Harbour Bistro

5 East Street, Ramsey, Isle of Man
☎ (01624) 814182
⌨ 50 🍽 £45
☺ Lunch 12-2, Dinner 6.30-10.30 ☹ Dinner Sun, 2 wks Jan, 1 wk Oct

European cooking, served in a relaxed and friendly atmosphere. Concise, reasonably-priced wine list.

Northern Ireland

Aghadowey Greenhill House

24 Greenhill Road, Aghadowey, Coleraine,
Co Londonderry, BT51 4EU
☎ (01265) 868241
6 £42 16 £35
☺ Dinner only at 6.30 ☹ Sun, Nov-Feb

The Hegarty family run their lovely Georgian home more as a guest house set on a working farm than as a hotel, the welcome is a warm one and the set dinners are exclusively for residents.

Ballymena Galgorm Manor

136 Fenaghy Road, Ballymena, Co Antrim, BT42 1EA
☎ (01266) 881001 (01266) 880080
23 £105 73 £70
☺ Lunch 12-2.30, Dinner 7-9.30 (Sun 6-9)

An attractive country house hotel situated just outside Ballymena in its own grounds on the banks of the River Maine. Bedrooms, suites and chalets are divided between the main house and separate buildings within the grounds. Good sporting facilities in the area. The elegant dining room provides a carte and a shorter, cheaper menu priced by the course.

Belfast Antica Roma

67 Botanic Avenue, Belfast, Co Antrim, BT7 1JL
☎ (01232) 311121 (01232) 310787
170 £55
☺ Lunch 12-3, Dinner 6-11.30 ☹ Lunch Sat, all Sun, 25 & 26 Dec

In a distinctly Roman setting (rich mosaic floor, murals and columns) this large restaurant offers set menus at lunchtime and an elaborate carte at dinner. There are plenty of imaginative dishes to choose from, and a fine range of Italian wines complements the cooking.

Belfast La Belle Epoque

61-63 Dublin Road, Belfast, Co Antrim, BT2 7AG
☎ (01232) 233244 (01232) 240666
78 £55
☺ Lunch 12-5.30, Dinner 6-11.30
☹ Lunch Sat & Sun, 25 & 26 Dec, 12 & 13 Jul

Sound French bistro-style cooking at this well-established restaurant – it's been going since 1986 and is run by 5 partners, though the kitchen comes under Alain Rousse.

Belfast Crown Liquor Saloon

46 Great Victoria Street, Belfast, Co Antrim, BT2 7BA
☎ (01232) 249476
🪑 85 🍽 £15
☺ Lunch 12-3, Dinner 7-11.15 ☹ 25 Dec

Great fun and one of a kind, the Crown Liquor Saloon is a fine example of High Victoriana (owned by the National Trust but operated by Bass). Described by some as a bit "in-your-face" – brightly coloured, overflowing with tiny decorative detail – but that really is the essence of its charm. In the snugs or at the bar, you can enjoy some fine ales, Irish food and most of all, the atmosphere of the place.

Belfast Dukes Hotel

65 University Street, Belfast, Co Antrim, BT7 1HL
☎ (01232) 236666 📠 (01232) 237177
🛏 21 £98 🪑 75 🍽 £55
☺ Lunch 12.30-2.30 (Sun 1-2.30), Dinner 6.30-10.15 (Sat to 10.45)
☹ Lunch Sat, Dinner Sun

Recently refurbished, bright and modern hotel set amidst a cluster of older (Victorian) buildings, Dukes has a high proportion of repeat business to its credit. First-timers can enjoy equally the good leisure facilities, a relaxing drink in the lounge, or an international-style menu in the restaurant.

Belfast Roscoff   ✿

Lesley House, Shaftesbury Square, Belfast, Co Antrim, BT2 7DB
☎ (01232) 331532 📠 (01232) 312093
🪑 70 🍽 £75
☺ Lunch 12.15-2.15, Dinner 6.30-10.30
☹ Lunch Sat, all Sun, 11 & 13 Jul, 24-26 Dec, 1 Jan

The Rankins have established Roscoff as Belfast's leading restaurant with its modern, minimal decor and stylish food. New ideas abound in Paul Rankin's repertoire: seared beef salad with celery, parmesan and truffle oil; herb and ricotta ravioli with walnut pesto and warm salad of crispy duck confit with olives and mushrooms show his style. Tenderloin of venison comes with a warm gratin of potato and cèpes; sautéed sweetbreads with pasta, bacon and roast garlic, spiced sesame-fried hake with stir-fried cabbage and ginger; and a rich ragout of seafood with lobster ravioli and saffron and coriander cream. Desserts are equally inspired and irresistible: a warm chestnut and amaretti soufflé, polenta cake with poached pears and crème fraiche, or a bitter chocolate sorbet with oranges. Fixed-price lunch and dinner menus are excellent value, as is the well-sourced, very comprehensive wine list.

Belfast Speranza

16 Shaftesbury Square, Belfast, Co Antrim, BT2 7DB
☎ (01232) 230213 📠 (01232) 236752
🪑 170 🍽 £40
☺ Dinner only 5-11.30 ☹ Sun, 3 days Xmas, 11 & 12 Jul

Large and busy trattoria-style restaurant with friendly staff offering a good range of Italian staples pasta and pizza, all at very reasonable prices.

Belfast Strand Restaurant

12 Stranmillis Road, Belfast, Co Antrim, BT9 5AA
☎ (01232) 682266 📠 (01232) 663189
🪑 55 🍽 £35
☺ Mon-Sat 12-11 (Sun 12-3, 5-10)
☹ 25 & 26 Dec, 12 & 13 July

A complete (one-course) meal for only £3.95 from noon to 11pm midweek or till 7pm on Saturdays must offer some of the best value in Northern Ireland! Beyond those times it's not much more expensive, as the carte has plenty of choice for most tastes at very reasonable prices. There's a fun atmosphere, and friendly service.

Belfast Villa Italia

39 University Road, Belfast, Co Antrim, BT7 1ND
☎ (01232) 328356 📠 (01232) 234978
🪑 180 🍽 £45
☺ Dinner only 5-11.30 ☹ 24-26 & 31 Dec, 12 Jul, Easter Sun

Relaxed Italian restaurant offering the traditional range of trattoria dishes. Good, friendly service and very reasonable wines: only champagne breaks the £20 barrier.

Crawfordsburn Old Inn

15 Main Street, Crawfordsburn, Co Down, BT19 1JH
☎ (01247) 853255 📠 (01247) 852775
🛏 33 £85 🪑 60 🍽 £60
☺ Lunch 12.30-2.30, Dinner 7-9.30 (Sun 5-7.30) ☹ 24-26 Dec

Another claimant to the title of oldest inn in Ireland – backed up by atmospheric decor of antiques, oak beams and gas lamps. It's a popular venue for business functions as well as wedding parties (try the Honeymoon Cottage); and all the bedrooms are non-smoking. Food tends towards the international rather than the purely Irish.

Dunadry Dunadry Inn

2 Islandreagh Drive, Dunadry, Co Antrim, BT41 2HA
☎ (01849) 432474 📠 (01849) 433389
🛏 67 £100 ♟ 132 🍽 £55

☺ Lunch 12.30-1.45, Dinner 7.30-9.45 (Sun 5.30-9.45)

☹ Lunch Sat, 24-27 Dec

A substantial hotel, popular with the business community as it's usefully located for the airport and Belfast city. Good conference and leisure facilities. A fairly international menu offered in the restaurant completes the appeal.

Helen's Bay Deanes on the Square

7 Station Square, Helen's Bay, Co Down, BT19 1TN
☎ (01247) 852841
♟ 40 🍽 £75

☺ Lunch Sun only 12.30-2.30, Dinner 7-10

☹ Dinner Sun, all Mon, 3 days Xmas, 2 wks Jan, 1 wk Jul

The unique atmosphere of a Scottish baronial railway station provides an interesting backdrop to Michael Deane's cooking. There's usually a choice of 5 or so dishes at each course of the set menu. Good range of farmhouse cheeses.

Holywood Culloden Hotel

142 Bangor Road, Craigavad, Holywood, Co Down, BT18 0EX
☎ (01232) 425223 📠 (01232) 426777
🛏 89 £157 ♟ 140 🍽 £65

☺ Lunch 12.30-2.30, Dinner 7-9.45 (Sun to 8.30) ☹ Lunch Sat

Just 5 miles from the centre of Belfast, this hotel is on the southern shores of Belfast Lough. Built of Scottish stone this baronial, neo-Gothic mansion was home to several bishops after it was conveyed to the church by the widow of its founder. Now much extended with a health and fitness centre, function rooms, 2 restaurants and a separate inn.

Holywood Sullivans

Sullivan Place, Holywood, Co Down, BT18 9JF
☎ (01232) 421000 📠 (01232) 421000
♟ 40 🍽 £55

☺ Lunch 10-2.30, Dinner 6.30-10.30

☹ Sun, 1 wk Jul, 25 & 26 Dec

Bring your own wine and enjoy Simon Shaw's good cooking at this convivial coffee shop by day which is transformed into a serious restaurant by night. Fixed-price menus offer great value, while the specials and the carte might make choosing difficult, though fun. Imaginative cooking, great atmosphere.

Londonderry Beech Hill House Hotel

32 Ardmore Road, Londonderry, Co Londonderry, BT47 3QP
☎ (01504) 49279 📠 (01504) 45366
🛏 17 £85 🍴 40 🍽 £65
☺ Lunch 12-2.30, Dinner 7-9.30 ☹ 24 & 25 Dec

A substantial country house that's a popular venue for functions and conferences. The Ardmore restaurant overlooks the lovely gardens, and is where you can enjoy a fixed-price menu of good Irish ingredients presented in modern style.

Portaferry Portaferry Hotel

10 The Strand, Portaferry, Co Down, BT22 1PE
☎ (01247) 728231 📠 (01247) 728999
🛏 14 £85 🍴 80 🍽 £62
☺ Lunch 12.30-2.30, Dinner 7-9 ☹ 24 & 25 Dec

The hotel overlooks Strangford Lough and is best reached by ferry from Strangford itself – this only takes 5 minutes. The Lough is a marine nature reserve and bird sanctuary, and nowadays the hotel also provides sanctuary for weary travellers. In the kitchen, fine local produce is treated in simple yet skilful ways to produce some interesting dishes.

Portrush Ramore

The Harbour, Portrush, Co Antrim, BT56 8BN
☎ (01265) 824313
🍴 85 🍽 £55
☺ Dinner only 6.30-10.30 ☹ Sun & Mon, 24-26 Dec

Everything about the McAlpins' Ramore is more like a trendy restaurant in a fashionable area of London than a harbourside location at the northern tip of Northern Ireland! From the decor to the menu and the bustling atmosphere, this is a unique place in an attractive setting. Roast red pepper and goat's cheese salad with basil pesto, rocket, parmesan and pine nuts; Dublin Bay prawns in lobster and chive sauce in a pot topped with puff pastry; fresh asparagus with egg-filled ravioli are examples of the inventive starters. Choose fresh fish dishes from the board or try confit of duck with armagnac, raisin and foie gras jus; rack of local lamb stuffed with spinach, wild rice, sultanas and pinenuts on caramelised tomato and cumin sauce; or escalopes of pork with fried greens, roquefort and bacon with parsley and garlic butter. No less detail on the puddings either: glazed orange pancakes with dark chocolate ice cream; cinnamon-flavoured bananas and pears en croute with kirsch and whipped cream; or perhaps a hot apple flan with vanilla ice cream and fudge sauce. A good wine list has many offerings at under £10.

Templepatrick Templeton Hotel

882 Antrim Road, Templepatrick, Ballyclare,
Co Antrim, BT39 0AH

☎ (01849) 432984 📠 (01849) 433406

🛏 20 £100 🍴 80 🍽 £50

☺ Lunch Sun only 1-2.15, Dinner 7-9.45 (Grill: 12-2.30 Mon-Sat, 5-9 Mon-Thu, 5-10 Fri & Sat) ☹ Hotel 25 & 26 Dec

A harmonious blend of ancient and modern (as is often true in the Province), the Templeton is especially suitable as a business venue, although there are also plenty of leisure visitors. Set menus are styled in the modern manner.

**BRITAIN'S TOP
INDEPENDENT BUTCHERS**
see page 9

Republic of Ireland

Adare Adare Manor

Adare, Co Limerick
☎ (061) 396566 📠 (061) 396124
64 £220 65 £80
😊 Lunch 12.30-2.30 (Sun to 3), Dinner 7.30-10

A Gothic-style mansion set in geometrically laid out gardens with the River Maigue meandering through its grounds. Inside are some admirable features – a fine oak staircase, an ornate gallery modelled on the great Versailles and no fewer than 50 carved fireplaces to enhance the bedrooms! In the equally grand restaurant, choose from fixed-price or à la carte menus with perhaps warm veal kidney salad tossed in wholegrain mustard dressing, or roast scallops and sun-dried tomatoes with honey and thyme dressing to start. Rich game stew flavoured with Poire William, grilled turbot with Parisienne potatoes and nut-brown butter or roast fillet of beef on celeriac rösti and confit shallots could follow. A good selection of puddings and home-made breads are hard to resist. If you book a private event you can choose to be entertained with traditional Irish music, 12 piece orchestra and choir, the Cork City Jazz Band, pianist, harpist, piper or string quartet. If variety be the spice of life, play on!

Adare Dunraven Arms

Adare, Co Limerick
☎ (061) 396633 📠 (061) 396541
43 £127 60 £60
😊 Lunch 12.30-2.30, Dinner 7.30-9.30 (bar food 12-6)
☹ Restaurant Good Friday

This popular sporting hotel has a greater number of bedrooms available this year, reflecting the increased interest shown by the clientele.
The choice of food is similarly wide, ranging from simple sandwiches to fairly elaborate dining room menus served in the Maigue Restaurant.

Adare Mustard Seed

Main Street, Adare, Co Limerick
☎ (061) 396451
50 £65
😊 Dinner only 7-10 ☹ Sun & Mon, Bank Holidays, Feb

Philosopher/patron Daniel Mullane knows his place; he believes a restaurateur should be a diplomat, a democrat, an autocrat and a doormat! He practises what he preaches at this pretty, cottage-style restaurant just outside Adare Manor itself. Fixed-price menus offer 4 courses with plenty of choice; and there's a good wine list which includes plenty of halves.

Ahakista Shiro

Ahakista, Nr Bantry, Co Cork
☎ (027) 67030
🪑 18 🍽 £85
☺ Dinner only 7-9

You need more than a little confidence to open a Japanese restaurant in Ireland. To open one seating just 18, on the western extremity of Co. Cork in a Georgian house overlooking Dunmanus Bay, could be considered as eccentric in the extreme: that's probably why it works! The husband-and-wife team of Werner & Kei Pilz are the brains behind this venture: long may they be here.

Ardee The Gables

Dundalk Road, Ardee, Co Louth
☎ (041) 53789
🛏 5 £34 🪑 34 🍽 £55
☺ Dinner only 7-10 ☹ Sun & Mon, 25 & 26 Dec, 2 wks Jun, 2 wks Nov

Michael & Glynnis Caine have run this French restaurant as a joint venture since 1978 – he cooks, she looks after front-of-house. Fresh, local seafood figures strongly, as does game in season, though always cooked and served in classic style.

Athlone Restaurant Le Chateau

Abbey Lane, Athlone, Co Westmeath
☎ (0902) 94517
🪑 40 🍽 £55
☺ Dinner 6-10.15 ☹ Sun in winter, 3 wks Jan

Excellent food cooked by patron Steven Linehan in this first-floor cottage-style restaurant near the Shannon. A choice of menus ranges from the early bird (great value), to set-price, to a la carte. A well-composed wine list similarly offers good value for money.

Athy Tonlegee House

Athy, Co Kildare
☎ (0507) 31473 📠 (0507) 31473
🛏 5 £60 🪑 40 🍽 £55
☺ Lunch by arrangement, Dinner 7-9.30 (Fri & Sat to 10.30)
☹ Sun, 24-26 Dec, Good Friday

Mark & Marjorie Molloy offer warm hospitality at their fairly small, carefully restored 18th-century house on the outskirts of town. Mark cooks for the restaurant, and is most strongly influenced by French food, though his home-made breads are definitely Irish and quite delicious.

Aughrim Aughrim Schoolhouse Restaurant

Aughrim, Nr Ballinasloe, Co Galway
☎ (0905) 73936
🏠 50 🍽 £45
☺ Lunch Sun only 12.30-3 (Tue-Sun Jul-Aug), Dinner 6.30-11
☹ Dinner Sun in winter, all Mon, 24-26 Dec

A simple philosophy of serving fresh food at sensible prices was adopted by Michael Harrison & Geraldine Dolan when they converted the old school into a restaurant on the Dublin to Galway road. They achieve their objective admirably with a choice of menus: early bird, table d'hote, à la carte. Several wines are under £10 a bottle and nearly all are under £20. Sunday lunch is a snip. There are definitely lessons to be learned from this example!

Ballina Mount Falcon Castle

Ballina, Co Mayo
☎ (096) 70811 📠 (096) 71517
🛏 10 £ £88 🏠 28 🍽 £60
☺ Dinner only at 8 ☹ Hotel Xmas, Feb & Mar

Built in neo-Gothic style in 1876, the 'castle' is now a comfortable hotel run by Mrs Constance Aldridge since 1932. There's superb salmon and trout fishing, and game shooting in the winter. Guests sit together at one large table for dinner, and enjoy the best of local produce.

Ballyconneely Erriseask House

Ballyconneely, Clifden, Connemara, Co Galway
☎ (095) 23553 📠 (095) 23639
🛏 13 £ £72 🏠 36 🍽 £75
☺ Dinner 6.30-9.30 ☹ Nov-Easter

Small, family-run hotel set in 50 acres of grass and marshland on the western shores of Galway. The Matz brothers bought the house in 1988 and have gradually developed it into one of the best hotels in the area. Comfortable bedrooms and sitting rooms, well-judged cooking for the dining room, carefully-chosen wines of good quality.

Ballydehob Annie's Restaurant

Main Street, Ballydehob, Co Cork
☎ (028) 37292
🏠 24 🍽 £55
☺ Dinner 6.30-10 ☹ Sun & Mon, 25 & 26 Dec, 3 wks Oct

David & Anne Barry no longer offer lunches, but there's an excellent-value set dinner in the evenings, as well as a coffee shop menu during the day, when you can have a light snack. Delicious home-made desserts and/or puddings.

Ballyferriter Tigh an Tobair (The Well House)

Ballyferriter, Co Kerry
☎ (066) 56404
🍴 30 🍽 £30
☺ Lunch 12.30-2.30, Dinner 6.30-9, (light meals 10-8) ☹ Jan & Feb

Louis & Elisabeth Mulcahy's Well House is at the opposite end of the village to his pottery, behind the grocery shop. Máire Hearty cooks wonderful Irish food, chalking up daily and seafood specials on a blackboard. There's an amazing range of cheeses, and the truffles which accompany coffee are also hand-made by Máire.

Ballyhack Neptune Restaurant

Ballyhack, New Ross, Co Wexford
☎ (051) 89284 📠 (051) 89284
🍴 45 🍽 £50
☺ Lunch Sun only 12.30-3, Dinner 6.30-10 (Sat to 10.30)
☹ all Mon (except Jul & Aug), Nov-Mar

Overlooking the harbour in the shadow of Ballyhack Castle, Pierce & Valerie McAuliffe's restaurant naturally looks to the sea for its inspiration. Good, local meat and game are also offered, as well as good selection of wines from around the world. A set-price menu is available until 8pm.

Ballylickey Ballylickey Manor House

Ballylickey, Bantry Bay, Co Cork
☎ (027) 50071 📠 (027) 50124
🛏 5 £ £99 🍴 25 🍽 £60
☺ Lunch 12.30-2, Dinner 7.30-9.30 ☹ Wed to non residents, Nov-Mar

Commanding fine views over Bantry Bay, this delightful family home is superbly furnished, and the Graves are charming hosts. There are 5 suites in the main house and simpler accommodation in 8 chalets in the grounds. The outdoor swimming pool is heated; and the restaurant is set in the middle of the lovely gardens, separate from the main house.

Ballylickey Larchwood House

Pearsons Bridge, Ballylickey, Co Cork
☎ (027) 66181
🛏 4 £ £45 🍴 22 🍽 £50
☺ Dinner only 6.30-9.30 ☹ Sun, 1 wk Xmas

The Vaughans' homely restaurant with rooms has fine views over river and mountain (the river actually runs through the garden). Sheila Vaughan produces an extensive, fixed-price menu using good produce in simple guises over 5 courses. The price of the meal is determined by the main course chosen. Comfortable bedrooms, good breakfasts.

Ballylickey Seaview House Hotel

Ballylickey, Nr Bantry, Co Cork
☎ (027) 50462 📠 (027) 51555
17   £100   45 £65
☺ Lunch Sun only 12.45-2, Dinner 7-9.30   ☹ Hotel mid Nov-mid Mar

This well-proportioned, white-painted house commands fine views over Bantry Bay, and Kathleen O'Sullivan makes everyone feel welcome in her efficiently-run hostelry. Comfortable rooms and Kathleen's excellent home cooking ensure the return of regular visitors. Local seafood is often featured. A good selection of wines is reasonably priced.

Ballyvaughan Gregans Castle

Ballyvaughan, Co Clare
☎ (065) 77005 📠 (065) 77111
22   £112   60 £80
☺ Lunch 12-3 in bar, Dinner 7-8.30   ☹ Hotel Nov-Mar

From Corkscrew Hill, this fine hotel overlooks Galway Bay in a unique landscape where the Gulf Stream creates a microclimate for the proliferation of some fascinating plant life. Bedrooms are comfortably furnished and mercifully free from TVs to disturb the tranquillity. For the restaurant, the emphasis is on fresh, local produce while the wine list travels the globe.

Baltimore Chez Youen

The Pier, Baltimore, Co Cork
☎ (028) 20136 📠 (028) 20136
45 £70
☺ Lunch 12.30-2.30, Dinner 6-11   ☹ 24 & 25 Dec, Nov

Certainly one of the finest seafood restaurants in Ireland, and Youen Jacob's popular place goes from strength to strength. Fixed-price menus offer an amazing range, all devised according to the latest catch. A bottle of crisp Gros Plant, and you could almost be back in Brittany.

Birr Tullanisk

Birr, Co Offaly
☎ (0509) 20572 📠 (0509) 20572
7   £76   30 £55
☺ Dinner at 8.15   ☹ 4 days Xmas

Delightful dower house in a beautiful setting with gardens and parkland all around. George Gossip prepares excellent, 4-course dinners that are served at large, communal tables. There's no choice, but dietary requirements are taken on board when booking, and vegetarians are well looked after.

Blacklion MacNean Bistro

Blacklion, Co Cavan
☎ (072) 53022
⏱ 35 🍴 £40

☺ Lunch Sun only 12.30-3.30, Dinner 5-10, (light meals 3-6)
☹ Dinner Mon (Tue & Wed in winter), 25 & 26 Dec, Good Friday

You could be forgiven for feeling somewhat disoriented when you read the menu at this small, family-run bistro in the main street, for there are some pretty exotic-sounding ingredients on offer: kangaroo, ostrich and bison to name but 3! Less adventurous gourmets can stick to the relatively tame (sorry!) choices instead. Young chef, Neven Maguire, was one of three Irish entrants chosen to go forward to the final of the Wedgwood Chef & Potter International Competition.

Butlerstown Dunworley Cottage

Dunworley, Nr Butlerstown, Clonakilty, Co Cork
☎ (023) 40314
⏱ 50 🍴 £60

☺ Lunch 1-3, Dinner 6.30-10 ☹ Mon & Tue, Nov, Jan & Feb

Healthy, local or home-produced ingredients are the essence of Katherine Noren's cooking at her neat, farmhouse restaurant in the wilds of Cork. You might even find a home-made, home-smoked, chunky salami on offer. Naturally, breads are superb. Every kind of exclusion diet (wheat, gluten, dairy, egg, diabetic) is accommodated with ease.

Caherciveen Brennan's Restaurant

13 Main Street, Cahirciveen, Co Kerry
☎ (066) 72021
⏱ 30 🍴 £55

☺ Lunch 12-2.30, Dinner 7-10 (early dinner 6-7.30) ☹ 24-26 Dec, Nov & Feb

Sound cooking in an unpretentious setting ensures the popularity of this small and friendly restaurant in the far west of Kerry. Dine before 7.30pm and enjoy amazing value for money. Dine a bit later and you still won't break the bank, though you'll have a greater choice of Conor Brennan's repertoire, which includes a good choice of fresh seafood and local produce, such as Kerry lamb.

Caherdaniel Derrynane Hotel

Caherdaniel, Co Kerry
☎ (066) 75136 📠 (066) 75160
🛏 75 £ £60 ⏱ 100 🍴 £45

☺ Lunch 12.30-2, Dinner 7-9 ☹ Oct-Apr

Simple, but efficiently-run modern family hotel which enjoys spectacular views over the sea and the Kerry coast. A small garden turns out good produce for the kitchen.

Carlingford Jordan's Bar & Restaurant

Carlingford, Co Louth
☎ (042) 73223
🛏 7 £50 🍴 34 🕐 £55
☺ Lunch Sun only 12.30-3.30, Dinner 7-10 (Sun from 6.30)
☹ 25 & 26 Dec, 3 wks Jan, 25 & 26 Dec

Harry & Marion Jordan's popular restaurant now has the added advantage of bedrooms which overlook the harbour. This small medieval town also houses a whiskey distillery and its own oyster beds. It's not too difficult to imagine what you should best spend your time doing here.

Carrigaline Gregory's

Main Street, Carrigaline, Co Cork
☎ (021) 371512
🍴 45 🕐 £50
☺ Lunch 12.30-2.30 (Sun to 3.30), Dinner 6.30-10
☹ Lunch Sat, Dinner Sun (except Xmas & high summer)

Gregory Dawson has quickly established himself as a force with which to be reckoned in his unpretentious restaurant. Lunch offers tremendous value, especially considering the standard of cooking. A simple wine list is well composed.

Cashel Cashel House

Cashel, Co Galway
☎ (095) 31001 📠 (095) 31077
🛏 32 £149 🍴 70 🕐 £70
☺ Lunch 1-2 (in bar), Dinner 7.30-8.30 (Sun 7.30-9) ☹ 10-31 Jan

The menus at Dermot & Kay McEvilly's Victorian country house understandably feature plenty of fish dishes – the Atlantic virtually laps at their door. There's still plenty of choice, though, within the fixed-price menus. The children's tea menu is worth leaving home for!

Cashel Chez Hans

Rockside, Cashel, Co Tipperary
☎ (062) 61177
🍴 60 🕐 £70
☺ Dinner only 6.30-10 ☹ Sun & Mon, Bank Holidays, 3 wks Jan

Victoriana in a converted chapel where proprietor Hans Matthiä cooks, concentrating on seafood. Produce is sourced locally when possible, poultry is free-range, while all herbs and most vegetables are produced in his own gardens and greenhouses. Some good value on the well-composed wine list.

Castlebaldwin Cromleach Lodge

Castlebaldwin, Via Boyle, Co Sligo
☎ (071) 65155 📠 (071) 65455
🛏 10 £120 🍴 50 🍽 £80

☺ Lunch by arrangement, Dinner 7-9 (Sun 6.30-8) ☹ Xmas, 3 wks Jan

A unique hotel, owned and run by Christy & Moira Tighe, offering stunning views from its hillside location. It's modern, yet sympathetic to the environment as well as the times, and the commitment given by Christy and Moira guarantees a warm welcome, high standards of service throughout and excellent food and wine in the delightful restaurant. Moira heads up a female kitchen team and produces her own distinct interpretations of classic dishes using good local ingredients. You might try flaked duck confit layered on crispy galette potato, followed by fillet of Sligo beef on a sauce of Roquefort cheese and finish with one of the delicious desserts on offer such as local organic raspberries layered on hazelnut wafers and cassis cream. Go there and enjoy!

Castledermot Kilkea Castle

Kilkea, Castledermot, Co Kildare
☎ (0503) 45156 📠 (0503) 45187
🛏 45 £190 🍴 65 🍽 £70

☺ Lunch 12.30-2.30, Dinner 7-9.30 ☹ 25 Dec

A genuine castle, possibly haunted, certainly old, possibly the oldest castle in Ireland that's still inhabited. Extensive grounds around the imposing frontage, including a river aspect. There's a well-equipped health and fitness club as well as facilities for golf, and business facilities are also very good.

Clifden O'Grady's Seafood Restaurant

Market Street, Clifden, Co Galway
☎ (095) 21450
🛏 11 £50 🍴 50 🍽 £65

☺ Lunch 12.30-2.30, Dinner 6.30-10 ☹ Sun in summer, 6 wks Feb/Mar

Traditional seafood menu using fresh local produce to good effect, prepared and served by the O'Grady family since – oh, since time began. Try a One Plate Special in the Piano Bar, for a change!

Clondalkin
Kingswood Country House/Restaurant

Naas Road, Clondalkin, Dublin, Co Dublin, 22
☎ (01) 459 2428 📠 (01) 459 2428
🍴 50 🍽 £60

☺ Lunch 12.30-2.30, Dinner 6.30-10.30

☹ Lunch Sat, Dinner Sun, Good Friday, 25 & 27 Dec

Comfortable, small hotel not far from Dublin and handy for the airport. Cosy bedrooms are well furnished, and the dining room offers a high standard of home cooking with good, home-baked bread and friendly service.

Collooney Glebe House

Collooney, Co Sligo
☎ (071) 67787
4 £30 40 £45
☺ Lunch by arrangment, Dinner 6.30-9.30 ☹ 2 wks Jan

A restaurant with accommodation provided in comfortable rooms, the friendly hospitality coming from owners Marc & Brid Torrades. On a very reasonable fixed-price menu there is some inventive cooking; accompanied by good-value wines.

Cong Ashford Castle

Cong, Co Mayo
☎ (092) 46003   (092) 46260
83 £265

George V Room
135 £100
☺ Lunch 1-2.15, Dinner 7-9.30

Connaught Room
40 £110
☺ Dinner only 7-9.30

A unique hotel created within the walls of a splendid castle with 13th-century origins. Sheer luxury is all around, from the elegant lounges to the spacious bedrooms and suites. There are plenty of outdoor sporting facilities and 2 restaurants in which to satisfy the appetite you will thus have built up. Dennis Linehan supervises both. Substantial wine list is long on France but doesn't ignore the rest of the world. Impeccable service.

Cork Arbutus Lodge

Montenotte, Cork, Co Cork
☎ (021) 501237   (021) 502893
20 £80 50 £80
☺ Lunch 1-2, Dinner 7-9.30 ☹ Sun, 1 wk Xmas

High above the city, surrounded by terraced gardens which naturally boast an arbutus tree in their midst, Declan Ryan has established this hotel as one of Ireland's best-loved, popular with locals and visitors alike. The cooking relies on the quality of the raw ingredients, on them being perfectly cooked, and complemented, not swamped, by other flavours. The wine list leaves nothing to be desired – except, perhaps, the opportunity and the purse to taste every wine on it!

Cork Bully's

40 Paul Street, Cork, Co Cork
☎ (021) 273555 📠 (021) 273427
🪑 40 🕛 £40

🙂 12-11.30 🙁 25 & 26 Dec, Good Friday

Eugene Buckley and chef Rocca Crea run this friendly little Italian restaurant, handily located by a multi-storey car park. Pasta and pizzas (cooked in a wood-burning oven) are the mainstay, supplemented by Bully Burgers and fresh local seafood.

Cork Cliffords

18 Dyke Parade, Cork, Co Cork
☎ (021) 275333
🪑 45 🕛 £75

🙂 Lunch 12.30-2.30, Dinner 7.30-10.30
🙁 Lunch Sat & Mon, all Sun, Bank Holidays, 2 wks Aug

Housed in the Georgian-style civic library which has been simply but tastefully modernised, Cliffords displays the work of contemporary Irish artists on the walls. Michael Clifford himself is in charge of the cooking, and uses fine, local ingredients with great skill. Deirdre Clifford runs front-of-house with great attention to detail. The small bistro next door, recently opened, is also enjoying great success (see below).

Cork Crawford Gallery Café

Emmet Place, Cork, Co Cork
☎ (021) 274415
🪑 70 🕛 £45

🙂 Lunch 12-2.30, Dinner 6.30-9.30, (light meals 9-5)
🙁 Sun, Bank Holidays, 2 wks Xmas

Alongside the Opera House in the city centre, this simple café comes with a fine pedigree: it's part of the Ballymaloe empire which is based at Shanagarry. From substantial breakfasts to short but inventive lunch and dinner menus, the food is of high quality. Wonderful puds, and breads from Ballymaloe.

Cork Flemings

Silver Grange House, Tivoli, Cork, Co Cork
☎ (021) 821621 📠 (021) 821800
🛏 4 £64 🪑 50 🕛 £55

🙂 Lunch 12.30-2.30, Dinner 6.30-11 🙁 Hotel 24-26 Dec, Good Friday

Just outside Cork city, this fine Georgian house stands in extensive gardens which include an area set aside for vegetables, thus ensuring a supply for Michael Fleming's needs in the kitchen. A la carte or fixed-price menus offer plenty of choice; the style is mostly French.

Cork Harolds Restaurant

Douglas, Cork, Co Cork
☎ (021) 361613
🪑 51 🍽 £55
☺ Dinner 6-10 ☹ 24 & 25 Dec

A relatively recent arrival at Cork's gourmet scene, Harold's has quickly become established as a serious contender for attention. Stylish, modern decor and a menu to match, cooked by Harold Lynch while partner Beth Houghton looks after front-of-house. Dishes vary in origin from a fairly international repertoire, and there's a concise list of well-priced wines.

Cork Isaacs

48 MacCurtain Street, Cork, Co Cork
☎ (021) 503805
🪑 90 🍽 £45
☺ Lunch 12-2.30, Dinner 6.30-10.30 (Sun to 9) ☹ Lunch Sun, 5 days Xmas

Canice Sharkey cooks at the Ryans' city-centre restaurant, offering Mediterranean-style menus which include good options for vegetarians. Lighter meals are also available at lunchtimes.

Cork Ivory Tower Restaurant

35 Princes Street, Cork, Co Cork
☎ (021) 274665
🪑 36 🍽 £55
☺ Lunch 12-4, Dinner 6.30-11 ☹ Sun & Mon

Seamus O'Connell is actually very down-to-earth and produces some interesting dishes on fixed-price and à la carte menus. Special themed Thursday evenings are very popular, as are the displays of work by local artists, which changes regularly.

Cork Jacques

9 Phoenix Street, Cork, Co Cork
☎ (021) 277387   📠 (021) 270634
🪑 55 🍽 £60
☺ Lunch 11.30-3, Dinner 6-10.30
☹ Dinner Mon, all Sun, Bank Holidays, 10 days Xmas

Chef/partners Eithne & Jacqueline Barry, here since 1980, offer some great-tasting French and Mediterranean cooking on daily-changing menus. Seafood is a speciality, and with advance warning they are happy to cater for most dietary requirements. Desserts are a strong point.

Cork Michael's Bistro

4 Mardyke Street, Cork, Co Cork
☎ (021) 276887
🍴 27 🍽 £45

☺ Lunch 12-3.30, Dinner 6-10.30 ☹ Sun, Bank Holidays, 2 wks Aug

Michael Clifford's newer, smaller establishment offers a simple menu supplemented by blackboard specials, but the style of cooking is as accomplished as ever, within a less formal setting. Super range of Irish cheeses.

Dingle Beginish Restaurant

Green Street, Dingle, Co Kerry
☎ (066) 51588 📠 (066) 51591
🍴 52 🍽 £55

☺ Lunch 12.30-2.15, Dinner 6-9.30 ☹ all Mon, mid Nov-Mar

Fish naturally takes pride of place in the Moores' comfortable restaurant which also has accommodation in the apartments next door. An extensive lunch menu offers light dishes at very affordable prices. In the evening, it's the turn of a more elaborate Mediterranean-influenced range.

Dingle Doyle's Seafood Bar & Townhouse ❀

4 John Street, Dingle, Co Kerry
☎ (066) 51174 📠 (066) 51816
🛏 8 £ £62 🍴 50 🍽 £65

☺ Dinner only 6-9 ☹ Sun, mid Nov-mid Mar

Still a favourite after more than 20 years, when the Doyles first carved a niche which anticipated good luck as well as foresight! The catch of local fishermen dictates the menu but they rarely fail to deliver an outstanding range of produce. It's a considerable bonus that you can stay in the townhouse next door, so you can get more than one shot at this intriguing, superbly-cooked menu and its aptly compiled wine list.

Dingle Half Door

John Street, Dingle, Co Kerry
☎ (066) 51600 📠 (066) 51206
🍴 50 🍽 £50

☺ Lunch 12.30-2.30, Dinner 6-10 ☹ Tue, Nov & Jan-Easter

Superb range of seafood at Dennis & Teresa O'Connor's friendly local restaurant, though there are some meat dishes for dedicated carnivores, and although in the 18th Century the area had a long history of smuggling, they'll be brought to your table openly and proudly, as they are confident of the reliability and consistency of their suppliers.

Dingle Lord Baker's Bar & Restaurant

Main Street, Dingle, Co Kerry
☎ (066) 51277
🍴 85 🍽 £50
☺ Lunch 12.30-2.30, Dinner 6-10 ☹ 25 Dec

Is this the oldest pub in Dingle? Now there's a question that could occupy you for several sessions in the bar, fuelled by enthusiasm and international-style food and wine as well as by fine ales and stouts.

Donegal St Ernan's House Hotel

St Ernans Island, Donegal, Co Donegal
☎ (073) 21065   📠 (073) 22098
🛏 12 £130 🍴 28 🍽 £65
☺ Dinner 6.30-8.30

A unique location on a wooded tidal island, reached by a causeway, yet located only 2 miles from Donegal. Delightful and relaxing individually-styled bedrooms. Fixed-price dinner menus make the most of the local catch, alongside plenty of meat dishes.

Dublin Berkeley Court

Lansdowne Road, Dublin, Co Dublin, 4
☎ (01) 660 1711   📠 (01) 661 7238
🛏 187 £220 🍴 60 🍽 £80
☺ Lunch 12.30-2.15, Dinner 6.30-10.15 (Sun to 9.15)

International, flagship hotel of the Doyle Hotel Group. Luxuriously appointed public and private rooms, with function facilities for up to 400 people

Dublin Blooms Hotel

6 Anglesea Street, Temple Bar, Dublin, Co Dublin, 2
☎ (01) 671 5622   📠 (01) 671 5997
🛏 86 £140 🍴 70 🍽 £55
☺ Lunch 12.30-2, Dinner 5-9.45   ☹ Lunch Sat & Sun, 24-26 Dec

Named after the hero of James Joyce's "Ulysses", this comfortable hotel is close to Dublin Castle and Trinity College. The bar and lobby have recently been refurbished, and there's a nightclub for those who wish to dance the night away.

Dublin Chapter One

18/19 Parnell Square, Dublin, Co Dublin, 1
☎ (01) 873 2266   📠 (01) 873 2330
🪑 100 🍽 £55

🙂 Lunch 12-2.30, Dinner 5.45-11
☹ Lunch Sat, all Mon, Bank Holidays, 1 wk Xmas

Ross Lewis, Martin Corbett & Eammon Walsh are the partners at this interesting restaurant in the vaulted cellar-basement below the Dublin Writers Museum (on the ground floor, the café and garden are also run by the trio). An international menu has some unusual flavour combinations which work very well.

Dublin The Commons Restaurant

Newman House, 85-86 St Stephen's Green, Dublin, Co Dublin, 2
☎ (01) 475 2597   📠 (01) 478 0551
🪑 60 🍽 £85

🙂 Lunch 12.30-2.15, Dinner 7-10   ☹ Lunch Sat, all Sun, Bank Holidays

Another unique location, this time within Newman House which was the original home of University College, Dublin. The elegant, Georgian houses have been completely restored and now serve as an important architectural monument and cultural centre. The stylish dining room is classically furnished, and adorned with fine paintings by Irish artists. Assuming your soul is restored by the surroundings, some good modern Irish cooking then nourishes the body.

Dublin Hotel Conrad

Earlsfort Terrace, Dublin, Co Dublin, 2
☎ (01) 676 5555   📠 (01) 676 5424
🛏 191 £230 🪑 50 🍽 £75

🙂 Lunch 12.30-2.30, Dinner 7-10.30   ☹ Lunch Sat, all Sun

Well-sited for business or leisure visitors, the modern-style Dublin Conrad is a match for any in that group. Large, beautifully-furnished bedrooms and suites have all the necessary luxuries, and conference facilities are extensive. Choose between 2 restaurants: the Alexandra offering formal, modern cuisine and the Plurabelle brasserie, which is open all day. Alternatively, relax in Alfie Byrne's pub, which is also on the premises.

Republic of Ireland 347

Dublin Cooke's Café

14 South William Street, Dublin, Co Dublin, 2
☎ (01) 679 0536 📠 (01) 679 0546
🍴 40 🍽 £70
☺ Lunch 12.30-4 (Sun to 3.30), Dinner 6-11 (Fri & Sat to 11.30, Sun to 9.30), (light meals 8am-12 midnight May-Sep) ☹ Bank Holidays

Café is something of an understatement as a description of John Cooke's ever-popular city-centre restaurant. From his open-plan kitchen he produces an interesting range of modern-style dishes well presented and tasting as good. Fixed-price menus for lunch and early evening are good value – make sure you book, though, at any time. Buzzy atmosphere.

Dublin Le Coq Hardi

35 Pembroke Road, Ballsbridge, Dublin, Co Dublin, 4
☎ (01) 668 9070 📠 (01) 668 9887
🍴 50 🍽 £100
☺ Lunch 12-2.30, Dinner 7-11
☹ Lunch Sat, all Sun, Bank Holidays, 1 wk Xmas, 2 wks Aug

A classic restaurant in its decor, its style, its cuisine, its service and its wines: Le Coq Hardi is for serious dining. Chef/patron John Howard offers a large menu with more than a nod towards France for inspiration linked with a strong desire to utilise superb Irish produce in the creation of his dishes. Smoked wild Irish salmon comes with a confit of citrus fruits, steamed Howth lobster with tarragon butter sauce, a navarin of Wicklow lamb; even Clonakilty black and white pudding sounds more evocative when described as boudin blanc et noir! Though the menu is extensive it competes with a memorable wine list that lists everything that you have ever wanted to drink though perhaps fewer that you can afford. Catherine Howard ensures the smooth running of the impeccable dining room.

Dublin Davenport Hotel

Merrion Square, Dublin, Co Dublin, 2
☎ (01) 661 6799 📠 (01) 661 5663
🛏 120 £135 🍴 100 🍽 £65
☺ Lunch 12.30-2, Dinner 5.30-10.30 ☹ Lunch Sat

Now marketed as a global partner of the Inter-Continental group, this elegant and impressive hotel is located close to the National Gallery and Trinity College. Some of the business suites are named after famous Dublin architects (Lanyon, Gandon). International menus are offered in the restaurant, and there's a fine range of wines by the glass.

Dublin L'Ecrivain

109 Lower Baggot Street, Dublin, Co Dublin, 2

☎ (01) 661 1919

🍴 40 🍽 £65

☺ Lunch 12.30-2, Dinner 6.30-11 ☹ Lunch Sat, all Sun

The move to new premises next door for Derry & Sallyanne Clarke means that more people can now enjoy their classic French cooking on daily-changing seasonal set and à la carte menus. Some excellent home-made breads are quite delicious.

Dublin Les Frères Jacques

74 Dame Street, Dublin, Co Dublin, 2

☎ (01) 679 4555 📠 (01) 679 4725

🍴 55 🍽 £80

☺ Lunch 12.30-2.30, Dinner 7.30-10.30 (Fri & Sat to 11)

☹ Lunch Sat, all Sun, Bank Holidays, 25-29 Dec

Classy restaurant opposite Dublin Castle. Table d'hote lunch and dinner menus offer great value, and are complemented by the short carte. The speciality of the house is the vivarium, from which you may choose your own lobster. Wine list of appropriate stature, professional yet friendly service.

Dublin Grey Door

22 Upper Pembroke Street, Dublin, Co Dublin, 2

☎ (01) 676 3286 📠 (01) 676 3287

🛏 7 £98 🍴 50 🍽 £60

☺ Lunch 12.30-2.15, Dinner 7-11 (Bistro 6-11.30)

☹ Lunch Sat, all Sun, Bank Holiday

Attractive, small hotel and restaurant with very comfortable, well-maintained bedrooms and attentive service. Blushes Restaurant has been revamped totally and is now Pier 32, an authentic West of Ireland-style seafood pub and restaurant. This gives greater flexibility to the service available to either individuals or business groups.

Dublin Jury's Hotel & Towers

Pembroke Road, Ballsbridge, Dublin, Co Dublin, 4

☎ (01) 660 5000 📠 (01) 660 5540

🛏 398 £168 🍴 86 🍽 £60

☺ Lunch 12.15-2.30 (Sun from 12.30), Dinner 6.15-10.15 (Sun to 9.30)

Surprisingly personal for a hotel of its size, Jury's offers a warm Irish welcome to all. There's always plenty of life in the public areas and bedrooms are comfortable and well appointed. The Towers offers a rather more tranquil environment. Excellent leisure, banqueting and conference facilities. Don't miss the Jury's Irish Cabaret evenings, which are nothing short of sensational.

Dublin Kapriol

45 Lower Camden Street, Dublin, Co Dublin, 2
☎ (01) 475 1235
🍴 30 🍽 £65
☺ Dinner only 7.30-12 ☹ Sun, Bank Holidays, 2 wks Aug

Long-established (since 1978) traditional Italian restaurant in the city centre, where pasta is home made, local game is sourced when in season (but cooked and served Italian-style), and the set-price menus offer excellent value for money.

Dublin Lobster Pot

9 Ballsbridge Terrace, Dublin, Co Dublin, 4
☎ (01) 668 0025
🍴 40 🍽 £70
☺ Lunch 12.30-2.30, Dinner 6.30-10.30
☹ Lunch Sat, all Sun, Bank Holidays, 1 wk Xmas

Thomas Crean and his loyal team celebrate 15 years at this cosy, first-floor restaurant where you can enjoy traditional fish specialities as well as excellent meat and game. This is one of Dublin's most dependable venues.

Dublin Locks

1 Windsor Terrace, Portobello, Dublin, Co Dublin, 8
☎ (01) 454 3391 📠 (01) 453 8352
🍴 47 🍽 £65
☺ Lunch 12.30-2, Dinner 7.15-11
☹ Lunch Sat, all Sun, Bank Holidays, 1 wk Xmas

Claire Douglas's attractive canalside restaurant is popular with locals who know good value when they see it. Fixed-price modern-style lunch and dinner menus have good variety, and a carte is also offered. Service is efficient without being in any way hurried, and there's a private dining area for larger parties. Reasonably-priced wine list.

Dublin Longfield's Hotel & No 10 Restaurant

Fitzwilliam Street Lower, Dublin, Co Dublin, 2
☎ (01) 676 1367 📠 (01) 676 1542
🛏 26 £ £96 🍴 40 🍽 £80
☺ Lunch 12.30-2.30, Dinner 6.30-10 (Fri & Sat to 11)
☹ Lunch Sat & Sun, Bank Holidays, 25 & 26 Dec

A Georgian town house just off St Stephen's Green with comfortable bedrooms. It also has the lower ground floor Number Ten restaurant, which features Irish produce.

Dublin Old Dublin Restaurant

90-91 Francis Street, Dublin, Co Dublin, 8
☎ (01) 454 2028 📠 (01) 454 1406
🍴 65 🍽 £60

☺ Lunch 12.30-2.30, Dinner 6-11   ☹ Lunch Sat, all Sun, Bank Holidays

An old-style, international, Eastern European-influenced cosy restaurant. Set and à la carte menus. Extensive range of fine wines.

Dublin Patrick Guilbaud   ✤

46 James Place, Off Lower Baggot Street, Dublin, Co Dublin, 2
☎ (01) 676 4192 📠 (01) 660 1546
🍴 60 🍽 £100

☺ Lunch 12.30-2, Dinner 7.30-10.15   ☹ Sun & Mon, Bank Holidays

A touch of Paris in Dublin, M. Guilbaud's well established sanctuary of gastronomy maintains its standards. Guillaume Lebrun guides his kitchen brigade through ever-busy routines with great aplomb, and consistency is the keynote to the deserved success of this fine restaurant. Patrick guides his customers through the menu with equal panache. Try foie gras of duck cooked in its own fat; warm, wild Irish salmon with potato blinis and lemon butter; or a warm salad of vegetables cooked in olive oil and coriander to start. Follow with a pink breast of wild duck with prune and lime compote; a young chicken cooked in a salty crust served with garlic butter; or a simple fillet of John Dory served with pimento oil dressing. Pain perdu with caramelised apples, bitter chocolate tart with pistachio ice-cream or perhaps the nage of mandarins on a honey sauce are typical puddings. Faultless service and fine wines round off a great experience.

Dublin Roly's Bistro

7 Ballsbridge Terrace, Dublin, Co Dublin, 4
☎ (01) 668 2611 📠 (01) 660 8535
🍴 120 🍽 £50

☺ Lunch 12-3, Dinner 6-10 (Sun to 9)

☹ Lunch Sat, 25 & 26 Dec, Good Friday

Packed since the day it opened, Roly's is the place to be in fashionable Ballsbridge opposite the American Embassy. It's hardly surprising that the place is so successful when you consider the fact that two of Ireland's best restaurateurs teamed up with one of the country's most talented chefs to create a very user-friendly bistro. On 2 floors there is room for around 100 diners, and there are usually 100 more waiting so book a table! Colin O'Daly's kitchen produces a true bistro menu with an unusually high proportion of dishes that you actually would like to try and considering the quality, prices are very reasonable for Dublin. Wines are also moderately priced with few bottles on the list exceeding £20 and around a dozen house selections at under £10. Superb fresh breads from their own bakery are a meal in themselves but try the specialities such as Colin's prawn bisque, monkfish with almonds, honey and dates flavoured with whiskey and mustard seeds or roast fillet of pork with black pudding and chicken sausage in thyme jus. Friendly service under Roly's guidance rounds off the experience. Lunch is the best deal in Ireland!

Republic of Ireland

Dublin Shelbourne Hotel

St Stephen's Green, Dublin, Co Dublin, 2

☎ (01) 676 6471 (01) 661 6006

164 £226 85 £60

☺ Lunch 12.30-2.30, Dinner 6-10.30 (Sun 6-10)

One of Dublin's best-known hotels has seen more than its share of visitors over the years. Spacious, well-appointed rooms and suites have all imaginable creature comforts and the hotel's 2 bars (the Horseshoe and the Shelbourne) are busy meeting places for locals and visitors alike.

Dublin La Stampa

35 Dawson Street, Dublin, Co Dublin, 2

☎ (01) 677 8611 (01) 677 3336

160 £60

☺ Lunch 12.30-2.30, Dinner 6.30-11.30 (Fri & Sat to 12)

☹ Lunch Sat & Sun, 2 days Xmas, Good Friday

A large, humming restaurant with unusual paintings and stylish decor, great atmosphere and excellent cooking from Paul Flynn's kitchen. Start with dishes like angel-hair pasta with olive oil and feta, warm pigeon salad and feuilleté of mushrooms and onions, then perhaps char-grilled, skewered lamb with a sweet salsa, pan-fried sea trout with citrus beurre blanc, or fillet of beef with chicken mousseline and blue cheese. Finish with meringue and hazelnut roll, and go straight to heaven.

Dublin Stephen's Hall Hotel & Bistro

14-17 Lower Leeson Street, Dublin, Co Dublin, 2

☎ (01) 661 0585 (01) 661 0606

37 £143 48 £50

☺ Lunch 12.15-2.30, Dinner 6.15-9.30 (Fri & Sat to 10)

☹ Lunch Sat, all Sun, 1 wk Xmas

Dublin's first all-suite hotel has a good range (of prices and facilities) within that description. If you don't want to cook for yourself, dine in the Bistro (formerly the Terrace) from a wide choice of imaginative dishes, arranged on à la carte and set menus.

Dublin Thornton's

1 Portobello Road, Dublin, Co Dublin, 9

☎ (01) 454 9067 (01) 454 9067

40 £80

☺ Lunch 12-3.30, Dinner 5.30-12 (Thu-Sat till 1am)

☹ Good Friday, 25 & 26 Dec

Informal, modestly-decorated newcomer to Dublin, split into bar downstairs and two dining areas upstairs, and home to Kevin Thornton's innovative and modern cooking. Carefully-chosen wine list and welcoming staff make this well worth a visit

Dublin The Westbury

Off Grafton Street, Dublin, Co Dublin, 2
☎ (01) 679 1122 📠 (01) 679 7078
▫ 203 £189 🛏 100 🍽 £85
🙂 Lunch 12.30-2.30, Dinner 6.30-10.30 (Sun to 9.30)

A large hotel in a prime location just off Grafton Street, with Dublin's entire shopping centre laid out before you – even though there's a shopping mall within the hotel, too. Competent cooking of international dishes is served up in the Russell Room restaurant.

Dun Laoghaire De Selby's Restaurant

19 Patrick Street, Dun Laoghaire, Co Dublin
☎ (01) 284 1762
🛏 120 🍽 £50
🙂 Lunch Sun only 12-10, Dinner 5.30-11
☹ Good Friday, 3 days Xmas

De Selby was a character in a book *"The Third Policeman"*: he had something interesting to say about almost every subject. At the restaurant, John MacManus & Eleanor Connolly have something interesting at every course on the menu, which is full of traditional Irish favourites. It's ideal for families, and an outside eating area recreates an Irish street of 40 years ago.

Dundalk Cellars Restaurant

Backhouse Centre, Clanbrassil Street, Dundalk, Co Louth
☎ (042) 33745
🛏 130 🍽 £25
🙂 12-2.30   ☹ Sat & Sun, wk after Xmas

Tiny establishment with restricted opening hours, run by George & Alison O'Shea. A short menu is offered at exceptionally reasonable prices, served up in a friendly, relaxed atmosphere.

Dunkineely Castle Murray House

Dunkineely, Co Donegal
☎ (073) 37022 📠 (073) 37330
▫ 10 £48 🛏 45 🍽 £50
🙂 Lunch 1-2.30, Dinner 7-9.30
☹ Lunch Wed-Sat, all Mon & Tue in winter, 24 & 25 Dec, 2 wks Feb

Superb cliff-top setting for this small hotel and restaurant. Chef/patrons Thierry & Claire Delcros offer French cooking and French hospitality, though they cannot resist the attractions of Irish farmhouse cheeses, which actually sit alongside the rest of the menu very well indeed.

Durrus Blairs Cove House Restaurant

Blairs Cove, Durrus, Nr Bantry, Co Cork
☎ (027) 61127
🍴 59 🍽 £60
☺ Dinner only 7.30-9.30 ☹ Sun (also Mon Sep-Jun), Nov-Feb

Philippe & Sabine de Mey's Georgian manor has a charming apartment above the restaurant, where the lucky diner who first booked can stay overnight and thus take full advantage of the delights of the wine list and the vaulted and beamed restaurant, which offers a wide range of dishes making the most of local produce. Puddings are displayed on the grand piano, and coffee is served from a copper Turkish pot.

Enniskerry Enniscree Lodge

Glencree Valley, Nr Enniskerry, Co Wicklow
☎ (01) 286 3542 📠 (01) 286 6037
🛏 10 £ £55 🍴 40 🍽 £55
☺ Lunch 12.30-2.30, Dinner 7.30-9.30 (Sat to 10, Sun to 9)
☹ Mon-Thu in Jan & Feb

Comfortable old inn set in some staggeringly beautiful scenery in the Glencree valley, less than 30k from Dublin. The owners offer a friendly welcome and are good hosts. A short menu at lunchtime offers a few simply-cooked dishes; while the more extensive dinner menu gives you imaginative cooking of good local ingredients.

Foulksmills Horetown House

Foulksmills, Co Wexford
☎ (051) 63771 📠 (051) 63633
🍴 45 🍽 £50
☺ Lunch Sun only 12.30-2.30, Dinner 7-9
☹ Lunch Tue-Sat, Dinner Sun, all Mon, Bank Holidays, 1 wk Xmas

This 18th-century manor house is a residential equestrian centre, but there's also the Cellar Restaurant where you can enjoy some good cooking, Sunday lunchtime being especially popular as it includes, for the kids, a complimentary trot around on a pony while parents relax. Sounds like a great idea – unless little Lilly then pesters Dad for a pony of her own.

Furbo Connemara Coast Hotel

Furbo, Nr Galway, Co Galway
☎ (091) 92108 📠 (091) 92065
🛏 112 £ £120 🍴 120 🍽 £55
☺ Dinner 6-10 ☹ 25 & 26 Dec

Large, modern hotel on the shores of Galway Bay, especially popular for business and conferences as large numbers can be accommodated with ease and there are good leisure facilities. Good choice of bedrooms, lovely views from lounges.

Galway Casey's Westwood Restaurant & Bars

Dangan, Upper Newcastle, Galway, Co Galway
☎ (091) 21442
🪑 120 🍽 £60
☺ Lunch 12.30-2.15, Dinner 6.30-10 ☹ 3 days Xmas, Good Friday

The Casey family's unique brand of hospitality is a much-loved feature of this part of Galway. More relaxed eating at lunchtimes, slightly more formal in the evenings.

Gorey Marlfield House

Gorey, Co Wexford
☎ (055) 21124 📠 (055) 21572
🛏 19 £154 🪑 60 🍽 £90
☺ Lunch 12.30-2, Dinner 7-9.30 ☹ 10 Dec-31 Jan

Stylish hotel run by the Bowe family, well-situated less than 2 miles from the sea. Inside, it's beautifully furnished and richly decorated, and a new wing provides good business facilities. The light and airy Victorian conservatory-style dining room is a fine setting for some excellent 5-course dinner menus. At breakfast, there's an irresistible range of home-made breads.

Greencastle Kealy's Seafood Bar

The Harbour, Greencastle, Co Donegal
☎ (077) 81010
🪑 40 🍽 £45
☺ Lunch 12.30-5, Dinner 7-9.30
☹ Mon, 1 wk Mar, 1 wk Oct, 25 Dec, Good Friday

Friendly service and serious food at this small, harbourside restaurant where the simpler lunchtime menu gives way to a well-conceived and quite extensive choice for dinner – it's mostly fish, of course, but meat-eaters are not neglected. Puddings are a strong point, too.

Greystones The Hungry Monk

Greystones, Co Wicklow
☎ (01) 287 5759
🪑 40 🍽 £55
☺ Lunch Sun only 12-8, Dinner 7-11
☹ Dinner Sun & Mon-Wed in winter, all Mon, 25 Dec, Good Friday

A homely, first-floor restaurant with all creature comforts, warmly lit by candles in the evening. Helen Ward trained with Declan Ryan at Arbutus Lodge, and her careful cooking of local fish and game has quickly established her reputation. Prices are very reasonable, and the excellent wine list offers great variety and good value.

Howth King Sitric

East Pier, Harbour Road, Howth, Co Dublin
☎ (01) 832 6729 📠 (01) 839 2442
🍴 70 🍽 £70

☺ Lunch (Seafood Bar 12-3 May-Sep only), Dinner only 6.30-11
☹ Sun, Bank Holidays, 10 days Jan, 10 days Easter

Sitric, a Danish king, contributed much to the development of Howth over the years; but it could be argued that Aidan & Joan MacManus have contributed even more by establishing this harbourside seafood restaurant, overlooking Balscadden Bay. The fleet delivers straight to the kitchen door and so it's not far on to the plate – you can't get fish much fresher than this.

Inistioge The Motte

Inistioge, Co Kilkenny
☎ (056) 58655
🍴 24 🍽 £60

☺ Dinner only 7-10 (Sun to 9) ☹ Bank Holidays, 1 wk Xmas

A very attractive, well-run restaurant in a lovely village where you can enjoy some excellent hospitality and fine cuisine from the stove of Alan Walton. Fixed-price menus change with the seasons. It's not a large room, so book in advance.

Kanturk Assolas Country House

Kanturk, Co Cork
☎ (029) 50015 📠 (029) 50795
🛏 9 £110 🍴 25 🍽 £65

☺ Dinner only 7-8.30 ☹ Hotel Nov-Mar

A comfortable, creeper-clad mansion house situated alongside a tributary of the River Blackwater, where the Bourke family offer splendid hospitality and fine cooking. Lots of home-grown and local produce are the basis of Hazel Bourke's progressive Irish cuisine, which is served in the elegant dining room. Fine wines complement the food.

Kenmare d'Arcy's

Main Street, Kenmare, Co Kerry
☎ (064) 41589 📠 (064) 41589
🛏 5 £29 🍴 40 🍽 £70

☺ Dinner 7-9 (5-10.30 in summer)
☹ Mon-Wed winter, 24-26 Dec, 2 wks Jan/Feb

Matthew d'Arcy has sensibly rechristened the Old Bank House which he opened in 1992, and the added identity has lent greater confidence to his cooking. Aileen d'Arcy looks after customers at front-of-house, surely with a great deal more sympathy than was ever dished out by the original bankers! Few of the 50-odd wines should break the bank.

Kenmare The Lime Tree

Shelbourne Street, Kenmare, Co Kerry
☎ (064) 41225
🪑 45 🍽 £50
☺ Dinner 6.30-9.30 ☹ Nov-Easter

In a former life, the building was the rent office and temperance hall for the Lansdowne Estate; and it was from here, during the famine, that almost 5,000 Irish secured free emigration to the USA. It then became a school, now a restaurant, where fortunately there's no sign of famine or temperance! The menu includes some interesting dishes that balance both modern Mediterranean and traditional Irish influences. The decor is stylish and lively (exposed stone walls, pine wood and modern art) and the service is friendly.

Kenmare Packie's

Henry Street, Kenmare, Co Kerry
☎ (064) 41508
🪑 35 🍽 £45
☺ Dinner only 5.30-10 ☹ Sun, Nov-Easter

Tom & Maura Foley (formerly at the Lime Tree) run this popular bistro, offering Irish and international eclectic menus that change seasonally, though specials change daily. Starters are cutely called small dishes, reflecting their versatility. A moderate wine list has some interesting choices.

Kenmare Park Hotel Kenmare ❀

Kenmare, Co Kerry
☎ (064) 41200 📠 (064) 41402
🛏 50 £ £272 🪑 80 🍽 £90
☺ Lunch 1-1.45, Dinner 7-8.45 ☹ Hotel mid Nov-Xmas, 4 Jan Easter

Any youngster who wants to learn about how to run a hotel should ask Francis Brennan to give him lessons. Francis bought this old railway hotel in the late '70s and since then has gradually established it as one of Ireland's very best. There's impeccable attention to detail in all aspects of housekeeping: the bedrooms are spacious and bathrobes, slippers, mineral water, books and fresh fruit are provided for guests' comfort. In the restaurant Brian Cleere cooks while Jim McCarthy looks after the diners, a happy combination that sees some excellent dishes on fixed-price menus. Rillettes of duck with a pan-fried duck breast and sherry vinegar dressing, a nage of prawns and scallops flavoured with chervil might precede a cream of broccoli soup or gazpacho. Sole in champagne sauce with a mushroom sabayon, roast baby chicken on a bed of lentils with thyme sauce or a trio of lamb dishes – a pan-fried noisette, navarin of the shoulder and a crumbed breast – served on a rosemary jus are main dishes. The wine list perfectly complements the food with ample range from French classics to a vast choice of Californian and other European delights.

Kenmare Sheen Falls Lodge

Kenmare, Co Kerry
☎ (064) 41600 📠 (064) 41386
🛏 40 £ £257 🍴 120 🍽 £90
☺ Lunch Sun only 1-2, Dinner 7.30-9.30 ☹ Dec-Feb (open Xmas)

A magnificent setting – Kenmare Bay on one side, Sheen Waterfalls on the other – is an idyllic location within 300 acres of grounds for this exquisite hotel. Bedrooms and suites lack nothing in comfort, and there's a well-equipped leisure and fitness centre, as well as facilities for outdoor sports including fishing. If you like, they'll smoke your catch for you! Modern Irish cuisine in La Cascade restaurant.

Kilkenny Lacken House

Dublin Road, Kilkenny, Co Kilkenny
☎ (056) 61085 📠 (056) 62435
🛏 8 £ £60 🍴 35 🍽 £65
☺ Dinner 7-10.30 ☹ Dinner Sun & Mon, 1 wk Xmas

Eugene & Breda McSweeney offer hospitality here in a small but comfortable restaurant with rooms, which they have run since 1983. They describe the cooking style as progressive Irish, which I think is a lovely phrase! Changes also reflect the seasons, naturally, and set-price menus offer particularly good value.

Killarney Aghadoe Heights Hotel

Aghadoe, Killarney, Co Kerry
☎ (064) 31766 📠 (064) 31345
🛏 60 £ £190 🍴 84 🍽 £100
☺ Lunch 12.15-2, Dinner 7-9.30

Wonderful views over Lake Killarney and the surrounding mountains for this hotel, well equipped for sport and leisure. Lounges are relaxing and comfortable, to take advantage of the setting. Fredrick's Restaurant (see also Maidenhead, England) offers set menus of modern cooking with an international flavour.

Killarney Dingles Restauraunt

40 New Street, Killarney, Co Kerry
☎ (064) 31079
🍴 45 🍽 £45
☺ Dinner 6-10.30 (light meals 12-10) ☹ Dinner Sun, Xmas-Feb

Simplicity is the keynote, in both decor and food at the Cunninghams' welcoming restaurant. Good, fresh produce is carefully prepared by Marion in traditional style. A carefully-chosen wine list has something for everyone.

Killarney Gaby's Seafood Restaurant

27 High Street, Killarney, Co Kerry
☎ (064) 32519 📠 (064) 32747
🪑 65 🍽 £60

☺ Lunch 12.30-2.30, Dinner 6-10 ☹ Lunch Mon, all Sun, Feb

The menu relies on the success of the Kerry fishing boats for inspiration, though Geert Maes will always transform the catch into a delightful dish, whatever it should be. Simple lunches, more elaborate evening meals, and on the wine list a fine variety at reasonable prices.

Killarney Strawberry Tree

24 Plunkett Street, Killarney, Co Kerry
☎ (064) 32688 📠 (064) 32688
🪑 30 🍽 £65

☺ Lunch by arrangement, Dinner 6.30-10.30 ☹ Jan-Feb

A rare opportunity to taste food as it should be, as the Strawberry Tree serves only organic and free-range produce. All suppliers have signed certificates confirming their status. The breads are really delicious, and the early-bird menu is exceptionally good value.

Killorglin Nick's Restaurant

Lower Bridge Street, Killorglin, Co Kerry
☎ (066) 61219 📠 (066) 61233
🪑 80 🍽 £65

☺ Dinner only 6-10 ☹ Mon & Tue Jan-Easter, Nov

Good, family-run restaurant which specialises in seafood based on the daily catch, but also includes several choices for meat eaters, especially venison in season. Wines are just as fine, with a good range from the Loire and Alsace alongside plenty of quality New World bottles.

Kinsale Blue Haven Hotel

3 Pearse Street, Kinsale, Co Cork
☎ (021) 772209 📠 (021) 774268
🛏 18 £ £96 🪑 45 🍽 £60

☺ Dinner 7-10.30, (conservatory 10.30am-9.30pm, teas 3-5)
☹ 2 days midweek in winter, Hotel 25 Dec

Accommodation at the Cronins' cheerful hotel has almost doubled in size, and all rooms now have ensuite bathrooms. The menu served in the cosy bar would be the envy of many restaurants, though here it is served throughout the day. In the evening, the main restaurant is open for dinner with a separate menu, though both rely heavily on the nearby Atlantic for their fish and shellfish. You can even fish for your own supper in the hotel's own boat, the *Peggy G*.

Kinsale Chez Jean-Marc

Lower O'Connell Street, Kinsale, Co Cork,
☎ (021) 774625 📠 (021) 774680
🍴 55 🍽 £55

☺ Lunch 12.30-3 (Sun only, in winter), Dinner 6.45-10.30 (winter 7-10)

☹ Dinner Sun, all Mon winter, Xmas, Feb (open w/ends)

Jean-Marc Tsai now offers the choice of the established, cottage-style restaurant on the ground floor, or the bistro/brasserie upstairs. Traditional French cuisine below, a more international theme above. Great atmosphere in either room.

Kinsale Man Friday

Scilly, Kinsale, Co Cork
☎ (021) 772260
🍴 80 🍽 £55

☺ Lunch by arrangement only, Dinner 7-10

☹ Sun in winter, 24-26 Dec, Good Friday

Considering the relatively small population of Kinsale, the town supports a remarkable number of good restaurants, and Man Friday has long been a favourite. This cluster of small dining rooms is above the quay, and serves – lots of fish! The accompanying well-balanced list of around 100 wines is very reasonably priced.

Kinsale Max's Wine Bar

Main Street, Kinsale, Co Cork
☎ (021) 772443
🍴 40 🍽 £40

☺ Lunch 1-3, Dinner 6.30-10.30 ☹ Nov-Feb

Actually, it's Wendy Tisdall's and has been since 1975, though the cooking is done by Jane Barrett. It's international in style and changes intermittently. The early-bird menu (£12 before 8pm) is very popular.

Kinsale Old Presbytery

Cork Street, Kinsale, Co Cork
☎ (021) 772027
🛏 6 £48 🍴 14 🍽 £50

☺ Dinner only open to residents ☹ Sun, 1 wk Xmas

Ken & Cathleen Buggy have run this lovely place since 1983, near St John's Church in this quaint fishing village. Each bedroom is individually decorated in traditional style with a warm, welcoming atmosphere, big beds and crisp Irish linen to give you a "real old sleep". Menus change daily and, naturally, feature plenty of fish.

Laragh Mitchell's of Laragh

The Old Schoolhouse, Laragh, Co Wicklow
☎ (0404) 45302 📠 (0404) 45302
🛏 5 £36 🍴 30 🍽 £45
🙂 9am-10pm (Sun to 9)
🙁 Dinner Sun, Lunch Wed in winter, Bank Holidays, 4 wks winter

There's a homely feel at the Mitchells' converted schoolhouse, where the cooking is imaginative and exemplary. Set-price menus offer plenty of variety and good value – eat on the patio if the weather's fine. Stay in one of the comfortable bedrooms and then you can enjoy a splendid breakfast. They also hold exhibitions of the work of local artists.

Letterfrack Rosleague Manor

Letterfrack, Connemara, Co Galway
☎ (095) 41101 📠 (095) 41168
🛏 20 £110 🍴 60 🍽 £65
🙂 Lunch 1-2.30, Dinner 8-9.30 (Sun to 9) 🙁 Hotel Nov-Easter

Brother and sister Anne & Patrick Foyle have been running Rosleague since 1970, keeping a constant eye on standards and continually refurbishing as necessary. The Regency-style manor is set in 30 acres of its own grounds and you can stroll right down to the sea. French-style menus use fresh seafood daily, and Connemara lamb in season.

Limerick Castletroy Park Hotel

Dublin Road, Limerick, Co Limerick
☎ (061) 335566 📠 (061) 331117
🛏 107 £131 🍴 70 🍽 £65
🙂 Lunch 12.30-2, Dinner 7-9.30 🙁 Lunch Sat, Dinner Sun, 24 & 25 Dec

A large, well-designed hotel popular with business people, offering extensive conference facilities, a leisure complex, the Merry Pedlar Bar, and McLaughlin's Restaurant. Bistro food is served in the former while in the latter (named after Thomas McLaughlin who first generated electricity in Ireland using the waters of the Shannon), the menu is based on classic dishes served with Mediterranean touches.

Limerick Restaurant de La Fontaine

12 Upper Gerald Griffin Street, Limerick, Co Limerick
☎ (061) 414461 📠 (061) 411337
🍴 40 🍽 £60
🙂 Lunch 12.30-2.30, Dinner 7-10 🙁 Lunch Sat, all Sun, Bank Holidays

A touch of France in Limerick, with classic menus that make a few concessions to modern fashions. You can put your meal together either by individual courses, or treat the choices as a table d'hote for a set price. Good range of French wines.

Malahide Bon Appétit

9 St James Terrace, Malahide, Dublin, Co Dublin
☎ (01) 845 0314   📠 (01) 845 0314
🪑 55 🍽 £55

☺ Lunch 12.30-2, Dinner 7-11
☹ Lunch Sat, all Sun, Bank Holidays, 1 wk Xmas

Patrick & Catherine McGuirk have been wishing you good eating here since 1989 and it's no surprise to encounter a French menu. Fixed-price offers good value – 5 courses are only £20 + service. There's an excellent wine list with great depth and variety.

Malahide Roches Bistro

12 New Street, Malahide, Co Dublin
☎ (01) 845 2777   📠 (01) 324147
🪑 35 🍽 £55

☺ Lunch 12-2.30, Dinner 6-10.30
☹ Dinner Tue & Wed, all Sun & Mon, Bank Holidays, 2 wks Jan

An authentic, family-run bistro with a congenial atmosphere and sound cooking from Orla Roche. The small, cheerful dining room with its open fire and checked cloths could easily be in France, a feeling shared by Orla from her open-plan kitchen from where she turns out some French-inspired bistro dishes that use good local produce when possible.

Mallow Longueville House

Mallow, Co Cork
☎ (022) 47156   📠 (022) 47459
🛏 16 £116 🪑 45 🍽 £65

☺ Lunch 12.30-2, Dinner 7-9   ☹ Hotel 20 Dec-mid Mar

This homely Georgian manor house set in 500 acres of woodland is owned by the O'Callaghan family, whose ancestors built it in 1720. There are good antiques and fine paintings, and the dining room has a collection of portraits of several of the Presidents of Ireland, which explains the room's name. William O'Callaghan presides over the kitchen and offers fixed-price dinner menus with a few supplementary house specialities such as a delicious ravioli of prawns scented with basil to start, and noisettes of milk-fed Longueville lamb in herb breadcrumbs with tarragon sauce as a main course. Aisling O'Callaghan looks after the restaurant while the hotel is Jane's domain. Lord of the Manor Michael knows a thing or two about wine and luckily shares his findings with guests. He imports many of the wines himself and even has what is possibly Ireland's only vineyard on the estate.

Moycullen Drimcong House Restaurant

Moycullen, Co Galway
☎ (091) 85115
🍴 50 £65

☺ Dinner 7-10.30   ☹ Sun & Mon, Bank Holidays, Jan & Feb

Gerry Galvin creates some exciting dishes in the tall, white-painted house just outside Galway. There's a cosy atmosphere in the comfortable restaurant where Marie Galvin looks after the guests. The weekly menu will feature what's best amongst local produce (much of it organically grown) and a 5-course vegetarian option is just as inspired as the regular menu. A concise wine list gives good value.

Newmarket-on-Fergus Dromoland Castle

Newmarket-on-Fergus, Co Clare
☎ (061) 368144   📠 (061) 363355
🛏 73 £269 🍴 90 £115

☺ Lunch 12.30-2, Dinner 7-10.30

The name almost conjures up Disney-like images, but this castle is very real, though it is fairy-tale attractive. The present building dates from 1826 and was converted into a hotel in 1962, and now offers extensive business and leisure facilities in decidedly grand surroundings. The Gallery features a collection of family portraits, the Drawing Room is the place for afternoon tea, and the elegant restaurant a perfect setting for careful Irish cooking.

Newport Newport House

Newport, Co Mayo
☎ (098) 41222   📠 (098) 41613
🛏 20 £124 🍴 39 £70

☺ Dinner only 7.30-9.30   ☹ Hotel 7 Oct-18 Mar

A characterful mansion where you'll find fishing is an integral part of life, with plenty of different angles from which to choose. The hotel is tastefully furnished and the Thompsons are good hosts. The kitchen produces substantial dinner menus of 6 courses with, naturally, plenty of fish! Commensurate wine list.

Oughterard Currarevagh House

Oughterard, Connemara, Co Galway
☎ (091) 82312   📠 (091) 82731
🛏 15 £92 🍴 28 £50

☺ Dinner only at 8   ☹ Hotel Nov-Mar

Early Victorian manor set in acres of woodland on the shores of Lough Corrib, comfortably furnished and hospitably run. Simple, no-choice dinner menus take advantage of good, local ingredients, good-value wine list.

Oysterhaven The Oystercatcher

Oysterhaven, Begooly, Co Cork
☎ (021) 770822
⋔ 30 🍴 £65

☺ Lunch by arrangement for parties of 7 or more, Dinner 7-9.30
(bookings only in winter)

The Pattersons' popular seafood restaurant features strong French influences (though the cheeseboard is 100% Irish and the wine list ranges around the world. It has a lovely setting by a creek, and is quite small so booking is advisable.

Rathmullan Rathmullan House

Rathmullan, Nr Letterkenny, Co Donegal
☎ (074) 58188   📠 (074) 58200
🛏 23 £104 ⋔ 60 🍴 £60

☺ Lunch Sun only 1-1.45, Dinner 7.30-8.45   ☹ Hotel Nov-mid Mar

Well-established, Georgian mansion on the shores of Lough Swilly in the so-called forgotten country of Donegal. The hotel boasts Egyptian baths, comprising an indoor pool of ionised salt water, steam rooms and sauna which overlook the splendid gardens. In the Arabian-style silk-tented dining room you can enjoy Irish country house cooking and a fine wine list.

Rathnew Tinakilly House

Rathnew, Wicklow, Co Wicklow
☎ (0404) 69274   📠 (0404) 67806
🛏 29 £116 ⋔ 50 🍴 £75

☺ Lunch 12.30-2, Dinner 7.30-9

A substantial, Victorian mansion set in attractive gardens. Many of the bedrooms have sea views, and all are spacious and comfortably furnished. The kitchen produces some well-judged dishes on table d'hote and à la carte menus. The location, just an hour from Dublin, makes Tinakilly ideal for small conferences.

Rosses Point The Moorings

Rosses Point, Co Sligo
☎ (071) 77112
⋔ 90 🍴 £45

☺ Lunch Sun only 12.30-2.30, Dinner 5.30-9.30   ☹ Mon winter, 1 wk winter

Cottage-style dining room overlooking Sligo Bay, offering uncomplicated cooking of a wide range of fish and grills. Sunday lunches are especially popular, and represent good value. Concise and useful wine list.

Roundwood Roundwood Inn

Roundwood, Co Wicklow
☎ (01) 281 8107
🍴 45 ⏱ £60
☺ Lunch 1-2.30, Dinner 7.30-9.30 (Sat to 10)
☹ Dinner Sun, all Mon, 25 Dec, Good Friday

One of Ireland's best inns is run by Jürgen & Aine Schwalm, who provide exactly the sort of food you want to find in an inn but so rarely do. In the bar, there's a big selection of hearty dishes ranging from soups to sandwiches to ragouts. The dining room has an even more extensive menu, and a long wine list tempts you to stay around.

Schull Restaurant in Blue

Gubbeen, Nr Schull, Co Cork
☎ (028) 28305
🍴 30 ⏱ £50
☺ Dinner 7.30-9.30 ☹ Sun-Wed off season, early Jan-14 Feb

A comfortable, relaxed atmosphere pervades this cottage-style restaurant furnished with antiques, run by chef Burvill Evans with Christine Crabtree in charge of front-of-house. I suspect Burvill is a surgeon "manqué" as so many of his meat dishes are boned before service! Daily-changing menus are chalked up on a blackboard. Light desserts, good coffee.

Scotshouse Hilton Park

Scotshouse, Nr Clones, Co Monaghan
☎ (047) 56007 📠 (047) 56033
🛏 5 £111 🍴 12 ⏱ £65
☺ Dinner 8-9.30 ☹ Oct-Easter

600-acre estate about half-way (2 hours) between Belfast and Dublin airports, currently being run by the 8th generation of the Madden family. You can swim in the lake, if the weather is warm enough! The hotel is not suitable for young children, though babes in arms are accepted.

L!VE TV: THE FACTS
see page 21

Shanagarry Ballymaloe House

Shanagarry, Co Cork
☎ (021) 652531 📠 (021) 652021
30 £120 90 £80
☺ Lunch 12.30-2 (Sun at 1), Dinner 7-9.30 (Sun buffet only at 7.30)
☹ Hotel 24-26 Dec

Long-established institution where you can go to relax in a quite unique atmosphere that is almost homely though the house is very professionally-run at the same time. Bedrooms are in the main house or the coachyard. They vary between traditional and modern decor, but all are comfortable and welcoming. The food is at first glance surprisingly simple, relying on superb ingredients rather than complex sauces or combinations. However, as soon as you take the first bite, you realise the care that has gone into the preparations. A perfect watercress soup, hot buttered oysters on toast, sole meunière, an omelette of chanterelles, roast pheasant with Cumberland and bread sauces, game chips and red cabbage or perhaps fillet of pork en croûte with apple sauce and celery are just some examples. Puddings usually include some home-made ice-creams, fruit pies, compotes, meringues and tarts. Delicious home-baked bread and vegetables from their own garden emphasise the heartwarming nature of the cooking: everything tastes how it should, so why mess about with it? Even breakfast seems to be rather more memorable than in most other places - delicious bacon and eggs, home-made marmalade and locally-ground oatmeal in the porridge. Children have a special tea party at 5.30 with all the kinds of choices that they would list on a dream menu; father has a wine list that will make his dreams come true as well. The Allen family work together to make all of this wonderful place run smoothly, including the farm, cookery school, craft shop and of course, the hotel.

Skibbereen Liss Ard Lake Lodge

Skibbereen, Co Cork
☎ (028) 22365 📠 (028) 22839
10 £200 25 £80
☺ Dinner only 7.30-9.30 (except for residents) ☹ Tue (except for residents)

Large, Victorian house set in gorgeous gardens on the shores of Lough Absidealy. Spacious rooms, half of them reserved for non-smokers, are luxuriously furnishes and have fine views of the surrounding countryside. A set-price dinner menu offers 6 courses with restricted choice and often without dairy products and largely vegetarian, but the food is well-balanced and superbly cooked. A relaxed breakfast the next morning will set you up.

Straffan Kildare Hotel

Straffan, Co Kildare
☎ (01) 627 3333 📠 (01) 627 3312
🛏 45 £250 🪑 70 🍽 £100
☺ Lunch 12.30-2, Dinner 7-10 ☹ Lunch Sat

Without doubt a top quality hotel with much money lavished on the main house and courtyard apartments. Luxury throughout, yet still maintaining a friendly, relaxed atmosphere coupled with top class, professional service at all levels – from the general manager to the gillie, who will arrange your fly fishing for you. The Byerley Turk restaurant, home to chef Michel Flamme, offers some interesting and imaginative dishes with a French slant, more often than not using first class Irish produce. Set in stunning surroundings (which include the Arnold Palmer-designed golf course with its separate facilities) this is a hotel that is heading for the very top.

Thomastown Mount Juliet Hotel

Mount Juliet, Thomastown, Co Kilkenny
☎ (056) 24455 📠 (056) 24522
🛏 56 £195 🪑 55 🍽 £80
☺ Dinner only 7-10

A very stylish country house that has been converted into a luxury hotel sparing little expense to ensure that original facilities have been retained while facilities are enhanced. Spacious bedrooms in the main house, 3 delightful suites in the separate Ballylinch House which also has a personal housekeeper and a private room for the chauffeur! Top-notch sports facilities – Jack Niklaus designed the golf course. The Lady Helen Dining Room is elegantly furnished in shades of blue with crisp Irish linen and shining crystal, or you can try less formal Irish meals in the Loft restaurant.

Tuam Cré na Cille

High Street, Tuam, Co Galway
☎ (093) 28232
🪑 45 🍽 £50
☺ Lunch 12.30-2.30, Dinner 6-10 ☹ Sun, Bank Holidays, 24-27 Dec

It's small wonder that this unpretentious restaurant attracts a busy lunchtime trade when you study the prices and variety on the menu. In the evening, it moves up a gear to a more sophisticated level, and the cooking is more adventurous. Puddings are especially tempting, Produce is sourced locally, organically-grown and carefully prepared.

Waterford Dwyer's Restaurant

8 Mary Street, Waterford, Co Waterford
☎ (051) 77478
🕴 30 🍽 £55

☺ Dinner only 6-10 (set dinner 6-7.30)

☹ Sun, 1 wk Xmas, Good Friday, 2 wks Jul

Serious cooking by Martin Dwyer in the unlikely setting of a converted barracks! The short menu offers plenty of interesting dishes, prepared in modern/classic style.

Waterford Waterford Castle

The Island, Ballinakill, Waterford, Co Waterford
☎ (051) 78203 📠 (051) 79316
🛏 19 £ £220 🕴 60 🍽 £80

☺ Lunch 12.30-2, Dinner 7-10 (Sun to 9)

This castle is set on its own island: you're brought across on the hotel's private ferry to the 300 acre-estate which includes a golf and country club. Bedrooms and suites enjoy splendid views, lounges are historic and comfortable, and in the elegant dining room set-price and à la carte menus take you a timeless era of charming service and good living.

Wicklow Old Rectory

Wicklow, Co Wicklow
☎ (0404) 67048 📠 (0404) 69181
🛏 5 £ £90 🕴 12 🍽 £60

☺ Dinner only at 8 ☹ Hotel Nov-Mar

Pretty, pink Victorian former rectory hosted by Paul & Linda Saunders. A good time to visit is during May/June during the Wicklow Garden Festival (book early): the floral display in the dining room is likely to be totally edible! Linda's cooking makes much use of such unusual ingredients. Paul's wine list has been equally carefully chosen, with over 20 quality Spanish wines at reasonable prices. A crowning glory is the Swiss Champagne Breakfast in Bed.

Youghal Aherne's Seafood Restaurant

163 North Main Street, Youghal, Co Cork,
☎ (024) 92424 📠 (024) 93633
🛏 10 £ £100 🕴 60 🍽 £60

☺ Lunch 12.30-2.15, Dinner 6.30-9.30, (bar food 11-10.30) ☹ 5 days Xmas

There are so many excellent seafood restaurants in Ireland and yet Aherne's still manages to stand out. It has been in the same family, the Fitzgibbons, for 3 generations, and they continually seek to improve standards. Excellent raw ingredients, perfectly cooked, lovingly served. An overnight stay in one of the letting bedrooms completes the experience of a visit here.

The Academy of Food & Wine Service

The Academy of Food & Wine Service was formed 7 years ago as a joint initiative by the Hotel and Restaurant Industry and the Wine and Spirit Trade.

The objective of the Academy is to increase the level of knowledge, and in particular, service skills, of those waiting staff employed in restaurants throughout the United Kingdom to benefit both the Industry and, more importantly, the Customer, by ensuring that there develops a network of waiting staff throughout the country who have been trained to National Vocational Qualifications Standards, initially at levels One and Two, and ultimately to even higher levels.

The Academy first set about this task by producing an open learning programme for Wine Waiters, which is available as a complete self-study pack, including a skills video, knowledge competence book and work book. This programme has been greeted by the Industry with much enthusiasm and has encouraged the Academy to further pursue research into a similar open learning programme on Food Service. Development of this new initiative is now completed and the pack is currently available.

This edition of The Ackerman Guide to the Best Hotels & Restaurants in Great Britain sees another step forward for the Academy. Readers will notice that certain symbols are marked with the symbol ❖. This denotes that the establishment employs a current member of the Academy or works closely with the organisation and supports its aims and objectives.

You will be able to identify our members by a small uniform lapel badge - green and gold for food service associate members, burgundy and gold for wine service associate members and a combined burgundy, green and gold badge for a full member. Membership is only available to those members of the waiting profession who have been trained and assessed to a National Standard and on whom you should rely for professional service when you are dining out. Please look out for these badges recognising competence and skills and start to demand that your favourite restaurant employs these dedicated, professional staff.

If you would like to obtain further information on the work of the Academy of Food & Wine Service, or as an employer wish to become an Establishment Member and involve your own staff in the training programmes, please contact the Academy at the address below:

The Academy of Food & Wine Service
Chelsea Chambers
262a Fulham Road
London SW10 9EL
Tel: 0171-352 6997 Fax: 0171-351 9678

NEWS FLASH

Britain's Top Independent Butchers

Who are the country's top butchers? Where are they? How can you be sure you're getting top quality, best advice and a service you can be confident of from a butcher?

These questions and more will be answered in the 1997 edition of the Ackerman Guide. Details have now been agreed on inspection criteria that will enable inspectors to visit independent butchers throughout the UK and determine which are good enough to be included in our Guide.

They will be listed in next year's Guide.

Scotch Beef Club

A welcome addition to this year's Guide is the inclusion of the Scotch Beef Club. Initiated by the Scotch Quality Beef and Lamb Association to promote quality beef from Scotland, members of this prestigious Club make no compromise when it comes to quality.

Scotland is justifiably proud of the centuries-old reputation of its beef industry and only the finest, genuine Scotch Beef – naturally produced to the highest farming and quality standards – is served in Scotch Beef Club member establishments.

Originally started in Italy, the Scotch Beef Club has spread across Europe and now boasts members in France, Germany, Belgium and Holland. The UK Club membership reads like a veritable "who's who" of top restaurants and hotels nationwide.

Scotch Beef's traditional worldwide reputation for quality, tenderness and flavour is further enhanced by today's chefs in the skill and innovation used by Scotch Beef Club members in preparing the Scotch Beef dishes on their menus.

Discerning diners, particularly those who appreciate the taste and succulence of quality Scotch Beef, should look out for the Black Bull symbol which identifies members of the Scotch Beef Club throughout the Guide.

L!VE TV: THE FACTS

- L!VE TV is Britain's first national 24-hour live cable exclusive entertainment channel

- L!VE TV is owned by Mirror Television, part of the Mirror Group

- L!VE TV is carried by 96% of cable systems as part of the basic package and as such is free to over <u>1.25 million cable viewers</u>

- L!VE TV broadcasts all day, every day, from both a multi-million purpose-built in London's Canary Wharf and roving broadcast vans

- L!VE TV has both national network and local versions, including Birmingham and Westminster Live

- Investment in L!VE TV is over £30m

- L!VE TV produces virtually all of its output using an in-house staff of trained TV professionals

Index

Index

A

Abbey Court, W2, 24
Abbey Hotel, Penzance, 217
Absolute End, St Peter Port, 319
L'Accento Italiano, W2, 24
Adam's Café, W12, 24
Adare Manor, Adare, 333
Adlard's, Norwich, 211
Aghadoe Heights Hotel, Killarney, 357
Aherne's Seafood Restaurant, Youghal, 367
Airds Hotel, Port Appin, 299
Al Bustan, SW1, 24
Al San Vincenzo, W2, 25
Alastair Little, W1, 25
Alastair Little Lancaster Road, W11, 26
Alba, EC1, 26
Albero & Grana, SW3, 26
Alderley Edge Hotel, Alderley Edge, 109
Alexander House, Turners Hill, 250
Alfred, WC2, 26
Allt-Nan-Ros Hotel, Onich, 298
Allt-Yr-Ynys Hotel, Walterstone, 254
Alp-Horn, Edinburgh, 281
Altnaharrie Inn, Ullapool, 302
Amberley Castle, Amberley, 111
Andrew Edmunds, W1, 27
The Angel, Burford, 137
Angel Hotel, Bury St Edmunds, 139
Angel Hotel, Midhurst, 203
Angel Inn, Hetton, 175
Angel Inn, Stoke-by-Nayland, 237
Anna's Place, N1, 27
Annie's, Moreton-in-Marsh, 205
Annie's Restaurant, Ballydehob, 335
Annie's Restaurant, Swansea, 315
Antica Roma, Belfast, 326
Appleby Manor Hotel, Appleby-in-Westmorland, 112
Arbutus Lodge, Cork, 341
Arcadia, W8, 27
Ardanaiseig, Kilchrenan, 292
Ardsheal House, Kentallen of Appin, 292
Arisaig House, Arisaig, 273
The Ark, Erpingham, 159
The Ark, W8, 27
Armathwaite Hall, Bassenthwaite, 118
Armless Dragon, Cardiff, 306
Armstrongs, Barnsley, 116
Arundell Arms, Lifton, 191

Ashdown Park Hotel, Wych Cross, 267
Ashford Castle, Cong, 341
Ashwick House, Dulverton, 156
Les Associés, N8, 28
Assolas Country House, Kanturk, 355
At the Sign of the Angel, Lacock, 185
Atelier, W1, 28
The Athenaeum, W1, 28
The Atrium, Edinburgh, 281
The Atrium, SW1, 29
Au Jardin des Gourmets, W1, 29
L'Auberge, Edinburgh, 281
Aubergine, SW10, 29
Auchendean Lodge, Dulnain Bridge, 279
Auchterarder House, Auchterarder, 273
Audleys Wood, Basingstoke, 117
Aughrim Schoolhouse Restaurant, Aughrim, 335
Aval Du Creux, Sark, 323
L'Aventure, NW8, 30
The Avenue, SW1, 30
Avenue West Eleven, W11, 30

B

B Square, SW11, 30
Bailiffscourt, Climping, 149
Balbirnie House, Markinch, 295
Balcary Bay Hotel, Auchencairn, 273
Balgonie Country House, Ballater, 275
Ballathie House, Kinclaven by Stanley, 294
Ballylickey Manor House, Ballylickey, 336
Ballymaloe House, Shanagarry, 365
The Balmoral Hotel, Edinburgh, 281
La Barbe, Reigate, 222
Barnard's, Denmead, 154
Basil Street Hotel, SW3, 31
Bath Place Hotel & Restaurant, Oxford, 214
Bath Spa Hotel, Bath, 118
Baumann's Brasserie, Coggeshall, 150
Bay Horse Inn, Ulverston, 253
Bay Tree, Burford, 137
Bear Hotel, Crickhowell, 308
Bear Hotel, Woodstock, 264
Beech Hill House Hotel, Londonderry, 330
Beechfield House, Beanacre, 120
Beetle & Wedge, Moulsford-on-Thames, 206
Beginish Restaurant, Dingle, 344
Bel Alp House, Haytor, 173
Belfry Hotel, Handforth, 170

Index

Belgo Centraal, WC2, 31
Belgo Noord, NW1, 31
The Bell Inn, Aston Clinton, 114
The Bell Inn & Hill House, Horndon-on-the-Hill, 178
La Belle Epoque, Belfast, 326
The Belvedere, W8, 31
Benihana, SW3, 32
Bentley's, W1, 32
The Berkeley, SW1, 32
Berkeley Court, Dublin, 345
Berkshire Hotel, W1, 32
Bertorelli's, WC2, 33
Bettys, Harrogate, 171
Bettys, Ilkley, 180
Bettys, Northallerton, 210
Bettys, York, 268
Bibendum, SW3, 33
Bibendum Oyster Bar, SW3, 33
Big Night Out, NW1, 34
Billboard Café, NW6 34
Billesley Manor, Billesley, 122
Bishopstrow House, Warminster, 255
Le Bistro, Hull, 179
The Bistro, Harrogate, 171
Bistro at Fern Grove, Kilmun, 293
Bistro Montparnasse, Southsea, 234
Bistrot Bruno, W1, 34
Bistrot 190, SW7, 34
Black Bull, Moulton, 206
Black Swan, Beckingham, 121
Blackgate Restaurant, Newcastle-upon-Tyne, 208
Blairs Cove House Restaurant, Durrus, 353
Blakes Hotel, SW7, 35
Blooms Hotel, Dublin, 345
Blostin's Restaurant, Shepton Mallet, 231
Blue Elephant, SW6, 35
Blue Haven Hotel, Kinsale, 358
Blue Print Café, SE1, 35
Bodysgallen Hall, Llandudno, 310
Bombay Brasserie, SW7, 35
Bon Appetit, Malahide, 361
Bon Appetit, Stourbridge, 239
Bond's, Castle Cary, 141
The Boot Inn, Barnard Gate, 116
Borthwick Castle Hotel, North Middleton, 297
Boscundle Manor, St Austell, 228
Restaurant Bosquet, Kenilworth, 183
La Bouchée, SW7, 36

Box Tree, Ilkley, 181
Boyd's, W8, 36
The Brackenbury, W6, 36
Le Braconnier, SW14, 37
Braeval, Aberfoyle, 271
Belle Epoque Brasserie, Knutsford, 185
La Brasserie, SW3, 37
Brasserie Forty Four, Leeds, 188
Brasserie St Quentin, SW3, 37
Brasserie on West Regent Street, Glasgow, 287
Brasted's, Norwich, 212
Breamish Country House Hotel, Powburn, 219
Brennan's Restaurant, Caherciveen, 338
Bridge End Restaurant, Hayfield, 173
Brighton Thistle Hotel, Brighton, 129
Brockencote Hall, Chaddesley Corbett, 142
Brown's, Worcester, 266
Brown's Hotel, W1, 37
Browns, Oxford, 214
Browns Bistro, Clitheroe, 149
Brundholme Country House Hotel, Keswick, 183
Bryan's Fish Restaurant, Leeds, 188
Bubb's, EC1, 38
Buchan's, SW11, 38
Buckland Manor, Buckland, 137
Bully's, Cork, 342
Burgh Island Hotel, Bigbury-on-Sea, 121
Burnt Chair, Richmond, 223
Burts Hotel, Melrose, 296
Butlers Wharf Chop-house, SE1, 38
Butley-Orford Oysterage, Orford, 213
Buttery, Glasgow, 287

C

Cadogan Hotel, SW1, 38
Le Cadre, N8, 39
Café dell'Ugo, SE1, 39
Café du Marché, EC1, 39
Café Flo, NW3, 39
Café Flo, Richmond, 223
Café Niçoise, Colwyn Bay, 307
Café Royal Grill Room, W1, 40
Calcot Manor, Tetbury, 246
Caledonian Hotel, Edinburgh, 282
Callow Hall, Ashbourne, 113
Camden Brasserie, NW1, 40
Cameron House, Alexandria, 272
Cannizaro House, SW19, 40

Index

The Canteen, SW10, 40
Cantina del Ponte, SE1, 41
The Capital, SW3, 41
Le Caprice, SW1, 42
Carnegie Club London Outpost, W3, 42
Carved Angel, Dartmouth, 153
Casale Franco, N1, 42
Casey's Westwood Restaurant & Bars, Galway, 354
Cashel House, Cashel, 339
Le Cassoulet, Cardiff, 306
Castle Hotel, Taunton, 245
Castle Murray House, Dunkineely, 352
Castleton House, Glamis, 287
Castletroy Park Hotel, Limerick, 360
Cavendish Hotel, Baslow, 117
Ceilidh Place, Ullapool, 303
Cellar, Anstruther, 272
Cellars Restaurant, Dundalk, 352
Celtic Manor, Newport, 313
Ceruttis, Hull, 179
Champany Inn, Linlithgow, 295
Champany Inn Chop & Ale House, Linlithgow, 295
Champers, Cardiff, 307
Le Champenois Restaurant, West Mersea, 257
Le Champignon Sauvage, Cheltenham, 145
Channings, Edinburgh, 282
Chapeltoun House, Stewarton, 301
Chapter 11, SW10, 42
Chapter One, Dublin, 346
Chapters, Stokesley, 237
Charingworth Manor, Charingworth, 144
Charlotte's Place, W5, 43
Restaurant Le Chateau, Athlone, 334
Chateau la Chaire, Rozel Bay, 321
Hotel Chateau Valeuse, St Brelade, 321
Chatters, Dunoon, 280
Chedington Court, Chedington, 144
The Chelsea, SW1, 43
Chelwood House, Chelwood, 146
Cherwell Boathouse, Oxford, 214
Chester Grosvenor, Chester, 147
Chesterfield Hotel, W1, 43
Chewton Glen, New Milton, 208
Chez Gerard, W1, 43-44
Chez Gerard, WC2, 44
Chez Hans, Cashel, 339
Chez Jean-Marc, Kinsale, 359
Chez Liline, N4, 44

Chez Moi, W11, 44
Chez Nico at Ninety Park Lane, W1, 45
Chez Nous, Plymouth, 218
Chez Youen, Baltimore, 337
Chiaroscuro, WC1, 45
Chimneys, Long Melford, 193
Chinon, W14, 45
The Chiswick, W4, 46
Christian's, W4, 46
Christopher's American Grill, WC2, 46
Churche's Mansion, Nantwich, 207
Churchill Inter-Continental Hotel, W1, 46
Chutney Mary, SW10, 47
Cibo, W14, 47
Cisswood House Hotel, Lower Beeding, 195
Claire du Lune, Bruton, 136
Claridge's, W1, 47
Clarke's, W8, 48
Cliffords, Cork, 342
Clifton Hotel, Nairn, 297
Cliveden, Taplow, 244
Clos du Roy, Bath, 118
The Close, Tetbury, 247
Cnapan Restaurant, Newport, 313
Coast, W1, 48
Cobwebs, Cowan Bridge, 152
Cockle Warren Cottage Hotel, Havant, 173
Coed-y-Mwstwr Hotel, Coychurch, 308
Collin House, Auchencairn, 273
Collin House, Broadway, 134
Combe Grove Manor, Monkton Combe, 204
Combe House, Gittisham, 164
Comme Ça, Chichester, 148
The Commons Restaurant, Dublin, 346
Compleat Angler Hotel, Marlow, 200
Congham Hall, Grimston, 168
The Connaught, W1, 49
Connemara Coast Hotel, Furbo, 353
Conrad International London, SW10, 49
Conrah Country Hotel, Aberystwyth, 306
Hotel Conrad, Dublin, 346
Cooke's Café, Dublin, 347
Coppid Beech Hotel, Bracknell, 126
Le Coq Hardi, Dublin, 347
Cork & Bottle, WC2, 49
Corse Lawn House, Corse Lawn, 151
Cotswold House, Chipping Campden, 148
The Cottage, Shanklin Old Village, 231

Index 379

The Cottage in the Wood, Malvern, 198
Coul House, Contin, 277
Country Friends, Dorrington, 155
County Hotel, Canterbury, 141
Courtney's, Newcastle-upon-Tyne, 209
Crab & Lobster, Asenby, 113
Crabwall Manor, Chester, 147
Craigendarroch Hotel, Ballater, 275
Crannog Seafood Restaurant, Fort William, 286
Crawford Gallery Café, Cork, 342
Cré na Cille, Tuam, 366
Creag Mor, Gairloch, 286
Creggans Inn, Strachur, 301
Crinan Hotel, Crinan, 278
Cringletie House, Peebles, 298
Cromleach Lodge, Castlebaldwin, 340
Cromlix House, Dunblane, 280
Croque-en-Bouche, Malvern, 198
Crosby Lodge, Crosby-on-Eden, 152
The Cross, Kingussie, 294
The Crown, Southwold, 234
Crown at Whitebrook, Whitebrook, 317
Crown Liquor Saloon, Belfast, 327
Crowthers, SW14, 50
Culloden Hotel, Holywood, 329
Culloden House, Inverness, 291
Currarevagh House, Oughterard, 362
Cwrt Bleddyn Hotel, Llangybi, 311

D

D'Arcy's, Glasgow, 287
d'Arcy's, Kenmare, 355
Dalmahoy Hotel, Golf & CC, Kirknewton, 294
Dan's, SW3, 50
Danescombe Valley Hotel, Calstock, 140
Danesfield House, Medmenham, 201
Daphne's, SW3, 50
Davenport Hotel, Dublin, 347
De Cecco, SW6, 50
De Selby's Restaurant, Dun Laoghaire, 352
De Vere Grand, St Helier, 322
De Vere Mottram Hall, Mottram St Andrew, 205
De Vere Royal Bath Hotel, Bournemouth, 125
Deanes on the Square, Helen's Bay, 329
Del Buongustaio, SW15, 51
dell'Ugo, W1, 51
Denzlers 121, Edinburgh, 282
Derrynane Hotel, Caherdaniel, 338

Design House Restaurant, Halifax, 170
Devonshire Arms, Bolton Abbey, 124
Dew Pond, Old Burghclere, 213
Dingles Restauraunt, Killarney, 357
The Dining Room, Hersham, 174
The Dining Room, Reigate, 222
Dixcart Hotel, Sark, 323
Dolmelynllyn Hall, Dolgellau, 308
Don Pepe, NW8, 51
The Dorchester, W1, 52
La Dordogne, W4, 52
Dormy House, Broadway, 134
Dorset Square Hotel, NW1, 53
Dovecliffe Hall, Stretton, 241
Dower House, Muir-of-Ord, 296
Down Hall, Hatfield Heath, 172
Downstairs at 190, SW7, 53
Downstairs at Thackeray's, Tunbridge Wells, 249
Doyle's Seafood Bar & Townhouse, Dingle, 344
Drewe Arms, Broadhembury, 134
Drimcong House Restaurant, Moycullen, 362
Dromoland Castle, Newmarket-on-Fergus, 362
Drum & Monkey, Harrogate, 171
Drumnacree House, Alyth, 272
Dryburgh Abbey Hotel, Dryburgh, 279
Dukes Hotel, Belfast, 327
Dukes Hotel, SW1, 53
Dunadry Inn, Dunadry, 329
Dunain Park, Inverness, 291
Dundas Arms, Kintbury, 185
Dunraven Arms, Adare, 333
Dunworley Cottage, Butlerstown, 338
Duxford Lodge, Duxford, 156
Dwyer's Restaurant, Waterford, 367
Dylanwad Da, Dolgellau, 309

E
The Eagle, EC1, 53
Eastwell Manor, Ashford, 114
L'Ecrivain, Dublin, 348
Egerton Grey, Porthkerry, 314
Elena's L'Etoile, W1, 54
Restaurant Elizabeth, Oxford, 215
Elms Hotel, Abberley, 109
English Garden, SW3, 54
English House, SW3, 54
Enniscree Lodge, Enniskerry, 353
Enoteca Turi, SW15, 54

The Enterprise, SW3, 55
Epicurean, Cheltenham, 145
Erriseask House, Ballyconneely, 335
L'Escargot, Herne Bay, 174
L'Escargot, W1, 55
Esseborne Manor, Hurstbourne Tarrant, 180
Est, W1, 55
L'Estaminet, WC2, 55
Ettington Park, Stratford-upon-Avon, 240
Evesham Hotel, Evesham, 160

F

Fairyhill, Reynoldston, 315
Farlam Hall, Brampton, 128
Farleyer House, Aberfeldy, 271
Farmhouse Hotel & Restaurant, Lew, 190
Fat Boys, W4, 56
Feathers Hotel, Ludlow, 196
Feathers Hotel, Woodstock, 265
Fen House Restaurant, Ely, 159
Ferns, Louth, 194
Fifehead Manor, Middle Wallop, 203
15 North Parade, Oxford, 215
Fifty Five BC, Bearsden, 276
Fifth Floor Restaurant, SW1, 56
Fins Restaurant, Fairlie, 285
Fischer's Baslow Hall, Baslow, 117
Fisherman's Lodge, Newcastle-upon-Tyne, 209
Fishes, Burnham Market, 138
Flemings, Cork, 342
La Fleur de Lys, Shaftesbury, 230
Flitwick Manor, Flitwick, 162
Florians, N8, 56
Restaurant de La Fontaine, Limerick, 360
Food for Thought, Fowey, 163
Formula Veneta, SW10, 56
Forsters, East Boldon, 156
47 Park Street, W1, 57
42 The Calls, Leeds, 189
Fosse Manor Hotel, Stow-on-the-Wold, 240
Fountain House & Dedham Hall, Dedham, 154
Four Seasons Hotel, W1, 57
Fouters Bistro, Ayr, 274
Fox and Goose, Fressingfield, 164
Francs, Altrincham, 110
Francs, Chester, 147
Frederick's, N1, 58
Fredrick's, Maidenhead, 197

La Frégate, St Peter Port, 319
French House Dining Room, W1, 58
French Partridge, Horton, 178
The French Brasserie, Altrincham, 110
The French Restaurant, Altrincham, 110
Les Frères Jacques, Dublin, 348
Fulham Road, SW3, 58

G

The Gables, Ardee, 334
The Gables, Billingshurst, 122
Gaby's Seafood Restaurant, Killarney, 358
Galgorm Manor, Ballymena, 326
Galley, Swanage, 243
Garden Restaurant, Bramley, 127
Le Gavroche, W1, 59
Gay Hussar, W1, 59
Geales Fish Restaurant, W8, 60
Gee's Restaurant, Oxford, 215
Gemini Restaurant, Tadworth, 244
George & Dragon, Rowde, 227
Georgian House, St Anne, 319
The George of Stamford, Stamford, 236
Gidleigh Park, Chagford, 143
Gilbert's, SW7, 60
Gilpin Lodge, Bowness-on-Windermere, 125
Glasgow Hilton, Glasgow, 288
Glebe House, Collooney, 341
Gleneagles Hotel, Auchterarder, 274
Glenelg Inn, Glenelg, 290
Glenfeochan House, Kilmore, 293
Gliffaes Country House Hotel, Crickhowell, 308
The Gloucester, SW7, 60
Goff's Restaurant, Nether Langwith, 207
Gordleton Mill, Lymington, 196
The Gore, SW7, 60
The Goring, SW1, 60
Grafton Manor, Bromsgrove, 136
La Grande Mare Hotel, Castel, 319
The Grand, Brighton, 129
Grand Hotel, Eastbourne, 157
Grange Hotel, York, 268
Grange Inn, St Andrews, 300
Granita, N1, 61
Grapevine Hotel, Stow-on-the-Wold, 240
Gravetye Manor, East Grinstead, 157
Restaurant Gravier, Kingston-upon-Thames, 184
Great House, Lavenham, 186

Green's Restaurant & Oyster Bar, SW1, 61
Greenhead House, Chapeltown, 143
Greenhill House, Aghadowey, 326
Greenhouse, W1, 61
Greens Seafood Restaurant, Norwich, 212
The Greenway, Cheltenham, 145
Gregans Castle, Ballyvaughan, 337
Gregory's, Carrigaline, 339
alistair Greig's Grill, W1, 61
Grey Door, Dublin, 348
Greywalls Hotel, Gullane, 290
Griffin Inn, Fletching, 162
Grill St Quentin, SW3, 62
Grosvenor House, W1, 62

H
The Halcyon, W11, 62
Haley's Hotel, Leeds, 189
Half Door, Dingle, 344
The Halkin, SW1, 63
Hall Garth Hotel, Coatham Mundeville, 150
Halmpstone Manor, Bishops Tawton, 123
Hambleton Hall, Hambleton, 170
Hamiltons, Twickenham, 250
Hampshire Hotel, WC2, 63
Hanbury Manor, Thundridge, 248
Harbour Bistro, Ramsey, 324
The Harley, Sheffield, 231
Harolds Restaurant, Cork, 343
Harry's Place, Great Gonerby, 167
Hartwell House, Aylesbury, 115
Harveys Restaurant, Bristol, 131
Hatton Court, Gloucester, 165
Haven Hotel, Poole, 219
The Haycock, Wansford-in-England, 254
Heathcotes Brasserie, Preston, 220
High Moor, Wrightington, 266
Highgrove House, Troon, 302
Hilaire, SW7, 64
Hilton International Regent's Park, NW8, 64
Hilton Park, Scotshouse, 364
Hintlesham Hall, Hintlesham, 176
Holbeck Ghyll, Windermere, 260
Hole in the Wall, Bath, 119
Hollington House Hotel, Woolton Hill, 265
Holne Chase Hotel, Ashburton, 114
Homewood Park, Freshford, 163
Honours Mill Restaurant, Edenbridge, 158

Hooke Hall, Uckfield, 251
Hope End, Ledbury, 187
Horetown House, Foulksmills, 353
Hotel L'Horizon, St Brelade's Bay, 321
The Horn of Plenty, Gulworthy, 169
Horsted Place, Uckfield, 251
Horton Grange, Seaton Burn, 230
Hospitality Suite, EC3, 64
L'Hotel, SW3, 65
The Hothouse, E1, 65
Howard Hotel, WC2, 65
Howard's, Bristol, 131
Howard's House, Teffont Evias, 246
Hundred House Hotel, Norton, 211
Hungry Monk Restaurant, Jevington, 182
The Hungry Monk, Greystones, 354
Hunstrete House, Hunstrete, 179
Hunt's, Bristol, 131
Hunters, New Alresford, 207
Hunts Tor House, Drewsteignton, 156
Huntsham Court, Huntsham, 180
Hyatt Carlton Tower, SW1, 65
Hyatt Regency, Birmingham, 123
Hyde Park Hotel, SW1, 66

I

Idle Rocks Hotel, St Mawes, 228
Inchalla Hotel, St Anne, 319
L'Incontro, SW1, 66
Inter-Continental London, W1, 67
Interlude de Chavot, W1, 67
Invercreran Country HouseHotel, Appin, 272
Inverlochy Castle, Fort William, 286
Isaacs, Cork, 343
Isle of Eriska, Eriska, 285
Ivory Tower Restaurant, Cork, 343
The Ivy, WC2, 67
Ivy House, Braithwaite, 127

J

Jack Fuller's, Brightling, 129
Jacques, Cork, 343
Jarvis Elcot Park, Elcot, 158
Jarvis International Hotel, Solihull, 233
Jenny's Seafood Restaurant, Liverpool, 193
Jersey Pottery Garden Restaurant, Gorey, 320
The Jew's House, Lincoln, 191
Joe Allen, WC2, 68

Joe's Café, SW3, 68
Jordan's Bar & Retsaurant, Carlingford, 339
Julie's, W11, 68
Jury's Hotel & Towers, Dublin, 348

K

Kalamaras, W2, 68
Kapriol, Dublin, 349
Kartouche, SW10, 69
Kaspia, W1, 69
Kealys Seafood Bar, Greencastle, 354
Kelly's, Edinburgh, 283
Kensington Place, W8, 69
Kildare Hotel, Straffan, 366
Kildrummy Castle Hotel, Kildrummy, 292
Kilfinan Hotel, Kilfinan, 293
Kilkea Castle, Castledermot, 340
Killiecrankie Hotel, Killiecrankie, 293
King Sitric, Howth, 355
Kinghams Restaurant, Shere, 231
King's Head, Richmond, 223
Kingshead House, Birdlip, 122
Kingswood Country House, Clondalkin, 340
Kinloch House, Blairgowrie, 276
Kinloch Lodge, Sleat, 301
Kinnaird, Dunkeld, 280
Kirroughtree Hotel, Newton Stewart, 297
Kitchen at Polperro, Polperro, 218
Knipoch Hotel, Oban, 297
Knockie Lodge, Whitebridge, 303
Knockinaam Lodge, Portpatrick, 299
The Knowle, Higham, 175

L

Lacken House, Kilkenny, 357
Ladyburn, Maybole, 296
Lainston House, Winchester, 259
Lake Country House Hotel, Llangammarch Wells, 311
The Lake Isle, Uppingham, 253
Lake Vyrnwy Hotel, Llanwyddyn, 312
Lamb Inn, Burford, 138
Land's End Hotel, Land's End, 185
Landgate Bistro, Rye, 227
The Landmark London, NW1, 69
The Lanesborough, SW1, 70
Langan's Bistro, W1, 70
Langan's Brasserie, W1, 70
Langar Hall, Langar, 186

The Langham Hilton, W1, 71
Langley House, Wiveliscombe, 263
Langshott Manor, Horley, 177
Larchwood House, Ballylickey, 336
Launceston Place, W8, 71
Laurent, NW2, 71
The Leatherne Bottel, Goring-on-Thames, 165
Leeming House, Ullswater, 251
Leigh Park Hotel, Bradford-on-Avon, 126
Leith's, W11, 72
Leodis Brasserie, Leeds, 189
Restaurant Lettonie, Bristol, 132
Lewtrenchard Manor, Lewdown, 191
The Lexington, W1, 72
Liaison, Stratford-upon-Avon, 241
Lime Tree, West Didsbury, 256
The Lime Tree, Kenmare, 356
Linden Hall Hotel, Longhorsley, 193
Lindsay House, W1, 72
Linthwaite House, Bowness-on-Windermere, 125
Liss Ard Lake Lodge, Skibbereen, 365
Little Barwick House, Yeovil, 267
Little Thakeham, Storrington, 238
The Little Angel, Remenham, 222
Llangoed Hall, Llyswen, 312
Llechwen Hall, Abercynon, 305
Llyndir Hall, Rossett, 315
Lobster Pot, Dublin, 349
The Lobster Pot, St Ouen, 322
Loch Fyne Oyster Bar, Cairndow, 276
Loch Fyne Oyster Bar, Elton, 158
Locks, Dublin, 349
London Hilton on Park Lane, W1, 73
Longfield's Hotel & No 10 Restaurant, Dublin, 349
Longueville House, Mallow, 361
Longueville Manor, St Saviour, 322
Lord Baker's Bar & Restaurant, Dingle, 345
Lords of the Manor, Upper Slaughter, 253
Lou Pescadou, SW5, 73
Lovelady Shield Country House Hotel, Alston, 109
Lovells at Windrush Farm, Minster Lovell, 204
Lower Pitt, East Buckland, 157
Lower Slaughter Manor, Lower Slaughter, 195
Luc's Restaurant & Brasserie, EC3, 73
Lucknam Park, Colerne, 151
Lygon Arms, Broadway, 135
Lynton House, Holdenby, 176
Lynwood House, Barnstaple, 116

M

Mabey's Brasserie, Sudbury, 242
MacNean Bistro, Blacklion, 338
Maes-y-Neuadd, Talsarnau, 316
Magno's Brasserie, WC2, 73
Magpie Café, Whitby, 257
Magpies Restaurant, Horncastle, 177
Maison Talbooth, Dedham, 154
Mallory Court, Leamington Spa, 187
Malmaison Hotel et Brasserie, Glasgow, 288
Malmaison, Edinburgh, 283
Man Friday, Kinsale, 359
Manleys, Storrington, 239
Le Manoir aux Quat'Saisons, Great Milton, 167
Manor House, Castle Combe, 142
Manor House, Walkington, 254
Mansion House, Poole, 219
Manzara, W11, 74
Manzi's, WC2, 74
Le Marché Noir, Edinburgh, 283
The Marcliffe at Pitfodels, Aberdeen, 271
Marco's, Norwich, 212
Restaurant Marco Pierre White, SW1, 74
Market Restaurant, Manchester, 199
Markwicks, Bristol, 132
Marlfield House, Gorey, 354
Marsh Country Hotel, Eyton, 161
Marsh Goose, Moreton-in-Marsh, 205
Martin's, Edinburgh, 284
Maryculter House, Maryculter, 295
Master McGrath's, Scarisbrick, 229
Mauro's, Bollington, 124
Max's Wine Bar, Kinsale, 359
Maxine's, Midhurst, 203
May Fair Inter-Continental, W1, 75
McClement's, Twickenham, 250
McCoy's, Staddlebridge, 235
Melton's, York, 268
The Merchant House, Ludlow, 196
Le Meridien, W1, 75
Meridien Waldorf, WC2,
Mermaid Inn, Rye, 227
Meson Don Felipe, SE1, 75
Le Mesurier, EC1, 76
Meudon Hotel, Mawnan Smith, 201
Mezzo Restaurant, W1, 76
Michael's Restaurant, Bristol, 132
Michael's Bistro, Cork, 344

Michael's Nook, Grasmere, 165
Michels', Ripley, 224
Middlethorpe Hall, York, 269
Milk House, Montacute, 204
Mill House Hotel, Kingham, 184
The Mill at Harvington, Harvington, 172
Miller Howe, Windermere, 261
Mimmo d'Ischia, SW1, 76
Mims Restaurant, New Barnet, 208
Miskin Manor, Miskin, 312
Mr Underhill's, Stonham, 238
Mitchell's of Laragh, Laragh, 360
Mock Turtle, Dorchester, 155
Mon Plaisir, WC2, 77
Le Monde, Cardiff, 307
Monkeys, SW3, 77
Montagu Arms, Beaulieu, 121
Montcalm Hotel, W1, 77
The Moon, Kendal, 182
The Moorings, Rosses Point, 363
The Moorings, Wells-next-the-Sea, 256
Morston Hall, Morston, 205
Mortimer's on the Quay, Ipswich, 181
Mortimer's Seafood Restaurant, Bury St Edmunds, 139
Mortons House Hotel, Corfe Castle, 151
Mosimann's Club, SW1, 78
Moss Nook, Manchester Airport, 199
Motcomb's, SW1, 78
The Motte, Inistioge, 355
Mount Falcon Castle, Ballina, 335
Mount Juliet Hotel, Thomastown, 366
Mulberry House, Torquay, 248
Murray's, Cuckfield, 152
Murrayshall House, Scone, 300
Le Muscadet, W1, 78
Muset, Bristol, 133
Museum Street Café, WC1, 78
Mustard Seed, Adare, 333

N

Nansidwell, Mawnan Smith, 201
Nare Hotel, Veryan, 253
Le Nautique, St Peter Port, 320
Neal Street Restaurant, WC2, 79
Neil's, Bristol, 133
Neptune Restaurant, Ballyhack, 336
Netherfield Place, Battle, 120
New Hall, Sutton Coldfield, 243

New House Country Hotel, Cardiff, 307
New Mill Restaurant, Eversley, 160
The New Moon, Bath, 119
Newport House, Newport, 362
Newton's, SW4, 79
Nick's Restaurant, Killorglin, 358
Nico Central, W1, 79
Nicole's, W1, 80
Nightingales Restaurant, Taunton, 245
Nikita's, SW10, 80
Restaurant 19, Bradford, 127
19 Grape Lane, York, 269
Normandie Hotel, Bury, 139
Northcote Manor, Langho, 186
Norton House, Ingliston, 291
Norton House, Mumbles, 313
Number One, Swansea, 315
Number Thirty Three, Perth, 298
Number Twenty Four, Wymondham, 267
Nunsmere Hall, Northwich, 211
Nuthurst Grange, Hockley Heath, 176

O

O'Grady's Seafood Restaurant, Clifden, 340
Oakley Court, Windsor, 262
Oaks Hotel, Porlock, 219
Ockenden Manor, Cuckfield, 152
L'Odéon, W1, 80
Odette's, NW1, 81
Odin's Restaurant, W1, 81
Old Bakehouse Restaurant, Little Walsingham, 192
Old Beams, Waterhouses, 255
Old Bridge Hotel, Huntingdon, 179
Old Chesil Rectory, Winchester, 259
Old Church Hotel, Ullswater, 251
Old Coach House, Barham, 116
Old Court House Inn, St Aubin, 321
Old Dublin Restaurant, Dublin, 350
Old Fire Engine House, Ely, 159
The Old Forge, Storrington, 239
Old Government House, St Peter Port, 320
Old House Hotel, Wickham, 258
Old Inn, Crawfordsburn, 328
Old Manor House, Romsey, 226
Old Mansion House, Auchterhouse, 274
Old Monastery Restaurant, Drybridge, 279
Old Parsonage, Oxford, 216
Old Plow Bistro & Restaurant at Speen, Speen, 235

Old Presbytery, Kinsale, 359
Old Rectory, Campsea Ashe, 140
Old Rectory, Llansanffraid Glan Conwy, 311
Old Rectory, Wicklow, 367
Old Station Restaurant, Spean Bridge, 301
Old Swan Hotel, Harrogate, 171
Old Vicarage, Ridgeway, 224
Old Vicarage, Witherslack, 263
Old Vicarage, Worfield, 266
Old Woolhouse, Northleach, 210
Olde Ship Hotel, Seahouses, 229
Olde Stocks Restaurant, Melton Mowbray, 203
Olive Tree, Leeds, 190
Olivo, SW1, 81
On The Park, Cheltenham, 146
One Devonshire Gardens, Glasgow, 288
192, W11, 82
Orsino, W11, 82
Orso, WC2, 82
L'Ortolan, Shinfield, 232
Osteria Antica Bologna, SW11, 83
Ostlers Close, Cupar, 278
Over the Bridge Restaurant, Ripponden, 225
The Oystercatcher, Oysterhaven, 363

P

Le P'tit Normand, SW18, 83
Packie's, Kenmare, 356
Painswick Hotel, Painswick, 216
Le Palais du Jardin, WC2, 84
Paris House, Woburn, 264
Park Hotel Kenmare, Kenmare, 356
The Park Lane Hotel, W1, 84
Parkhill Hotel, Lyndhurst, 197
Partners Brasserie, Sutton, 243
Partners West Street, Dorking, 155
Patrick Guilbaud, Dublin, 350
Paul Heathcote's Restaurant, Longridge, 194
Paul's, Folkestone, 163
Pear Tree, Purton, 221
The Peasant, EC1, 84
The Peat Inn, Peat Inn, 298
Pelham Hotel, SW7, 85
Penally Abbey, Penally, 314
Penrhos Court, Kington, 184
People's Palace, SE1, 85
Percy's Restaurant, North Harrow, 210
Perkins Bar & Bistro, Plumtree, 217

Perry's, Weymouth, 257
Petersham Hotel, Richmond, 223
La Petite Auberge, Great Missenden, 168
Le Petit Canard, Maiden Newton, 197
Pheasant Inn, Keyston, 183
Pheasants, Ross-on-Wye, 226
Phoenicia, W8, 85
The Phoenix, SW15, 85
Pied à Terre, W1, 86
The Pierhouse & Seafood Restaurant, Port Appin, 299
Piermasters Restaurant, Plymouth, 218
Pig'n'Fish, St Ives, 228
Pink Geranium, Melbourn, 202
Plas Bodegroes, Pwllheli, 314
Plumber Manor, Sturminster Newton, 242
Poissonnerie de l'Avenue, SW3, 86
Polmaily House, Drumnadrochit, 279
Pomegranates, SW1, 86
Le Pont de la Tour, SE1, 87
Pool Court at 42, Leeds, 189
Pophams, Winkleigh, 262
Poppies Restaurant, Brimfield, 130
Portaferry Hotel, Portaferry, 330
La Porte des Indes, W1, 87
Porters, Taunton, 245
Porters English Restaurant, WC2, 87
Porth Tocyn Hotel, Abersoch, 305
Hotel Portmeirion, Portmeirion, 314
La Potinière, Gullane, 290
La Poule Au Pot, SW1, 88
Le Poussin, Brockenhurst, 135
Preston Marriott, Broughton, 136
Priory Hotel, Bath, 119
Priory Hotel, Wareham, 254
Puckrup Hall, Puckrup, 220
Puppet Theatre, Glasgow, 289

Q

Quaglino's, SW1, 88
Quails Restaurant, Chobham, 149
Quality Chop House, EC1, 88
Queensberry Hotel, Bath, 119
Quince & Medlar, Cockermouth, 150
Quincy's, NW2, 89
Quincy's, Seaford, 229
Quorn Grange, Quorn, 221

R

Radisson Mountbatten Hotel, WC2, 89
Radisson SAS Portman Hotel, W1, 89
Raemoir House, Banchory, 275
Ram Jam Inn, Stretton, 242
Ramore, Portrush, 330
Rampsbeck Country House, Hotel, Ullswater, 252
Rankins, Sissinghurst, 232
Ransome's Dock, SW11, 90
Rathmullan House, Rathmullan, 363
Read's, Faversham, 162
Red Fort, W1, 90
Regatta, Aldeburgh, 109
Los Remos, W2, 90
Remy's Restaurant Français, Torquay, 249
Hotel Renouf & RenoufsRestaurant, Rochford, 225
Restaurant in Blue, Schull, 364
Riber Hall, Matlock, 201
Richard's Bistro Restaurant, Llandudno, 310
Ristorante Bari, York, 269
Ritchers Restaurant, Wells, 256
The Ritz, W1, 91
Riva, SW13, 91
River Café, W6, 92
River House, Lympstone, 197
River House, Thornton-le-Fylde, 247
Riverside Hotel, Abersoch, 305
Riverside Hotel, Evesham, 161
Riverside Inn, Canonbie, 277
Riverside Restaurant, Bridport, 128
Roadhouse Restaurant, Roade, 225
Rocher's, Milford-on-Sea, 204
Roches Bistro, Malahide, 361
Rococo, King's Lynn, 184
Rogano, Glasgow, 289
Roger's Restaurant, Windermere, 262
Roly's Bistro, Dublin, 350
Roman Camp Hotel, Callander, 276
Rombalds Hotel, Ilkley, 181
Rookery Hall, Nantwich, 207
Rosa's Place, Ballasalla, 324
Roscoff, Belfast, 327
Rose & Crown, Romaldkirk, 225
Rösers Restaurant, Hastings, 172
Rosleague Manor, Letterfrack, 360
Rothay Manor Hotel, Ambleside, 111
Round Table, Edinburgh, 284
Roundwood Inn, Roundwood, 364

Royal Berkshire, Ascot, 113
Royal Crescent Hotel, Bath, 120
Royal George, Tintern Abbey, 316
Royal Oak, Sevenoaks, 230
Royal Oak, Yattendon, 267
RSJ, SE1, 92
Rules, WC2, 92
Rumbles Cottage, Felsted, 162

S

La Sablonnerie Hotel, Sark, 323
St Andrews Old Course Hotel, St Andrews, 300
St Benedicts Restaurant, Norwich, 212
St David's Park Hotel, Ewloe, 309
St Ernan's House Hotel, Donegal, 345
St George's Hotel, W1, 93
St James Court, SW1, 93
St Olaves Court, Exeter, 161
St Pierre Park, St Peter Port, 320
St Tudno Hotel, Llandudno, 310
Sambuca, SW3, 93
San Frediano, SW3, 93
San Lorenzo, SW3, 94
San Martino, SW3, 94
Sandrini, SW3, 94
Santini, SW1, 94
Sardis, Darlington, 153
Saverys Restaurant, Frampton-on-Severn, 163
Les Saveurs, W1, 95
The Savoy, WC2, 95
Scalini, SW3, 96
Scarista House, Scarista, 300
Scott's Restaurant & Oyster Bar, W1, 96
Sea Crest, St Brelade, 321
Seafood Bar, Falmouth, 161
Seafood Restaurant, Great Yarmouth, 168
The Seafood Restaurant, Padstow, 216
Seaview Hotel, Seaview, 230
Seaview House Hotel, Ballylickey, 337
Restaurant Sebastian, Oswestry, 214
Seiont Manor, Llanrug, 311
The Selfridge, W1, 96
September Brasserie, Blackpool, 124
Seymour House, Chipping Campden, 148
Sharrow Bay, Ullswater, 252
Shaw's, SW7, 96
Sheekey's Restaurant, WC2, 97
Sheen Falls Lodge, Kenmare, 357

Sheila's Cottage, Ambleside, 111
Shelbourne Hotel, Dublin, 351
Shepherd's, SW1, 97
Sheraton Park Tower, SW1, 97
Shieldhill, Quothquan, 299
Shiro, Ahakista, 334
The Shore Bar & Restaurant, Edinburgh, 284
Signor Sassi, SW1, 98
Simply Nico, SW1, 98
Simpson's Restaurant, Kenilworth, 183
Simpson's-in-the-Strand, WC2, 98
Singing Chef, Ipswich, 182
Snows on the Green, W6, 99
Soho Soho, W1, 99
Sonny's, Nottingham, 213
Sonny's, SW13, 99
Soughton Hall, Northop, 313
Sous le Nez en Ville, Leeds, 190
South Lodge, Lower Beeding, 195
Spaghetti Junction, Teddington, 246
Speranza, Belfast, 328
Spinnakers, Salcombe, 229
Splinters Restaurant, Christchurch, 149
Sportsman's Arms, Wath-in-Nidderdale, 256
Spread Eagle, Thame, 247
The Square, SW1, 100
The Stables, Ayr, 274
The Stafford, SW1, 100
Staithes Restaurant, Cheltenham, 146
Stakis St Ermin's, SW1, 100
La Stampa, Dublin, 351
Stane Street Hollow, Pulborough, 221
Stanneylands, Wilmslow, 259
The Stannary, Mary Tavy, 200
Stanwell House Hotel, Lymington, 196
Stapleford Park, Stapleford, 236
Star of India, SW5, 100
The Starr Restaurant with Rooms, Great Dunmow, 166
Stephen Bull, W1, 101
Stephen Bull's Bistro, EC1, 101
Stephen's Hall Hotel & Bistro, Dublin, 351
Steppes Country House Hotel, Hereford, 174
Stock Hill House, Gillingham, 164
Stocks Hotel, Sark, 323
Ston Easton Park, Ston Easton, 237
Stone Hall, Welsh Hook, 316
Stone House, Rushlake Green, 227
Stones Restaurant, Avebury, 115

Stonor Arms, Stonor, 238
Stour Bay Café, Manningtree, 200
Strand Restaurant, Belfast, 328
Stratfords, W8, 101
Strattons Hotel, Swaffham, 243
Strawberry Tree, Killarney, 358
Studley Priory, Horton-cum-Studley, 178
Sullivans, Holywood, 329
Summer Isles, Achiltibuie, 271
Summer Lodge, Evershot, 160
Sundial Restaurant, Herstmonceux, 175
Le Suquet, SW3, 102
Swallow Hotel, Birmingham, 123
Swallow Royal Hotel, Bristol, 133
Swan Diplomat, Streatley-on-Thames, 241
The Swan, Bibury, 121
The Swan, Lavenham, 187
The Swan, Southwold, 234
Sweetings, EC4, 102
Swinton House, Stow Bridge, 239
Swynford Paddocks, Six Mile Bottom, 233
Sykes House, Halford, 169

T

Le Talbooth Restaurant, Dedham, 154
La Tante Claire, SW3, 102
Tanyard Hotel, Boughton Monchelsea, 125
Taychreggan Hotel, Kilchrenan, 292
Taylor's, York, 269
Templeton Hotel, Templepatrick, 331
Thackeray's House, Tunbridge Wells, 249
Thainstone House, Inverurie, 291
Theobald's, Ixworth, 182
Thierry's, SW3, 103
36 On The Quay, Emsworth, 159
Thomas Luny House, Teignmouth, 246
Thornbury Castle, Thornbury, 247
Thornton's, Dublin, 351
Three Chimneys Restaurant, Colbost, 277
Three Lions, Stuckton, 242
Three Main Street, Fishguard, 309
Thruxted Oast, Chartham, 144
Tigh an Tobair (The Well House), Ballyferriter, 336
Tinakilly House, Rathnew, 363
Tonlegee House, Athy, 334
Tophams Ebury Court, SW1, 103
Topps Hotel, Brighton, 130
Tottington Manor, Edburton, 158

Toxique, Melksham, 202
The Traddock, Austwick, 115
Trebrea Lodge, Tintagel, 248
Trenchers, Whitby, 258
Truffles Restaurant, Bruton, 137
Tufton Arms, Appleby-in-Westmorland, 112
Tullanisk, Birr, 337
Tullich Lodge, Ballater, 275
Tummies Bistro, Slough, 233
Turnberry Hotel, Turnberry, 302
Turner's, SW3, 103
21 Queen Street, Newcastle-upon-Tyne, 209
Twenty Trinity Gardens, SW9, 104
22 Chesterton Road, Cambridge, 140
Two Fat Ladies, Glasgow, 289
Tyddyn Llan, Llandrillo, 310
Tylney Hall, Rotherwick, 226

U

Ubiquitous Chip, Glasgow, 289
Underscar Manor, Applethwaite, 113
Uplands, Cartmel, 141

V

Veronica's, W2, 104
Victor's Restaurant, Darlington, 153
Victoria & Albert Hotel, Manchester, 199
Victorian House, Thornton Cleveleys, 248
Villa Italia, Belfast, 328
Village Bakery, Melmerby, 202
Village Green, Trellech, 316
Village Restaurant, Ramsbottom, 222
Village Taverna, SW10, 104
Villandry Dining Room, W1, 104
Hotel du Vin & Bistro, Winchester, 260
Vine House, Paulerspury, 217
Vintners Room, Edinburgh, 285

W

Wagamama, WC1, 105
The Waldorf Meridien, WC2, 105
Wallett's Court, St Margaret's, 228
Walnut Tree Inn, Abergavenny, 305
Waltons of Walton Street, SW3, 105
The Waterside Inn, Bray-on-Thames, 128
Wateredge Hotel, Ambleside, 112
Waterford Castle, Waterford, 367
Weavers, Diss, 155

Weavers, Haworth, 173
Welford Place, Leicester, 190
Well House, Liskeard, 192
Well View Hotel, Moffat, 296
West Lodge Park Hotel, Hadley Wood, 169
The Westbury, Dublin, 352
The Westbury, W1, 106
Westerwood Hotel, Cumbernauld, 278
Weston Park, Shifnal, 232
Whipper-In Hotel, Oakham, 213
White Hart Hotel, Coggeshall, 150
White Horse Inn, Chilgrove, 148
White House, Herm, 320
White House, Williton, 258
White House Manor, Prestbury, 220
White Moss House, Grasmere, 166
White Tower, W1, 106
Whitechapel Manor, South Molton, 233
Whitehall, Broxted, 136
Whitstable Oyster Fishery Co, Whitstable, 258
Whittington's, EC4, 106
Wickens, Northleach, 210
Wig & Mitre, Lincoln, 191
William Harding's House, Penkridge, 217
The Willows, Ashington, 114
Wilton's, SW1, 106
Windmill, Burgh le Marsh, 138
Winterbourne Hotel, Bonchurch, 124
Winteringham Fields, Winteringham, 263
The Witchery by the Castle, Edinburgh, 285
Vodka, W8, 107
Wood Hall, Linton, 192
Woodhayes, Whimple, 257
Woods, Bath, 120
Woolley Grange, Bradford-on-Avon, 126
Wordsworth Hotel, Grasmere, 166
Wyck Hill House, Stow-on-the-Wold, 240

Ye Olde Bell, Hurley, 180
Ye Olde Bulls Head Inn, Beaumaris, 306
Yetman's, Holt, 177
Ynyshir Hall, Eglwysfach, 309

Zani, SW3, 107
Zoe, W1, 107